Hurley's Journal

Hurley's Journal

TWENTIETH ANNIVERSARY EDITION

ESSAYS & EXPEDITIONS

1995 to 2003

MICHAEL HURLEY

RAGBAGGER PRESS

CHARLESTON

Hurley's Journal
Copyright © 1995-2015 by Michael C. Hurley

www.mchurley.com

Published in the United States by

Ragbagger Press
Post Office Box 70
Ridgeville, SC 29472
U.S.A.

Front and back cover illustrations by S. J. Stout
Cover design by Danijela Mijailovic

All rights reserved in accordance with the
U.S. Copyright Act of 1976

All rights reserved. Written permission must be secured from the publisher to use or reproduce any portion of this book except for brief quotations in critical reviews and articles. For information address the publisher. The material in this book was originally published in Paddle & Portage, Hurley's Journal, and Hurley's Pack & Paddle from 1995 to 2003. The essays were originally published in 2005 under the title, *Letters from the Woods*. All photos and illustrations are by the author except as otherwise credited.

Library of Congress Control Number: 2015936712

Hurley, Michael C., 1958-
Hurley's Journal
Michael Hurley
ISBN 10: 0996190104
ISBN 13: 978-0996190107
1. Family 2. Nature 3. Spirituality I. Title

Printed in the United States of America
10 9 8 7 6 5 4 3 2 1

Extraordinary Praise for
HURLEY'S JOURNAL

"One of those books you pick up like a comfy old shirt to relax in. . . Whimsical . . . elegiac . . . Hurley writes in the grain of Annie Dillard. Like Dillard—or like Hemingway in his Nick Adams stories—his immediate subject is nature but his deeper subject is often something else. The canoe trip becomes a small simulacrum of the larger spiritual journey . . . Hurley, like Hemingway, glories in the job cleanly done."
—*Wilmington Star-News*

"Pointed, personal, and poignant. A deep and passionate tale of wilderness adventures. A celebration of universal truths. Well worth reading."
—*Raleigh News & Observer*

"Like a visit to the campfire with an intelligent friend, this book will waft you into the woods and streams."
—*Paddler Magazine*

"This book could prompt others to step back and rethink ways to bring more balance into their lives."
—*ForeWord Magazine*

"[T]he essays offer tranquil and touching insight into life, love, faith and family from the vantage point of wilderness peace."
—*Adirondack Life Magazine*

"One of the best outdoor writings released this year."
—*Carroll County Times*

"I'm embarrassed to admit that as a long-time canoeist, I had never heard of Hurley's journal. Now after reading a sample of Hurley's work, I'm really sorry that I hadn't. Turns up a little gem of an insight that gives meaning to the simple pleasures of life in the woods."
—Ron Watters Chairman, National Outdoor Book Awards

"His writing style is pleasing and intimate, and it is obvious that the writer of this work is quite familiar with the pen. It is a pure and simple joy to read his words."
—*Café Libri Reviews*

"Hurley tells us the secret of life. You'll be happy to possess it, too."
—*Colorado Daily*

*To Kip and Caroline,
to help them find their way.*

TABLE OF CONTENTS

Foreword	xix
Caveats for Trip Planning	xvii
A Poem: The Campfire	xxx

ESSAYS

On Cochran's Pond	1
The Secret Life of Mud Daubers	6
A Question of Character	12
The Secret of Life	17
Northern Dreams	22
My Girl	27
Fear and Fear Itself	33
Paddling by Ear	38
A Dream of Spring	43
While Ye May	49
The Living Wilderness	52
Traveling Light	58
Memories of Maine	63
The Adventurous Life	68
The Simple Life	73
The Kindness of Strangers	78
Return to Still Pond	84
"We Few, We Happy Few"	90
What, Me Worry?	94
On Solitude	100
Breaking Camp	106
A Perfect World	111
Time and Tide	117
A Young Man's Fancy	123
The Old-Timers, The Old Times	128
Law and Wilderness	131

On Simplicity	137
Time, Speed & Distance	143
The Gypsy in Me	147
A Boy's Life	153
The View from Here	159

PHOTOGRAPHS   167-295

EXPEDITIONS

James River	299
Fish Creek Ponds Loop	303
White Oak River	307
Brice Creek	314
Lake Moomaw	317
Merchants Mill Pond	320
Rappahannock River	322
Allagash Wilderness Waterway	330
Pocomoke River	348
Crooked Lake Circuit	353
Cedar Creek Canoe Trail	362
Nottaway River	367
Bog River/Oswegatchie Traverse	373
Shenandoah River, South Fork	390
Potomac River	399
Broad River	406
Lake Opeongo	412
Sequatchie River	422
Batsto River	427
Roanoke River	436
Moose River Bow Trip	443
Allegheny River	453
Fulton Chain to Tupper Lake	461
Tyger River	484

Lac LaCroix Circuit	490
Suwannee River	503
Fontana Lake to Hazel Creek	513
New River	520
Big South Fork Cumberland River	525
St. Croix River	533
La Vérendrye Réserve Faunique	538
Upper Pasquotank River	548
Lake Lila Primitive Area	557
Antietam Creek	565
Little Tupper Lake	572
La Costa Island	581
Grass River	591
The Lobster Trip	600
Calderwood Lake	611
Green River	617
Route of the Seven Carries	627
Peace River	635
Mullica River	646
Delaware River	654
Temagami Canoe Country	662
North Nest Key Loop	673
Lumber River	680
Bear Island Canoe Trail	688
Edisto River North Fork	693
Lake One/Snowbank Lake Circuit	701
Saranac River & Lakes	713
Sylvania Wilderness	724

APPENDIX

Loading the Duluth Kitchen Pack	735
The Tandem Outfit	738
The Solo Outfit	741

The Spartan Outfit	743
Hobo Pie	745
World Famous Canoe Stew	746
Spicy Campfire Popcorn	747
How to Filet a Northern Pike	748
About the Author	749

EXPEDITIONS BY STATE/COUNTRY

Florida

Suwannee River	503
La Costa Island	581
Peace River	635
North Nest Key Loop	673

Kentucky

Big South Fork Cumberland River	525
Green River	617

Maine

Allagash Wilderness Waterway	330
Moose River Bow Trip	443
St. Croix River	533
The Lobster Trip	600

Maryland

Pocomoke River	348
Potomac River	399
Antietam Creek	565

Michigan

Sylvania Wilderness 724

Minnesota

Crooked Lake Circuit 353
Lac LaCroix Circuit 490
Lake One/Snowbank Lake Circuit 701

New Jersey

Batsto River 427
Mullica River 646
Delaware River 654

New York

Fish Creek Ponds Loop 303
Bog River/Oswegatchie Traverse 373
Fulton Chain to Tupper Lake 461
Lake Lila Primitive Area 557
Little Tupper Lake 572
Grass River 591
Route of the Seven Carries 627
Saranac River & Lakes 713

North Carolina

White Oak River... 307
Brice's Creek 314
Merchants Mill Pond 320
Broad River 406
Fontana Lake to Hazel Creek 513

North Carolina (continued)

New River	520
Upper Pasquotank River	548
Calderwood Lake	611
Lumber River	680
Bear Island Canoe Trail	688

Pennsylvania

Allegheny River Islands	453
Delaware River	654

South Carolina

Cedar Creek Canoe Trail	362
Tyger River	484
Edisto River North Fork	693

Tennessee

Sequatchie River	422
Big South Fork Cumberland River	525

Virginia

James River	299
Lake Moomaw	317
Rappahannock River	322
Nottaway River	367
Shenandoah River, South Fork	390
Roanoke River	436

Canada

Lake Opeongo (Ontario)	412
La Vérendrye (Quebec)	538
Temagami (Ontario)	662

Also by Michael Hurley

The Vineyard

The Prodigal

Once Upon a Gypsy Moon

Letters from the Woods

Hurley's Journal

Foreword

As a boy, I used to think I would grow up to be president. Looking back, that seems like such a ridiculous and improbable dream, but it is one that was shared in some form or another by millions of children of the Baby Boom generation. We were raised to believe that anything was possible in America. The towering achievements of my peers in science, technology, the arts, letters, and the law, not to mention the many spectacular failures, attest to the overarching grandeur and underlying pathology of our ambition. The gauntlet was thrown when we heard President Kennedy ask for the moon, then taken up as Neil Armstrong gave it to us on a hot July day in 1969. I was eleven, absorbing those indelible, grainy television-images with wide eyes, standing in dripping wet swim trunks.

Freedom. Adventure. Exploration. These were the values instilled in a generation of seekers, and a sense of wonder ran through it all. After Kennedy published an article entitled "The Soft American" in *Sports Illustrated* in 1960, he gave a speech proposing the idea of completing a fifty-mile hike in one day as a test of fitness for Marines. In response, Dr. Carl Zapffe, the beloved scoutmaster of Baltimore's Troop 35, called the entire troop into the pre-dawn darkness to light out for York, Pennsylvania—forty miles away—on foot. Kennedy later established the Presidential Physical Fitness Award, and as a result, I along with millions of other elementary schoolchildren did jumping jacks in footie pajamas to the tune of "Go

You Chicken Fat Go"—the song written for Kennedy's program—in sweaty school gyms across America. The "forty-miler" hike was an annual event by the time I joined Troop 35 in 1969. I was among the stragglers, but I made it—breathless and blistered—into the dark streets of York after thirteen hours.

In those days, America seemed still fresh. Her frontiers and ours were limitless. In the sixties, we played outside from dawn till dark and rode forever on our bikes. The Wilderness Act was passed in 1964. When the mighty Susquehanna River froze, we skated it for

miles in one direction. The world was ours for the taking.

In the seventies we followed Thoreau and *The Waltons* into the woods, where Euell Gibbons fed us dinner, Bradford Angier taught us to survive, and the *Foxfire* books taught us to prosper—even if it was only for a weekend. The rivers and lakes were jammed with canoes. The backpacking craze was born alongside the streaking craze and the jogging craze and the sexual revolution. Billie Jean King defeated Bobbie Riggs in the Battle of the Sexes, and lines formed at tennis courts everywhere.

Even as the struggle for civil rights was raging, Nixon and Vietnam were imploding, and the cities were burning, we were drinking life to the full and pushing every convention, every boundary, to its limit.

Those sapling years came to an abrupt end for me in 1981 in the stacks of a law school library and the concrete forests of the city where I later went to work. I toiled for long hours that ran seamlessly into weeks, then years. In one four-year period I took not a single day of vacation. But then the nineties arrived, and something remarkable happened: I became the father of a laughing baby boy and, eighteen months later, a beautiful baby girl.

As my children grew into toddlerhood, I began to hear the small voice of those carefree days again, calling me back to the Neverland of my own childhood. One day, when my son Kip was five years old, the world of woods and waters reappeared before me as invitingly—and, though I did not know it then, as fleetingly—as Brigadoon. I bought a canoe, and this journal was born.

We began taking trips, and I began writing about them in the essays and stories collected in this book. I took a camera into the woods and shot most of the photos, aided by paddling companions who either aimed my camera when I was in the shot or sent in their own photos, for which they are given due credit in this book. Afterward, I would retrace each voyage in hand-drawn maps that were scanned and published in the journal.

A physician in Houston who received one of the few early issues I printed for family and friends sent back an unsolicited check for ten dollars with a note of thanks and a request that I keep the stories coming. I happily did just that.

The journal began as *Hurley's Pack & Paddle* and at one point took the loftier moniker *Paddle & Portage*, but it was always known as *Hurley's Journal*. Before long, word got out that a tiny, homespun magazine with no ads,

published quarterly, was celebrating the forgotten lore of woodsmoke, campcraft, and voyaging by canoe. Subscribers nostalgic for a glimpse of their own past appeared almost magically, including famed philanthropist and conservationist Laurance Rockefeller, who signed his renewal forms simply "L" and sent a check each year faithfully from the Rockefeller Trust. Before long, the paid readership had grown to more than ten thousand souls in forty-eight states and overseas, and the days my children and I were spending in the woods

creating stories for the journal added up to nearly two months each year.

But with parenthood comes the need to provide, and to do that I needed to work for more money than what a kitchen-table gazette could supply. My love was for woods and boats and wild places, but my labor was in the law. I managed by necessity to build a career as a defense lawyer that eventually took me to a large law firm in the city of Raleigh, North Carolina, where my particular skillset as a litigator was in high demand. I remember well

the day the managing partners of the law firm called me in for my first annual salary-review. The year was 1998, and I was still publishing the canoeing journal I had started three years earlier. My children were seven and eight years old. After the usual buildup of attaboys and accolades, the partners proposed to raise my pay by ten thousand dollars if only I would become "more productive." The deal they offered was unspoken but clear: more billable hours and fewer wilderness days.

There aren't many times in my life when I can say that

Northern Dreams

It had seemed a long drive from suburban Baltimore to Deer Creek, the "designated trout stream" where, my father had somehow learned, the fishing was fast and furious. Along the way we stopped at a tackle shop to purchase a bamboo fishing pole—my first—that came with an impossibly large bobber and braided line of the type in wide use before the advent of monofilament. I was nine or ten years old. Except for a few, blurry flashes of earlier memory, it was the first outing with Dad that I can recall.

Sons of absent, alcoholic fathers will understand too well the hope and unease that surrounds such reunions. Without the usual, day-to-day exchange between parent and child to define for me who and what my father was, he became in my mind an amalgam of the stories—part truth, part fancy—told by and about him. Those stories often revolved around the culture which he and his brothers shared with other families of Irish ancestry who found success in large cities early in this century. There were whispers of the money his father had made and somehow lost as an executive in the canning business. There were stories of the privileged youth he and his brothers spent in private schools and summers at Indian Lake; of his brother's 40-foot wooden yawl "Signet," the Larchmont Yacht Club, and a garment business with offices in the Empire State Building; of his college days at Columbia and nights spent busing tables for the glitterati at the 21 Club; of the letter of acceptance from Harvard Law School that came after his father's money had run out; and, finally, there were those stories held in common with a nation of that long, dark tunnel called World War II.

After he was tested at the Battle of Peleliu and other venues of the U. S. Marines in the South Pacific, the stories which followed my father were mostly about the drinking. But hope springs eternal in a young boy clutching his first fishing pole on a brisk march through the tall grass to his first trout stream, and the stories I chose to remember then were about the Adirondacks.

I doubt I knew where or what the Adirondacks were, at my age, beyond the image of a vaunted, shining wilderness filled with fish, game, and fresh air. My father called this place repeatedly to mind, however, in contrast to the place where we happened to be. The trout fishing on Deer Creek, several days after the spring opener, was neither fast nor furious. Some locals finally explained to my father the routine: Hatchery trout are no sooner poured from buckets upstream than they are ignominiously hoisted from the water on bait of kernel corn by hordes of fishermen crowded along the downstream shoreline.

(Continued on back page)

I did or said something that truly astonished anyone, but I did that day. I thanked the partners for the praise but passed on the raise. I explained that they were already paying me a gracious plenty, that I wanted to continue publishing the journal, and that I would feel guilty taking the time to do so if I let them up the ante.

Parenthood lasts forever, but as every parent soon learns, we have only a few precious years while our children are truly ours alone. As my children grew into their teens, the voice that had called them and me into the woods together grew quiet, then altogether silent—drowned out by the deafening roar of adolescence. That is as it has always been and ever must be.

I went on to accept a partnership in my law firm and, in 2003, publish the final issue of the journal. I left the firm after eleven years to build a practice of my own, then retired six years after that. The world of work and worry often weighed heavy in those years, but the journals remained as a relic to which I often returned on quiet nights, unfolding yellowed pages and bringing those adventures back to life for a few hours—a reminder of my children's wonder years and my own, relived.

This is the story of *Hurley's Journal*. It stands as a testament to the smartest decision I ever made: to linger awhile in the woods and follow the poet's admonition to "gather ye rosebuds while ye may." I joined with Thoreau in his pledge, "For I'd rather be thy child, and pupil in the forest wild, than be the king of men elsewhere, and most sovereign slave of care." Thoreau had his priorities straight—in theory if not always in practice.

I suppose I'll never be president, which is just fine by me and, no doubt, most of America. But in gathering my own rosebuds into the pages of this book, it occurred to me that they comprise exactly eight years of my life—two terms, to be exact. That's as much glory as any president can hope for and more than some will get. Of all the legacies I might have chosen, none can compare with the chance to hold a little child's hand along a woodland path, beside a river, where the wild things of the world remind us of the meaning of life itself.

Michael Hurley
March 20, 2015

Caveats for Trip Planning

When *Hurley's Journal* first appeared in 1995, one reason for its popularity was the use of detailed directions and maps in the trip reports contained in each issue. It was easy to find good reference books on what sections of a river to run in an afternoon or a day, where to find the "best" whitewater, and even where to find an established park with improved camping facilities nearby, but *Hurley's Journal* was unique in its mission to take readers far off the beaten path and leave them there.

That was then, and this is now—twenty years later. It would not be possible to run every river and lake covered in each issue of the eight-year span of the journal to update landmarks, put-ins, take-outs, and camping and navigational directions in the *Expeditions* section of the book that begins on page 299. Instead, what is presented in these pages is a look-back at the expeditions as reported in their original form in a journal that will gain more nostalgic and historical importance and less accuracy for planning purposes with each passing year.

Additionally, references in the essays and trip reports to page numbers pertain to pages of the issue of the journal in which those stories originally appeared, not the pages of this book. The trip reports originally contained telephone numbers with contact information readers could use in planning their own trips, but most of these numbers—now long outdated and likely reassigned to other people—were removed from this collection.

References in this book to outfitters, suppliers and such are left unchanged from the time the journal was originally published. Some of these people may have since gone out of business, and some, no doubt, have since gone to their Maker. The names and faces will continue to change as time passes.

All of the maps accompanying the trip reports were hand drawn by me—sometimes rather crudely—using USGS topographical maps, park brochures, or whatever else was available as a reference. The maps have not been updated since their original publication and were not, even then, intended for navigational use but rather as an aid to planning. Likewise, land ownership and rights of access along some rivers may have changed in the years since the trips covered in the journal were made. Never camp on private land without asking, first.

This homage to memory is intentional. Having now turned my pen toward novels, I haven't the time to perpetually update a canoeing guidebook. But the primary reason is nostalgia. After all, what joy would there be in reading *Nessmuk's* Adirondack letters today, or Thoreau's *The Maine Woods,* if their words were overlaid and cluttered by footnotes, asterisks and revisions about the highways, boat ramps, merchants and other alterations in the physical and societal landscape of their adventures?. So too, a hundred years from now, readers may marvel to read that their favorite river is just as I described it or lament to learn what has been altered beyond recognition. In any event, I urge and caution the reader to consider this journal more of an historical marker than a guide. Set out upon your own adventures anew, with just as much care and no less wonder. The yearning for discovery that calls to you is the same unchanging summons heard and answered by the earliest explorers of the age.

The Campfire

A Poem by

Michael Hurley

A weary dusk drifts down in silken mists,
And clouds float their burdens upon the tide.
A flame of white-hot birch defies the gloom
with dancing fists.
Yet alas, this fight must too subside.
It was ever thus and will remain.
Sleep we all against the dawn,
Our voyage to begin again.

ESSAYS

On Cochran's Pond

The door to the house was impressive if not a little intimidating. I had never come this far up the hill, before—all the way to the large, brick mansion that overlooked the patch of woods known to the kids in the apartments where I lived, nearby, as Cochran's Pond. I knew somehow that the people who lived here owned this land, where for the last five of my thirteen years I had dawdled and explored, played hooky and hockey and spent a goodly part of each day pretending this was a real wilderness—like the kind I had seen only in pictures—and not just a woodlot tucked within Baltimore's ever-growing suburbs.

Christopher Robin may have had his hundred-acre wood, and the Swiss Family Robinson their island, but I had Cochran's Pond. It was a place big enough for pretending. If you knew where to pick up the trail in the forest behind the neighborhood swimming-pool, you didn't need a key to get past the chain-link fence. In the summertime, it was just a short walk before you were completely hidden by the low branches of silver maple, white oak and hickory as you climbed the hillside above the pond. There was one tree in a clearing that must have been a variety of chestnut or hazelnut. I never could find the species in the field guide at the library, but its fruit made a tolerable meal for roasting over an open fire, whatever it was.

Higher on the hill, in the woods above the pond, fallen giants left hollow spaces in the ground, filled with the sweet smell and inviting *crunch* of leaves. As hiding places these were ideal. I would tuck myself in and sit for hours, waiting for the regular appearance of a red fox at dusk from his den in the earth beneath another fallen giant, just where the trees give way to a small cow-pasture. Imagine, if you will, cows not three miles from the city and not eight miles from the stadium where Brooks Robinson played third base. I didn't have to imagine—it was real to me, with a real bull that chased me and my pals. We snuck inside the pen and waved our arms to see whether there was any truth to those cartoons about bulls and the color red. I remember how utterly unexpected it was when he came barreling at me. Charging, angry beasts were not every day fare in these parts. I ran for all I was worth—getting that second leg above the top fence-rail not too very much ahead of the moment of pressing need that I do so. What an odd obituary it would have been, otherwise: "Baltimore boy trampled to death by raging bull behind apartment swimming-pool."

The woods of Cochran's Pond served as the backdrop for an array of boyhood adventures too numerous to recount—woodland and otherwise. There was bow-fishing for carp and the lessons on refracted light that I no longer remember. (Must one aim *below* the place where the fish appears to be, or is it *above?*) There was the other mansion—the haunted one that had fallen to ruins decades earlier and seemed to be littered as much with history as mystery. We boys had discovered the remains of a bowling alley among the creaking timbers of the basement. There wasn't much in life that seemed more unattainable to us at the time than having your own private bowling-alley, and finding it here only fanned the flames of imagination. But apart from these occasional trespassory episodes, the real attraction of the pond was the opportunity it offered to while away hours that might otherwise have been spent on schoolwork with my fingers dug into the mud, instead. I marked the first Earth Day in 1970 in solemn ceremony, here. I came to understand the Mississippi Delta from the sand that the stream left where it settled into the pond. Most often, I looked at the waters of Cochran's Pond and imagined the lakes and woods of a faraway wilderness and the wild fish—the big ones—that lay hidden, there. I would have traveled to such places if I could, but the options open to a thirteen-year-old son of a single, working mother being what they were, I resolved instead to make a sanctuary of Cochran's Pond. And so I stepped up to the door of that imposing mansion at the top of the hill, whose occupants did not know me from Huckleberry Finn nor I them, and knocked.

I knew I was out of my element when the butler met me at the door, though how I recognized his occupation I am not sure—he being the only butler I had ever seen. He greeted me, and the unexpected happened as it so regularly did in this enchanted forest. I was asked in to meet the master of the house, the courtly Mr. Merrick, and his wife. Before I knew it I was seated at a formal dining table in my rumbled dungarees being offered—*I shall never, ever forget it as long as I live*—a dinner of lobster Newburg.

In my memory the place was resplendent with Persian rugs and had the smell of mahogany, leather and wool that, I would later come to know, is so telling of Old Baltimore. I don't recall the taste of the lobster or the homemade jam in little jars sealed with wax, but I remember Mr. Merrick listening with flattering interest to my plans to dredge Cochran's Pond and stock it with bass—at his expense. What I lacked in funds I made up for in chutzpa.

The pond was silting in from street-water runoff that came rushing down the creek, I explained (with studious comparisons to the hydrology of the Mississippi Delta). I proposed to take bids to dredge the bottom and oversee the project. He agreed, and in a matter of a few months, a man was reporting every day to operate a huge crane on the bank. In the bucket would go and up it would come on a wire cable, dumping its contents onto a growing moonscape of muck on shore.

The dredging project took weeks to finish, and it all must have seemed a little surreal to my grandmother. Fearing that I had perpetrated an expensive hoax, she intercepted a telephone call from Mr. Merrick one morning to ask whether he was aware that his foreman was only in the 7th grade. He said that he was, and he asked to speak to me. These were heady times for a thirteen-year-old boy.

Mr. Merrick and his patch of woods entered my life only briefly, but I was so much the better for it. The first *hard* job I ever had was splitting logs for firewood, on his woodpile. What I know of the simple art of building a campfire I perfected there. But larger lessons were underway. Not until I was much older did I appreciate the man who invited me in for dinner and took on my plan to save Cochran's Pond: Robert G.

Merrick, Sr., a decorated veteran of World War I, a Ph.D. economist, a distinguished alumnus and benefactor of Johns Hopkins University, a scion of Wall Street, and for thirty-five years the president of Equitable Trust, one of Maryland's largest and most trusted banks.

Mr. Merrick is gone, now. Cochran's Pond has since been acquired by a nearby country club. The new owners have cleared part of the surrounding forest and encircled the pond with a more secure fence. Though I doubt many young interlopers will find a way in there to play, at least the pond lives on as a natural place of beauty. We are poorer today for the loss of other places like it.

As a nation we have done much to save the great open spaces, and it is well we should do more; but there is something special about the neighborhood woodlot. There is no pond in my children's neighborhood, and they have no secret woods. They have paddled and camped on more rivers than most men will see in their lifetimes, yet I wish for them that one patch of woods they could know better than anyone—a place they could cherish and nurture for their own.

When I look back, now, I see what Mr. Merrick must have seen. I think of all the other paths a boy might have taken, and I am glad I took the one that led up a hillside beside a pond, where fallen giants had left hollow places for hiding, where the red fox came each day at dusk, and where life was sweet with the smell of leaves.

THE SECRET LIFE OF MUD DAUBERS

For this season's issue, I had long planned an opening essay on a lovely little pond and patch of woods that occupied a special corner of my boyhood. Then came the massacre at Littleton, Colorado, followed a month later by a similar attempt in Georgia. These events bring to me the palpable sense that at this time in our nation's history, reminisces on the lighter delights of a childhood spent outdoors are a sort of fiddling while Rome burns. I have even felt a tinge of guilt that, with the very fabric of society seeming to fray ever closer to the seam, the days we *grownups* spend relaxing in woodland camps are perhaps a little too self-indulgent. There's a war on for the hearts and minds of our children, and trivial pursuits are unbecoming of a people at war.

As I write these words I can hear the ready rejoinder of many of you that, had those boys in Littleton only spent more time in the Great Outdoors than in the darker alleys of the Internet, their hearts and minds would have been drawn to high ideals. The sort of thinking in that response is nothing new, of course, and I will be the first to speak up for the many spiritual gifts imparted by a closeness to the land. But the grotesqueness of what happened in Littleton suggests to me that there is something amiss in our nation's life that cuts far deeper than what songs around the campfire or any number of miles washed down the wake of a canoe can heal. The beauty of nature and the deprivations of camp living that we cheerfully endure are a powerful therapy. They remind us of the important things in life. But is that enough? Where do we—and our children in particular—discover what the important things are to begin with?

Last year I took my children to our state museum of natural science and made just such a discovery. We had the good fortune to stumble into a fascinating presentation put on by a talented curator who seemed to be enjoying his job greatly out of proportion to what we, the taxpayers of North Carolina, were paying him. He was unfolding a story for the enraptured children in the audience about the life of mud daubers—those wasp-like bugs that build clods of mud in organ-pipe formation in rafters and caves everywhere in the South.

It seems that the humble mud dauber is a rather busy and thoughtful fellow. In the earthen catacombs that it constructs it lays the eggs that will become the next generation of mud daubers, but it hardly leaves the fate of that generation to chance. A good deal of the mud dauber's day is spent accumulating a cache of spiders which with to feed its brood, and feed them in a rather strange and mysterious way. You see, the eggs take a fairly long time to hatch—at least in comparison to the shelf-life of dead spiders. If the adult mud dauber simply killed the spiders and stuffed them in the nursery like Twinkies in a lunchbox, they would decay too much to provide a balanced, healthy diet by the time the babies were hatched. As the curator explained how the daubers get around this problem, his words made the hair on the back of my neck suddenly stand on end.

The adult mud daubers prevent the spiders from decomposing during the time it takes for gestation by catching them without killing them, then injecting them with exactly enough venom—not too much, mind you, but just the right amount—to paralyze them. This ensures that the spiders will sit patiently still, helpless but very much alive, as they wait to become the hatchlings' first meal.

Three truths occurred to me from this story. The first of these, and what gave me the willies right off the bat, is that this rather sophisticated bit of engineering in food-storage science by mud daubers is no accident. It is possible to sing hymns and hallelujahs all one's life and never really come to terms with the awesome reality of a Creator, but often the greatest truths lie hidden in the smallest details. One cannot consider the attention that God has paid to the proper care and feeding of the humble mud dauber and not shudder with the realization of what he must expect of us, whom he has made in his own image.

The second truth is born of pity for the poor spider. After all, the God who created the mud dauber also gave us Charlotte's Web and the clever engineer behind it. Do we suppose the life of mud daubers to be a cruel imposition on the life of spiders, and should we expect to find spiders railing against nature in anger or wandering in bewilderment as to the injustice of it all?

The truth evident in the spider's fate is that all life on Earth is temporary and incomplete. Whether one is a mud dauber, a spider or a king, the temporal world in the end does not offer a meaning for one's existence.

I have heard some in the media ask in vain, in the wake of the terrible events of this year, "why bad things happen to good people." There is a book by that title which I have not read, but the questioner's premise is that, in the natural order of things, health and well-being should reward the Good on this earth. The horrors of Littleton, therefore, necessarily represent a disturbance in that natural law. This way of thinking inevitably comes to grief in the death of an innocent child or a senseless accident. To seek a well-ordered justice in this world is an invitation to bitterness. Whether we find ourselves on the mean streets of the city or gazing at the moon from the shores of the wilderness, life all around us is brutal by nature.

There will always be those with romantic notions of human law and civilization, whose illusions about the power of politics and policy to shape behavior will be shattered in places like Littleton and Somalia and Rwanda. Better that we should find, in this parable of the mud dauber, a quiet reminder of our faith—a remembrance that we are only pilgrims in this land, placed here awhile for a particular purpose that is certainly not to rant at our own misfortune or to crave an illusory justice.

The third truth revealed in the mud dauber's lot is a lesson for parents. I was struck by the planning of which a tiny insect is capable to ensure the safety and survival of its offspring. It really is quite remarkable when you consider how many other ways a mud dauber might choose to spend its time. But when it comes to the question of what we humans should be doing to keep another schoolyard massacre from happening, don't expect to hear exhortations from me about gun control, the importance of good schools, coaching your kids' soccer team, being a stay-at-home mom, V-chips, or any of the conventional wisdom. And don't expect me to tell you that if you make sure your kid grows up camping and canoeing with mom and dad, he'll never shoot up his school. This is where the analogy between men and mud daubers ends. Each one of these initiatives has its value, but ultimately our children's souls cannot be purchased at the paltry cost of a parent's time, better movies, or a well-planned and well-provisioned childhood.

I speak with some authority on this subject from my own experience. I grew up the happy child of a single mother who worked nights and weekends to make ends meet, and I was often home alone. I made not one camping trip with my father, for whom alcoholism was an ever-present reality. I attended public schools where drinking, drug-use and racial tension were neither rampant nor rare. Though I have no qualms about gun control, I was an enthusiastic hunter and spent my summers on a farm around enough firepower to kill every squirrel in the county, twice. One man's experience is not necessarily a lesson for all, but neither will I ignore what is obvious to me from my experience.

What was clear to me that day in Raleigh, as my children and I contemplated the secret life of mud daubers, is that there is a purpose to Creation. Knowing this, we are called by faith to enlist our lives in the service of that purpose. When we fail to heed that call, our lives turn down paths that are empty of lasting meaning—paths that lead to places like the tragedy at Columbine High. A life without faith is a life without hope. Children feel that lack of hope most acutely and are honest enough to ask: "If this is all there is, why should I care?"

I realize that all of this may sound pretty corny to some, and my wife, who worries constantly about what each of you thinks of this journal, will chastise me for writing another homily. But make no mistake, Littleton was a clarion call to our nation. It poses a question that each of us fails to answer at his peril. We are called to remember that in the final analysis, life on this earth—with its pleasure and inevitable pain—is not about this earth. We may exult in the time we spend with our children and take them camping and fishing all over creation, but the enjoyment of these blessings is an aid to our faith, not the aim of our existence. May we and our children remember what elaborate plans God made for the life of mud daubers, and never despair or doubt what he has in store for us.

A QUESTION OF CHARACTER

The rain, cold and fog were an inescapable state of affairs and had been so for days—long enough to dim the memory that there had ever been a sunny day or a balmy breeze on these waters. I was alone aboard the 28-foot sloop *Intrepid* on a broad reach into Pamlico Sound, an estuary so vast that European explorers first mistook it for another ocean. It was not a pleasure cruise. My appointed task was to deliver the boat to a berth twenty-five miles away in the coastal town of Oriental.

You could look at any point of the compass that December day and find no vision to relieve the gloom and gray. But there was one thing to be thankful for—a gentle, quartering breeze—were I inclined toward thankfulness at the time. I was not. Instead, I was underdressed for the weather, cold, and worried with good reason that I would not make the channel in sufficient daylight to stay off the shoals. The only thing that seemed possibly worse than sailing through this soup was spending the night aground in it. Then, slowly through the fog of my distemper came the bow of a little ship to port.

He passed close enough to speak, and through his yellow weathers I distinctly saw a smile. It was not the smile of a madman but of one who had learned how to smile when all impulses are to the contrary.

As he took my leave he lifted his mug to the rainclouds and remarked with wry enthusiasm, "What a great day!" I shouted my agreement without hesitation and meant it. His greeting had reminded me in an instant that, given all the things a human being could be doing on the planet at that moment, we were lucky men, indeed. I sheeted in the jib and headed to weather.

The lesson shared between those boats in the fog will play out sooner or later in every endeavor of our lives and is one we never master. For those of us who journey through wild places by canoe, it is a lesson we have the privilege to practice almost daily.

Companions suspect it may be some particular disfavor I have engendered with the gods, but whatever the reason, rare is the journey I make that is not attended by its own special tests of character. An extended canoe-trip compresses in time and space much of the epic of life. We plan, study and equip ourselves for a passage to unknown places. To succeed in this passage we must summon the resolve at each new landing in the forest to construct a shelter, gather fuel for warmth, secure our provisions against predation by wild beasts and the elements, and plan for the journey ahead. A team of voyagers as any other group must constitute and obey some hierarchical system of government, and those charged with the governance of the voyage must judge wisely or subject the entire company to dire and immediate consequences. We may think it is just another canoe trip, but in these daily rituals we repeat a liturgy that is at the very foundation of every successful civilization in history. The driving spiritual force at the heart of that liturgy—the strength of which will ultimately foretell the success or failure of the venture—is character.

Character is nothing less that the gift to experience the present reality not as a moment fixed in time but as a part of a larger and more complex whole. Character is that faithful remembrance of the past and unshakable confidence in the future that sustains us through the deprivations of the present. It matters little where or how tests of character come; the mettle required is always the same. The ability to look past the occasional deficits of a marriage and see the value appreciating over the long term is the same ability which compels us to add one paddle stroke to the next, even when it seems that the sum of our efforts will be too little, too late to purchase our goal against the surcharge of wind, weather and fatigue.

There have been many times—more than I care to recall nor would have space in this journal to recount—when life has presented me with a bill that I had insufficient funds of character with which to pay. That I preferred my personal pleasure over volunteering to serve my country as a younger man is chief among a myriad of errors of omission whose reparation now forever eludes me. But in looking back at every instance in which we are put to the test, the conflict is always the same: the temptation to despair and fly from a present, certain duty strains against the will to persevere toward a future, unseen goal. Would that God had granted us the ability to see the future, but thanks be given for the gift of character to guide us in its stead.

I did not set out to make wilderness canoeing a

salve for my spiritual angst or a regimen for personal improvement. My reasons were much more banal: it was the fishing. Yet I cannot help but notice the character-building effect of these journeys. Indeed, in the work-a-day world carried on largely within air-conditioned offices and upon cushioned furniture, I would soon lose my bearings if I did not regularly retreat to a place where life is reduced to its fundamentals.

One of my more formative lessons in the fundamentals of life came during a summer in the Adirondacks. I was alone on the first leg of a ninety-mile journey from Old Forge to the town of Saranac Lake that was expected to last eight days. It seemed that the heavens had reserved the entire world's allotment of rain to follow me through those woods. The carry from Eighth Lake to Browns Tract Inlet was thick with mosquitoes and seemed interminable. As, discouraged and tired, I shoved the bow of my canoe through the dusk into Raquette Lake, the sky opened again—with an added insult of lightning. That night, I shirked the usual duties of an evening in camp and crawled into my tent to brood. The next day, I packed up and paddled to the nearest road, caught a ride back to my car, and drove home. None would blame me. The awful weather was expected to continue for days.

After returning home, a strange sense of remorse came over me. The sun eventually came out, and tired muscles soon recovered, but I was not happy to be in the comfort and warmth of my living room. I wanted to be back at that rain-soaked camp in the Adirondacks—back at that moment in time when I still had a chance to look a fight in the eye with fists raised and say "Try me!" But it was too late. The water was under the bridge, and other duties intruded. The memory of that regret chiseled this rule into my wilderness lectionary: once begun, never turn from a journey to follow your ease.

Some say we remember discontented days in the woods more fondly in hindsight because we choose to forget our pain. I disagree. It is not that we fail to recall hardship, rather only that with the passage of time it occupies a rightly smaller place in the larger landscape of life's joys. Character is simply the vision to see that landscape through the fog of the moment and say, with conviction, "What a great day."

The Secret of Life

It is no small sign of the fundamental goodness of mankind that utter strangers sit quietly by when I play the guitar in public places. Yes, our friends, neighbors, and all but the most determined passersby now surely know that the classical guitar is my newfound obsession. A Christmas gift from my wife almost two years ago, in the time since it has carved out that space in my evening hours that formerly belonged to the glowing, blue tube in our living room. It has rekindled my interest in music that began on the piano, thirty years ago. My son the violin player has taken on the guitar as a second instrument. Both children and I are accomplices in a nightly conspiracy to push the envelope of bedtime. They know that the last inkling of the day can be postponed almost indefinitely by asking Daddy, who waits expectantly at the foot of the bed with guitar in hand, to play "Mamas, Don't Let Your Babies Grow Up to Be Cowboys" one more time.

People may suspect that Willie Nelson can't really sing, but there's no doubt at all about me. So, it was especially heartwarming that at this summer's rendezvous in the Adirondacks, the band of paddlers assembled for the last night around the campfire let me howl on in good measure. To their credit, a few even crooned along for a few bars of "Puff, the Magic

Dragon," the "Garden Song" and "What a Day for a Daydream." It was great fun—for me, at least, and if not for others they were kind enough not to show it.

Driving home from the rendezvous through the mountains of Pennsylvania, I was listening to the country station as I am now wont to do, always looking for new material. A song came on the radio that I had heard, before, but the words struck me differently, this time. You may have heard it yourself. Sung by Faith Hill, it is entitled "The Secret of Life," and what a melancholy treatment of the subject it is.

As the song goes, the nightly ritual of a couple of regulars at the "Starlight Bar" is interrupted when one of them laments the pointlessness of their lives of "workin' and drinkin' and dreams." This leads to a chorus of metaphors such as one might imagine would be offered up by bar chums at just such moments of introspection. Before the song is over, the secret of life is said variously to be found in a good cup of coffee, Monday Night Football, the inviting gaze of Marilyn Monroe, a well-made martini, getting up early, staying up late, and so on in a series of banalities. Ultimately, despondently, the singer tells us that "the secret of life is there ain't no secret, and you don't get your money back." It just goes to show you what a rough day in the saddle can do to a songwriter's mental attitude.

As for me, I thought smugly as I drove along, I had certainly found the secret of life. After all, unlike all those poor devils back in Raleigh, working themselves to death in the drudgery of full-time law practice, I had chosen to absent myself from the partnership track to devote more time to enjoying life—time I have spent paddling all over this country, writing this journal, and lately learning classical guitar.

In my self-satisfaction, I recalled the sad story of a well-known and very successful attorney who found himself terminally ill at a young age. When I heard that his final words were of regret for never having made a trip that he and his young son had long dreamed of taking together, I mentally crossed that one off of my own list of possible regrets. Name a state, name a river, and there's a fair chance that my kids and I have been there in a canoe. Come to think of it, I would now cross off learning a new musical instrument from my list of "things to do before I die." "Yessiree," I told myself. "I'm a heck of a lot smarter than all those money grubbers who haven't figured out that it isn't the guy who dies with the most toys who wins—it's the guy who makes the best use of his leisure time." Isn't that right? And don't you readers of this journal know this same secret: getting out to enjoy God's creation while you still can, as often as you can, and soaking in all the beauty of the world? Whether it be canoeing, saving the whales, surfing the eddies, golfing or what-have-you, find your thing in life and do it to the hilt. Isn't that what life is all about?

Well, actually—no. To tell you the truth, I met the secret of life when I was very young. She was a child at a home for sick children in Baltimore that our youth group visited one Christmas when I was about sixteen. She had a rare disease that withered the skin from her face so that she literally appeared to be a skeleton. It required a conscious effort on my part just to look at her, but she was as happy and as talkative and as wrapped up in the coming of Christmas as any child I ever met.

In that child's smile, I knew even then that I had found the secret of life, but in the years that followed I was certain that if I looked hard enough I could find that secret in other places more pleasing to the senses: in the right woman, enough knowledge, a brilliant career, hard work, a nice home, a comfortable salary, and—yes—beside a campfire, under the stars, in a forest that one can reach only by the silent thoroughfares of the canoe. But the secret of life is no more to be found in those places than in a country song.

Let me tell you the secret of life, friends. I certainly make no claim to the discovery of this knowledge. I am only happy to possess it. It makes for uninteresting copy in this Enlightened Age, but it is, I assure you, the bona fide secret if you can accept it. No, it is not the dip of a well-turned paddle or the call of a loon. It is not the smell of balsam or the dancing light of a campfire. It is only this, and nothing more: that we should love God with all of our heart and mind and soul, and love our neighbor as ourselves. Study that line, once more. It's old news, but good news just the same. What does it mean?

Some of you, I know, are reading this and asking why I cannot just stick to paddling and leave the Almighty out of it. That is, of course, the Great Lie of our times: that we shall have a civil society apart from God. It is not just freedom *of* religion, but freedom *from* religion that so many in our nation now seek. We have already begun to see the fruits of that lie in places like Columbine and pop idols like Eminem. After all, if the only moderating influence in our civic life is no longer a divine imperative, if we make a deity of our free will and a dogma of our pleasure, who is to say that one man's deity won't be another man's death, or that one man's pleasure won't be another man's pain? Take a trip to your local movie theater, sometime, and you'll get a good idea of how the experiment is going, so far. The ideals that make for a civil society—kindness, compassion, self-sacrifice—are anchored in the faith that there is a purpose and a recompense to life on Earth that is greater than our collective quest for personal satisfaction while we are here.

It is well that we should repair to the wilderness to refresh our minds and bodies, and there the beauty of life we shall surely find. But the secret of life, life's very goal, is closer at hand. The love of neighbor is not just a warm welcome to our friends but a hand stretched out to our enemies. It is food to a hungry and undeserving stranger, clothing to a poor and illegal immigrant, and a life lived in service of a purpose broader than our own families.

Imagine, if you will, that we have been put on this earth to accomplish only this and nothing more in our days, here: to love and obey God, and to love and serve our neighbor as ourselves. Imagine that all creation redounds to those two objectives. Imagine that, and do me this favor: find me twenty years from today, and ask not how many rivers I have paddled, but how well I have kept the secret of life.

NORTHERN DREAMS

It had seemed a long drive from suburban Baltimore to Deer Creek, the "designated trout stream" where, my father had somehow learned, the fishing was fast and furious. Along the way we stopped at a tackle shop to purchase a bamboo fishing pole—my first—that came with an impossibly large bobber and braided line of the type in wide use before the advent of monofilament. I was nine or ten years old. Except for a few, blurry flashes of earlier memory, it was the first outing with Dad that I can recall.

Sons of absent, alcoholic fathers will understand too well the hope and unease that surrounds such reunions. Without the usual, day-to-day exchange between parent and child to define for me who and what my father was, he became in my mind an amalgam of the stories—part truth, part fancy—told by and about him. Those stories often revolved around the culture which he and his brothers shared with other families of Irish ancestry who found success in large cities early in this century. There were whispers of the money his father had made and somehow lost as an executive in the canning business. There were stories of the privileged youth he and his brothers spent in private schools and summers at Indian Lake; of his brother's forty-two-foot wooden sailboat, *Cygnet*, the Larchmont Yacht Club, and a garment business with offices in the Empire State Building; of his college days at Columbia and nights spent bussing tables for the glitterati at the 21 Club; of the letter of acceptance from Harvard Law School that went unanswered because his father's money had run out; and, finally, there were those stories held in common with a nation of that long, dark tunnel called World War II.

After he was tested at the Battle of Peleliu and other venues of the US Marines in the South Pacific, the stories which followed my father were mostly about the drinking. But hope springs eternal in a young boy clutching his first fishing pole on a brisk march through the tall grass to his first trout stream, and the stories I chose to remember then were about the Adirondacks.

I doubt I knew where or what the Adirondacks were, at my age, beyond the image of a vaunted, shining wilderness filled with fish, game and fresh air. My father called this place repeatedly to mind, however, in contrast to the place where we happened to be. The trout fishing on Deer Creek by the time we arrived, several days after the spring opener, was neither fast nor furious. Some locals finally explained to my father the routine: hatchery trout are no sooner poured from buckets upstream than they are ignominiously hoisted from the water on bait of kernel corn by hordes of fishermen crowded along the downstream shoreline.

When my father and I arrived, there were no other fishermen and, it soon seemed apparent, no fish. Nonetheless, Dad schooled me in the proper technique. Creeping cautiously up to the bank and shushing me to make no noise, he directed my cast toward a likely looking pool. Nothing. Another pool, another cast, and again, nothing. And so it went for the afternoon until the fishing fell into reminisces about days he and his brothers spent bushwhacking along little streams in the Adirondacks. "If there were a fish in there," he would say, "as soon as your fly hit the water—POW!" I was eager for the "pow" part to begin, but as it turned out my first fish would be not nearly so lofty as a native Adirondack brook trout.

Hillary Sullivan and I were the kind of friends known only to the Neverland of boyhood. But of all the adventures, schemes, and misdemeanors we shared, rising at dawn to pursue the carp of Lake Roland was not to be one of them. Hillary rolled over when the alarm went off, but I got rigged and ready. Carrying the same unlucky bamboo pole from my father and a bag of dough balls concocted of white bread, vanilla extract, molasses and sugar, I set out for glory. It was a testament to my disbelief that I carried nothing with me in which to keep a fish if I actually caught one.

The sun rose over the lake while I patiently stared at my bobber ten feet out from a well-worn spot on shore. A man passed by and, asking what I was after, commented that a carp would break my pole when I caught one. That seemed a little over the top to me at the time, given that I'd never caught a fish, much less one capable of any such destruction. Not ten minutes later, however, my bobber shot south. I reared back on the skittering bamboo pole, which promptly split down its length and became as limp as a blade of grass. Others might have taken that cue to surrender, but I had something to prove. Wallowing waist deep into the cold water of early spring, I snatched the broken tip of my pole as it was being towed out to sea. Then, stumbling and sloshing backwards towards shore, with the bare line in my hand, I soon had a fat, two-pound carp flipping on the ground at my feet. Winning the lottery could scarcely compare to my sense of incredible luck and euphoria at that moment. It was not a trout nor even a bass, but I walked two miles back to Hillary's house with that trophy clasped to my chest. When I called my father for instructions on how to clean and cook a carp, he responded with an old saw: "Boil it for two hours in a pot filled with water and a large rock. Then, eat the rock." And while even I appreciated the wisdom of that recipe after the bony dish was served, to his credit Dad joined me in the feast.

After those days, I encountered other fruitless, well-trodden streams, but occasionally there would be that experience which seemed to recall the mythic promise of the northlands. It was those experiences, like the time-worn stories of my father's glory days, that I chose to remember. Those higher hopes, not the failures and the disappointments, were always brought to the fore as each new adventure was planned.

In the spring of this year, now five seasons since my father's death, I finally reached the headwaters of the legendary Oswegatchie River—a proving ground of trout fishermen in decades past. Whether my father ever walked these virgin woods it is too late to ask, but doubtless he saw others like them. There, deep in the heart of this most primal region of the Adirondacks, I crept quietly upon a rock below High Falls. Spotting a likely looking pool, I cast my lure. No sooner had I turned the handle of my reel, when—POW! An exquisite specimen of the famed Adirondack brook trout, not more than eight inches long, was wriggling at the end of my line. I eased it back into the river, there to grow not nearly so fast as it will in my memory. For what I choose to recall of this and every trip is neither the size nor the number of fish, neither the pain of the portage nor the chill of the wind, neither the luckless days nor the cloudy skies, but rather that vaunted, shining wilderness which is every sportsman's highest ideal and dearest dream.

My Girl

In the heat of a Virginia summer, as we lay beneath a canopy of leaves on a ridge in the Shenandoah Mountains, the two of us heard the noise begin slowly. It started as just a distant rustling of the brush in the early morning, long before dawn, but became steadily, unmistakably closer. We either had no tent or had chosen not to pitch it in the sweat and swelter—I cannot remember now, seventeen years hence. But given what little we did have in the first months of our marriage, it would not surprise me to recall that we were just doing without.

We had certainly done without the night before. After borrowing my sister's VW wagon to make the trek from our apartment in Maryland for a "honeymoon" weekend of backpacking in Shenandoah National Park, we had arrived in Front Royal too late to hit the trail. A cheap hotel would have to do.

Were it not for the innkeeper's taxidermy displays that recalled Hitchcock's *Psycho* too vividly in Julie's mind, we would have had better sense than to walk away from the last vacant room in town. After whiling away another hour of fruitless searching, Julie relented and we returned to ask Mr. Bates for the room—only to find that one gone, too.

The back of a VW wagon is not quite five-feet-ten-inches long, but I am. And getting married was supposed to mean never again having to say "Gee, honey, this parking lot looks dark enough," but we did that night. My plan, if the Hardee's manager came out to complain about our being parked there too long, was to tell him in no uncertain terms that Julie's father was the executive vice president of the company (true) and that she had the pull to have a mere store manager summarily dismissed if he didn't back off and leave us alone (not even close to true). Thankfully, I never had to explain to the manager of the Front Royal Hardee's—or to my wife, for that matter—why we were sleeping in a borrowed VW in the parking lot of a hamburger stand, in the first place.

The long answer to that question is still in the rough-draft stage, but the short answer was "the money." Young, fearless, and high on the challenge of making a life together, we were determined to starve our own way. We had held onto hope against hope for a honeymoon at a cottage in the Adirondacks, that summer, but we just couldn't swing it. I still have the now-tattered brochure that shows an aerial photo of Raquette Lake amid a carpet of woods spreading out for miles. The little cottage in another picture, set back in the trees on Pine Island, seemed as quaint as you might imagine. I don't know why the owner didn't tell us it was our tough luck for canceling our reservation so late in the season, but we were more glad than he could know to have our deposit back.

When dawn came, we fired up the VW with the thirty-nine-dollar Earl Scheib paint job (Gatorade green) and sputtered away before the breakfast crew got suspicious. At the park gate, the ranger gave us the scare report about lions, tigers and bears, which we blithely ignored. By mid-morning, we were already deep in the woods, casting for trout with a fishing rod I had given Julie for her twenty-first birthday. (Yes, I was an incurable romantic even then.)

It is easier to get lost on foot in the woods than in a canoe on a lake where, sooner or later, one will bump into the shore. The lesser-used trails we had chosen (of course) were overgrown and hard to follow. More than once I humored Julie in her insistence about which way to go to regain our bearings, only to come to the unspoken realization that she had been right all along. Everything I needed to know about married life was revealed to me in the woods that weekend, slow though it has been to sink in.

What rare spasm of forethought had prompted me to hang our pack from a tree, that night, I am not sure. At the age of twenty-three, I planned for few things in advance. We were well off the trail in a hardwood forest, sleeping on a bed of dry leaves, when the noise in the blackness changed unmistakably to footsteps.

I was no Daniel Boone, but my subconscious mind apparently could not reconcile the pace and rhythm of the noise with the usual motions of the night forest. When my deductive powers finally stumbled to the conclusion that this was indeed the sound of four heavy legs, I woke up. My arm shot out and pinned Julie to the forest floor beside me. She was so very pleased to be there at the time, as I recall.

Exactly how the sacrament of marriage imparts to the union of two people a strength greater than the sum of their fears is one of the mysteries of Faith. Many, many times since that summer have I reached out and found uncommon courage to face life's twists and turns in the simple gesture of touch between a man and wife. It also helps to hang your food pack in a tree.

Apparently finding nothing to eat but the two stiff, moribund creatures on the forest floor—and they thankfully not to his liking—the beast wondered off. In the morning we found our way out of the woods in time to save fond memories of the experience. The VW started on the first crank, and we began the ride home listening to the radio play the John Denver tune, "Some Days Are Diamonds, Some Days Are Stone." So it has been these seventeen years, much more for the better than the worse.

Just a few months ago a letter arrived from a concerned reader who hoped that the absence of my wife from many of the stories in this journal was not a sign of a decline in "friendly relations" between us. I bounded down the stairs from our home office to show the letter to Julie, who responded with characteristic bemusement. Having known me "when," she waits expectantly for the day when all of the present 5,000 readers of this journal will realize that I haven't the foggiest idea of what I am talking about and I am forced to slip quietly into a life of gardening and bridge.

But the reader's letter was an occasion for some reflection, as reader letters often are. I realize that many men have the company of their wives on trips into the wild. Is it a sign of some disaffection that I usually do not? I shouldn't think so. The reason has something to do with our basic assumptions about the individual in married life.

What I have learned about marriage after

seventeen years could have saved us a lot of the usual arguments and frustrations at the outset of that journey. It is a lesson I dare say that men—being self-absorbed by nature—are more in need of learning than women. Yes, it would please me greatly if Julie joined me whenever I went into the field. A photo on a recent cover of a men's magazine showing a comely young woman in a bikini, pulling a canoe through the marsh while her beau reclines in the stern, captured this fantasy quite nicely. (Wives everywhere, please take note.) What I enjoy most, though, are those long, where-will-life-take-us conversations around the campfire. That's what makes a trip meaningful, to me. But the elusive truth is that marriage is not about *me* or my personal satisfaction and never was. The object of the game is not my happiness or contentment—these are fringe benefits earned in the pursuit of a simpler but much loftier goal. That goal is the survival and success of the union, itself.

A pastor whom I greatly admire once observed that, in our narcissistic culture, we err by filtering the question of whether, when or how to obey God through our own myopic, mortal sense of what will bring us joy and contentment. We've got it exactly backwards. Joy and contentment, he would teach us, flow from an obedience to God if for no better reason than that He is God and we are not. What a profoundly repugnant notion that is, in a country which venerates the individual, self-determination, and personal freedom increasingly above all else, and where the "Me Generation" reigns supreme.

Two people are at first drawn to each other by physical attraction and the sense of personal affirmation that each derives from the other's companionship. We could hang together for scarcely ten minutes in the absence of these adhesives, but they make a poor mortar with which to build a life together. There will always be someone else who is more attractive, and Mr. or Ms. Right will eventually tire of the job of assuring our continual aggrandizement. Over the long haul, there will come a cold, sober moment when all that separates us from the abyss of self-indulgence is the power of the promise we have made to each other. From our commitment to obey the promise in that moment—if for no better reason than because it is a promise—comes a wife's trust and the sound sleep of little children. From that trust comes the freedom to celebrate each other's differences without fear of being divided by them. And in that freedom abides the peace, joy and contentment we have been searching for all long.

FEAR AND FEAR ITSELF

On a gray July afternoon, the waning daylight made silhouettes of a party of canoeists struggling to make headway against the Canadian wind. It was a north wind, for which Lake Opeongo is duly famous. We watched them from the warmth of our campfire, sheltered from the blow beneath a knoll of granite and moss. The smell of fresh, baked bread and cedar smoke wafted through the air. It was a good day to be in camp, and the youngsters in the approaching canoes knew that as well as anyone.

They were a group of a dozen boys, all about thirteen years of age, accompanied by two Toronto teachers working as counselors at a summer camp. For the last mile they had hunkered in the lee of the point of land on which we were camped, finding there some respite from the boarding waves in unprotected water. To our pleasant surprise, they chose not to round the point into the teeth of the wind but instead pulled into camp on the leeward shore. Apologies for the intrusion and assurances that they would stop only for a moment were cheerfully interrupted by an invitation to stay the night. They thanked us but deferred their answer, while their eyes moved from the map, to the lowering north sky, to the mound of split wood beside our campfire, then back to the map. Meanwhile, my son Kip and his cousin Bennett, at seven years apiece, were electrified into action by the arrival of the older boys. Various shells, bugs and rope projects were retrieved from around the camp and presented to the bewildered guests for inspection and approval. Bennett's father and I roused the fire a little higher while the young campers eagerly succumbed to offers of brownies and bread with jam. Wet jackets were hung on the clothesline, and soon every hand held a steaming mug of spiced cider. The leaders finally concluded that it was pointless to resist further and joined us for the night.

Later that evening, while the younger campers attended to roasting marshmallows, the leaders discussed with us their plans and the glories of living so close to such a boundless wilderness.

"Did you hear of the bear attack in the North Arm two weeks ago?"

We had not. The ranger had mentioned only that there had been some "bear problems" in the North Arm and told us to be sure to hang our food, at night. I thought it strange that she marked in large, black letters across our permit, "advised about bears," but precautions against food-pack raiders of all stripes were already part of our routine.

The men explained that the incident involved a group of boys from another summer camp in the area who were making their annual canoe-trip through Lake Opeongo into the interior of Algonquin Park. They had placed their food in canoes and moored the canoes out in the lake, to avoid bear problems. At about two o'clock in the morning, a bear came into the camp where an eleven-year-old boy from Montreal and two other children were sleeping in one of the group's several tents. The bear reportedly tore into the tent and began to drag the boy off by the foot. An intrepid counselor who heard the screaming smashed one canoe paddle over the bear's head, then bludgeoned it with a second paddle until it ran up a tree.

The counselors put the boy in a canoe and took him to a nearby campsite where a motorboat could be seen. He was rushed to the ranger station, and a call for help was made. According to the report in the *Toronto Star*, the boy will recover fully. Rangers confirmed that there was no food at the site where the bear attacked and could not explain the bear's behavior. They later found and shot a bear that they determined by the paddle marks on its skull had committed the attack. It was reported to be a healthy, normal animal.

Well, this certainly was food for thought as we contemplated retiring in the woods that evening. Still, I reasoned, we were at least four miles from the location of the attack. Then our guests began with the next, more horrible story.

"A lot of folks camp on islands out here, thinking they're safe from the bears," they explained. "But six years ago, a man and woman were found cached on Bates Island." ("Cache" is the word for a carcass which a bear has buried for a future meal.) Bates Island is a beautiful spot not more than a twenty-minute paddle from the ranger station. Kip had begged me to make camp there on our way out, but there was little firewood, and it is a busy spot. The island forms a bottleneck through which all traffic heading back to the road must pass. It seemed an unlikely place for a bear attack.

There are many things to fear in a canoe trip, but

seldom have my thoughts been pre-occupied with the risk of bears. I have long understood the importance of securing the food well up and away from the tent—chipmunks and raccoons are a ravenous bunch—but those things which I fear most relate to the safety of my children in the elements. Indeed, the sole consolation of a canoe trip without Kip—my even-keeled, ever-ready companion—is the leave which his absence grants to confront every rapid and squall with giddy abandon. A crossing with my wife and children is fraught with unspoken concern for my plan should the canoe become swamped in open water. Behind every sunny sky that heralds the departure of laughing children is a blackening storm that threatens disaster for their return. But still we go, because somehow we understand that a life without risk is a life not worth living. A child sheltered from all of life's dangers is one who will know few of its joys.

People who consider that in writing this journal I am living in the woods some two months out of the year often ask whether I carry a weapon for safety against black bears. I do not. The risk is too great that my wife, in a fit of sleep dementia, would take me for some Sasquatch on my return trip from the loo and blow me to kingdom-come before the first bear ever showed up. To be truly effective in a moment of urgent need, the gun would have to be left loaded in the tent at night, and loaded guns don't belong on canoe trips with kids. Despite the tragic exceptions, the real risk of encountering a predacious black bear in one's tent at night is small. *Field & Stream* has yet to recommend retiring to a tent with a gun in its annual issue on bear-hunting techniques.

Still, a father worries about his children. As I settled into our tent in the Canadian woods that night in July, I vowed that it will be an unfortunate bear that ever attempts to drag away a child of mine. But the better part of valor knows that a father cannot protect his child from every danger—animal or otherwise. Like the reassurance that FDR once gave a nation, more often the greater danger in the woods comes not from that which we fear but from the paralysis of fear itself. Pity the child who is never allowed the chance to face life's bogeymen and overcome them. With that in mind, I drifted off to a peaceful sleep.

PADDLING BY EAR

Amid the cobblestone streets of Baltimore's Mount Vernon section, where statues of our Founding Fathers festooned with pigeons have watched a century pass, the gargoyles guarding the entrance to the Peabody Conservatory of Music have watched along with them. Some thirty years ago they bit their tongues as a distracted young man passed those portals each week en route to a ritualized agony of childhood known as "piano lessons."

Actually, I loved the piano—still do. I picked out the notes of my first songs by ear on an instrument purchased for my sister Suzie and by third grade had learned a three-chord boogie-woogie well enough to be lead piano-banger in a trio of pals. At an early age I rarely missed tuning in to the Harley Show on AM radio at night to hear the riffs and rhythms of Oscar Peterson, Earl "Fatha" Hines, Fats Waller, and all the greats.

At eighteen, I was the only male student at Western Maryland College with his own key to the women's dormitory, where a concert-size grand piano beckoned me decidedly more often than the women did. I could hum more standards than Steely Dan tunes, was a fixture at sorority wine-and-cheese parties, and even did a stint for cash at Cockey's Tavern, but Peabody wasn't interested in any of it. Peabody was a place of notation and theory, of tempo, timbre and timing—of playing a piece exactly the way Bach wrote it and jolly well liking it, thank you. It was, ultimately, a place to which I was politely asked not to return after the exasperation proved too much for my instructors.

I used to waste time wondering what might have been "had I only applied myself," but one of the benefits of the passing years is that a pattern of this behavior eventually emerges, and, along with it, the means to rationalize most of life's left turns under the notion of "larger forces at work." In my case, those forces were at war against conformity, obedience, deference to authority, and many other core values of a well-ordered society. Their armies have been winning most of the skirmishes if not the war in my life, and this journal is among the spoils. By whose leave, after all, does an improbable voyageur from the suburbs of Baltimore presume to write "The Quarterly Journal of Traditional Canoe Camping"?

By whose leave, indeed. Giants have stalked the North Woods before us all—Bill Riviere, Sigurd Olson and Bill Mason to name a few of the latter-day saints. I have read but hardly studied their works, and I knew none of them. More to the point, I have carefully avoided following too closely any one man's particular approach to journeying in the wilderness—not that I wouldn't do well by a closer study of the masters, mind you. I simply believe that life is best lived at your own risk, as a process of creative error and rediscovery, not a calculated imitation of what has gone before.

In fact, I get a subtle sense of unease whenever I read someone else's idea of how, exactly, to negotiate a difficult piece of whitewater, as if it might deprive me of the satisfaction of taking credit for my own accomplishments. Some gain real benefit from careful study of proper form, but there are those of us who are hard-wired to extemporize everything in life. After all, what fun is there in going bleary-eyed trying to learn paddling maneuvers such as cross-braces and draws from confusing diagrams, when a sense of "what to do next" ultimately must come to you (or not) like an epiphany in the middle of a real set of rapids? I may have flirted with *Study and Planning*, but *Necessity*, and more often her sister *Dire Necessity*, have been the mothers of my inventions. That's why you will never see an article in this journal presuming to teach you the dance steps you'll need to go lightly over your next waterfall.

There is ample opportunity nowadays to get caught up in notions of the *right way* and *wrong way* of doing things in the wild. I remember a man who climbed into the bow of my canoe for a short paddle across the riffles to an island in the river, where we planned to saw up a boatload of driftwood for our fire. He had recently been to a high-flown paddling school—one of those places where kids in trick boats and wetsuits teach the "sport" of paddling to well-heeled suburbanites eager to catch on to the Next Big Thing. No sooner had we eased into the current than he became a tornado of activity, punching the water with his paddle on one side and then the other, angled this way and that way, in short bursts of surgical precision. You would have thought we were in the Olympic trials and that Hell Falls loomed just ahead. It was exhausting just watching him. I had never known how much difficult and complex work I had been missing in the simple task of moving from point A to point B. For the rest of the trip, I was sure I looked like a sloth on a barge.

A similar experience occurred when some friends first invited me up to their favorite river for an overnighter. These were students of the Old School. They had a curious paddling style I had not seen before but have since come to recognize as the North Woods stroke popularized by Bill Mason. Mason was to the Canadian canoeing tradition what Mickey Mantle was to baseball. Kids practiced swinging like Mickey, and wilderness-seekers everywhere still want to do most things as Mason did them. Clinics are regularly held at canoeing festivals to teach the North Woods paddling style, and those who claim to have mastered it swear by it. Most of the hotshots in the wilderness-canoeing biz paddle this way. You'll notice ads in canoeing magazines with paddlers posed in the turned-down-wrist finish that is characteristic of Mason's style. It's a fine style, at that.

No sooner had I started out on the trip with these fellows than I noticed that they had stopped ahead and were staring back as I came down the river. I began to feel like the only man in a sport coat at a black-tie affair. What they were watching was the way the editor of a journal of traditional canoe-camping paddled his canoe. What they were seeing was not Mason but a modified feather-stroke from the Boy Scout Handbook, with a little English thrown in. It is an ungainly sight, to be sure, but I can paddle in that groove from sunup to sundown, day after day, and never miss a beat. They tried to teach me the North Woods stroke, but I proved to be an incorrigible Old

Dog.

Here's the lesson, friends: When you listen to a cut of Oscar Peterson taking off for the stratosphere at the Blue Note, you know he's playing it the way he feels it—the way that no one, including Oscar himself, has ever played that piece before. That's his gift. You can't deconstruct it, you can't teach it, and you can't recreate it from a page of sheet music. You've got to feel it. *Feeling it* is all that you can really learn from any master. No one ever painted a Renoir by the numbers, and the art of the wilderness is not in how well you travel, but why. The great tradition to which this journal aspires is not a set of techniques to be memorized or gear to be accumulated. It is the freedom of every man to write his own opus across the tattered pages of the woods and play it as far and long as his imagination will carry him.

A Dream of Spring

"Ah, Fall." We say those words with bitter sweetness, as a father speaks the name of a wayward child who grew up and left him too soon. Only yesterday our world was sultry and serene, but now we are left to our early evenings beside the fire, sipping something warm and growing weary with regret for the lost love that was Summer.

Our journey through the seasons began with the first, tentative drips of thawing snow from the face of the Appalachian range, with its great ear cocked southward for the muffled cries of returning geese. The march of Spring gathered momentum on the flood tide of rivers grown wild and drunk with rain, where hungry trout, stacked cheek by jowl in the current, struggled for their place at the long-awaited banquet of flies—an abundance nearly forgotten in the months of ice and sleep, sleep and ice.

By July the journey slowed considerably and seemed to stand still in thick forests, dark and heavy with the smell of rain. There, you and I hung our tarps and found a tree good for leaning paddles, while we fetched supper from the bottom of a canvas pack. We dared not speak, that afternoon, of the impossibly blue sky, or of how the fish had been so easily fooled, or that in all the days that had been spent in the woods for a hundred generations, no one could have seen a finer example of a bull moose than the one that surprised us at the end of the portage. If we spoke of these things, perhaps they would disappear, we worried. Perhaps the weather gods might realize that they had overlooked our daily dram of misery for days on end, and it would blow a gale all the way to Kittery. So we smiled without a word as the woods beyond our campfire faded to grays and blues, and we slept like kings and emperors beneath a royal canopy of stars.

Deep within us we kindled a tiny flame of hope that this would be the year that the feast of our freedom would roll on forever. The immortal green of each leaf along the lake offered no hint of the dying golds and reds of autumn hidden within. The sunlight that painted the skies and the distant mountains betrayed no inkling of the planets above, quietly marking their appointed rounds through the portals of time, space and season. We had no cause to think of the end of things. Ours was only to begin anew each day—to swim, ebullient and naked, beneath the waterfalls. Ours was only to lie basking in the patch of sun that found its way through the fir tops onto the wide, flat rocks below. We had forgotten each and everything, all and anything, else. We had forgotten all of it because there was no one in the forest to remind us, and the sunshine made a hash of our memory.

Such luck, it was! Who knew that the Conservateur des Forêts would sign the wrong form for our camping permit—the blue one labeled "jamias plus" (evermore)—and thereby cede to us all of Quebec, in error? The general populace had no choice but to move away and take most of the mosquitoes with them. The two of us were left to paddle and camp over all three-hundred-twenty million acres, forever! Well, not forever, technically. You calculated that if we kept our pace we would reach the last lake in Quebec at about the same time the sun burned out. The whole affair caused a huge ruckus in Ottawa, but forms are forms, and the ones signed in triplicate, addressed to Her Royal Highness the Queen, can't be fixed. It was all ours.

In Summer, we were no different than the deer, the otter and the bear, you and I. We shared their world and for a week or two dared imagine that we belonged with them. After all, did not the paddle bend to our whim? Did not our slender canoe sweep beneath us like a woman who has danced with the same man all her life and is as easily led by his thoughts as by his hand? Masters of forest and stream, our serenade was the timeless song of the whippoorwill, and the barred owl invited us every day at evening to discuss with him the great issues of the age.

In that magic haze, in that place where we hung a rope over a deep hole for swimming, where all men are boys, time did stand still for us that day in July. It came at that same moment when you and I decide, as we do each year, that there shall be a Fall. Somewhere between the first cup of coffee and the last strip of bacon at breakfast, one day, we decide that there again must be taxes and traffic jams, mortarboards and mortgages, football and apple cider and pumpkins and shiny shoes on the feet of little schoolchildren. And so there are such things. Time marches on, they say, but Man is the grand marshal of his own parade through Time, and what if we forgot to call Time's tune? To what, then, would Time march?

I tell you, my friend, Pogo was right when he said, "I have met the enemy, and he is us!" If we had just kept our eyes open and our thoughts clear, if we had lived in that moment of joy and that moment alone, who can say that all of us—every last one of us—would not still be there beside a campfire, on a lake, beneath a July moon? No, you say? No? Ah, but so little faith in the magic of daydreams, there is. Who, after all, are you to say "no"—you who looked away, you who let Summer slip past us like a fickle schoolgirl? You've done it again, don't you see? She was too fast for you, and wiser than her years. You climbed the rock above the lake to pick a prize of blueberries for her, then lost yourself in the thicket of a long, sinking afternoon. By the time you finally stumbled out onto the other shore, fat and blue-faced, she had stolen your clothes and left with September. And now where have they gotten you, all of your promises of eternal love beneath an Adirondack moon?

Gather our paddles and let us go home. Enough of this fog. The tide is away, and Fall is upon us, with Winter on her heels. Let us finally say it and confront the bitterness of saying so: She is gone, our lovely summer. She is gone as a first kiss and the girl who gave it, and there is no turning back to either of them. Fond remembrance will warm us awhile but leave us colder still for the remembering. Like aging champions, we trundle through November along the paths of June, as the lakes close over again for spite at our inattention.

A day of unexpected warmth in December will tempt our memories, and we will pause for a moment at the edge of a field. We will crane our necks for a breath of Summer that travels on the wind like a lover's letter, but it will not be her. Tomorrow will be colder still. Soon there will be snow, and we will come at last to admit defeat at the grave of February.

What's that, you say? Kindle hope, you say? Why should we? She is gone, I tell you, and there is nothing but January and despair and ice in our boots. We had her beauty and all of Canada, too, and we gave them both up for this wind and bitterness. Leave me then to my pipe and fire, and do not torment me to speak of those halcyon days of August and the smell of pine in the noon sun.

Look, you say? Out there, in the distance? Look at what? There is nothing here but duty, news, and news of duty. There is much work to do, and I shall not go looking with you. Not at all. We had our chance.

Look, look farther you say, again? What is it that you see? I tell you she is gone, and the one you claim to see is a poor pretender to the throne of my heart. Her name is Spring you say, but I do not know her. I have eyes only for Summer, Summer, who left me to weep for her golden hair and bronzed shoulders. Do not tempt me with talk of hope, and leave me to my grief.

Will you not desist? Alright, then, I shall look for what little good it will do us.

But wait—what is it, there?

Yes, I now see what you see. She is shy, distant and pale—but how lovely! Spring, you say? I see her now, yes. Still months away, I watch as she slowly slips off her long white gown of snow and stands shivering in the flesh. Such full, firm breasts, and cheeks still flush from the cold. The gentle curve of her back meets her hips and forms the shape of a heart that would steal my own. She fixes my eyes like a talisman. I cannot look away. It is no use any longer to mourn. I am in love! I am in love, and her name is Spring! There shall never be another like her, and none so splendid or fine. We shall soon be wild and drunk with rain, she and I, on rivers of melting snow, in meadows where no man for a hundred generations has seen such sights as we shall find. Come with us, will you? We will not fail her, this time. To Canada! To Canada, boys! Spring is ours, and we are hers, and cruel December has lost its might.

WHILE YE MAY

As I prepared for our voyage in the Adirondacks this summer, I thought it behooved me to read an excellent book about the life and letters of one of the first white men to go venturing by canoe without a professional guide in this wilderness of upstate New York. The book is *Canoeing the Adirondacks with Nessmuk; the Adirondack Letters of George Washington Sears*, published by the Adirondack Museum at Blue Mountain Lake. It is edited by Dan Brenan, with revisions by Robert L. Lyon and Hallie E. Bond. The book compiles the several letters written by Sears in the 1880s for *Forest & Stream* magazine, under the Narragansett Indian pen-name "Nessmuk," about his canoe-camping adventures in the Adirondacks.

Editor Dan Brenan credits Nessmuk for the "democratization of wilderness travel" that has made outdoor recreation the industry and passion of millions today. In Nessmuk's time, those who came to the Adirondacks for its storied trout-fishing and deer hunting generally were "sports." They would hire a guide to transport them from lake to lake in a distinctively-shaped rowing canoe known as the Adirondack guide boat. Nessmuk clearly admired and revered the guides for their skill and knowledge of the woods, but he sought more to emulate than be served by them. At 5-feet 3-inches tall and 110 pounds, he could, one supposes, only with great difficulty portage a guide boat that typically weighed seventy-five pounds or more. Seeking a more self-reliant experience, he commissioned the construction of short, lightweight boats that later became commonly referred to as "pack" canoes. One such boat, which he named the *Sairy Gamp*, measured just nine feet and weighed ten-and-a-half pounds. The published letters of his Adirondack trips "going through alone" in these small boats fanned the popularity of the design and, Brenan concludes, helped to usher in the "golden age" of American canoeing.

Despite his determined independence, love for the outdoors, and remarkably skilled woodcraft, Nessmuk's poor health, Brenan notes, was a recurrent nuisance that sometimes interfered with or interrupted his adventures. He was afflicted by malaria and the respiratory illnesses common to that era. In his last years, Nessmuk wrote the following in a letter to a friend, who had invited him on a trip to seek respite from his condition: "I seldom get beyond the front yard, and the gun is of no further use to me, while I have not put the old rod together in two years. Time and 'physical disability' will . . . beat every mother's son of us and I do not complain. Few men have had as much of life in the woods as I have, and memory at least can not be taken away from me while my senses hold good . . . Ah me! How vividly I recall the visit, all too short, that we had at the Moose River years ago. *Tempus fugit.* Let him fly; let him flicker. I have been there, and done it; and if I were young again I would do it some more . . ."

In our age of vaccines, long life, and

unprecedented wellness, it is easy for us who are the progeny of Nessmuk's self-reliant ideal to forget that life holds no guarantees and that our own days of wilderness sojourning might not be long. I recall once telling an elderly woman about my idle dreams someday to cruise the world in a sailboat—a pursuit that Nessmuk had also enjoyed—but dismissing lightheartedly the notion that work and family ties would soon, if ever, permit such a trip. She paused to answer, and, with an abrupt seriousness and unsolicited concern for my plans, flatly said, "Go now."

It was clear to me from the depth of her glance, seemingly across the span of a lifetime, that she offered knowledge distilled from experience. *Tempus fugit.* It is said that no one on his death bed every wished for more time at the office. Our "Adirondack days," wherever they are spent among friends and family, are the ones that we, like Nessmuk, will treasure most in the end.

THE LIVING WILDERNESS

My grandfather George Washington LaCroix was raised on a farm near Pulaski, Tennessee. I have only a fleeting memory of him, from when I was two, as the old man in the bed on the second floor of my grandmother's house in Baltimore, just before he died. His younger brothers Jefferson Davis (Jeff) and Monroe (Monnie) had stayed and made a living through the Great Depression in the gentle hills where "George W" was born.

Right after Christmas in 1972, I left Baltimore and headed south for a visit with my grandfather's side of the family. In my mother's judgment, I was getting to an age, at fourteen, that demanded more freedom of movement than our small apartment in the suburbs could furnish. I was about to encounter, and be distinctly changed by, a world vastly different from the one that I knew.

The differences in that new world were apparent to my every sense from the first step I took inside Uncle Jeff's and Aunt Viola's tin-roof farmhouse, tucked back in Puryear Hollow. Theirs was a life lived very close to the land. The woodstove in the main bedroom provided the only, yet ample, heat in winter. The fields behind the house produced tobacco and cattle for the auction houses, hay for the animals in winter, and vegetables of every variety for the table.

For more than a century, the LaCroix family had trapped the creeks and streams of this area for mink and muskrat and hunted the hills all about for squirrel, rabbit and deer. Even among a rural community accustomed to such living, Jeff and Viola were widely noted for having raised their two giant sons largely on a diet of wild game.

There was a rugged honesty and toughness to this way of life that intrigued me. Although I was an athlete of average ability, the lifestyle I encountered among my grandfather's family demanded a different sort of grit. They had a mental and physical toughness forged by the elements and measured in terms more subtle than time, speed and points scored.

The days after Christmas are the last of the deer-hunting season in Tennessee and most everywhere else. I was outfitted with a brand new pair of leather, Herman Survivor boots and a goose down coat purchased for me by a neighbor who knew I had little of what I would need for a winter hunting trip. In my own mind, I was every inch of Davy Crockett, but that image quickly faded.

The LaCroix men weren't equipped the way I was or the way I expected them to be, nor did it seem to matter much. They had an eye for useful things, but not much use for luxury. While in the woods one day I was dressed to the nines and freezing my tail off, bouncing from one foot to the other to keep warm despite the goose down, leather gloves and forty-below-zero boots. At the same time my Uncle Monnie, a man then in his sixties, kept vigil in a light, cloth jacket, holding a cold rifle-stock in his thick, bare hands without complaint. How, in such circumstances, do you say to a man fifty years your senior that you are freezing and need to head in? Pride goeth, and I decided to follow. Monnie didn't mind, of course, but his seeming indifference to the elements left an impression on me.

I eagerly returned to Tennessee for the next two summers. In that time I learned a little more about life on the land and took my post as Defender of the Bean Fields against the willful incursions of cottontail rabbits. I would watch as Uncle Jeff, slowed only by the arthritis in his fingers, expertly dressed the fish and game that the earth yielded to us, to be breaded, pan-fried and served for supper. The leftovers were saved, reheated and served again at the next meal until all was gone.

"Wilderness adventures" in this world were not planned—they simply occurred. Jeff's son Charles and I once took off for someplace on the Little Tennessee River without much more than a boat and a bottle of peach soda between us. Neither he nor I can recall the spot, but I'll never forget the trip. When night fell, we found a high, rock ledge overlooking the river and laid our bedrolls on the open ground. Gazing up in the pitch black at the dazzling array of stars, we wondered out loud about Chariots of the Gods, life and the origin of things.

During an entirely different type of adventure, I got to know a tomboy who lived at the next farm up the road. Until then I had never even kissed a girl, but by the end of that first summer I was as certain as only a fifteen-year-old boy can be that I would never love another. Now married and a mother of two, she never knew that I stayed up all night before my flight home, scrawling elaborate plans at the kitchen table for an escape into the woods. There, in the name of true love, I intended to seek sanctuary from the cruel imperatives of growing up. It was only the certain knowledge that my sanity would forevermore be in doubt that persuaded me otherwise. Despite these reservations, though, I never paused to wonder whether the forest would provide for my needs.

Impossibly, it has been more than twenty-six years since that first Tennessee holiday. What you now hold in your hands is grown from the seeds of that experience. I often wonder whether we in this country are still planting such seeds, or enough of them.

Last summer, my eight-year-old son and I chanced to share a group campsite for one night with a patrol of boy scouts who, like us, were on a canoe trip through the Adirondacks. Notable in their routines was the complete absence of a campfire. Propane stoves and lanterns were humming everywhere, but not one stick of wood was kindled for cooking or camaraderie. Most of their food was reconstituted from plastic bags, all without preparation or cooking over an open flame. They did not occupy their time fishing for dinner, nor with pioneering. There was not an axe, saw, filet knife or Dutch oven to be found among them. They were *at* the woods but not *in* the woods.

A friend whose son is in the scouts explained to me that rustic camping has fallen out of favor with some wilderness advocates. He cited the growing sentiment in favor of banning cooking fires altogether and confining tent sites to designated platforms. As he described the various restrictive covenants of "low impact" camping, I had mixed emotions. At the age of these boys, my peers and I shared a fanatical devotion to leaving no trace of our presence, but being on our own in the wild and mastering the skills of the American frontier were matters of great personal pride. The yellowed pages of my 1972 edition of *How to Stay Alive in the Woods* are dog-eared and underlined. It occurred to me that, with a very different sense of themselves as aliens unwelcome to touch or tarry in this world, the "impact" of this new type of wilderness experience would be low, indeed—on the boys who were experiencing it. The magic of canoe-tripping, after all, lies in the re-creation of a way of life connected to the land, not the ability merely to "withstand" the elements through a brief triumph of portable technology.

I join with those who seek to reduce man's impact where the very notion of "wilderness" is threatened by it. There surely are wild places we have loved too much, but I wonder if the problem is so widespread as we suppose. Every year I paddle and camp extensively in varied parts of this country, and it is astounding in this age how often I am utterly alone. My abiding concern is less for canoeists' impact on the wilderness than that there are not enough children furloughed on a more regular basis from the malls, arcades and soccer fields to interact with, and be impacted by, the very places which we must look to them to preserve.

Do you remember the first time you saw the Great Smoky Mountains? Did you look out over the purple haze and imagine the world as it was before the first axe fell on these shores? Did you plan, as I did, to follow a tumbling, crystal stream to that place where the "big ones" were hiding? Did you dream of a hidden waterfall, the perfect cast, the impossible trout? If so, ask yourself: Do we allow such places to infect our children with the same incurable longing, or will brief, technological encounters with wild places leave no trace on their psyches? When duty calls this generation to fight the next wave of urban sprawl, will they have a romance with the woods worth fighting for?

Looking into the embers of our Adirondack campfire, I supposed it was useless to join the chorus of old codgers pining for the way things "used to be." Time marches on. Things change. Just then, my son Kip came into camp. By the firelight I saw that he had the face of a coal miner, and what clothes remained attached to his body were covered in mud. He would need a long swim in the morning, but he was asleep before his head hit the pillow. I decided that if what sticks to him in these woods never washes off entirely, that will be just fine with me.

Traveling Light

In my last year of law school, at the start of the final exam in one particularly difficult course, several dozen of my classmates and I were spaced evenly apart in the auditorium, each with nothing upon his desk but a pen and a blank exam booklet. This arrangement was designed to prevent cheating. The distance between students made it impossible for anyone to see what anyone else was writing in his exam booklet, and any extraneous material on one's desk would be easily spotted.

Before the start of the exam, I saw the professor approach one young man and ask to see a small card on his desk. It turned out to be a holy card. These are small cards illustrated with a scene from the Gospel and imprinted with a prayer. They are used by many Catholics as an aid to faith in times of need or special devotion. This being a Jesuit school, the professor was only too pleased to allow the card to remain.

As I said, it was a difficult course. Sometime during the test, I noticed the young man in question draw a card from his pocket. Whether it was the same card the professor had examined earlier I cannot tell you and am only too happy not to know; but the furtive manner in which it was retrieved and read suggested to me that the young man's purpose was something other than prayer. That image has endured in my memory because it was so starkly unexpected. He was one of the brighter students in the class.

In the years since law school I have preferred to give my classmate the benefit of the doubt. But whatever idealism I took with me on graduation day has been sorely tested in the ensuing fifteen years of trial practice and daily life. I have seen judges, lawyers, paupers and princes cheat with gusto and devotion. None of these sins was committed for a loaf of bread or medicine for a sick child. With few exceptions, they were lies told out of a desire for material gain or the fear of material loss—told by people who, like the young law student, were well able to achieve their desires and assuage their fears through honorable means.

It is symptomatic of our human nature, in general, and our American culture, in particular, that we seek to surround ourselves with a superabundance of material comforts. I need hardly bother to make this point heard above the deafening roar of Madison Avenue which shouts it every day. There are creams that make us look young and cars that make us look rich. There are houses that make us feel powerful and gadgets that make us feel smart. There are baubles and trifles and curios without number to clutter our cabinets and speak of our good taste, and there are malls without end to store and sell them. There are clubs and societies and schools and neighborhoods that make us feel well-connected or well-bred. And then there are the clothes and ornaments we find pleasing because they reassure us (and remind others) that we are the kind of people who would own the cars, go to the schools, belong to the clubs and live in such neighborhoods as we do. In this way are our days enslaved—not in a struggle against want but in a pledge of fealty to things of this world. What a fool's lot this is.

Lest my purpose be misunderstood, let me hasten to confess my full-paid, charter membership in this fraternity of fools. It is a decided minority in this country whose homes are not a palace, whose dinner tables are not a banquet, and whose furnishings are not a royal dowry in the currency of the wider world. If we are to hear the voice of Mr. Lincoln's "better angels," we must step away from the crowd. When we do, we will often find we have wandered into the wilderness.

My first encounter with the transforming power of wilderness happened to occur in a sailboat. I was with my brother on the South River of Chesapeake Bay in a Rhodes 19 that he had rented by the hour. The boat had no motor, but I recall looking over the bow at the unbroken horizon and realizing that it was within our power, at that moment, to sail as long and as far as the water and wind would bear us. What an epiphany that was to me, and how well it illustrates what I have recognized elsewhere in life's wiser moments. It is the promise of that which is sustainable, incorruptible, unfailing and unfettered which marks the eternal.

In the simple form of the canoe we find not only a means of travel and amusement but an opportunity to sever ties to a needlessly complex world. Less is truly more. Furnished in nothing more than what a common man's wages might buy, I have never known an hour of want in the woods. The excesses of domestic life may accumulate unnoticed in our closets, but in the middle of a day's fourth portage, any undue luxury in our packs will surely declare itself.

It is not to be all sackcloth and ashes, this life. There is a time to break out the best wine, strike up the band and let the good times roll. In the woods it has pleased me to fete friends and family with what luxuries I could conceive and the frame of a canoe could carry. Traveling alone, though, we have time and need for introspection. On a solo voyage a man has no one to please but himself, and his self-regard appreciates no flattery. It is fitting to travel light when traveling alone and to take only that which is needed or perhaps a little less—the better to discern our wants from our needs and steer a straighter course between the two.

Lately I have been amused by an advertisement for a financial service of some sort appearing in *The Wall Street Journal*. The caption, paraphrasing Henry David Thoreau's command, tells the reader to go confidently in the direction of his dreams. The man in the photograph is a study in the nonchalance of wealth, and he appears to be going confidently in the direction of a rather large, beachfront estate in the Hamptons. I wonder what the author of *The Maine Woods* would say to that. It will take a lot more than confidence to make headway in the direction of that particular dream. Yet this is the siren song of popular culture—mainstream culture, mind you—and every day another man drives his ship upon the rocks in pursuit of it. As often as you and I sleep beneath the trees, kindle a campfire for our comfort, and fish for our dinner, we will hear a different song.

In this season of penance, therefore, let me waste no time to make my pledge: I aspire to die a man of modest means in a modest house, having frittered away my chance for fame and fortune in the pursuit of quiet lakes, distant shores and deep woods. I aspire to know my family better than my friends and my friends better than my clients. I aspire to make something of my life, not something of myself. I aspire to be driving the same old Jeep long after the neighbors start whispering.

As well as I know the distance between my reach and my grasp, I know I will falter in these ambitions. It is no modest house I live in now, and no modest man who lives there. But if God should grant that you outlive me, heaven help me if when you come to pay your last respects you find only men and women of high esteem in attendance. Pray for me if there is not one there who can say that I gave him a dollar when he didn't really need it and my coat when he did. When the papers write that they found Hurley's last camp, let it be said that there was no more in his pack than was rightly needed for a good night's shelter, a warm fire, and a decent meal. Let it be said of me and of all of us that we traveled light through this world, ever mindful of the world to come.

MEMORIES OF MAINE

In the spring of 1977, I sat by the window of my dormitory room at Western Maryland College, unable to sleep at 3:00 a.m. one night. As I looked down on the little town of Westminster, at the foot of the Catoctin Mountains, my thoughts were not of school or studies but of the plans for the coming summer and where I would be. A well-worn James Taylor LP crackled wistfully in the background—the preferred mood-maker of my generation for just such late-night ruminations.

I don't recall today exactly what frame of reference I had for the State of Maine at the age of nineteen, having never traveled there before nor being able to name a solitary person who lived there, save someone named L. L. Bean. Perhaps I was inspired by the vintage photographs of my 1940s-era fishing encyclopedia, showing men in buffalo-plaid shirts and fedoras hoisting the coveted smallmouth bass—the harder caught, better tasting and scrappier fighter of the species—from clear, granite lakes amid the wilderness.

Perhaps it was an image I had conjured up from a decade of Bean catalogs of this hardy, fir-crested territory, populated by men who supped clam chowder and black coffee and lived the kind of authentic sporting experience that most suburban kids could only read about in the pages of *Field & Stream*.

Whatever my expectations were, by the morning I was busy calling and writing a dozen or more summer camps seeking employment as a counselor. One that replied and offered me a position overseeing a cabin full of junior campers was the venerable Kennebec boys' camp of the Belgrade Lakes region. Within a scant few days of my late-night insomnia, my plans for a summer in Maine were well in hand. Certainly it was not the first nor hardly the last of many wild hares I would conceive from thin air, unaided by the advice or experience of others. But if it was tradition, beauty and a flavor of old Maine summers I sought, I would find it there in spades.

I arrived at the Kennebec Camps with a battalion of other counselors and staff in early June to begin advance preparations for the season. Piles of equipment and gear were pulled out of cabins and sheds where they had been secured against the ravages of the Maine winter. The beachfront was readied for the campers at Salmon Pond, whose waters were so frigid that full wetsuits were required for the task of re-floating and securing the swim docks. Yard after yard of tape was carefully tapped into place on the only real clay tennis courts I had ever seen. Log cabins and pinewood mess halls were swept and cleaned. Dozens of canoes were gently set in place by the pond amid rows of paddles.

Salmon Pond, with its crystalline water and fir trees pointing like steeples to the sky around its shores, was a glorious sight to a boy from Baltimore. To this day it embodies my sense of the classic Maine lake country. It is no wilderness, to be sure, but as is often the feeling one gets elsewhere in Maine, the character and simplicity of its few cottages lend a certain charm all their own.

It was apparent to me, from the faded photographs lining the cabin walls, that the Kennebec Camps had been operating in much the same fashion for decades before I arrived. On each opening weekend old campers would return to their alma mater for a reunion, and in this particular year they came back in droves—platoons of old men with widening girths and bald heads made young again in Indian head-dresses and face paint, racing each other in war canoes down the pond to settle old scores. The traditions of this grand, old place were everywhere in evidence.

In sturdy wood-canvas canoes that had obviously delivered years of good service, with many more to come, we ferried young campers to the woods around Salmon Pond to spend nights in tents and sleeping bags that summer. The water was so clean we dipped it in buckets from the lake for drinking and dove for mussels from the sandy bottom.

The pond was deeper at the middle than I was ever able to fathom. Serious fishermen would occasionally glide by, and I once saw what appeared to be a near-record smallmouth that ambushed an angler from a granite ledge near our camp. I would later recall with incredulity that, in the entire summer I spent in this paradise in 1977, I never wet a line. My one encounter with a smallmouth bass was eye to eye, underwater, in the shade beneath the dock. While swimming there I stopped to notice a lunker finning his way idly by, with almost no concern for my presence. Perhaps the fish understood that I was of an age where matters of fishing and outdoor life had taken a back seat to romance. In any event, the bass population of Salmon Pond was no match for a young girl I had met at a church in Augusta, and to whom I beat a path whenever furloughed for an afternoon from my duties at camp.

One day this young lady and I traveled north to Bar Harbor to see the sights from atop the seaside mountains of that glorious venue. There is no place in America quite like it. On our way home, we encountered another enchanted place that now remains only in the Brigadoon mists of my distant memory and has never fully re-emerged. We stopped at a summer theater attended by, excepting ourselves, a rather well-to-do crowd. I recall neither its name nor its location within three hundred miles, but it was a large, white clapboard meeting house, theater or auditorium of some kind set amid rows of old trees and pathways that led through beautiful gardens and lawns. Perhaps it was somewhere near the French-speaking region of Maine, or perhaps I am mistaken. I wish I could find it again, but no one to whom I have spoken about my experience knows of such a place. We spent an evening, there, enjoying a live performance of Joseph Stein's *Fiddler on the Roof.* Many are familiar with this story of the character Tevye's lament. Amid my fading memories of this place, that day, and the girl I came with, the refrain of the booming ode to *tradition* in this musical remains clear. It was a stirring tribute, in this place so steeped in the traditions of summer, to a value that I did not fully appreciate at the time.

The summer passed too quickly, and I soon found myself headed back to the hills of Western Maryland.

Correspondence with the young lady from Augusta fell to a trickle, then stopped altogether, and later college summers were spent on other far-flung (though less enchanting) adventures. Still, the seeds of my own traditions had been sown, and fourteen years later I would return with my wife and infant son to a cottage from that earlier summer—more of a mind, at the age of thirty-three, to give the bass their due. I was not disappointed by the fish or the place, and I knew I would return again and again.

The Allagash voyage reported in this issue is a reprise of these earlier pilgrimages to Maine, now nearly twenty years after my first encounter with its granite lakes. Its magnificence is undiminished. As I sat atop the thundering Allagash Falls this summer, I marveled at the power of a tradition—conceived on a sleepless night two decades earlier and nurtured on the milk of memory—to draw me back to those hallowed woods.

THE ADVENTUROUS LIFE

In a hotel restaurant in downtown Houston, in 1988, I sat uneasily at the table with two attorneys from one of the nation's largest companies. Having just recently taken a leap of faith in opening my own law office after four years of employment with a firm, I faced the unfamiliar task of explaining why a thirty-year-old upstart with a one-room office and a computer was a good choice to handle litigation for a company that typically hires law firms with hundreds of employees.

The senior lawyer inquired as to the number of paralegals on my staff. I answered that there were none. Silence followed. I recovered with an anxious explanation of the wondrous capabilities of my new 8-megahertz PC and an astonishing program called WordPerfect. The other lawyer, who was a young friend of mine, volunteered some mitigators to my lack of staff. At length, though, the older lawyer eased back in his chair and asked me why I had done it—why I had left the security of a respected law firm and a steady paycheck to hit the street without a single case or client to my credit. My rather cavalier and hastily conceived answer to this man, who I would guess was some twenty years my elder, was that I did not want to spend my old age regretting that I had never tried. Again, silence. I'm sure at that point I must have begun looking among the dinner mints for a new career, but then I heard the man say that he often wished he'd done the same at my age. It was not the most digestible lunch I can recall, but I got the business, and my practice grew.

In the years that followed, relatives would visit and ask how business was going and whether I'd "made it" yet. When I would explain that there was no "it" to make—that success or failure in any professional practice was always looming in the next case—they clearly were unsatisfied. Their unease on the subject called to mind a crowd watching a Hail Mary pass by an untested quarterback. Hope and regret, glory and condemnation, are suspended together with the ball. But in life and business, the ball never really comes all the way back down, and the pass is not completed until the end of the game.

Not too long after that lunch I decided to show my gratitude to Anna, the young lawyer who had spoken for me, by torturing her and her fiancée on a weekend cruise. We were returning a sailboat from Port O'Connor to Houston. Landlubbers both, they had signed on for the voyage in the expectation that we would spend our time gliding up the Texas coast, waving ashore under puffy, white clouds and blue skies. But as many who have traveled with me can attest, the reality of life's adventures sometimes falls short, sometimes far exceeds, but is certainly always different from what we dream in sheltered evenings by the fireside. We soon found ourselves close-hauled and punching through long swells on a course headed offshore in the blackening night. When it was Anna's watch, she crawled out of the forward berth, where she'd no doubt taken a good head-pounding for the past four hours, and took a grip on the tiller. On the horizon, a light rose dimly out of the darkness. Those on shore might have remarked at what a pretty sight it was, but to Anna, in the fearsome, unforgiving darkness of a night at sea, it was a *blood red moon*.

Let purveyors of ocean-going adventure say what they will: riding a breakable, sinkable, fiberglass shell over fifteen fathoms of roiling, blue-green mystery, far from shore, is a marked risk. As I looked down from the cockpit that night at the sea whooshing past, just inches below the rail, I found no words for Anna to ameliorate the essential danger and uncertainty of our position. This was no thrill ride at an amusement park. That really was Davy Jones' locker below us, and yes, all that came between us and the briny deep were our nerve and a bit of plastic. Yet on my wall now hangs a painting given to me in found memory of that voyage. And who among us does not harbor a romantic notion of someday sailing to tropic seas in command of a tiny vessel?

The sense of those nights at sea came rushing back to me as we ventured steadily farther into the trackless wilderness of Northern Minnesota, last summer. We were placing ourselves in a circumstance of dependency on the elements and, with each paddle stroke toward the north, becoming a little less able to make radical or swift alterations in that dependency for whatever reason necessary. The vapor-thin, Kevlar hull of our rented canoe resounded with a sickening *crack!* over rocks in the shallow flows. Silently, I imagined permutations of various disasters: finding ourselves with an irreparable canoe on some forgotten beaver-flow a hundred miles from the nearest road; losing our provisions to bears; a broken leg or injured back halfway into the voyage; a sudden attack of appendicitis and a race against time to reach help.

On the third day of our Minnesota trip, after gorging ourselves on blueberries at the end of Sunday Lake, we set happily about a course on the Beartrap River that we expected would take us eventually north into Iron Lake. It was getting toward mid-afternoon on a cloudy, gray day. Slowly, the channel in the river grew narrow among the lily pads and grass, and then narrower still. Soon, we were straining to keep the canoe moving forward through barely visible water overgrown with thick vegetation. After it seemed clear that we had lost any discernible channel, we stopped. We looked at the map, then at the scene around us, then at the map. We stood up in the boat. No answers. The map depicted a clearly discernible ribbon of blue where the river was supposed to be—and no doubt was in colder months. But we were in the middle of a seamless marsh appearing to stretch for miles in every direction. If we chose to go on a given course to look for the channel and guessed wrong, it could be hours and near dark before we realized our error.

Although we weren't lost for long, had one of us not noticed some unusual topography on the map near the northward bend in the river and matched that to a bluff we could see in the distance, we might have been lost quite a while longer. In the moment we were stopped there, the sense of risk was palpable. There were no guarantees and no easy answers. No cheery words could remit the need to regain our course, nor soften the hazards of failing to do so.

In the woods as in life, it is instructive at times simply to stop and absorb the profound, unblinking reality of the world around us. There in the silence is a challenge that goads us to risk footless paths. "Do what you will," it says. "Find your way or not," it says. "I will be here as a witness to the ages; mute, pitiless and immovable." No man can foresee what that challenge portends for him, but in what we cannot foresee yet dare to discover lies the heart of adventure. And whether we succeed or fail in our endeavors, we shall always be glad to say that we attempted the journey.

The Simple Life

At a campsite along the route of the Adirondack Canoe Classic, a few years ago, I overheard a conversation between two of the participants in that three-day, ninety-mile marathon. One was an older gentleman, a veteran of many years in the race. His movements were deliberate and unhurried whether he was paddling or progressing through the familiar rituals of an evening in camp. That night his rumpled, old canvas tent was set up on the banks of Forked Lake. Everything in his outfit appeared well-worn, and I dare say he had not purchased a new item of gear in many years. As the two talked, the older man inquired about the younger fellow's career and his busy life back in the big city. The young man gave an accounting of how life had treated him since the previous year's race. As he did so, he mentioned with a sigh that there were of course a good many items of gear and other things he would like to acquire but for which there never seemed to be enough money or time. The older man was unmoved. Then he replied to his young friend with some advice that struck me as rather profound: "It's not how much money you have," he said, "but what you spend it on." Clearly the older gentleman had spent his money sparingly and wisely over the years on an outfit that continued to serve him well at little or no additional expense.

As I considered this man's advice, I began to realize how applicable it was across a wide set of circumstances. My wife and I married two weeks after graduating from college and resolved to put ourselves through law school without financial assistance from our families. In those years the only money we made was through student work-study programs and summer clerkships, all of which added up to less than the federal poverty level in our most prosperous year. I have a sense of the five loaves and two fishes now when I look back at our tax returns for those years and wonder how we ever made it, but at the time we felt solidly planted in the middle class. Our lives were less cluttered with things, our diversions were simpler, our commitments were fewer, and our time was our own. As the years went by we saw more prosperity, but we were no happier because of it.

When we finally entered private practice, we would occasionally rub elbows with some "high rollers" in the business and legal communities. As a rule they lived in huge, ludicrously expensive homes, and to me their private lives seemed to be guided by the most superfluous and trivial concerns. This predictably yielded for them more unhappiness in the form of broken hearts, drug and alcohol abuse, and depression than was usually visited upon serfs like us in our tiny apartments on tiny budgets. All of this was cause for frequent introspection on my part about the real meaning of the "American Dream" and my place within it. That introspection has yielded no easy answers but rather a number of observations.

There is a tendency toward voracious consumption

that is pervasive in our culture. The American dream in the minds of millions has come to mean a continually upward spiral of material largesse: a bigger paycheck, a bigger house on a larger lot in a better neighborhood, more clothes, more expensive vacations, and generally greater self-indulgence than our parents' generation could conceive. A love of spending for its own sake and a steady expansion in the inventory of our wardrobes, furnishings and accessories are articles of faith in the new American mall-culture. It has been reported that the average new home built today is some 40 percent larger than the average new home built in the 1950s, leaving one to wonder how Mom and Dad ever managed to raise a family for all those years in that little ranch house. Real estate agents now refer to a home that an upper middle-class family of the previous generation might have worked their entire lives to afford as a "good starter." Well, who moved the finish line?

It is not that our parents lived deprived lives: it is rather that our perspective has changed. The bar for an acceptable minimum lifestyle has been raised almost imperceptibly over the years by the steady march of Madison Avenue to the point where, now, life without two cars, two televisions, a microwave, videos, cable TV, frequent dinners out, seventy-five-dollar leather sneakers, health clubs, and a phalanx of scheduled activities for even the youngest of children is considered a hardship. Yet many of us who tend to accept this mentality as part of mainstream American culture—myself included—fail to appreciate the clutter and complexity, not to mention the expense, it contributes to our lives. Not surprisingly, frustration is rising over a sense of declining quality of life amid nostalgia for the less frenetic pace of earlier times. Standing in stark contrast to these phenomena are people like that Adirondack canoeist, with a rumpled tent, an old boat, a well-dented stew pot, and other coddled items of equipment acquired through the years, who remind us that living well is more about making good choices than making a fortune.

The canoeist's advice was called to mind again this winter as I accompanied Virginian Fred Ostrander down the Nottoway River. Fred made the trip in the Old Town Otca canoe that he and his father had bought new in 1939 for $210. My first thought upon hearing the price was how very cheap it was compared to the cost of such boats today. My second thought was that if the entire American public followed Fred's shopping regimen, there would be no economy left. As I considered it further, however, I realized that $210 was a tidy sum in the dark days of 1939. Yet, the money Fred and his father had invested in what may have seemed to some at the time a pricey extravagance had been money well spent.

I suppose that there is the slightest whiff of elitism in this whole business of canoeing in general and even more so in the rarefied world of traditional canoes. They are not inexpensive craft, but as with any classic, when the immediate cost is amortized across the timelessness of their appeal, they become almost inexpensive by comparison. Which of your present possessions can you say you will have thirty or fifty years from now and be truly enriched by the money you spent to acquire it?

What draws us to voyaging by canoe is a simple

elegance that has little to do in the long run with money or privilege. Once you have the boat and a paddle to make her go, the equation is fairly complete. There is more room for expense in the gear you take with you, but even this has its limit. Eventually you find that your needs are well met and that what remains is simply to go. If you set your sights on the essentials of the voyage and invest in equipment built to last, the return is exponential. Money could never purchase the glory of the sunrise over a remote, northern lake accessible only by canoe, or the thrill of coming face to face with a moose whose ancestors fed and clothed the earliest humans on the continent; yet for the small cost of pack, paddle and craft it is available to anyone who has the wisdom to gauge its real value.

THE KINDNESS OF STRANGERS

On our first trip into Boston's airport, Julie was three-months pregnant with our daughter Caroline. Together we were moving our one-year-old son and a mountain of luggage through cramped hallways, up and down escalators, and onto crowded shuttle buses. We had brought everything we could think of and then some for a two-week vacation at a tiny cabin on a lake in Maine.

I remember this trip not because the bass in the lake were the most gullible I have encountered, before or since. The picture of that trip in my mind is of a dark, early morning when I sat up beside the wood stove, while Julie and our infant son slept in the other room. Worried as I often was about cases and clients and employees back at our law practice in Houston, I could not sleep. A Federal Express package of papers to review and sign had arrived the day before. Another would go out that day. It was June 1991, and we had never been away from anything or anywhere for two weeks. While sitting in the dim, electric light of the cabin and jotting down "what if" scenarios on a scrap of paper, I conceived the idea that led, six months later, to the sale of our law practice, the move to North Carolina, a brief fling as a charterboat captain, and, in the fall of 1995, the first issue of this journal. There are three places where my life has made a dramatic, new beginning: one is the maternity ward at Johns Hopkins Hospital, circa 1958; one is the Sunshine Café in College Park, Maryland, where I proposed to my wife; and one is that cabin in Maine.

The driver who would bring the overnight packages to us and pick up the new ones was intrigued to be making deliveries to the banks of Knickerbocker Lake. He had a genuine concern for our affairs that was almost quaint. If he didn't thoroughly enjoy his own job and wasn't sincerely interested in making sure I could do mine, he was doing an awfully good job of faking it. Not so for some of the other New Englanders we met on that trip.

Passengers and employees in the Boston airport at our coming and going could not have better epitomized a Southerner's stereotype of "Damn Yankees." There was pushing and shoving and utter lack of pity for a young mother with a baby and her clearly inept husband, trying to wend their way through the maze of concourses, gates and lines. When at one point it became apparent that we had been deposited at the wrong end of the terminal and might miss our flight, the faces of those best able to help us could not have been more vacant of concern.

Not usually one to hold a grudge, I have made special exception for the Amtrak employees at Chicago's Union Station (another grim tale) and the folks Julie and I met in the Boston airport on that trip. And so it was with a sense of dread that I learned, on a return flight from Bangor this past summer that I would be taking an unexpected detour through Beantown.

I suppose there are more serious things that the

ground crew in Bangor could have forgotten to do than close the door to the airplane before we took off, but that was reason enough for the pilot to return to the airport. Back in Bangor, I was told that all of the available planes with fully closing doors were headed to Boston, where apparently they still have my name and photo on file under the words, "Do not help this man under any circumstance." I hopped aboard, made sure I heard the door slam shut, and hoped for the best.

It was par for the course that I would be the only one of twenty re-routed passengers to be given a voucher for a room that night in Boston at the "Parkway Plaza" hotel instead of the Ramada. I even shrugged it off when the Ramada shuttle bus promptly whisked all of the other passengers off to warm beds when we arrived at the airport at 1:00 a.m. A dark sense of destiny really didn't overcome me until I learned, at 2:00 a.m., that there *is no* Parkway Plaza hotel in Boston. There is a Parkway Plaza hotel somewhere in Wyoming—and a lovely place it is, no doubt—but the name is spelled differently. Spelling is unimportant to airline clerks but a matter of national security to hotel managers.

The night manager of the "Park Plaza" hotel, a $200-per-night affair in downtown Boston, made it clear when I called from the airport that they would not accept vouchers for similarly named establishments located in Casper, Wyoming. But when I showed up anyway at 3:00 a.m. in his gleaming lobby, strapped to a muddy Duluth pack and dressed in the same clothes I had worn for the past three days on the St. Croix River, a sense of imminent danger must have overtaken him. I was given a free room with breakfast service, and I took full advantage of both.

Feeling as rested as circumstances would allow, the next morning, I did my best to look inconspicuous as I portaged past the concierge to a taxi at the curb. Back at the airport, fatigue finally got the best of me.

After returning one of those rented push-carts to its carousel, I was too busy digging for my 25-cent refund to notice that my camera case, containing two-thousand-dollars-worth of equipment and all of the photographs you see in this issue, was still in the cart. I walked inside the terminal to a magazine stand to wait for my flight, not questioning why my hands were suddenly free to thumb thorough Claudia Schiffer's latest swimsuit pictorial.

You would have greater need for imagination in reading about the St. Croix River, in this issue, were it not for the kindness of a stranger at the airport in Boston—a resident of that fine city, no less. Having watched me leave the case in the cart, he had been looking for me for more than a few minutes when he walked up with my case in hand. Before the sudden rush that comes with disaster-nearly-missed would let me say more than "thank you," the man nodded with a smile and was gone. Never again will I paint all Bostonians with the same brush.

There is a lot of time for thinking on airplanes. On this recent trip from Boston I wondered why some of us hail the fellow-well-met in the wild, yet scarcely acknowledge those we meet on elevators, at intersections, and in airports. In gathering material for this journal I travel widely through the woods every year, often alone, in places I have never been before, and usually where I do not know a soul. The question

I often get from friends and family is, "Aren't you afraid out there, where you don't know who might come along?" The answer is no. I can honestly say that I am more relaxed and unafraid for my safety in the woods than on any city street. The people I have met canoeing over the last thirty years have a lot more in common with that helpful fellow in the Boston airport than with whatever ghoulish characters might live in your imagination. Perhaps one reason for this is that, in the woods, I am a less ghoulish fellow, myself.

From the very first, people have regularly come along to lighten my load. The bundle of dry firewood handed to me one cold, wet night on the Allagash; packs carried three miles across a portage in the Adirondacks by two men I'd never met; room made for me in someone else's camp when it was too late to find my own—these are but a few of many examples that come to mind. For my part, I have tried to show others in the woods a measure of that kindness. Ah, but how quickly the spell fades when we return to the *civilized* world, as one sad example in my own life too clearly shows.

Having been informed that I am the last man in America whose wife prepares a hot meal every evening, I come when dinner is called and remain until the cook is finished. Ringing telephones are never answered during this ritual, but a knock at the door one night could not be ignored. When I turned on the porch light and opened the door, there in the darkness stood a man my age. Immediately, I realized that he was selling something, and my defenses went up. From his pack he pulled several drawings, each carefully rendered with a talent far beyond my own, and each selling for less than I would have accepted for poorer work. Awkwardly, and sensing he would be granted little time, he held a few examples out to their best advantage in the dim light. I complimented his work but, eager to return to dinner, said I was "not interested" and bid him good night.

Sitting down, I looked across the table at the contented faces of my children. As I ruminated on the man's age and how badly I would have to need the money before I went door to door selling ten-dollar drawings, I realized there might be two similar faces looking across that man's table at an empty chair. I had turned away someone in need who had asked of me only a small measure of value for something of greater value in return. Had he wandered into my camp instead of my front yard, I would have known him as a friend. What is it in the city that closes men's hearts, or in the wilderness that opens them?

Returning to the door, I saw no one on our street. It hadn't been long. Perhaps a kinder neighbor had taken him in. Or perhaps he had come only to bring this message to me, and to you: There are no strangers in this world. If "there but for the grace of God go I," may we give grace to everyone we meet and leave none without the company of our kindness.

Return to Still Pond

When I was eleven years old, an exciting, new world opened to me, as it did for many young men in the pages of the magazine *Boy's Life*. Eagerly awaited each month, it was the official publication of the Boy Scouts of America, which I had recently joined in the hope of encountering, firsthand, the rugged individualism of the Great Outdoors. In its pages I studied the adventures of other boys my age and older in places known only to my imagination. In the classifieds, I ogled ads promising to give me the body of Charles Atlas alongside photographs of men struggling to lift enormous pike taken from far-flung lakes of the North Woods—and regarded them with equal suspicion.

But dreaming of doing bold, new things and doing them are, as I would soon discover, two very different propositions. After all, I was a child of the city of Baltimore and, only recently, its greener suburbs. I had never pitched a tent, lighted a fire, or tended to any of life's more delicate, daily necessities in anything other than civilized surroundings. These things would have to be learned, and scouting would teach me.

I have written in these pages, before, of my lifelong admiration for Dr. Carl Zapffe, the former scoutmaster of Troop 35. The father of seven daughters, he inspired generations of boys to reach for more than what the teenage imagination, left to its own devices, might choose to pursue. But the remarkable strength of that organization and of successful scouting programs everywhere is in the example offered by the older boys. For as every parent knows, there is no surer recipe for resistance than to tell a child that this is how his father or mother thinks things should be done or—worse still—how they did them when they were his age. Let a boy discover something on his own, however, and he will learn it for life. Still Pond would be the venue for the first of many such discoveries of mine.

Nestled in a little cranny of Kent County on the Eastern Shore of Maryland, Still Pond is not a *pond* at all but a picturesque, brackish estuary of Chesapeake Bay—filled with blue crabs and surrounded by woods and farms. It emerged each summer of my boyhood as a Brigadoon of youthful activity, a Never-Never Land of swimming, sailing, canoeing, yelling, laughing and general unrest.

The pond lies just off the Sassafras River, about ten miles north of the once-sleepy fishing village of Chestertown—a place since discovered by hordes of well-heeled Washingtonians looking for that authentic, Old Bay charm. By the good offices of our scoutmaster we had secured the permission of a local farmer to overrun, for two weeks each summer, a prodigious, rolling expanse of cow pasture and woods that looked out on the pond from a bluff high above.

It was any boy's Shangri La, this place. Well-worn trails meandered through the woods that rimmed the pasture, leading the way to an authentically rustic, timber-and-canvas "mess hall," where giant gobs of limp bacon and vats of pancakes, scrambled eggs and hash browns were served up each morning. Overlooking the pond, just west of the mess hall, was an outdoor chapel. There, with a feigned disinterest, I listened intently to one boy's father offer elegant homilies that seemed to flow directly, effortlessly from the inspiration of our surroundings. On the shore below, a wooden pier jutted some thirty yards into the water from a beach littered with the implements of adventure: long, aluminum canoes, Sunfish sailboats, and johnboats for oaring across the pond to weed beds, where twenty or thirty white bass could be taken at a time. But it was the catfish that I preferred.

In the idle hours of many afternoons, I would stand on the outermost corner of the camp pier and cast a bait of chicken livers or whatever else was available from the kitchen. Before long there would come the telltale shudder of the line—briefly, almost imperceptibly—followed by the slow, attempted escape of an unsuspecting catfish, his movement betrayed by the line rising from the surface of the water. I learned to wait breathlessly for the line to grow taught, then set the hook with a sharp, upward heave. This method never failed to retrieve a fat, sleek specimen writhing with indignation. Taking care to avoid the knife-like, venomous, pectoral fins of the species, I would remove the hook and dash up the hill.

The camp cook had a weakness for catfish filets sautéed in butter, and he seemed more than a little bemused at the skinny boy who shared this passion. I would sometimes bring the day's victim to the back of the kitchen, where he would dress it for me. As I saw it, this ritual passed in silent recognition of my status as a "real fisherman"—not just another feckless bluegill-hunter like so many of my peers. Once, the cook spoke affectionately of what an uncommon source of strength Dr. Zapffe had been to him when the cook's son lay dying with leukemia. He hardly needed to ask whether I knew what a special man Dr. Zapffe was. I most certainly did—all of us scouts did—with that infallible radar by which young boys everywhere are able to distinguish true leaders from pretenders. Troop 35 tried to mold young men of similar ilk, and one of the newly minted heroes was a fellow named Dave Doub.

Dave was an all-American type who would have been every mother's wish for her daughter's first date. He was certainly my mother's wish for her son's first camping trip. As the Eagle Scout designated to keep me from lighting my long underwear on fire or doing myself some other serious, bodily harm on my first campout, Dave came to our apartment to sort through the odd pieces of gear that I, in my eleven-year-old's imagination, had determined might be useful. He made a few adjustments and recommendations, all the while making me feel as if I had done a remarkable job of it on my own. That first outing in the woods at Still Pond went swimmingly and, well, the rest of the story you now hold in your hands.

I returned to Still Pond last fall with my son Kip, in his 10th year. We joined Dave and Billie Roberts, who live an idyllic life in the tiny town of Still Pond, proper. I first met Dave and Billie a few years ago, when I shared a campsite with them and a small band of like-minded paddlers in the Jersey Pine Barrens. Standing around a campfire on that trip, I described my fading memory of heading off in canoes from a scout camp on the Eastern Shore to a place away where—impossibly, it seemed—water rushed quickly past a sand bar like a mountain stream into Chesapeake Bay. A dozen of us kids had spent the afternoon, there, floating through the inlet on the swift, cool current, again and again. With time steadily fraying the picture of that day in my mind, I had come to believe it was a dream. Aging synapses, I supposed, had cross-linked my memory of some West Virginia whitewater float-trip with a day of crabbing on the bay. But when Dave overheard my story of this "river," he assured me it was real. I could not have been more surprised if a shadowy lamp-merchant had just offered to take me to Aladdin's cave. Churn Creek is the very place, he explained—a narrows through which the ebb tide hurries back to the bay, near the mouth of Still Pond. We made plans to go.

Every tragic figure has a fatal flaw, and mine is the inability to resist the siren song of a small sailboat on open water. It was unthinkable, therefore, that I would come to Dave's home on the bay and not bring our little sixteen-foot sloop, *Whisper*. Kip and I resolved to *sail* to Churn Creek, like a couple of old salts. Alas, we spent a day luffing around the Sassafras River with barely a breath of wind, then anchored that night in the same place we had started. A quick meal of noodles boiled while we hunkered in the cuddy cabin had to suffice, as a passing cold front brought rain and the first chill of winter. The next morning, we decided to light out for my old scout-camp in Dave's canoe.

Paddling hard into a wind that would have been welcome in the different vessel of a day earlier, I struggled to summon the thirty-year-old memory of a shoreline that would reveal the location of my old camp. Eventually the familiar profile of the pier—the very altar on which so many catfish had once been sacrificed—led us in. I bolted for the hill with Kip in pursuit and Dave a distant third. At the top, the view from the bluff where the chapel had once stood was mercifully unchanged and just as inspiring, but no trace of any recent encampment was to be found. The pasture and woods were similarly preserved. We even walked to the very place where, under the tutelage of a thoughtful mentor, I first pitched a tent.

Coming to the end of camp, I looked over the open water. Dave pointed out the location of Churn Creek, but it was too far off to see. On the bay, steep whitecaps promised to stymie our passage, and winter had already begun to whisper her injunctions. The creek, I knew, would elude me for another season. It was just as well. The legends of memory had been revived. A beautiful place where I had started out, in life, had been remarkably, improbably saved. I was a happy pilgrim to my own past, and this would be a pilgrimage to be savored.

"We Few, We Happy Few"

A favorite homily familiar to many tells the story of three stone-cutters in the Middle Ages. Working side by side, they do the same job. Each is asked in turn to describe what he does. The first, with his head down at his task, replies simply that he cuts rock out of the earth. The second looks slightly upward and replies that he shapes rock into a form suitable for building. The third puts down his tools, raises his eyes to the heavens, and with a swell of pride exclaims that he is building a great cathedral.

Perspective to see the passage of time and the slow march of ordinary events across a larger canvas is an elusive and rare gift. Kings and princes have paid handsomely for it for centuries. It cannot be acquired by intelligence or education or wealth or status, but in the solitude and simplicity of the wilderness it is often revealed. Rarely have I come back from even the most abysmal, rain-soaked misadventure in the wild without a sense of some needed course-correction or a renewed understanding of the reasons to press on.

It is clearly not only great fun to run rivers and explore wild places but instructive, as well, to re-encounter what life is like away from the din of civilized society. In that moment when we stand in a silent wood or beside a still lake, with nothing to keep us company but our thoughts and one another and nothing to *do* but take in the world around us, we taste something of the essence of man's life on Earth that has not changed across the millennia. We may pine for the comforts of modernity, but there are lessons to be learned in the starkness of nature that cannot be captured in the glow of our television sets. Among these are the lost art of conversation, the meditations of solitude, and a sense of our own insignificance in the larger order of things.

The rivers and lakes we paddle were here thousands of years before us, and they will remain thousands of years after we are gone. A mere hundred years after these words are written, none of those who first read them will walk this earth. If we are not by our daily labors building a cathedral somewhere in our lives, to what purpose do we work at all?

I came to ask that question of myself one day four years ago in Houston. In my mid-thirties, I had been cutting rocks steadily for ten years since entering law school, with no cathedral in sight. I was at an age and a point in my career when most lawyers were looking to move up to that *big* house, with the really *big* mortgage, followed in due course by longer hours at the office, the *big* ulcer, the twelve-step recovery program, and the rebellion of lonely children who never really became a priority in their parents' schedules. As the birth of my little daughter Caroline approached, there came an impending sense that life really is not a dress rehearsal, that one doesn't get a second chance to better raise one's children, or to be young and healthy, or to make the kinds of mistakes and try out the wild-eyed dreams that are forbidden to us in the frailty of old age. And so I sold our Texas law practice, took off for North Carolina, opened and failed in a sailboat-charter business, and later reopened a smaller law office. Here in the piney woods, the grand experiment of which this journal is a product continues.

Part of that experiment has happily been more time spent along the rivers and ponds depicted in this issue. These places and others to be covered in the seasons ahead offer an interesting contradiction to conventional wisdom. Expecting to find crowds of people in many wild places within a short driving distance of large cities, I have more often than not found myself alone in the woods, or nearly so. While many state and national parks are jammed with crowds of tourists of the worst ilk and overrun by day hikers, there seems to be less if not little competition—knock on wood—for the primitive campsites along canoe trails.

Some theorize that the rise of the two-earner household and the difficulty of coordinating an extended vacation for two workers at once has confined most of us to venues accessible within the time-span of a weekend. Travel experts have cited a trend towards shorter, two to five-day vacations. There are other explanations, too. Many would say that we have seen a growing crassness in a public which seems increasingly less in tune with what came to be coined in the 1970s as the "wilderness experience." Witness today the incessant whine of personal ski-boats circling like so many flies on the water and how infrequently one sees a canoe gliding by. In his book *Canoeing the Jersey Pine Barrens,* Robert Parnes wrote that "camping is not the same as it used to be. There are more people, and campers are more wasteful, leaving behind unwanted belongings, trash, and unsightly campfire pits." He is right, but elsewhere, on the game lands, in the national forests, and along established water trails, there is refuge. The key is to find those places where the facilities are primitive and the access is limited, which should be every canoe tripper's objective.

Two years ago, when planning a trip along the most storied canoe route of the Adirondacks in the height of the summer season, I was warned that vacant campsites would be few and far between. Instead, I found that few sites were occupied, and those people I did see were quiet and respectful folk. The same experience has been repeated elsewhere, including the rivers and creeks of the Croatan covered in this issue. There are pockets of wilderness everywhere. With the native people of this land long since displaced and the rest of America having safely retreated to the suburbs, who can say that on any given Wednesday afternoon in October you might not have the lake you paddle more to yourself than did the earliest explorers of our age?

Whatever the reason, those today who take to the wild by simple means, seeking simple pleasures, are clearly few in number. Let millions build an altar to MTV and the myriad distractions of modern life, but "we few, we happy few" can, with pack and paddle in hand, yet find that quiet, uncluttered exuberance which the poet promised us along the road less traveled.

WHAT, ME WORRY?

I have long been a hater of cell phones. It is true there was a time, when these devices first appeared on the market, when this was not the case. I was frantically trying to manage some semblance of a life apart from our law practice in Houston, in the late 1980s, and I carried a bulky apparatus (we called them "car phones" back then) similar to what the president now keeps at hand for launching global thermonuclear war. But for me, the bloom fell off the car-phone rose long ago. Readers of this journal know well the story of the (early) middle-age jitters that led me to abandon that fast-paced life and all of its symbols, including incessant, compulsive yakking on cell phones. ("Hello, Honey. I just wanted you to know that since pulling out of the driveway thirty seconds ago, I arrived at the end of the street and all is well. How's everything at home?") The latest technology be damned, I say! But as I would come to learn, technology is a jealous mistress.

It was to be just a quick trip in late March—a weekend jaunt on the Antietam Creek on the Maryland side of the Potomac River. The weather had turned favorably warmer the weekend before and, seeing a window of opportunity open, I decided on short notice to make the five-hour drive north to complete the trip featured in this issue. My daughter Caroline would join me for the drive as far as her cousin Emma's house in Silver Spring, Maryland.

A cold rain was falling as I drove the final fifty miles early on a Saturday morning from Silver Spring to Boonsboro. When throwing together the plans for this trip three nights before, I had found the web page of the local canoe-outfitter and the announcement that he would open for the season on the day I planned to arrive. With the bliss that is ignorance, I expected to arrange a shuttle when I got there. You can write the next line in this tale, no doubt.

I arrived at Devil's Backbone County Park in Boonsboro and stopped a kayaker making plans for the day's paddle. The fact that he was donning a wet suit as protection against cold-water immersion was not lost on me, in my long woolies.

"Do you know where the canoe-rental place is?" I asked. He pointed to a barn just across the street, on the bank of the river below the bridge. Other than a trailer full of canoes, there was no sign of the outfitter. It was ten o'clock in the morning, and another window of opportunity—enough daylight to complete the thirteen-mile paddle to the campground at the C & O Canal—was rapidly closing. I could have called the outfitter easily enough had there been a payphone at the park, but *easy* is a word not often associated with the trips I make for this journal. Instead, I hopped in my boat and paddled off under the assumption that I would find a payphone downriver at the National Park Service campground from which to summon the 82nd Airborne, if need be, to fetch me back to my car.

Part of being male is a physiological predisposition against fretting and worrying. As every wife knows, being a man is to live in an all-is-well, don't-worry-be-happy, let-the-devil-take-tomorrow, if-I-ignore-that-clicking-sound-it-will-probably-go-away state of mind. I like being a guy for this reason. My wife frets and worries far more than I do. She would have fretted and worried about making contact with the outfitter all the way down the river. No, she would have turned around and driven straight back home before heading off on the assumption that she would later somehow reach a person who could bring her back to her car. No, in fact, a hundred other worries would have kept her away from a cold, Western Maryland creek on a rainy day in the first place.

Worries rarely intrude on a man's thoughts until there is no longer anything he can do about them. By this time, they are more accurately described as *regrets*. Women may worry, but men have lots of regrets. Woman: "Shouldn't we look at the map, Dear, before we make this turn?" Man (two hours later): "I now *regret* that I didn't look at the map, Dear, *before* we drove one hundred miles in the wrong direction and missed your sister's wedding, but I was never *worried*."

My regrets on this trip started early. Upon encountering the first haystack in the chilly, not-quite-yet-in-season water of the Antietam, I realized that I had not spoken to a living human being about where the rapids are, how to run them, or whether I had any business at all being on this river alone in late March. Then again, years of paddling dozens of rivers and hundreds of haystacks just like this one had taught me a thing or two, by golly, and I surfed over the first ledge in fine form. Four hours later, I washed out into the Potomac and found the landing that leads to the campground. Life was good.

Coming up the bank to the towpath, I asked a day-hiker whether there was a phone nearby. "No," he said, "but you're welcome to use my cell phone." To my amazement he pulled one right out of his pocket. I used it to call my sister-in-law in Silver Spring. "I am at the Antietam Creek Ranger Station," I explained to Susan as I stood on the towpath reading a sign with those very words. "Call the outfitter and tell him he can pick me up here anytime tomorrow morning, and don't worry." I must say I now r*egret* not knowing, at that time, that the ranger station had recently been removed from the towpath, where the campground is located, and that the only ranger station in the area was four miles away, in Sharpsburg.

After an enjoyable evening camped alone above the banks of the Potomac—the only camper there—I allowed myself the luxury of sleeping late on a chilly, Sunday morning. Outside my bivouac I could hear the voices of day-trippers and kayakers assembling for the day to surf Furnace Rapids. Fearing that this might be my last chance for a phone call, I importuned one of them to let me use his cell phone. ("It's just a local call. Would you mind, terribly?") I reached my brother-in-law Michael, who was surprised to hear that the outfitter was not there. Michael promised to find out what happened, but the kayakers left for the river and took the cell phone with them. I was unable to call or be called, after that. I returned to my phone-less campsite and waited, not knowing that the outfitter would report to my family that he had arrived long ago at "the ranger station" as instructed, and found no sign of me.

The morning waned into afternoon as I waited resolutely in camp, heaping one log after another onto what, after several hours, had become the perfect campfire for roasting a small buffalo. The volunteer campground-host who had chatted with me the night before about wood-canvas canoes began to worry as the sky threatened rain. He offered to drive me back to my Jeep. I accepted, doused the fire, and left camp. Unbeknownst to me, not ten minutes later the outfitter would find my "abandoned" camp beside the towpath and, with growing alarm, alert the park service to a missing person named Mike Hurley. Maintaining steady contact with my sister-in-law on his cell phone, the outfitter assured her that he found "no sign of a struggle." Knowing that he had even thought to look for such a sign brought tears of worry to Susan, who wondered if I had met my doom on the Antietam.

Returning in my Jeep to break camp, I finally met the beleaguered owner of Antietam Creek Canoes, who refused my offers to pay for the shuttle. A young ranger stopped to ask my name, picked up her radio mike, and called off the search for the missing canoeist. When I got home, several plans for a cell-phone contract were waiting for my perusal. Never mind running from your past—the future will catch up with you a lot quicker.

Nowadays I am never without my little gray friend, but I worry more. I worry that my battery is either not charged or not achieving its true potential. I worry that messages I would earlier have let languish on my office voicemail might be too urgent to wait until the next morning, and so I call—twice a day. I worry that my wife will worry if I don't call, and so I do. I worry that

I am spending $59.95 a month for something that, if the truth be told, I will really *need* only once a year.

As I write this, a blinking green light signals that a cell tower, somewhere, knows where I am. No outfitter in North America is beyond my reach, and it seems the wilderness just got a little smaller. Call me anytime. I'll worry if you don't.

ON SOLITUDE

One of the unexpected lessons of this journal for me, as its creator, has revolved around the discipline of solitude. Having only recently enlisted the aid of contributing editors for the stories you read in these pages, for six years I have had the privilege and duty to travel to various parts of this country, making upwards of eight or nine trips each season to feature in the journal. The tyranny of the deadline often forced me to go at times when school or family schedules did not permit the company of my wife and children. Many of you may travel on business in circumstances where colleagues, airline stewards, and hotel clerks maintain at least a veneer of those relationships we call "society." It is quite another thing to leave behind both the comforts of home and the companionship of other human beings to enter a wilderness, alone. What is it like, you may wonder, to load one's provisions and shove off into a speechless void for days at a time? I am a family man and no advocate of the hermit's life, but I have found an unexpected virtue in the occasional necessity of solitude.

Sigurd Olson was said to possess a "wilderness within," and that is certainly a concept I have come to identify in my own life. Incidentally, those who grieve for the glory of this country's unspoiled frontier can find a reasonable facsimile of the pioneer experience surprisingly close at hand, when they paddle solo. I have been as desolately and completely alone on tiny streams not five miles from a major city as I have been on distant, windswept lakes in the Boundary Waters. My most surprising discoveries on these trips have come in the mental wilderness, not from my physical surroundings.

If you could sift from life all of its frenzy and detail as one might sift gold from sand, the gift of solitude would be among the treasures that remained. Entering the woods alone reduces daily life to an elemental level we scarcely recognize amid the traffic, television, appliances, and architecture of modern man. Seeing it for the first time through the door of a tent in a soft, lingering rain can be unsettling. In similar conditions at home, we might seek the narcotic effects of television to fill the hours and spare us the burden of creative imagination. Whether the solitary experience of wilderness becomes an ordeal or an epiphany depends on one's approach and perspective.

I had set out one summer for a week alone on the Canadian border when I encountered a large family traveling together. The children were thrilled to be free to swim and race around the woods while mom and dad lagged tiredly behind. I paddled not far from their camp, trolling for walleye for dinner and enjoying the excited shouts and antics of the children. The man noticed I was alone and, with a wistful look, remarked at how I must be enjoying the solitude in such a place. Just then, though, I had been imagining how much more I would have enjoyed playing with my own children and talking with my wife in that very spot. Two days later, I passed a young couple who had pitched their tent on a small lake which they had all to themselves. They were enjoying a veritable Garden of Eden without a stitch of clothing between them. As I kept paddling so as not to disturb their paradise, I was reminded, again, of the companion I had left at home. What fish I caught on that trip were mine alone to admire, and what wonders I saw it was pointless to exclaim. No one could hear me. After a while, an undisciplined mind in that circumstance will—as goes the song about Camp Grenada—begin to be more acutely aware of life's difficulties and less acutely aware of life's beauty. We are social creatures, to be sure. That being so, there is a natural temptation to despair in being alone, but the greater pity is to give in to despair and let that obscure the lessons that solitude offers.

The tradition of my Catholic faith is one of contemplation and reflection. We are constantly urged to repair to some quiet place to better discern the divine will, and we are reminded that Christ often did the same—in preparation for times of trial and uncertainty. The truth is that many who speak enthusiastically of their time in the wilderness never actually experience the rejuvenation it offers. A group of drinking buddies off for a week in the woods has merely taken a form of social interaction that might otherwise have occurred at a ballpark and improved the scenery a bit. That can be great fun, of course, but the hidden gift of wilderness is introspection. It is a cathedral created by God to bring us closer to him through a better knowledge of ourselves. Solitude accelerates the process of self-discovery by simplifying life's routine and reducing the number of demands on our senses.

There is no wilderness on earth so isolated as the sea, nor any the contours of which remain as unchanged by time and man. You can get a sense of that isolation in the story of Assateague Island, in this issue. Not far from that coast, my wife and children and I were very much *together* in the cramped space of a small sailboat for three days, this summer. We wended our way from the charming and historic town of St. Michael's on the Eastern Shore of Maryland to the equally charming and historic town of Annapolis. At night we lay at anchor on a huge air mattress in the cockpit, staring up at the moon and stars. We giggled uncontrollably when unexpected winds rocked the boat—tossing us around on the mattress like a trampoline. I felt a surge of pride when we sailed past the Thomas Point Lighthouse in Chesapeake Bay, and I called the children out on deck to make sure they witnessed the moment. Later that day, after we had dropped anchor in Annapolis Harbor, we strolled proudly down the streets of the city like Magellan and his crew in the South Pacific. I pointed out historic paintings of the lighthouse to Julie and the children. Seeing these sealed our collective memory that "We were there—together!" It would not have meant as much to me to have rounded that mark alone.

The plan for the remainder of this summer trip was for Julie and our children to see her sister's family while my brother-in-law joined me for the twenty-two mile sail between Annapolis and Baltimore's Inner Harbor. It had been my dream since I was a child to sail my own boat into the harbor where I was born. When my brother-in-law had to cancel at the last minute, I resolved to make the trip alone. Sailing a quiet ship was a distinct contrast to the preceding days full of conversation, laughter, and shared adventure. Then again, running against a gathering thunderstorm to find a tiny cove depicted on the chart, anchoring there in the moist, summer evening, and watching in silence as a storm of apocalyptic proportions passed over the bay were solitary experiences I will never forget. That I relished this interlude is no slight to the wonderful time I had with my family. The virtue I try to make from the necessity of solitude is an appreciation for each experience in life—realizing that the opportunity for that experience will soon pass, perhaps never to return.

In May of this year I celebrated twenty years of marriage to my college sweetheart. At forty-three, I am not far from that meridian past which the majority of my time on this earth will have been spent as someone's partner. It may seem strange in the afterglow of this milestone to ponder the subject of solitude, but marriage has taught me the importance of the individual. It takes a whole person to make half a marriage.

It was after sundown before I reached the inner harbor. When I arrived, the evening breeze was calm. My sails billowed only slightly, allowing me to cruise slowly enough to discover an unexpected anchorage right in the middle of the city. My little ship was one of only four boats anchored amid the spectacular display. The entire harbor was decorated in white lights. Paddle boats in the shape of sea monsters ghosted quietly about in the twilight, adding a dreamlike quality. Roots music from an outdoor concert drifted over the water, and it seemed as if I had suddenly arrived on another continent. "You can't believe how beautiful it is," I told my wife over the phone. "I'll be there tomorrow," she replied. We met the next morning like two young lovers on the docks, below the stern of a great sailing ship, and I showed her all the wonders I had found.

Neither a recluse nor a clinging vine will I be. For every one of life's treasures there is a season. What solitude invites us to discover, our hearts compel us to share.

Breaking Camp

As I poked at the embers on a midsummer evening, this year, a familiar companion emerged from the shadows and took his seat at the campfire beside me. It was the end of a glorious week in the wilds of Canada, near the end of a glorious season spent in many such venues on many evenings beside many campfires. But his entrance was not entirely unexpected. He seems to happen by at about the same time, every year. Whether we're standing on an ocean beach or perched on a rocky crag in the woods, he passes over many of us like a sudden change in the weather. The woods and waters never lose their luster, and the dawn may still sing its hallelujahs, but there slowly comes a difference in us. I'm talking about that old Puritan anxiety, that back-to-school, down-to-business, what-am-I doing-here-skipping-rocks-when-I've-got-work-to-do feeling that, try as we may, seems to be an inescapable appendage of the civilized psyche.

I am best acquainted with this emotion as it manifests itself in the waning days of a canoe trip. In children it is called homesickness, but as an adult with family, friends, and all the best parts of *home* gathered about me in the wild, it is something different altogether. It wells up from a campfire when the food pack finally lifts a little lighter and no more grand, culinary ambitions drive our efforts at the wood pile. It is the force that pauses the fisherman's hand upon the rod, once undeterred but now content to settle into the grain of the paddle on a steadier, homeward course. Rocks and pools that invited "just one more cast" at the start of the journey now slide by under an admiring but unstudied glance. Standing on the shore we cast our eyes farther into the distance than before, seeing neither the lake nor the river nor the trees but something out on the horizon of our lives: what will be, what remains to be done, what challenge awaits, what test is to be met, what greater purpose is to be answered. It is that familiar feeling of breaking camp, tinged less with sadness than with resolve and renewed purpose to shape our lives.

This is both the blessing and the curse of Modern Man. So many of those things that intrigue us and bring such challenge and excitement to our world—art, science, literature, theater, enterprise—derive from urban, social interaction. I have come to understand that this is precisely why wilderness, with its perfect simplicity of physical structure and predictable rituals of daily activity, offers the urban animal such an oasis. An oasis is by definition a thing of contrast, and without contrast it loses its meaning and preciousness.

In the fat happiness of July, my friend Tom Tompkins and I had wandered from our canoe near the ruins of Hazard Mill, on the South Fork of the Shenandoah River. We were searching half-heartedly for the reported location of an ancient Indian village recently unearthed by archaeologists. Not finding any sign or artifact of the encampment, and growing apprehensive of the poison ivy round about our ankles, we resolved to head back to the canoe and continue our journey homeward. As we began, Tom posed the question: "Could you have lived like that?" he asked, referring to the lives of the Indians of whom we had found no trace. We had fed ourselves to overfilling with fish from this river only the night before and had landed by canoe at a primitive camp in the woods, so it seemed to me at first that "living like that" was exactly what we had been doing for the past two days. But I had misunderstood his question, and he explained further: "I mean living in the woods permanently—making all of your tools, hunting and gathering all of your food, day in and day out, month after month, year after year."

I paused a while before answering Tom's question, as it was squarely one that I have considered yet never resolved to my satisfaction on every occasion I have gone into the woods. No matter how beautiful the surroundings, how glorious the fishing, or how fair the weather, there comes a point at which the isolation we once so highly prized becomes a source of small but undeniable concern for the routines we have left behind. The campfire on the last night of the trip burns never so brightly as on the first, and our sleep is never so free and easy as on those nights when we have just begun the voyage.

Most of us I would guess have had this emotion. It is perhaps the biological prompting of our ancestors, stored in our genes to wake us from the dangers of complacency. It stirs us in the lush of summer to remember and prepare for the lean of fall. It is the same feeling which, though it may hang like a pall over the gaiety of sun-kissed afternoons, still promises to invigorate us with the duties of autumn: school and studies, harvest time, putting up stores against the winter, and a return to the discipline of life indoors.

A child of postwar, suburban America, I am no foundling of the wilderness by any means. Long unseen family members who read this journal and recall my teenage years spent in the thrall of jazz piano and politics must wonder whether I have since resolved to quit civilization for life in a canoe. On the contrary, it is precisely the accoutrements of civilization that bring to the wilderness experience that depth of contrast which gives it clearer meaning and importance. Were it not for our urbanity, would there even be such a notion as "wilderness"?

Native peoples, it seemed, lacked the distraction and shortened attention span of modern life. To them the woods were home. George Washington Sears, the Adirondack explorer known by the name Nessmuk, observed in 1880 that an Indian baby "is not expensive in the way of playthings" and would sit "placidly content" for hours "gazing at the mysteries of the forest." We children of the modern world it seems are conditioned to require more varied and frequent stimuli.

Years ago on one fall afternoon, I felt compelled to gas up a battered VW wagon and chitty-bang my way with axe and saw up to the Catoctin Mountains of Maryland, near Thurmont. Under a cloudless, blue sky tinged with the cool portent of winter, I labored until I had gathered and split a trunk-load of firewood. Then, I lay back amidst the clean smell of wool, sweat, and pine to soak up what I feared might be the last, hospitable afternoon of the season. It was fitting work to be done on such a halcyon day. But as I lay there my thoughts wandered to apple-cider stands by the roadside, the smell of pigskin and parties on crisp dry leaves, and the jazz and ambiance of the King of France Tavern; to Thanksgiving feasts and bundled shoppers on city streets, and to the place where the wood at my feet would warm us. I hurried home.

Let us likewise make glad haste again in this fall season to break camp. Better for the journey and with a spring in our stroke we shall paddle home—home to the towns, halls, schools, and hubbub of modern life from whence the wilderness learns anew its precious worth.

A PERFECT WORLD

I spent the week before September 11 in a perfect world, and I had hoped to celebrate it with you now, in this column. It was and is a world of wilderness along the Grass River in New York. It is a place in kind and character familiar to most of you. In paddling through it I was struck as I often am, in such places, by the unfailing perfection of God's creation. Rivers like these run endlessly through the ages. Fish thrive, grasses grow redolent with blossoms, and trees find root and prosper. Seasons come and go in an infinite cycle of birth, decay, and renewal. Nothing lives or dies in the woods without a purpose. No life is taken in vain. There are no terrorists, here.

Each creature in the wild does exactly what God created it to do, which is to say it does exactly and only what is necessary to survive and ensure the survival of the whole. The wilderness presents a remarkable theorem of life that we cannot comprehend in its infinite detail but which is infallibly proved again and again with each new dawn. The wilderness is, indeed, a perfect world. It is a place very different from the one to which I returned on September 11. And the story I had hoped to tell you of that world seems to pale in irrelevance to the one in which we all live. Ours is a supremely imperfect world, and the history of it is sobering to contemplate.

It is a tale of a hundred woes and a thousand sorrows. It is the story of a child who has lost a father, a mother who has lost a son, and a man who has lost hope at the bottom of a bottle. It is a story of the cross, the tomb, the valley, and the abyss of despair. It is a tale of betrayals—of trust gained and broken, of unspeakable grief, of divorce and death, of lives ruined and lives wasted. It is a story of world wars, of madmen and heroes, and of unfathomable cruelty amidst inexplicable mercy. It is a story of Antietam and Gettysburg, of Auschwitz and Iwo Jima, of the frozen Chosin and Khe Sanh, and of Waco and Columbine. It is a story of the 7th of December, the 22nd of November, and now the 11th of September. It is the story of us. It is the story of this world as it has been, is now and ever shall be.

I have been thinking a lot, lately, of that familiar Bible passage in which Jesus, having languished in the desert for forty days and nights, is taken by Satan to the mountaintop and given a vision of all the kingdoms of the earth. Jesus was tempted, we are told, to exchange his divinity for the opportunity of an earthly kingship—an offer he refused in order to purchase, with his body and blood, a heavenly kingdom for us all.

To those of you who do not share the Christian faith, I mean no offense by these remarks. In moments of deepest doubt, we simply have no comfort or counsel to offer beyond what our own faith supplies. And by faith I believe that Satan's offer and Christ's refusal in the desert two thousand years ago provides us the perspective to understand what is happening in the deserts of Afghanistan, today.

What fascinates me about the Bible story of this

encounter between Good and Evil is that the gospel writers who tell it speak of Jesus being *tempted*. Imagine that, for a moment. It seems almost blasphemous to ascribe to Christ the uniquely human capacity for temptation, but his life without sin would be meaningless without that capacity. He was, I believe, both utterly human and utterly divine. Temptation implies a desire for that which we do not have, as temptation cannot exist without desire. What, then, could possibly have been *tempting* to Jesus? This was not a man whose life was marked by an interest in money or material possessions or political power. Indeed, he led his disciples in a headlong retreat from those ideals. One does not imagine that all of the gold or jewels or wealth of the world would have held any attraction for him. He would have seen the transience of all such things. What could Satan possibly have offered Jesus that Jesus did not have but valued and desired?

I imagine that what Satan showed Jesus in an instant on the mountaintop were not the riches of the world but the sorrows it would endure. I believe he saw, in that moment, the horrors of the Inquisition, the carnage of the Civil War, and the ravages of Hitler and Hirohito. I believe he saw the suffering of all disease and injury and the defilement of God's creation. I believe he saw the sorrows and pain that every one of us will face on the way to the grave, and I believe he saw the jets of September 11. If there was temptation in that moment for Jesus, it surely must have been not the desire to rule creation but to preserve it—to exchange his Father's heavenly paradise for an earthly one; to be our king on this earth and walk among us down through the centuries, to save us the pain of war, to heal not just the sick and lame of Galilee and Judea but all mankind of every affliction for all time. His temptation must surely have been to use the power that was awakening within him to alleviate the present, physical suffering of the world, but the price Satan demanded was nothing less that Christ himself—the very ransom for our souls. And in the choice Jesus made we find not only our salvation but also a lesson for the world in which we now live.

The human experience in this life will always be an imperfect story. That is the fundamental reality of this world and our time within it. Understand this when you see a child born with cerebral palsy, a young boy called to die for the cause of freedom, or a plane fly into a building full of people. We did not wake up on September 11 to a suddenly imperfect, often cruel and dangerous world. It has been so since the Fall of Man. But in our struggle against this latest enemy, we should not delude ourselves to think that we will ever find peace in mere physical safety or that the greatest dangers we face are from men who lurk in shadowy caves a world away.

What insight do our own travels in the wilderness offer us in this crisis? Perhaps, as Jesus did, we will find something eternal, there—something that affirms the divine spirit within all of us.

I remember standing with my son Kip, several years ago, at a scout camp. It was the first, big camping trip for many of the boys, and there were the usual fears to soothe about bogeymen in the woods. As the leader spoke, I found my eyes drifting to the distant forest. At first I noticed how foreboding it must have seemed to the boys—the trees densely draw together almost as a curtain, hiding a dangerous, unknown beyond. Then, I noticed something in myself. I recognized an impulse to explore deep within those woods and realized that I felt none of the anxiety of being alone in a dark forest that most folks—my wife chief among them—would consider part of being *normal*. In fact, I rarely feel as safe and sanguine as when I am utterly isolated in the wild. There is something in the wilderness—a sense of order, a fleeting image of the divine—that touches someplace deep within all of us. It speaks to a part of our souls that remembers who God is and yearns to see his face. It clears our mind and clarifies our choices. I suppose that is why, when I heard of a possible fourth plane on September 11 and wondered where the next strike would come, my mind wandered again to the edge of the forest.

When I think of safety, I think of a night beneath the stars, beside a waterfall in a river full of trout, and the dancing flames of a campfire. I think of my bare feet resting in a spot on the forest floor where the sun breaks through on a fall afternoon and warms the pine needles like toast. I think of thoroughfares that know no roads or runways or engines, where only boots and paddles can take you. I think of a perfect world, and I know that the world to which we must all return will never be so comforting.

It is well we should strive for Peace on Earth. That is, after all, the Great Commission. We in the United States have come closer to fulfilling that commission than any nation in history, but in this world it will always elude us. It is well we should strive to cure disease and ease suffering, but in this world man will die. It is well we should defend our families and our country, and may God have mercy on the souls of those who compel us to that task. But let us never forget that there remains a fate worse than death and a goal higher than our personal safety. Peace be with you, my friend, and peace be with our enemies. May you savor each day in this imperfect world and never lose hope for the perfection of the world to come.

TIME AND TIDE

Pulling onto Interstate 95 in the early morning hours, I looked for my place in the caravan of pilgrims heading south. We were on a journey to Mecca, all of us—strangers bound together by a ribbon of asphalt, rifling at a steady speed toward the warm, Florida sunshine. License plates from distant lands told the tale. We all hoped to find a few days of respite from the drear and humdrum days of work and darkness farther north. We would go and gather in the coming days like wheat, carefully savoring each moment and storing it away to feed our souls during the winter ahead.

Staring at the fleeting horizon of the highway, I kept up a steely indifference to the passage of time, looking neither to the right nor the left nor, for that matter, at what lay ahead. I could see the road well enough, but I was gazing more inside myself, toward a horizon of memory. Suddenly it was 1978 again, and I was a twenty-year-old officer candidate at the Marine Corps base in Quantico. In the hot, Virginia sun, the smell of freshly mowed grass mixed with the odor of tar melting on the tarmac beneath our boots. I stood with my platoon of an unlikely mix of college boys in starchy, new fatigues. The temperature rose to eighty, then eighty-five. Later that day, during drills, a black flag would rise above the base that would send us to our barracks for the afternoon to escape the heat—there to sit and polish belt buckles and boots to an astounding brilliance—but for now we stood erect and still in the gathering warmth.

The drill sergeant passed by our line slowly, menacingly, like a barracuda circling a reef. He was younger that the gunny whom we most feared, and he lacked that authentically callous manner of a seasoned Marine, but he carried the same authority over us. Coming to me, he paused, and I stiffened what few muscles were not already locked in readiness. You never looked at him—never. You stared ahead. You stared inside. You stared past the present moment. You stared at a mental image of your girlfriend on the distant tarmac, but never at him. A credit card emerged from his pocket, and he swiped it across my chin. It made an incriminating noise. He moved closer to speak to me—so close I could have seen every follicle in his jaw as clean and close as a baby's bottom. I had been shaving in earnest for only three years, then, but I had not done so that morning. There hadn't been *time*.

Time was the real luxury in this place, and a drill instructor has a special talent to suspend and accelerate the movement of it. He awakened us shortly after four o'clock each morning, just a few short hours (it seemed like seconds, really) after we hit the rack. No sooner had our feet touched the floor than we were running out of time to shower, shave and dress. I had skipped the shaving that morning, hoping that my anemic beard would not betray me so easily. I was wrong, and in the years since I have become much more accomplished at the quick shave. But in those days, at that place in memory, *time* was an unforgiving master.

In the classroom that afternoon, an M-16 rifle lay on the desk before each man as it had every day before. At the head of the room, a Special Forces expert with a stopwatch in his hand lorded over all of us. *Click*, he pressed the watch, and we began the hurried work of disassembling the pieces of the M-16 and arranging them all neatly on the desk. *Click*, and we made the weapon whole again. *Click*, and we did it still faster the next time. I was fast. I was very fast. And when the captain sent the whole platoon on a long-distance run, I made it back to base ahead of the pack—*way ahead*. The physical part of OCS was a cakewalk compared to my experience on soccer and lacrosse teams in high school and college, but in officer candidate school, the compression of time and the constraints on the freedom of a self-absorbed twenty-year-old are a powerful voodoo. Stupidly, but perhaps inevitably, I left the program and elected not to return the following summer, thus abandoning the prize of a commission as a second lieutenant.

Whether I would have made a good Marine or even had any business applying for the job are open and exceedingly unimportant questions, now. All I can say is that there are three moments in my life that I would like to have back, and one is the day when I walked away from Quantico. All three have in common a failure to master the tyranny of my own impatience and the inability to imagine what lay beyond a given point in time.

What I have learned since those younger days is that we do not pass through life. Instead, life passes through us at a steady and predictable rhythm, like a tide. We must have the patience to wait for its arrival and the wisdom to act at the fullness of the swell. On its flood ride life's opportunities. With its ebb go the choices we make. Some moments of decision return to us for further deliberation while others are swept out to sea, gone forever in an instant.

Four hours flew by almost imperceptibly, and a tiny yellow light began to glow from my dashboard somewhere in southern Georgia. I needed gas. At one of those endearingly tacky, roadside shops off of Interstate 95, I noticed an empty can of "Florida Sunshine" for sale next to the rows of pecan divinity. I wouldn't need a can, I thought. The sunshine where I was going would be stored in memory for decades to come.

Arriving at the last toll booth before Key Largo, I switched the radio dial to a lively, Cuban station. Hearing Spanish spoken fluently for the first time in a long while, I could scarcely understand it. A succession of power poles raced past my headlights in the darkness of the Keys Highway. Eager vacationers crowded my bumper, but signs cleverly spaced in single file along the shoulder offered these words of encouragement. "Patience . . . pays . . . Only . . . three . . . miles . . . to . . . next . . . passing . . . zone." As a singer on the radio crooned "Tu eres el mejor," I recalled my first, halting efforts to learn a foreign language in Puerto Rico, during the summer of 1972, from the dog-eared pages of a Spanish-English dictionary.

My old Jeep finally rattled to a stop in from of the Caribbean Club in Key Largo at midnight. Though dawn came early the next morning, I had no complaint. My kayak eased forward, and the waters of Florida Bay bubbled up around my waist—warmer than I had expected. A steady thrust of the paddle divided the unfettered hours into a purposeful rhythm. I passed an entire family fishing from a boat anchored in the inlet. The ebb tide swirled around their transom and fled seaward. A gray-haired grandmother, easily in her eighties, stared silently at a thin line of monofilament that disappeared beneath the mangroves. I coasted past them effortlessly on a flying ribbon of green water.

When I finally drifted into the pale-blue shallows of North Nest Key, I saw no one at first. Then, rounding the southern tip of the island, I encountered a man and his wife fishing from a boat. They were surprised to see me in this deserted place. The woman hurriedly pulled a towel over herself but then, concluding that I posed no danger, resumed her worship of the setting sun. Later, I saw their boat fade into the distance as I pitched my tent on the sand. Storm clouds gathered far away in the gulf.

That evening, rain and wind roared across the tiny, emerald strands that lie scattered along this turquoise sea. With nowhere to go on my island home, I relished several hours of unplanned rest and introspection. At midnight, when it seemed as if the wind might lift up my bivouac and hurl it into the mangroves, I wondered if my stay might be prolonged. I had little food but plenty of water and, certainly, no cause for worry. The air of the storm was balmy and sweet. The sand was harder than expected, but I was not anxious for sleep. Somewhere in the twilight, between my thoughts and my dreams, it occurred to me that time has taken on a warmer hue with the passing years. All but gone now is the impetuous boy I once knew. I have come to find, in places of quiet solitude like this, a recompense for the haste of my adolescence and the hope of wisdom in my old age. Time and tide, it is said, waits for no man, but the wise man waits for the tide.

Dawn brought blue skies and fair winds to my camp on North Nest Key. In my kayak again, I was born softly off the sands by gentle waves. A blister in my hand, unaccustomed to the turn of the double paddle, stung slightly in the salt water, but it would heal. So too will all hearts, with time. I paused awhile beside the mangroves to rest. It was good to feel the sunshine. It was good to wait, in this place. The tide had changed, and so had I.

A Young Man's Fancy

I await the spring eagerly every year now just as I did as a boy. Back in those days, when I lived in Maryland's northern counties above Baltimore, my winter penance sometimes would not fully subside until mid-May. Before then, the fishing and everything else that one might plan for a day in the outdoors were shrouded in doubt for what tantrums the weather gods might throw our way.

In every place I have lived, from St. Louis to Houston to the coast of North Carolina, I have heard the locals describe their climate by the phrase, "If you don't like the weather around here, wait a minute." But Baltimore, nestled between the Chesapeake Bay to the south and east and the Pocono and Appalachian mountains to the north and west, truly lives up to that reputation. It is a reputation never better deserved than in the springtime.

Unlike my peers, in the spring of my sixteenth year I had very little interest—well, no interest, really—in the usual objects of what Lord Tennyson so aptly described as a "young man's fancy." My fancy, then, was the rise of a trout and the slow approach of a largemouth bass. In fact, when my sixteenth birthday arrived, I didn't know how to dance or drive a car. I hadn't even bothered to get a driver's license. There was no need. Shepard Pratt Pond was an easy bike ride from my house and a short walk from the home of my pal Barry Skinner. The Shepard Pratt estate had long ago been turned into a mental-health institution. Happily, its sweeping pastures and woods had been preserved for the relaxation of its patients and the trespassory adventures of kids in the neighborhood who knew the pond's secret: bass. Big bass. You could fish all season at Loch Raven Reservoir out in the county and never come across lunkers like those hiding under the great, fallen tree that stretched halfway across the dark water of the pond. Branches fingered out into the murky depths, offering excellent hiding places for the swarms of fingerlings that would swiftly grow to impressive size.

The first book I ever wrote was a pamphlet I published myself at about the age of thirteen, entitled "101 Ways to Better Your Bass Fishing." Whatever became of it I do not know—I don't even have a copy—but as I recall one of its imperatives was temperature. The surface temperature of the water had to rise to sixty degrees before the bass would come into shore, where a boy with no boat could get at them. Until then, they stayed in the deep holes out in the middle, mostly dormant and uninterested in feeding. It seemed an eternity before the water was warm enough. I would pass the same maple tree on the way home from school each day, marking the slow arrival and increase of its green buds as the calendar passed the Ides of March. Indian summer weather would briefly appear and retreat throughout April in a pattern that kept the water much colder than the air. I carried a thermometer in my pocket and would stop by any streams or ponds I passed to watch for the telltale warming.

As kids, Barry and I had perfected the art of using a flashlight covered with red cellophane to spot the giant night crawlers that came out of his yard after a rain. His father was a sportsman who regularly took Barry and his pals fishing and hunting on the Eastern Shore. Perhaps for this reason, his mother was more tolerant of the muss and mud and clutter of boyhood than anyone we knew. She let Barry keep a huge tub full of earth and worms in the basement. It was all the ammunition we needed.

The approach was always the same: a single, barbed 2.0 hook, no leader, tied to eight-pound test line. We clipped the knot close to the eye of the hook, so as not to give any opportunity for grass to catch on the line and give us away. The worm was impaled in the "collar" and nowhere else, so he could writhe long and well, calling to our prey in the dark and deep. If you had enough line on the reel, the weight of the worm alone would carry a high, long cast to the middle of the pond. The enticing *plip* of the worm on the surface would summon our audience from within the tree branches. Down, slowly down went the worm. The line steadily sank back toward us until, suddenly, it would shudder to a stop and, after a moment's pause, reverse course, pulled by a bass swimming toward the tree. *One, two, three* we would count, then pull back for all we were worth, and the fight was on. I watched once as Barry performed this ritual and lifted from the pond a five-pound largemouth—the biggest I had ever seen then or since. To this day I have never caught a fish as big, and I hope I never do. The grandest achievements of later life are never so dear as the apogees of your youth.

Time passed, and other springs came and went. I met a girl. I learned to drive. We, who were fools for fishing and truants from our teenage rites of passage, passed through those portals late, but we passed through them just the same. Barry became a star attackman for our high school lacrosse team and I a midfielder of lesser ability. College, fraternities, parties, marriage and law school loomed closer then than I knew. My fancy having turned with a vengeance, the assorted packs and traps of my bygone adventures gathered dust in my mother's locker and, eventually, were passed on to those more likely to make use of them. A young man's fancy, indeed. But what of the young man who grows older, still?

As I write this, a poor, misguided robin is spending the day, as he has spent each day for the last seven days, flying a short course from the oak tree that rises in front of our house to the second story window. I now await the arrival of spring from my home in Raleigh, where the season comes a little sooner than it does farther north but never soon enough. Perhaps I will retire one day to Florida and find my impatience for fairer weather finally sated, there, but until then, cabin fever will take its yearly toll. Some ornithological strain of the disease surely has dealt a hard blow to the red-breasted dive-bomber who sits outside my window. The little bird's hopeless protest against the transparency of glass is marked by a *tap-tap* of its beak that grows more tedious by the day. This is followed by a flutter of wings as it regains its composure on the windowsill for just a moment before circling off for another sortie against our castle. (What was that song about a Billy goat and a hydroelectric dam?)

My wife has become strangely empathetic toward the bird and, with a chauvinism I did not let pass unmentioned, assumed it to be a female looking for a lost chick. She was appropriately outraged when she spied me with our son Kip, one morning, crouched on the sidewalk below the window, planning the bird's assassination with a Daisy BB rifle. After several unsuccessful attempts, at last I had the little pecker in my sights. Then, as I began to squeeze the trigger, I noticed the striking orange of his chest feathers, the "fuller crimson" of which Tennyson wrote, which distinguishes the male of the species. This bird was no anomaly of nature—just another fool for spring, like myself. I lowered the rifle and went inside to finish this essay. Live and let live, I say. It's spring at last!

THE OLD TIMERS
THE OLD TIMES

Every once in a while I catch a whiff of that special mixture of woodsmoke, coffee, gunmetal and boot-leather that takes me back there. Way down in Puryear Hollow, about twelve miles out in the country beyond Pulaski, Tennessee, lies a shrine of my boyhood of the kind that too few young people seem to find, anymore. It was a little house on the farm where my grandfather was born, planted mostly in tobacco and beans, with plenty of woods, hills, and creeks and enough stories for a lifetime. It had wood heat, no indoor bathroom, no air conditioning, no television, and water you carried uphill in buckets from a clear, cool, spring when the pump wouldn't prime.

In short, it was heaven.

It was there that I came to know my uncles Jefferson Davis LaCroix and Monroe LaCroix, their sainted wives Viola and Lucille, and other assorted descendants of the Frenchmen in my mother's family who first came to farm and trap those Tennessee foothills two hundred years earlier. I tagged along for two summers and one deer season as a youngster with Uncle Jeff as he held court under the shade trees, in the feed stores, and along the roadsides of Giles County for friends, neighbors, and kids like me. I remember how boys and grown men alike listened to him with the unspoken understanding that here was one of the real old-timers, the genuine article, someone who could talk with authority about the old days and who for the most part still lived them.

I got to know Jeff's grown sons Jerry and Charles. Jerry had fun once handing me a green, horned tobacco-worm for bream bait and watching for my reaction when he casually mentioned that they didn't bite "real hard." Charles' dead aim with a gun, the story went, had gotten him banned from every turkey-shoot in the county. With my own eyes I watched him throw a bright, copper penny up in the air as high as he could, then shoot it out of the sky with a .22 rifle. Incredulous, I retrieved the twisted coin and mailed it back to my brother in Maryland, enclosed with a letter containing a breathless account of this feat. "Could that kill a deer?" I asked Uncle Jeff, as I admired this amazing weapon in his hands. "Not likely unless you hit him in the head," he replied, "but it will kill you deader than a mackerel." Then he handed me the rifle I would learn to respect, that summer, while plinking tin cans on the hillside.

Those were summers filled with preachin' and sweet harmony on Sundays, hauling hay at three cents a bale, baths in the creek, biscuits for breakfast, Sun Drop at lunch, and beans of every species with dinner. Were it not for the considerable time I spent mooning around Farmer Long's pretty daughter up the road, I might never have come out of the woods.

I took away from those summers an understanding of a few of life's rules that have never failed me: that being a lawyer is a whole lot easier than farming; that "Love Lifted (Even) Me"; that there is always room for more chess pie; that farmers' daughters are a fickle breed; and that there is nothing like the great outdoors.

As my son Kip and I glided down the James River in our canoe last weekend, I wondered what he would take with him, and where his shrines will be. These days it seems our approach to the great outdoors has changed from what it was even when I was growing up. We have mostly forgotten the lure of campfires, woodsmoke, black coffee and flapjacks on a camp stove. Today's adventurer wears neon, fleece outfits and sandals that the old guys wouldn't have been caught dead in. He eats "Power Bars" for lunch, and fishing holes are what he's hell-bent to get through as he races down the river for the maximum adrenaline-rush before heading back to the office. Piles of guidebooks written today will tell you which sections of a river you can run in an afternoon and where to buy a hamburger on your way home, but few will tell you where to pull up and camp. Enter this humble journal.

Let these pages be a guide to the low-tech, high-adventure, wilderness experience we need more of. Drop your pack. Pull up your boat. Have a cup of black coffee and a biscuit by the campfire, and watch out for those green, horned worms.

LAW AND WILDERNESS

As I have related in the story about Maine that begins on the next page of this journal, the writings of Henry David Thoreau had an influence on my life that began early and lasted long. He sounded the clarion call to simplicity long before the Kennedys gave us casual chic. Minimalism was his watchword decades before that concept came to symbolize a hip design trend in upscale furniture and art, popularized mostly be people with non-minimalist incomes and lifestyles.

Simplicity and minimalism were for me, in my growing years, mottoes of convenience. It is easy to be simplistic and a minimalist when one hasn't the means to be otherwise. But for all that Thoreau so eloquently tried to tell us about those virtues, I was more struck by Thoreau himself and the ethos of the intellectual rebel that he seemed to embody. His life, more so as I imagined it than likely as he lived it, seemed so fearlessly defiant of convention; and convention, to a teenage boy, is a Lord High Master to be feared and obeyed above all else. To know this we have only to recall our darkest fears of wearing the *wrong* outfit to the dance, getting the *wrong* haircut before going back to school, and saying something stupid in front of the whole class. Thoreau's quiet world on Walden Pond seemed to shrug off all of that, and the notion that someone could live that way, with only his thoughts and principles to condemn or acquit him, was intoxicating to me as I contemplated the power in my hands to shape my own life.

That notion that we have complete autonomy and the absolute power to shape our own lives is, of course, the fleeting illusion of youth and the brief luxury of old age. Somewhere in the middle of our lives, we are overtaken by events that shape and form us until the mold hardens around our heads, immovable and unyielding. The tyranny of the human condition and our need for food, clothing, and comfort lead us onward. Decisions are made. Choices are foregone. Doors close softly behind us. Accidents of geography and genetics work their quiet influence. Soon the trail has narrowed beneath our boots, and before we know it, we can only gaze upon the distant mountains to which other paths less traveled might have led. It was there, on those distant peaks, where Thoreau seemed to stand and beckon to me, an idealistic student reading these words:

Let us consider the way in which we spend our lives . . . I foresee that if my wants should be much increased, the labor required to supply them would become a drudgery. If I should sell both my forenoons and afternoons to society, as most appear to do, I am sure that for me there would be nothing left worth living for. I trust that I shall never thus sell my birthright for a mess of pottage. I wish to suggest that a man may be very industrious, and yet not spend his time well. There is no more fatal blunderer than he who consumes the greater part of his life getting his living.

These are lofty ideals, to be sure. What I failed to see as a younger man, though, was a certain hypocrisy in Thoreau's words that became clearer to me as a husband and father. Thoreau's own father had sold pencils from his home to support young Henry's ascent to Harvard and beyond, and I dare say he didn't do it for the love of wood and lead. He did it for the love of Henry, as do we all, in our daily labors, for the love of the children and families we are privileged to call our burden. Still, I am not prepared even at this jaded age to toss Thoreau onto the ash heap of youthful illusions. What Thoreau tried to express was a sentiment more purely distilled in the famous essay of his contemporary and fellow-philosopher, Ralph Waldo Emerson, entitled "Self Reliance":

There is a time in every man's education when he arrives at the conviction that envy is ignorance; that imitation is suicide; that he must take himself for better or worse as his portion; that though the wide universe is full of good, no kernel of nourishing corn can come to him but through his toil bestowed on that plot of ground which is given to him to till. The power which resides in him is new in nature, and none but he knows what that is which he can do, nor does he know until he has tried.

As for me, growing up in an alcoholic family on the outskirts of normalcy, the plot of ground I was given to till, as it were, seemed covered in brambles. There was never enough money—or any money. I harbored this deep-seated suspicion that the other guy *really was* smarter than me, and that unlike him, I would become Thoreau's "fatal blunderer," who sells his birthright for a pottage. It was not until I had blundered my way through two colleges, abandoned two majors, and turned four years of undergraduate study into five that the lights came on in my head.

In 1981, I had landed, most improbably, with a wife and a U-Haul van at a Jesuit university in St. Louis to study law. Terrified and broke, I applied myself. Astonished, I succeeded in small ways where I had once been accustomed to failure. Encouraged and emboldened, with the support of a wife who loved and believed in me, I applied myself harder still. Doors opened, and the path beneath my boots widened a bit.

That golden moment of epiphany about life's limitless possibilities, which comes to most of us in some form or fashion, came to me in March 1983. I was approaching the podium of the law school courtroom. All around me were seated assorted dignitaries of the bench and bar and academe as well as family members, including my own mother, who had traveled great distances to witness the occasion. There were four of us—my partner Brian Konzen and I and our two opponents—nervously shuffling papers at the counsel tables. Law school faculty members whose sandal straps we were not worthy to unfasten sat in the audience to witness the spectacle, as if any of the four of *us* could possibly have anything important to say to *them*.

I had stolen away, hours before, to a classroom in the library just to collect my thoughts. I was alone and trying my best to bring the enormity of what I was about to face down to size. I had never *won* anything before. In fact, I had never been in a position to compete for the prize. Over the preceding months, dozens of my fellow students—many from prominent, successful families and exclusive, private schools—had reached for and fallen short of the goal that now lay before me. Gradually, round by winning round, I gave up my suspicion that we were succeeding only by some happenstance of good fortune. I was not even close, after all, to the top of my class. Were it not for an unexpected friend and unfailing ally I had encountered along the way, I might have crumpled at the podium when Justice William Rehnquist of the United States Supreme Court finally called upon me to deliver the respondent's argument. That friend and ally is *the law*. It was then and has been lo these many years a marvel to me, a fearsome tool, and a thing of beauty in its own right. It is the great leveler of kings and commoners, and on that night in St. Louis it elevated a nervous young man from the brambles of his upbringing to the pinnacle of a legal education.

In the years since, I have taken the memory of our victory in that competition into dozens of other courtrooms, before the mightiest of opponents, and before judges who wielded terrible, awesome power. And in each of these arenas the miracle of our democracy, which is to say the rule of law, not men, has given me the confidence of David before Goliath. This is how I have chosen to spend my life, by and large. Although it has not been the career of contemplative solitude to which Thoreau beckoned me, at Walden Pond, it has had such moments. In fact, I have come to appreciate in my journey through the law that the wilderness is, likewise, a leveler of men.

The wilderness respects no title, fears no enemy, and grants no special privilege. To the unwary or unprepared it is unflinching and unforgiving. It offers no remedy or relief beyond what the laws of nature will allow. But for any mother's son who will apply himself to learn its precepts, great rewards await. You can lose your life in the woods if you are careless, but you can find life's meaning there, too. If you will but study and plan, map your course and prepare for the journey, you can make your way through any forest of life or nature, no matter what difficulties or delays you have encountered on your journey, thus far.

Remember to scout the rapids and carry the rough ones. It is best to rise early and find camp before twilight. Gather your firewood before the rain comes, and share it with those who have none. Pitch your tent on high ground, and leave each camp a little better than you found it. These are the laws of the wilderness. These are the laws of life, as well. They are one and the same, and I have been privileged to measure myself by them.

ON SIMPLICITY

Lovers of wilderness paddling and all the wonders it entails—breathtaking scenery, fresh air and solitude being just a few—tend to be lovers of simplicity. Thoreau's exhortation to "simplify, simplify, simplify" might well be the voyageur's credo. After all, we do not take to the woods in buses but in slender vessels of far more limited capacity. The beauty of a canoe lies not in its versatility but in its singular aptitude to do one thing well and unfailingly, with elegance and grace.

Like many of you, I am one who secretly aspires to a much simpler life. Even so, as I look within a three-foot radius of the computer on which I type the words you now read, I see a veritable storehouse of supplies inessential to life on Earth. There are assorted brass curios, pens that have long since gone dry, books I will never read, copies of useless documents, and file cabinets to keep it all in pointless order. In the rooms beyond my office, the stockpile of life's miscellany expands further still.

Perhaps it is the clutter and complexity of civilized life that compels us to the woods. Set his feet in a canoe, and even the most prodigious packrat among us must be content with a mere ration of the impedimenta considered "essential" to life at home. When I empty the contents of my pack in search of some item at the bottom, often I will pause to marvel at how Spartan are the tools of the outdoor life. With one eye to the portage that lies ahead, I cast the other critically upon any goods that I might have weeded out, vowing next time to be more vigilant against such needless excess. When we are in the woods for more than a few days' duration, we eat less and more simply, and what we have in abundance are not possessions but our thoughts and the time to think them.

My fascination with the ideal of simplicity began early, thought it would lie fallow for many years thereafter. It was 1964, at the World's Fair. New York seemed to me, as a six-year-old, an exceedingly long distance from my home in Baltimore, though it was probably not much more than a three-hour drive. I don't recall being a party to any lengthy preparations to go (I was not consulted about such matters), only that it was dark and traffic was busy on St. Paul Street when suddenly I found myself in the back of the family car at an hour well past my usual bedtime.

The World's Fair itself is mostly a blur in my memory. I have a vague recollection of people in strange, African dress beating out a rhythm on native drums of some kind—pretty exotic stuff for a little boy from Baltimore. I also recall the giant, steel globe of planet Earth, placed prominently at the entrance to the fairground, which was the most visible symbol of something momentous and important going on.

Something momentous and important, indeed. Yes, I understood even then that it was not an everyday thing to go to a World's Fair. It was a wonderland, for sure—a bazaar filled with intricate, native crafts of every description. Yet for me, the most enduring memory of the trip is what little I brought home. Of all the trinkets and souvenirs that the world had laid before me at the fair, I chose nothing more than one carved, wooden donkey made in a pueblo in South America. It was smaller than the palm of my hand.

I recall thinking how pitiful it was that a child should return from so grand an adventure with so meager a trophy. I also distinctly remember knowing, at the time, that my self-pity was contrived. My mother and sisters had asked me more than once whether that was all I really wanted. Determined to play the martyr, I reveled in my self-imposed deprivation. No grasping, gluttonous striver was I—no sir! I would learn to be content in my state of want, however imaginary it might be.

All of my false piety aside, there is, undeniably, a quiet power that resides in poverty. Part of that power is drawn from the virtue of a simple life. What we don't have cannot be taken from us, and what cannot be taken from us we need not fear having to do without. This was the wisdom of Rabbi Schachtel, now also the words of a pop song: "Happiness is not having what you want, but wanting what you have."

A sailor and favorite author of mine, Don Casey, tells a story of the first Dole plantation in the South Pacific: "None of the islanders came back to work after the first two weeks, having earned enough money in their first paycheck to buy everything for sale in the stores of their village." Casey wryly observes that if there had been a Wal-Mart on the island, many of them would still be working. Perhaps that is the story of our island.

The bedrock of the American economy is freedom,

growth, and prosperity—freedom to pursue a prosperity measured by growth in the number and value of our possessions. The lifestyle we encounter in the wilderness is the antithesis of this principle. There, in place of *things* we find a seamless harmony of life, death, and regeneration. The qualities we seek in the wilderness have nothing to do with the number or value of the possessions we take with us. *Growth* in the wild takes on a new meaning. The forest is always growing, but left unattended a mature wilderness will appear very much the same in a hundred years as it does today. How does your neighborhood look, compared to a hundred years ago? In place of luxuries, afield, we carry tools, implements, and vessels of practical and necessary use. Typically, the inventory of equipment one brings to the woods will shrink, not grow, with time and experience. Look around your house: is there more or less stored there, today, than a decade ago?

How do we reconcile the complexity of our civilized world with the simplicity of the wilderness that we so admire and love? There was a time when I would have met that dichotomy with the youthful zeal of absolutism—with exhortations to sell up, pare down, cut back, and go native. But I have grown more skeptical, in my forty-five years, of the absolutist. Life's answers rarely are so obvious.

Consider again our friend, Mr. Thoreau. More than merely an apostle of simplicity and leisure, he stood atop the shoulders of a prosperous, young nation to condemn the very industry that bore him to those heights. Were it not for the hard labor of nameless cobblers, farmers, miners and sailors and the bloody shores of Bunker Hill where many of them died, Thoreau's neck might have been beneath the boot of a British soldier instead of craning to hear the call of the whippoorwill on the Allagash. He traveled to the North Woods on wheels of iron, dug from the earth by men who scarcely knew a summer's day of ease, and tempered by fire in the choking smoke of Pennsylvania foundries, a far cry from the tufted parlors of Concord and Cambridge. Many of us are no different than he.

Statistically speaking, that some of us even live, today, is a study in complexity of the highest order. Who discovered the vaccines that saved you from polio and smallpox and measles? Who built the laboratories in which they were conceived? Who mined the sand which became the glass which became the test tubes in which these miracles took shape? Who built the machines by which these materials were mined or the roads over which they came to market? What of the workers who made all of this happen? Do we suppose that they were paid in platitudes and psalms? Was it not money they sought—money to buy comfort and ease and vaccines for their own children; money which paid the salary of the brilliant scientist, who paid his carpenter, who built his lovely home, who by his wages sent his own child to college, and who by that child's industry added to the body of science and, in turn, to our abundance?

Most of us well know the parable of the rich young man, who refused to sell all of his worldly goods and give the proceeds to the poor. Some mistake this story as a call to universal poverty, but implicit in Christ's instruction to the rich man is the necessity of a willing buyer. Unless we suppose that Christ intended the rich man's obedience to be the occasion of another man's sin, we must conclude that it is not in owning things that we falter, but in things owning us. Real virtue lies in our state of mind, not in the quantity of our goods, however many or few. It takes a simple man to know the difference.

Time, Speed & Distance

Dressed in battle gear of Bean Boots and old chinos, I sat perched behind the window of my office. A gray, winter sky loomed above downtown New Bern. A Jeep in the parking lot, below, waited at the ready, fully packed for a weekend on the Cape Fear River. But as I looked across town, a freezing downpour continued to tap out a steady reminder of the impudence of nature. The Cape Fear is new water to me, and the guides warn of "an absolute keeper hydraulic" in periods of high water, which is a way of describing a big nasty spot in the water offering a one-way swimming invitation. Class II rapids are reported along the route, flooding to Class III with rain.

Having long since put my young son's outfit back in the shed, promising him later adventures in calmer, warmer waters, I was still loathe to surrender the two free days set aside for this trip. I had lifted the canoe onto the Jeep under a clear, moonlit sky the night before, but the rain thudding on the roof by dawn told the tale. Maybe it would clear, I thought. Then again, the neighbors would think I'd finally lost my mind if I drove through our little town in that weather with a canoe on top of the car. "Was that Mike Hurley I saw headed off in a freezing gale with a canoe?" I carried it back to the shed.

My computer's cursor blinked at me impatiently, and I glanced out the window for any break in the clouds. The rain came harder and with more purpose. It is springtime in the South. Tulips and azaleas must be given their due, and fair weather waits for no man. Thus are we all reminded that the pace of nature is not the pace of clocks and deadlines, weekends and holidays. For most of man's days on this earth he has kept in rhythm with the natural cycles of time. Life's routine was clearly divided by light and dark, warm and cold, wind and calm. Ours is now a world that heats and cools its air to order, lights its cities all night long, and moves us about in aerodynamic bullets along smooth, paved roads. Into this even order comes the effrontery of rain clouds, hurricanes and blizzards, running through precious free-space on the calendar while we can only wait.

It rained a little harder, still. I stayed inside. Bean Boots soon grow hot, indoors. There would be no trip, today.

It was another rainy morning in September 1994 when I eased the bow of an old fishing canoe over the lawn of the town pond in Old Forge, New York. Two hundred fifty paddlers, myself among them, awaited the start of the Adirondack Canoe Classic—a 90-mile, three-day dash across the ancient "highway" of fur traders and Indians. We all clung to coffee cups and shuffled our feet to stave off the morning chill. The weekend after Labor Day had brought fall to this country as surely as the mail.

As my eighty-pound, fifteen-foot tandem canoe readily attested, I was not hoping to win the race but only to finish. A veteran of the event passed by, stopping to examine my canoe. "Are you planning to race in that thing?" he wondered. It was not a question, but an admonition. Summoning an unwarranted bravado, I said yes. He then asked to shake my hand with the kind of rueful admiration accorded to doomed men on the eve of battle. I got the point. And though I smiled and tried my best to shrug it off, I was conspicuously the only solo contestant paddling a two-man fishing boat with a full pack lodged in the bow for weight. This would not be pretty.

It wasn't that bad in the end. In fact, I rather enjoyed the challenge of paddling and portaging that old barge for three days from Old Forge to Saranac Lake. It was one of the few times that I had traveled through the woods with a real sense of purpose to move across a span of time and distance. As brisk, blue skies broke through and the sun rose over the water, it was a great day to be alive and straining behind the ash. Yet, unlike the average day of canoeing spent idling for fish and pleasure, the limitations of a paddle applied at a given speed over a span of time and distance are immutable in a race. Stroke, glide, correct, stroke. Miles away, the end of a lake comes ever so slowly closer. Throughout most of history on this highway of the Adirondacks, there was no accelerator, no cruise control, and no amount of anxiety that could propel the trappers and the Mohawk any faster toward their goals—nothing but the unerring addition of stroke to stroke.

The raw boundaries of the natural world and the limits of traversing it under one's own power are no more in evidence than on a portage. A particularly brutal one of nearly two miles around Raquette Falls, mostly up the side of a mountain, waited for us on the second day of the race. Years ago, I had often pursued the limits of my physical endurance on the lacrosse field, but I believe I found those limits at last on the Raquette Falls portage, beneath an eighty-pound canoe. It seemed as though it would never end, but each time I dropped the weight from my aching shoulders, subconsciously seeking to plead for some compromise, none was granted. A distance remained to be crossed, and only the steady application of time to speed would span it.

Ultimately, the simple propulsion of paddle and muscle fetched Saranac Lake with a seeming swiftness, in hindsight, that was not discernible in the medium of the moment. My mother often remarks when she looks at my wisp of a daughter that she remembers herself as just such a little girl "like it was yesterday." The same laws of memory must be at work in the paddle.

It is still raining outside, but in my mind's eye I remember the glint of the water at the end of the portage below Raquette Falls. I am content to wait. The time and distance from rain to sunshine, from winter to summer, from youth to old age, are just so many paddle strokes subtracted from the number God has given us. We all get there eventually. What's our hurry, anyway?

THE GYPSY IN ME

In the eulogy to my father, which I struggled to read through an unexpected wave of emotion eleven years ago at Arlington, I felt compelled to remind myself and my siblings that "[s]ooner or later, we have to come to terms with our roots. We did not invent ourselves. We are the sons and daughters of our parents. And if today my brother and sisters and I dream great dreams and seek the adventure in life with a childlike faith in the future, we would be only fooling ourselves not to acknowledge the dreamer and adventurer who has gone before us, the tragedy of whose alcoholism stood between him and his dreams." A year ago this May, with the passing of our mother, I had occasion to contemplate these words anew.

All of us struggle, at this milestone, to gain some perspective on that chapter of life which is our own childhood—a chapter whose last, enduring symbol vanishes with the death of our parents. The memories of those days lie scattered on the floor awhile, as we search for a theorem of remembrance, a box of sorts, constructed of the questions and answers that will both contain and explain our past. Not until these images are given order and meaning can they be safely stored in the closets of our minds, where we are free to return from time to time in search of answers to the questions in life that lie ahead.

Like many of her generation, my mother was not a coddler or a nervous hen. By necessity more than design, she gave me, a latchkey kid from a young age, a degree of personal freedom that I found absolutely delicious. The world really was my oyster. Each sunny afternoon and every creek and woodlot beckoned me with undetermined potential. I can't help but notice the evolution in parenting styles since those years. Whereas children once revolved in orbit around their parents' lives and thus learned the crucial lesson that they are not the center of the universe, parents' lives today revolve in orbit around their children, who not surprisingly have an inflated sense of their own importance. At a school athletic-awards banquet I recently attended, there was more effusive praise for the talent of sixth-grade outfielders than I suspect Willie Mays heard during his induction into the Hall of Fame.

Parents in the sixties, my mother included, worked all week and looked forward to a little R&R for themselves on the weekend. As kids, we pretty much did our own thing. Sometimes we got gloriously into trouble, but we acquired a sense of adventure and a capacity to dream that children now, in their over-scheduled, over-supervised lives, have been denied. Tell a ten-year-old child of today's soccer moms just to go out and play and you might very well get a blank stare.

Looking back at that first eulogy from the distance of eleven years, the image of the dreamer and adventurer in both of my parents remains bright. That, I suppose, is their legacy to me. For my father, the product of a privileged upbringing and an Ivy League education, alcoholism barred the way to any lasting accomplishment in life. Still, he retained an indefatigable and, at times, infuriating optimism—a belief that he would strike gold in the Rockies, finally develop a system for picking ponies at the track, or make it big, overnight, in business. He was no model father, by any means, yet I cannot help but smile when I think of him celebrating his move to Mazatlan, in his late seventies, to the tune of "Who needs you, I've got Mexico." If I hit rock bottom, someday, and need to reach for that kind of chutzpah to pull myself up, I hope I find it as readily as he did.

For my mother, herself the child of an alcoholic, her gender and the tenor of her times, the unexpected birth of the youngest son of a failed marriage, and a limited education should have defeated her, but she succeeded remarkably in spite of these obstacles. She worked two jobs, leaving me and the family dog alone in our apartment to a world of late-night Elvis movies and frozen TV dinners. She found a niche in federal civil service, moved us to the suburbs, and made a fatherless childhood seem as close to normal as she reasonably could, given our circumstances. Through it all, she kindled a wild and almost tragically comic desire for wealth and notoriety, just as she remained committedly skeptical of our well-to-do neighbors and the veneer of normalcy that distinguished their lives from ours.

One of the second jobs my mother took to make ends meet was a position in the admitting office of Johns Hopkins University Hospital, where I was born in 1958. Diaper service for her new son was a luxury beyond her means but not her imagination. She offered to slip the driver of the diaper truck the names of new mothers coming home from the hospital. The diaper service gained an uncanny intuition for finding new customers, and I got all the free, clean diapers I needed. It was part of a pattern of benign subterfuge that, I would later come to recognize, marked her approach to many things in life. She was a Gypsy at heart, just like the Irishman she married. If she dreamed of wealth and comfort, it was only to be a wealthier and more comfortable Gypsy—never a matron of the stuffy, polite society she loathed. This definition of her nature eluded me until, earlier this spring, I recalled the story she often told of her encounter with a kindred spirit: the Gypsy Queen.

She was an ancient woman of Eastern European heritage who arrived at Johns Hopkins Hospital with an entourage. It fell to my mother, as the admissions officer, to gather all of the particulars. When she asked for the woman's age, however, her co-workers gasped and summoned her out of earshot of the waiting family. "Do you know who that is?" they whispered. "She's the queen of the Gypsies! You don't ask them for her age! She has no age. They believe she is immortal." Composing herself, my mother returned to her desk and proceeded with the interview, omitting any further references to age.

As word spread that the Gypsy Queen was a patient at the hospital, telegrams began arriving from around the world as did throngs of well-wishers and van loads of flowers. As days passed, the outlook became increasingly grim. Then, news came that she had passed away. One caller demanded to know the name of her attending physician, which my mother obligingly provided. Minutes later, the physician appeared at the window of the admitting office, ashen faced. "Don't tell anyone I was her doctor," he begged. "Why ever not?" my mother asked, still not fully aware of the stature of this patient. "Because immortals are not supposed to die."

The hospital waiting room was soon filled with the cacophony of mourners who arrived in droves from New York in long, black Cadillacs. The attending physicians snuck out through the back entrance to avoid them. The Gypsy Queen was no more, or so it seemed.

In 1976, I left our two-bedroom apartment on a bus for college, the last of four children and the youngest by ten years. For the first time, at age 55, my mother was on her own. She wasted no time. She bought a new car, moved to a rented house in a tony suburb on the outskirts of Washington, D.C., and began a long-awaited adventure in independence. She traveled widely in her work for the government, visiting elderly shut-ins in little country towns to help them qualify for social security benefits. It was a Gypsy life, and she loved every minute of it. She often supplemented her expense account to gain a taste of the good stuff at fancy restaurants and stay at finer hotels.

When I got a job after law school, I would try to impress my mother with expensive dinners. "I've had better," she would quip. My mother was always a little rough around the edges and a little insecure—even rude at times—but her message rang true: live life to the hilt, and don't be fooled by appearances.

Eight months after my mother's death, my twelve-year-old son and I stood on a dock in Charleston contemplating the purchase of "Moonlighter," a 32-foot sailboat built in 1979 that I hoped would take us on our own Gypsy adventures, someday. She was a little rough around the edges and lacked the finer appointments of a proper yacht, but she seemed sound. The surveyor said her hull was "as hard as a New York sidewalk," but the clincher was on the abstract of title. The original owner had named her "The Gypsy in Me." In a nod to seagoing superstition against re-naming boats, I took a part of each name and christened her the "Gypsy Moon." Friends and I sailed her offshore to North Carolina over three cloudless days and two moonlit nights. Along the way I drank a toast to the Gypsy in me, and to the mother of adventure in all of us. Long may she live.

A BOY'S LIFE

What a remarkable voyage it has been. My son Kip turned thirteen in June of this year. As we paddled together in August, just the two of us, for eight days and seven nights through that holy wilderness of Northern Minnesota, I scarcely recognized the powerful figure in the bow of the canoe. There, where for years had sat a little towheaded boy playing with frogs and bugs and hardly ever noticing a paddle, was a solid, young man matching me stroke for stroke. It has been a change long in coming but so quick in its passing that, lately, I have felt the urge to rub my eyes in disbelief. My elders used to preface their observations of me with the words "it was only yesterday," and now I know the derivation of that phrase.

We have been through countless adventures afloat, the two of us. On innumerable lakes, rivers and two oceans, through capsizings and storms, suffering rains that lasted for weeks and reveling beneath eternal, sunny skies, Kip has been my most faithful companion. We don't choose our fathers, but the choice made for us holds the potential to color all that we do and are. A fisherman's son will learn to fish, and a sailor's son to ply the wind. He may travel on to other skills and interests, but the avocations of his youth will always bear a fond familiarity. Like a first instrument in the hands of its former student, the memories of those days will play sweeter still in the distant years of old age.

Many readers who love the voyageur's life as I do would suppose that Kip Hurley is living a charmed youth, but to Kip it is the only life he has known—no more or less charming than any other he might imagine. Watching the moon rise over a dot of water in a distant forest; savoring the taste of a fish grilled only moments after it was caught; listening to stories beside a crackling campfire in a home built of canvas and canoe paddles; drifting off to sleep, night after night, to the peaceful serenade of running water—these glories have simply been part of the wallpaper of his boyhood. He has splashed and played in a hundred waterfalls more spectacular than any theme park, but like every child he pines for the day his parents will take him to ride the log flume at Disney World. I jokingly tell him and his sister that they've been living in Disney World all these years without knowing it, and they groan.

Through it all I have been cognizant of Kip's silent and oblique observation of my habits, the way a cottontail rabbit sees our approach without turning its head to look. I have worn uncomfortably the mantle of fatherhood, ever doubtful of God's decision to cast me as a leading man in the drama of a child's life. There are, after all, no dress rehearsals, and the critics can be brutal.

It occurred to me, as we wound our way through the spectacular scenery of the Boundary Waters, this summer, that Kip's adolescence would be not only his rite of passage, but mine, as well. I had been called to be a beacon and a guide to this child before I had yet escaped the fog of my own boyhood, and it would be my challenge to steer us both clear without running up on the rocks. Unanswerable questions disturb my peace of mind: Will there be problems with drugs or alcohol? Will he talk to me? Will I find the words to help? Will my own example inspire or discourage him? Will he choose wisely? Will he find good friends to ground him? In moments of doubt, will he find faith?

I am mindful that questions such as these are no less pertinent to that tousle of blonde hair, freckles and elbows that is my eleven-year-old daughter, Caroline. Nor do I suppose that the kindly offices of a father extend only to a son's coming of age. Caroline is the patient student of all that I attempt to teach her, but for now at least, the storms in her life are mostly those peculiar to the lives of little girls. In such matters her mother offers a steadier hand on the tiller. I suffer the disadvantage of inexperience. What I happily give her is a willing ear, a hand to hold, and a welcome shoulder. What she will take from me, ultimately, is nothing less than the standard by which, for good or ill, she will measure every other man she encounters in life. Whether in the end I rise to that challenge or falter beneath it is not my essay to write.

The eternal question that confounds fathers and sons is simply this: What does it mean to be a good man? The lives of great men in history offer us examples to follow, of course, but the devil lives in the interpretation of example. One might suppose that at least the outer markers of right and wrong are visible to all, but I grow less certain of that with time.

A few months ago I was on my way to work on a

two-lane road when the driver of a shiny, black BMW to my left veered suddenly toward me. Inches away from his passenger door I jammed my brakes hard and steered to the right. I avoided what would have been a bad wreck for both of us, but the right wheels on my car bent when I hit the curb. The driver of the BMW stopped and accepted responsibility for the damage. Dressed in a suit and presenting a business card that revealed him to be a high-ranking bureaucrat in state government, he implored me to replace my battered wheels and send the bill directly to him—asking that I not involve his insurance company. I thankfully agreed, and we shook hands. After I replaced the wheels and sent him the bill a few days later, I received a reply from his attorney, denying responsibility for the accident. With no police report and no witnesses, I realized I had foolishly trusted in the value of something I assumed to be priceless: a man's word, sealed by a handshake.

Examples of this sort of deceit and far worse are hardly newsworthy, but it is always startling to encounter it in one's own affairs, behind a smiling face. Kip, who lovingly guards my car out of longing for the day when he will be allowed to drive it, was incensed by the man's deception. The whole experience was little more than an annoyance, but it taught us a valuable lesson. We were reminded that every man must choose to put personal responsibility ahead of personal advantage. Although I am ill-qualified to make pious claims of selfless virtue, I can say with confidence that Kip has learned never to shake a man's hand with the intention to deceive him. That particular shoal in life, for now, should be plainly in view. Others will be less easily spotted. My sobering duty as his father will be to guide him chiefly by example. In this daunting task, I solicit your prayers.

As Kip and I headed out from Thomas Lake last August on the morning of our sixth day in the Boundary Waters, we celebrated our uncommon, good fortune. The weather and the fishing could not have been better. Well rested and refreshed, we boldly decided to paddle all the way to Disappointment Lake, that day, and set up camp for two nights. Moving westward, however, we began to encounter other parties of canoes, and it became clear that there would be fierce competition for campsites at the end of the day. We resolved to stop before reaching Disappointment Lake and take the next campsite we saw, possibly on Ahsub Lake.

As we paddled on, I noticed an older man. Traveling with his grandchildren, he had given us a wide smile when we first saw him, earlier in the week. On this day he was having trouble staying ahead of Kip and me. Catching his breath at the end of one portage, he struck up a conversation and asked where we intended to camp. I told him that Ahsub Lake was a possibility. He took out a rumpled map that looked like it might have made this trip twenty years ago, and pointed to one of only two sites on Ahsub Lake. "That's where we'd like to camp," he said. His boys looked worn out. I knew we could beat them there and that the old man was asking me, as best his pride would let him, to pass up that site. I assured him that we were going much farther, that day.

When Kip and I arrived that afternoon at the head of the last portage, we were spent. Three couples sat at the waters' edge, watching us as we came ashore. They told us they were camped nearby and felt sure that all the sites on Disappointment Lake were taken. "Hence the name," I said. They laughed. One of them complimented Kip on the broken fishing pole we had splinted together with sticks and duct tape. He squirmed at the attention and hurried down the trail. I followed with our canoe on my shoulders. As we paused at the other end to make a plan for that night, we heard something behind us. There, coming across the portage on the shoulders of the couples we had just met, were the rest of our heavy packs. It was a welcome reprieve. Not long thereafter, we found the best campsite of the trip. Things often seem to work out that way. My hope is that the years ahead offer Kip many such reasons to recall that a good man seeks something higher than his own advantage, and that a good life is its own reward.

THE VIEW FROM HERE

It has been more than eight years since that summer in 1995 when, camped alone under a full moon on the shores of Long Pond, in the St. Regis area of the Adirondacks, I got the wild hare to write and publish a canoeing journal. I was euphoric finally to be doing at age 37 what I had only imagined as a boy, and I wanted to tell the world. I hoped to create something that would serve not merely to chronicle my personal adventures but to sing the glories of wilderness voyaging. It was apparent to me that the romance of travel by paddle and portage had somehow been lost on the over-engineered, hyper-technical camper of today, whose chief aim, it seemed, was to put as many layers of Gore-Tex as possible between himself and an authentic, wilderness experience. I wanted to restore through the olfactory of language that whiff of woodsmoke, balsam, hot coffee and bacon frying on an open fire that was all but unknown to a new generation of shopping-mall adventurers.

This lark on the banks of Long Pond was not the first time I had indulged delusions of journalistic grandeur. There had been flashes in the pan, before: various impromptu college newspapers, occasional magazine articles, and a homemade press-pass that let me inside the police line at the ERA rally in Washington, where I got to shoot pictures of Marlo

Thomas deliciously eating an apple and gaze in amazement at Bella Abzug's enormous hat. There were daydreams, when I should have been studying for finals, about launching this or that magazine. The bug to write for public consumption had bitten me early in life, and recovery from infections of this sort is usually hopeless.

Mine was an unusual strain of the writer's virus which compelled me to instruct readers in a subject as a means of coming to understand it for the first time, myself. Thus did I find the chutzpah to write, at the grizzled age of thirteen, a pamphlet telling others how to improve their bass fishing when I had scarcely caught a dozen, respectable fish of my own. The journal you now read was cut from the same cloth. Someone once said, "Act like you know what you're doing, and the world is your oyster." I can think of no better credo for trial lawyers, politicians, or outdoor writers.

The truth is that I knew precious little about canoe camping when I set out to publish a quarterly journal on the subject, and I still know less than most of you. Although I paddled occasionally as a boy scout on camping trips, canoe travel in the tradition of North Woods voyageurs was something beyond my understanding.

An opportunity arose one year to join other scouts on a much-ballyhooed trip to the Boundary Waters Canoe Area Wilderness in Minnesota, but lack of money to travel such a long distance (well before the days of discount airfares) kept me and many others at home. Sitting with my fellow wallflowers in the dark, on the dusty, wood floor of the church hall where the scout troop spent Friday nights, I watched as a clackety projector produced a flickering, black-and-white movie of two boys canoeing through Canada. They carried their gear in great, canvas packs and dined off of their talents at the rod and reel. Seeing this mode of travel for the first time, I was transported. I dreamt of the day I would experience similar adventures on my own.

The dreams of one's early boyhood fade quickly, alas. I became an athlete and an inveterate Romeo in high school and college. This transformation was followed rapidly by other head-snapping bends in the road: marriage at twenty-three, law school immediately thereafter, and then a career as an associate in a big law firm. I was nearly thirty before I took my first day of vacation. It was not until after I had a son of my own and he turned four that my old dream of a loaded canoe, a placid lake, and a waiting wilderness came rushing back like a torrent.

I was in Rocky Mount, North Carolina, at the time, at a discount warehouse store. My wife casually pointed out a fifteen-foot red Coleman canoe hanging from the rafters. I should have suspected that there was some voodoo afoot when she did this. After all, she is the non-sailor who casually mentioned, one day in Houston, that we might visit the sailboat store behind our tiny apartment. The thought of buying a sailboat had never occurred to me. Four years and two boats later, we still had not bought a house. Four years after that, we sold our first house and moved to the coast of North Carolina so that I could chase the life of a professional sea captain.

It was the first canoe I had ever seen for sale in a store. In the places I had lived -Maryland, Missouri,

Texas and North Carolina, in that order -there were row boats and rafts aplenty on display at sporting goods outlets, but never a canoe. That day in Rocky Mount, where others saw merely another boat, I saw a $350 magic carpet—a lifetime pass to all of the wilderness adventures I had imagined as a child. People in the store were walking right by it, oblivious to its beguiling invitation, but it called to me like a genie in a bottle. I bought it, of course. Had I not, this might have been a journal about stamp collecting, instead.

A polyethylene-over-aluminum frame "Ram-X" is hardly the stuff of legend. Sigurd Olson and Bill Mason did not wax poetic over the good ol' Coleman canoe. It is, nonetheless, the preferred battle-wagon of southern float fishermen everywhere—those determined fellows, fueled by little cans of Vienna sausages and beans, who will beat any boat to within a skinny inch of its life in pursuit of stringers of bass and bream. If there is poetry in such a vessel, it is a short work. Before long, though, I was experimenting with various ideas for making a silk purse out of a sow's ear and a wilderness-tripping canoe out of my investment.

I tried all kinds of gear and packing strategies, including portage wheels, cargo nets, and five-gallon ice-cream buckets with water-tight lids. After a while, I discovered that there is usually more science than sentiment in traditional ways of doing things. The reason the canvas Duluth pack, portage yoke, and campfire tent have been around for more than a century is that they all do simple jobs well. And however much we improve and innovate modern methods and materials, there will never be a vessel made of plastic that dips and sways so sweetly, or rests so beautifully in the eye of the beholder, as a wooden canoe. This journal became a compendium of such lessons as I learned them and a celebration of traditions that have stood the test of time.

But I digress. I did not begin this final essay to write the last thirty-four essays over again. If you have been with me for the journey, you know these stories, and I hope they have brought a smile or two. What perhaps you don't know, and what I am coming to learn only lately myself, is the driving force behind them.

The journal has been for me the literary equivalent of two soup cans strung together between twenty yards of cord. The excitement at seeing a personal daydream come to fruition, in print, is something akin to hearing your pal's voice echo on the other end of that cord, even though he's standing in a tree house close enough to shout the message to you just as clearly. I could have written these stories and essays for any number of canoeing publications and perhaps made a larger reputation for myself—not to mention more money—but they would not have held the same thrill for the writer. A child could more efficiently navigate a river in a store-bought skiff than to spend the better part of an afternoon lashing together logs, but he would not as easily conjure the spirit of Huckleberry Finn.

At the heart of every pamphleteer and kitchen-table publisher, whose exemplar is Benjamin Franklin, is a yearning to do something large in a small and unexpected way. Therein lies the reason this journal bears more in common with Poor Richard's Almanac than the typical, *Hook 'em & Cook 'em* outdoor-magazine of today's Madison Avenue publishers. Nothing in all of the outdoors more readily deflates my spirit than a fast, shiny boat, bristling with horsepower and electronics, varooming off in pursuit of some testosterone-charged ideal of a wilderness experience. I would rather command the helm of a single clipper ship in a modern-day reprise of the East Indian spice-trade than a fleet of luxury ocean-liners. A penchant for the unlikely conquest, for self-expression unbounded by convention, is what has driven me to write—and I dare say what compels you to read—this pamphlet of mine. What I have been attempting almost unawares to express on these pages is an argument for choosing the path less traveled. I have trod upon, turned from, and regained that path dozens of times, myself. Every word I have written has been taken from the same, unfinished essay that I now see, looking back from the perspective of these past eight years, I have been writing all my life.

Long-time readers of this journal will know the story of my decision at age thirty to leave a comfortable existence on the partnership track of a law firm in Houston to begin, without a single client or a single case, a firm of my own in 1988. It was not an entirely new idea. I had stumbled upon and quickly devoured a book in law school entitled *How to Go Directly Into Solo Practice Without Missing a Meal*. Only through the gentle persuasion of my ethics professor, Dennis Tuchler, had I foregone the idea of starting my own practice right after graduation. "Are you worried I won't have any clients?" I asked. "No," he said. "I'm worried you'll have too many." I recall to this day the kindness of his concern as much as the enormity of his intellect.

After four years at Hays, McConn, Rice and Pickering, with a half-dozen jury trials under my belt and an over-inflated opinion of my abilities, I left to open the law offices of Michael C. Hurley. At an open house for my new office, pals from my old firm gave me a gift that well expressed the inauspiciousness of the moment: a plaque that read "cash only—no checks, please." The ripple effect of that decision to strike out on my own still astonishes me, and in the process I learned that America is yet a Land of Opportunity for all. Within three years we had become the husband and wife firm of Hurley and Hurley, employing six attorneys and as many staff, and ranked 41st on the "Houston 100" list of the fastest growing businesses in the fourth largest city in the nation. We moved into new offices in a gleaming, glass tower on the fashionable side of town, with hardwood floors, oriental rugs, and spacious views of the Texas plain to the west. One of the old-line firms in town offered us a handsome partnership to subsume our practice into theirs, and we turned them down flat. Our collections approached a million dollars a year. I was no wealthier than most of my peers, but I was at one of the higher ledges near the top of Unlikely Mountain, and the sky was the limit. No sooner had the paint dried on the walls of our new office, however, than a feeling of unease overtook me—a clutch in my gut that made me wonder whether I really wanted to be where I was at the time and what I might rather be doing with the rest of my life.

Julie planned to leave the firm indefinitely with the birth of our second child, but that alone was not reason enough for me to sell our practice, fold up our tent, and move away to become a sailboat charter captain in a tiny town on the coast of North Carolina. At the time

I could have given you any number of reasons why I had decided to leave, including the honest desire to spend more time with the fascinating little human beings our children were becoming. Such a cataclysmic change, though, would hardly be necessary to achieve those aims. Looking back at those days, now, I have to wonder if the force at work was not an abiding distrust of power, privilege, largesse, and conformity. Some might call it a fear of success or a low threshold for boredom, but I would disagree. It is the same force that has propelled this improbable publication to kick against the goad of convention. Who, after all, would suppose that anyone cared to read a homespun, black-and-white, low-budget journal on canoe-camping in this age of glossy, color magazines and high-tech extreme sports? More than ten thousand of you, in fact, cared enough to subscribe, and I have been more flattered than you know to be your poet and guide.

My bohemian impulses have been constrained for a little while by the loving necessity to provide bed and board for two special children, but time marches on. Out there, somewhere, I can hear the faint, distant beat of a different drummer. I am headed his way. Keep a lamp lit for me, my friends, and for the adventures in life that still await us all.

PHOTOGRAPHS

Kip Hurley (foreground) and his cousin Bennett Rosenthal beach their canoe on the Green River in Kentucky.

*Above: Becky Cox navigates a riffles on the
Peace River in Florida.
Below: The author comes ashore on Attean Pond for the first
night of the Moose River Bow Trip in Maine.*

Above: Nick Mathews, Missy Hutchison, son Zach Mathews, and the family dog on the Bear Island Canoe Trail in North Carolina. Below: A scene along the Bear Island Canoe Trail.

Kip Hurley with a smallmouth bass he caught and landed by himself on the South Branch of the Potomac River.

Smallmouth bass taken on Lake Opeongo in Algonquin Provincial Park, Ontario.

Above: Kip Hurley holds his first pike, caught and released in La Réserve Faunique Vérendrye, Quebec. Below: The author's and Kip's camp on Long Lake, Adirondacks, 1998.

*The author with a pike taken in
La Réserve Faunique Vérendrye, Quebec.
(Photo by Robin Lauer)*

The author with a pike taken and released on Hudson Lake in the BWCA. (Photo by Kip Hurley.) Below: Sam Heller (left) and Kip Hurley wait for supper on the Allegheny River in Pennsylvania.

Readers of Hurley's Journal gathered for a rendezvous in the Sylvania Wilderness of Michigan's Upper Peninsula. From left to right: Linda and Jim Kumler, Ken and Dan Brown.

On the Allagash River in Maine, near Henderson Brook.

Bennett Rosenthal (foreground) and Kip Hurley play on driftwood in our sandbar-camp on the James River, in 1995.

Kip Hurley (left) and Sam Heller play at our camp on Thompson's Island in the Allegheny River Islands Wilderness of Pennsylvania.

Above: Caroline and Kip Hurley ready for battle with the black flies on Raquette Lake in the Adirondacks. Below: A cow moose wades toward our canoe on the Allagash River in Maine, ready to defend her calf, nearby.

Above: The author camped on Polliwog Pond near the St. Regis Canoe Wilderness, Adirondacks. Below: The author's camp on Forked Lake, Adirondacks.

*Above: the author's camp on the Green River in Kentucky.
Below: (left to right) The author, Kip Hurley, Bennett Rosenthal,
Michael Rosenthal, and Robin Lauer in La Vérendrye, Quebec.*

Caroline Hurley wears Daddy's hat on the Cedar Creek Canoe Trail, Congaree National Forest, South Carolina.

The author, age 21, on Hazel Creek in the Great Smoky Mountains of North Carolina, holding a rainbow taken on a gold Little Cleo spoon with a trusted (and much missed) green Heddon spinning reel.

Above: The author's solo camp in the BWCA.
Below: Kip and Caroline make a birch bark fort on Forked Lake, Adirondacks.

Dusk falls on an unnamed brook running into the northwest corner of Grass Pond, near Low's Lake, Adirondacks.

Will Mistrot (above) and Kip Hurley explore a stream leading from Small Lake to Diamond Lake in the Temagami Canoe Country, Ontario.

Above: The author and Kip, at first light on the James River in 1995. (Photo by Michael Rosenthal) Below: The author and Kip overlooking the Delaware River. (Photo by Dick Powers)

*Above: Beaver dam near Little Tupper Lake, Adirondacks.
Below: Robin Lauer (left) and the author camped at the Raquette
Falls lean-to, Adirondacks, on December 12, 1998.*

*Caroline Hurley climbs a beaver dam
near Little Tupper Lake, Adirondacks.*

A railroad trestle appears early in the trip down the Mullica River in the New Jersey Pine Barrens.

Above: Wright Shields (bow) and Mike Avery shoot the rips on the Grass River, Adirondacks. Below: the author in camp in the BWCA. (Photo by Kip Hurley)

The author's canoe on the Delaware River.

The author using Cabela's tripod campfire irons and Lefebvre's reflector oven to heat water for the dinner dishes and bake dessert.

Above: This photo of a huge smallmouth bass caught and released by the author on Whitefish Lake was published in the trip report on the Sylvania Wilderness with a request for readers to estimate its weight. The consensus was four pounds. Below: The author stands on the American side of Crooked Lake, BWCA overlooking Curtain Falls. (Photo by Brad Peacock)

Above: Curtain Falls, Crooked Lake, BWCA. Below: A falls where the author's party went for a swim in La Vérendrye. Another view of this falls is shown on p. 200.

Above: The author prepares to break camp at Camel Rips on the Moose River in Maine. Below: Ragmuff Creek on the West Branch of the Penobscot River in Maine, where Thoreau's Indian guide went in search of moose.

*The author stands beside Allagash Falls in 1996.
(Photo by Michael Rosenthal)*

The view from the pool below a waterfall great for swimming in La Vérendrye, Quebec.

Above: Slickrock Creek as it meets Calderwood Lake, in North Carolina. Below: Lower Basswood Falls in the BWCA.

Above: Kip Hurley cruises for blueberries on an island in Lake Opeongo, Ontario; Below: The Big South Fork of the Cumberland River, on the Kentucky/Tennessee border.

*Mike Avery guides Caroline Hurley on a
leaf hunt along the Tyger River in South Carolina.*

Caroline Hurley flees from a bee chasing her at our lunch stop on the West Branch of the Penobscot River, Maine.

Above: The Suwannee River in Florida is famous for powder-white beaches and beautiful woods. Below: Tom Tompkins fishes the South Branch of the Shenandoah River. The author's Cheemaun wood-canvas canoe, which Tom built by hand, is in the foreground of both photos.

Above: The day's catch on Iron Lake in the BWCA. Below: (From left to right) Bennett Rosenthal, Caroline Hurley, and Kip Hurley paddle the South Branch of the Potomac River.

Eel grass in the upper reaches of the St. Croix River, Maine.

*The author camped on the Delaware River.
(Photo by Dick Powers)*

The Boundary Waters Canoe Area Wilderness.

*Above: Stopped for lunch at an island in the James River.
Below: An overturned canoe, stabilized with logs, makes
an excellent table for preparing meals and keeping
kitchen utensils off the ground. Here the author
is breading fresh caught mussels for the pan.*

*Kip Hurley, age 5, and Jingles inspect
their catch on the James River.*

Kip Hurley, age 5, hits the trail a little overloaded in the Joyce Kilmer preserve of Cherokee National Forest, North Carolina.

Above: Kip Hurley in the Allegheny River Islands Wilderness. Below: Kip hunts for blueberries on an island in Long Lake, Adirondacks.

Above: Kip Hurley waits for mussels to steam in Temagami, Ontario. Below: Kip on the West Branch of the Penobscot River in Maine.

The author's Old Town Camper canoe on Churchill Lake, Allagash Wilderness Waterway, Maine.

From left to right: Caroline Avery, Claire Shields, Caroline Hurley, Chase Barden, Kip Hurley, and dads Mike Avery and Wright Shields stop for lunch in the shallows of the Tyger River.

Above: Brad Peacock readies his gear at the end of the portage over Curtain Falls on Crooked Lake, BWCA.

Above: Canoes congregate at the end of a portage in the BWCA. Below: A native brook trout caught and released by the author at High Falls on the Oswegatchie River, Adirondacks.

The author paddles Lake Opeongo, Algonquin Provincial Park, Ontario. (Photo by Michael Rosenthal)

Above: A four-thousand-year-old Indian painting of a moose on a rock high above the narrows of Crooked Lake, BWCA. Below: Kip Hurley and Bennett Rosenthal paddle Calderwood Lake, Cherokee National Forest, North Carolina.

*Above: A campsite on Little Tupper Lake, Adirondacks.
Below: The author in camp on Lac LaCroix in front of the
"Hurley Canoe-to," a canvas lean-to made to the author's
specifications and sold commercially by a Canadian supplier.*

Above: The author's solo campfire on the Lumber River. Below: Caroline Hurley inspects lily pads on Little Tupper Lake.

After a long morning in the bow of a canoe, Kip stretches his legs running up a meadow in La Vérendrye.

Above: Kip Hurley returns for the food pack on the carry from Little Long Pond to Bog Pond, on the Route of the Seven Carries, Adirondacks. Below: A moose wades out into Churchill Lake on the Allagash Wilderness Waterway, Maine.

Above: The author paddles the exquisite, 15-½ foot wood-canvas Cheemaun built for him by reader Tom Tompkins of Virginia Beach. Below: A moose spotted by Caroline Hurley wanders into camp at Boom House on the Lobster Trip in Maine.

*Above: A loon nesting on Lake Opeongo, Ontario.
Below: A brook trout caught and released on
the Moose River below Camel Rips.*

*Above: An otter spotted our canoe on the West Bank of the Penobscot River in Maine.
Below: Kip Hurley on the Route of the Seven Carries.*

Above: The author's great uncle Jeff LaCroix—trapper, farmer, moonshiner, storyteller, and beloved friend of children—on the family farm in Puryear Hollow, Tennessee, in 1973. Below: John Ward overlooks the Bog River in the Adirondacks.

From the Tennessee summer relived in "The Old Timers, The Old Times," the author's great uncle Monroe LaCroix, his wife Lucile, and Spec, who loved squirrel hunting more than life itself.

*Above: The author and Caroline Hurley camped on Thoreau's Island, West Branch of the Penobscot River in Maine.
Below: Two boys on a school trip on the Moose River in Maine.*

Will Mistrot (left) and Kip Hurley dive for mussels in Temagami Canoe Country, Ontario.

*Above: Wright Shields guides Caroline Avery (middle) and Claire Shields on the Tyger River in South Carolina.
Below: on Falls Lake near Raleigh, North Carolina, Kip and Caroline Hurley paddle the plywood/fiberglass/epoxy canoe made from a kit by their dad as a scout project, assisted by Jim Bullard and others. It was named "Doubtful" out of worry that, at ninety-five pounds, it would be too heavy to float.*

Michael Rosenthal and son Bennett on the Potomac River.

Above: A canoe comes through Little Falls on the St. Croix River, seen from the Canadian side. Below: Caroline Hurley chooses Harry Potter over the scenery on the West Branch of the Penobscot River in Maine.

Above: Robin Lauer (stern) and Kip Hurley head for Obabika Lake, Ontario, in Robin's Chestnut Prospector canoe. Below: Michael Rosenthal guides daughter Emma on the South Branch of the Potomac River.

Overlooking the Oswegatchie River in the Adirondacks.

Rapids on the Big South Fork of the Cumberland River.

Above: John and Suzy Ward lift over a beaver dam on the Oswegatchie in the Adirondacks. Below: The view at dusk from the Five Finger Brook campsite on the Allagash River.

Above: The Big South Fork of the Cumberland River on the Kentucky/Tennessee border. Below: Tom Tompkins navigates a rock garden on the South Fork of the Shenandoah River in Virginia.

*The author (stern) and Brad Peacock paddle past Indian rock paintings on Crooked Lake in the BWCA.
(Photo by Becky Rich)*

Kip Hurley hunts for the perfect skipping stone on the Allegheny River in Pennsylvania.

Kip Hurley heads for a swim near our island camp on the Allegheny River in Pennsylvania.

Above: Fred Ostrander takes a break on the Nottaway River in Virginia. Below: Tom Tompkins paddles a Cheemaun wood-canvas canoe built in his shop in Virginia Beach.

Above: Fred Ostrander paddles the Old Town Otca wood-canvas canoe that his father bought in the 1930s for $210. Old Town still makes and sells the Otca today for nearly $10,000. Below: John and Suzy Ward clear a blow down left by a devastating microburst over the Oswegatchie River.

Above: A weary group of campers and their counselors coming up Lake Opeongo in Quebec were hailed to spend the night in our campsite, from which this picture was taken. Below: The South Fork of the Shenandoah River in Virginia.

Above: Fossils and people who come out on weekends to pan for them like gold abound in the Peace River, in Florida. Below: Kip Hurley (left) and Robbie Fralick opt for a water war on the Peace River.

After high winds prevented passage across Chamberlain Lake in the Allagash Wilderness Waterway for two days straight, canoe campers holed up in the Gravel Beach site—including this father and daughter—made a dash for the portage in the welcome stillness of dawn.

Robin Lauer, standing before his classic Chestnut canoe, tries one more cast from our camp in La Vérendrye, Quebec, before supper.

Above: The author guides while Michelle Paul reaches for Jingles and Caroline Hurley stays the course on the Upper Pasquotank River in North Carolina. (Photo by Kathy Paul)
Below: Kip Hurley and Jingles in the Congaree National Forest of South Carolina.

*Above: The author using the invaluable Schmidt Pack Saw in the Camel Rips campsite on the Moose River in Maine.
Below: The author paddles a one-man canoe on the Saranac River, Adirondacks.
(Photo by Graham Barden)*

From left to right: Caroline Avery, Caroline Hurley, Kip Hurley, and Chase Barden test an improvised seat of PFDs with a rope swing on the Tyger River in South Carolina.

Robbie Fralick swings out over the Peace River.

Canoes lined up at the end of the portage below Allagash Falls in Maine.

Michael and Bennett Rosenthal and Kip Hurley stop for lunch on the Mullica River in the New Jersey Pine Barrens.

The Congaree National Forest of South Carolina has some of the tallest tress in the East, including this pine.

Above: A box turtle suns himself on the Batsto River in New Jersey. Below: Tom Tompkins wades the shallows of the South Branch of the Shenandoah River.

Above: Kip Hurley (left) and Chase Barden overlook Middle Saranac Lake from Norway Island. Below: The author and Kip cross Middle Saranac Lake en route to Tick Island. (Photo by Graham Barden)

Emma Rosenthal and Caroline Hurley at a campsite overlooking the South Branch of the Potomac River.

Above: The author puts "the Spartan List" to use on Antietam Creek, Maryland. Below: Bennet Rosenthal and his sister Emma play in the South Branch of the Potomac River.

Michael and Susan Rosenthal and daughter Emma wave to a passing train on the South Branch of the Potomac River.

The author with a pike taken on a silver spoon near Hocum Point Island, Lower Saranac Lake, in 1996. (Photo by Graham Barden)

Above and below: The author and son Kip on the Broad River in North Carolina. (Top photo by Kathy Paul)

Above: Eric Paul guides Kip Hurley and Michelle Paul on the Broad River. Below: (From left to right) Kip Hurley, Michelle Paul, and Kiersten Paul wade the Broad River.

*Above: Kip Hurley (left) and Jamie Luther
make camp on the New River in North Carolina.
Below: Kip Hurley paddles while Caroline Hurley plays on the
Big South Fork of the Cumberland River.*

Everything seems to be going well for this couple on the Big South Fork of the Cumberland River, but the photo on the next page tells the tale.

Above: While running a ledge on the Big South Fork of the Cumberland River (preceding page), this couple snags a rock that swings and swamps their canoe. Below: Caroline and Kip Hurley make the best of Daddy's cooking in Congaree National Forest.

The author with a smallmouth bass caught and released on the Broad River in North Carolina. (Photo by Eric Paul)

Above: Caroline Hurley keeps a lookout from the bow on the Tyger River in South Carolina. Below: Readers of Hurley's Journal gathered for a rendezvous on Lake Lila in the Adirondacks.

Caroline Hurley stakes her claim to an island on Raquette Lake in the Adirondacks.

Chase Barden (left) and Kip Hurley test the theory that a watched pan of pudding never sets, on Saranac Lake in the Adirondacks.

*Above: Tom Tompkins navigates the James River in Virginia.
Below: (left to right) Graham Barden, Chase Barden, Kip
Hurley, and the author camped on Duck Island,
Lower Saranac Lake, Adirondacks.*

Caroline Hurley goes out on a limb on Little Tupper Lake.

Caroline Hurley puts a brave face on breakfast on the Upper Pasquotank River in North Carolina.

Above: Kip Hurley and Dad in La Vérendrye, Quebec. Below: Kip Hurley (left), the author, and Bennett Rosenthal celebrate a cherry pie dessert fresh from the reflector oven.
(Photos by Michael Rosenthal)

Above: Robin Lauer's hoists Kip Hurley's biggest smallmouth ever—a six pounder—on Wakimika Lake, Ontario. Below: Kip Hurley and Will Mistrot go for a swim in Lake Temagami, Ontario.

Above: Readers of Hurley's Journal gathered for a rendezvous on the Peace River, Florida. Below: Kip Hurley (left) and Will Mistrot hunt for blueberries in Temagami, Ontario.

The author and Kip Hurley push through a rainy patch on the Edisto River of South Carolina (above) to make it to a dry camp for the night (below). (Photos by Rick Wylie)

Above: Becky Rich with a bass taken on Fourtown Lake in the BWCA. Below: The Lower Beartrap River. All of the trees seen here were destroyed in a fire a few years after this photo was taken.

*The view from Lower Basswood Falls, BWCA,
looking toward the narrows of Crooked Lake.*

Brad Peacock with pike taken on Thunder Lake in the Boundary Waters, including one pike that bit and latched onto the tail of another as it was being reeled into the canoe.

Above: (left to right) Becky and Terry Rich and Brad Peacock rest on an improvised "couch" in an island campsite overlooking Crooked Lake, BWCA. Below: The author prepares a shore lunch on Lake Temagami, Ontario. (Photo by Robin Lauer)

Above: The author's solo camp on the Lumber River in North Carolina. Below: The author approaches the head of the carry around Raquette Falls in the Adirondacks.
(Photo by Robin Lauer)

Above: Caroline and Kip Hurley follow in the footsteps of Thoreau up Ragmuff Creek on the West Branch of the Penobscot River in Maine. Below: Unaware that their flashlight will go out inside, Kip Hurley (left) and Bennett Rosenthal make their way into a cave off the Green River, in Kentucky.

Caroline races up the hill for ice cream at The Store, a favorite stop that awaits paddlers near the end of the Lobster Trip, in Maine.

Caroline Hurley paddles the Lobster Trip, in Maine.

Caroline Hurley heads back from the brink on Little Tupper Lake in the Adirondacks.

Above: Calderwood Lake seen from a road in the mountains.

Above and below: Kip Hurley and Bennett Rosenthal play in the falls where Slickrock Creek meets Calderwood Lake.

Above and below: Kip and Bennett on Slickrock Creek.

Above: A moose on the Lobster Trip in Maine pauses for a closer look. Below: Readers of Hurley's Journal gathered for a rendezvous on the Mullica River in New Jersey.

Above and below: On the Green River in Kentucky.

Above: Readers of Hurley's Journal gathered for a rendezvous on Tupper Lake in the Adirondacks. Below: Kip and Caroline Hurley with Dad on Thoreau's Island on the West Branch of the Penobscot River in Maine.

Kip Hurley (left) and Bennett Rosenthal discover a lake hidden in a cave just off the Green River in Kentucky.

After portaging their canoe over from the adjacent Green River, in Kentucky, Kip Hurley (left) and Bennett Rosenthal take it for a spin on a hidden cave lake.

The author and Kip Hurley on "Kip's Island," Disappointment Lake, BWCA.

Caroline Hurley waves goodbye to Dad before setting off with Kip and friends Caroline Avery, Chase Barden, and Claire Shields on the Tyger River in South Carolina.

Above: Kip Hurley loads his canoe on Second Lake in the BWCA; Below: the author.

EXPEDITIONS

JAMES RIVER

SCOTTSDALE TO BREMO BLUFF

Not far southeast of Charlottesville, Virginia, we encountered a shining, wooded river that we scarcely recognized as the muddy slough that crosses under I-95 at Richmond. Where we put in at Scottsville, Virginia and surely for many miles farther upriver, the James is a free-flowing, picturesque, canoe-camper's dream.

The most popular trip on this river, we were told, is to put in at Scottsville and take out at the first state boat-ramp on the left bank near where the Hardware River comes in, after about a 3-hour paddle. For some miles before this boat ramp, islands in the river begin to emerge, several with gravel bars and high ground suitable for camping. We found one such island at the end of the first day and had a couldn't-be-better moonlit night enjoying a dinner of steak and potatoes by a crackling campfire of driftwood. Couldn't be better that is, except for our oversight in failing to pack a single cold beverage other than the boys' milk and Tang to wash down the meal. Perhaps it was just the ninety-degree heat over Labor Day, but an enterprising drink-salesman could have made a bundle off of us then, to be sure. The night air soon grew cooler as it does on clear summer nights, though. My son Kip, his cousin Bennett, Bennett's dad Michael, and I slept soundly under the protective eyes

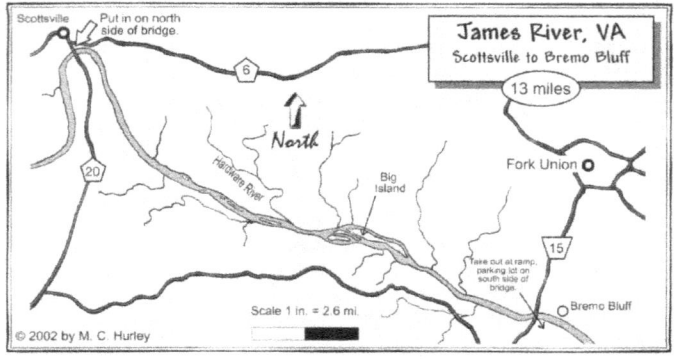

and ears of Jingles, our beagle-cum-canoe-dog, who kept watch against all invaders on her island kingdom.

The benefit of camping on a gravel bar is that one can cook, set up and break camp, and sort gear without getting mud everywhere. The drawback has to be that when a sudden thunderstorm raises the level of the river, you may find yourself sleeping on the wrong side of the waterline. For us that night, the red sunset, cool, still air, and starry night-sky gave no threat of rain. Had that been a concern, though, other campsites on higher ground were certainly available.

This trip down the James is a kid's paradise. If you have been looking for a good trip to introduce a youngster to the sport, this has to be it. The river at what appeared to be its mean level, during our trip, ran three to six feet deep in the middle at most spots, with lots of riffles and eddies from ankle high to waist deep where younger kids can swim and splash with confidence. The water is remarkably clean. We could see the bottom of sand, gravel, and boulders during the entire trip. The water temperature reminded us that this river's origins are not far off in the Blue Ridge mountains, but it was not so cool as to be uncomfortable.

The James is widely reputed as an excellent

smallmouth-bass river, and it did not disappoint on this trip. This was late summer, though—not the best time for catching smallmouth—and the serious fishermen we saw were happy with one or two good fish. Most of them were using what the locals call "mad toms," which are catfish fingerlings. They were lip hooked and cast without a weight in the fast water above waterfalls, then allowed to drift down into the pool below. Another popular bait on the James is hellgrammites, which are available locally. We were fishing only artificial lures and didn't do too badly, either. We had all the pan size bluegills we could handle. They would hit a little Beetlespin with telltale ferocity and put up a terrible fight all the way to the boat. The kids were entertained. By the time we got to the second night's camp just above the bridge at Bremo Bluff, we had caught two nice smallmouth on the same lure, and we fried them with the bluegills for dinner. It had been some time since I'd cooked up a mess of bluegills, and I must say that I'd forgotten how good this ubiquitous little fish can taste when pan-fried with nothing more than a little salt, pepper, and oil.

After the first night, we passed the first take-out and continued downstream through what turned out to be some mildly challenging class-1 riffles. Large boulder fields in this section afforded some of the best scenery of the trip—long after I had shot the last bit of film in my pack, unfortunately. The river current never gets much above three miles per hour, and even in the trickiest sections there is ample room for a canoeist of average strength to back-paddle away from the rocks.

This Labor Day we opted for a three-day, two-night trip with time for the kids to goof off. It would be just as easy to camp where we did the first night and canoe all the way down to Bremo Bluff for a late-afternoon take-out on a regular weekend. One thing to remember if you plan to camp for two nights: The number of islands suitable for camping diminishes to none about half-way between the first take-out and Bremo Bluff. There is one nice island to your left as you come over the last riffles before the high-rise bridge at Bremo, and we had a lovely river-side campsite there, complete with a rushing waterfall that the kids must have ridden downstream a hundred times. If you go that far before setting camp and that small island is occupied, however, you're out of luck. To be assured a campsite you may want to shorten your second day's paddle time and choose one of the many islands available farther upstream.

Whether you need to rent one or a dozen canoes, the friendly folks at James River Reelin' and Rafting in Scottsville will be happy to accommodate you. They also run shuttles to take-out locations on the river. When we went, their basic rate was $27.50 per day for a nice Old Town Discovery canoe. They also run a supply store with a fair selection of the kinds of lures that work in the river as well as live bait. If you forget your socks or a coat or some other essential piece of gear, Coleman's store up the street can probably fill the bill. Coleman's also sells fishing licenses if you need one.

Unlike the Adirondack voyage featured in this newsletter, this trip on the James River can be comfortably made with ordinary gear that most folks have around the house for camping in their local state park. By all means carry a cooler—or two—loaded with ice, steaks, and cold drinks, and take full advantage of that old scout motto: "Nothing you can do for yourself is too good, when you're in the woods."

FISH CREEK PONDS LOOP

ADIRONDACK PARK

I f you want to get an idea of the size of Adirondack Park in Upstate New York, consider that Yellowstone, Grand Canyon, and Glacier national parks combined would fit comfortably within its six-million acre boundaries. It is a breathtaking place that amazes the uninitiated to think that such large tracts of northern forest and clear, clean water can still be found in one of the nation's most populous states, just a seven-hour drive from Manhattan. In fact, most people outside New York seem to have only a vague sense that the area exists, much less the quality of wilderness that waits to be explored, there.

Adirondack Park is unique in that not all of the land within its boundary lines is wilderness—there are towns, roads, and houses aplenty in some areas. Against a tide of increasing development in the early part of this century that threatened to destroy the wild character of the area forever, the State of New York took the unusual step of demarcating a park-boundary that included both developed and undeveloped land. Its long-term goal was to control further development, preserve the wilderness that remained, and eventually return much of the area to wilderness status. Some of the areas inside the park had by then already developed into communities like Saranac Village and Old Forge, which remain busy resort-towns today. Since the beginning, however, state and private agencies have been steadily acquiring land and adding acreage to the wilderness side of the ledger in the hope that the Adirondacks might be "forever wild."

The trip covered in this issue can be paddled in three days and two nights very comfortably. It covers about 25 miles of lakes and ponds through a variety of terrain, including general-use areas as well as canoe-only wilderness. The portages are numerous but mostly quite short.

The trip begins in the northern end of the park, about 17 miles above the Village of Tupper Lake on State Route 30. There on the north shore of Fish Creek Ponds is Hicok's Boat Livery, whose owners will let you park your vehicle in their lot for a small fee paid in advance. They also rent Old Town canoes, sell fishing licenses, and have a well-stocked tackle shop. A little ham-and-egg place across the street opens at 7:00 a.m. and offers a welcome last-taste of home cooking.

From the dock at Hicok's, as shown on the map at page six, you head left down Fish Creek Pond. Cottages along shore begin to taper off where Spider Creek comes in. This creek like many others was obstructed by beaver dams. In all but the most remote areas, though, dams are usually cleared well enough to allow a canoe to float or shimmy over.

Spider Creek passes under a roadway and comes out on beautiful Follensby Clear Pond facing the high country to the east. Were this pond not such an early stop on the day's itinerary, I would have been happy to explore it all day. As you enter the pond, head north toward the mountains. There is a campsite on the north end of the island farthest west in this first section of the pond. It's wide and level, with a gradually sloping beach and a beautiful view of the water. Continue to the north end of Follensby Clear Pond past several islands, keeping generally to the western shore of the pond. At the end you'll see the white sign on a tree marking the portage to Polliwog.

There are a number of drive-in campsites on a jeep trail that runs between Polliwog and Floodwood ponds, so you're likely to see some other canoes on the water, here. There are several nice canoe-in sites farther out on Polliwog, though. Polliwog and Follensby Clear ponds are both good places to spend the first night.

As I scouted the portage between Polliwog and Hoel ponds that evening, a large game bird of some kind exploded from the brush, puffed his chest up, and came hissing and bluffing several feet down the trail toward me before flying off. While making trips over the same portage the next day, a large deer broke the morning stillness with a deafening snort not ten yards from the trail and bolted off. The hair on my neck still hasn't gone down.

At Hoel Pond you enter the canoe-wilderness area, where no motorized traffic is allowed. Here you begin to see fewer people. The still, quiet world I encountered in this area en route to Long Pond was a treat. Good campsites are at the northern end of Long Pond. Be sure to leave time to climb Long Pond Mountain and fish the creeks and beaver ponds, here.

The portage between Long and Floodwood ponds is the longest of the trip at a little over a mile. Half-way down, I stood with my broken reel staring at the prettiest beaver pond I've ever seen, feeling cursed. Ah, well, so it goes.

At Floodwood you'll see the log cabin used as an outpost by St. Regis Canoe Outfitters. This is a good place to resupply if need be. Owners Dave and Kathy Cilley are a font of information about the entire park. They can plan a trip for your time and ability, sell you the

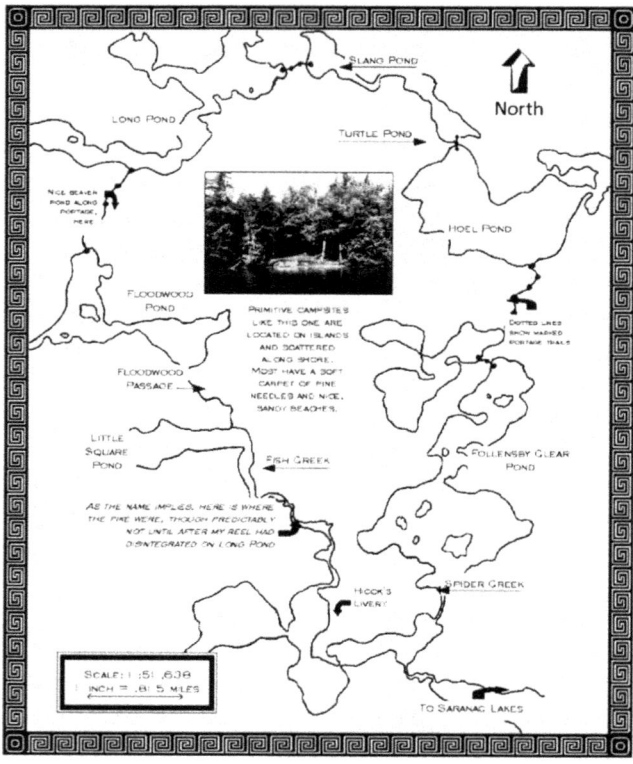

maps and books you'll need, and outfit your entire party with ultralight gear.

At Floodwood Passage you leave the canoe-wilderness area. This shallow creek has a few log jams. As you enter Little Square Pond, turn hard left to head down Fish Creek. Toss your buzz-bait here among the weeds and pull up a nice pike, as I saw a youngster do. Watching him I figured my reel was meant to be broken. Now I'll surely be back someday for that pike, or perhaps for his larger cousins in rivers and lakes farther still into the remoteness of this special place.

WHITE OAK RIVER & BRICE CREEK

CROATAN NATIONAL FOREST

Croatan National Forest, stretching inland from the beaches of Carolina's Crystal Coast, is a forbidding and varied wilderness of lowland swamps, southern pine plantations, and pocosin hardwood-forests. Though ranging over 157,000 acres and encompassing over 30,000 acres of designated "wilderness" lands, it is largely unsung outside the small towns of Eastern North Carolina that surround it. This is no doubt due in large part to the warnings that typically accompany any Croatan travelogue: Go only in the off-season to avoid the bugs and wear your snakeproof leggings. Such publicity and the impenetrable swamp forest have worked to preserve the remote character of this area's many canoeable streams.

The advice to go in the off-season, after the bugs depart, is well-heeded. As for the snakes, while they are certainly present, the threat they pose to those who give them a wide berth is largely overblown. I've often thought that if someone offered me a million dollars to walk these woods until I were bitten by a snake, I would probably die shoeless and poor.

The Croatan by virtue of its dense woods is well populated with game and is hunted heavily during deer and bear seasons. It is one of only ten game lands in the state where the North Carolina Wildlife Resources Commission permits unrestricted, primitive camping. Campfires may be built with caution anywhere on forest lands provided that they are fully extinguished and covered afterward.

There are a number of canoeable streams and wilderness lakes in the Croatan. The waters covered in this issue are selected because their length, wild character, and proximity to forest service land makes them attractive for a two or three day trip. Keep in mind, however, that the demarcated boundary of the national forest includes private land, and maps should be carefully consulted along with USFS boundary markings to determine which shorelines are "campable." Both USGS and Forest Service maps of the area are available. Contact the U.S. Forest Service office at 435 Thurman Rd., New Bern, NC 28560, to request the color map of the entire forest that shows the grids for ordering USGS and Forest Service maps for particular areas. Forest Service maps distinguish federal and private lands within national forest boundaries. Some forest service roads may require four-wheel drive during rainy periods.

WHITE OAK RIVER

The White Oak between Belgrade and Haywood Landing is a fairly popular trip in this area, apparently owing to the deservedly high praise given it in Benner & McCloud's *A*

Paddler's Guide to Eastern North Carolina (Menasha Ridge Press, Birmingham, Al., 1987). The book contains a helpful guide to this section of the river,

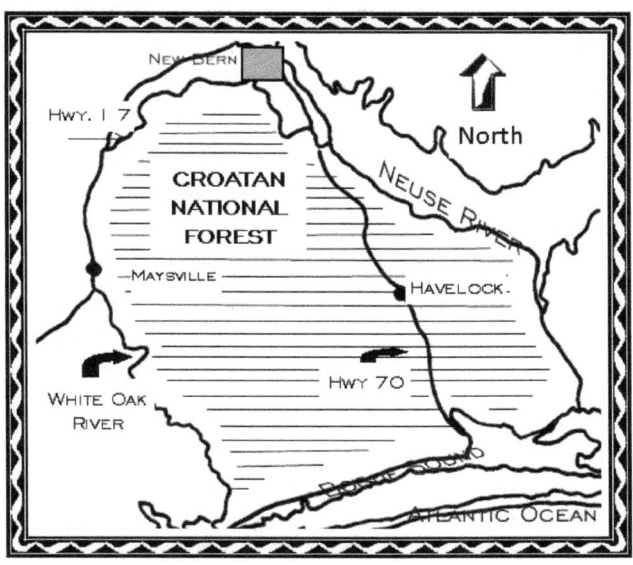

although I would allow more than the three-and-a-half hours of paddling time which the authors estimate for the trip. Unless you're in a kayak or stroking hard downstream in a light boat at high water, you'll probably find that the trip requires four to five hours of steady paddling. This is particularly true if you start the trip as far upriver as the Hwy. 17 bridge and encounter the headwinds commonly faced in the last few miles before the take-out, where the river widens on its approach to tidewater.

As I paddled the White Oak under azure blue skies on an Indian Summer weekend this fall, it occurred to me that I have not seen a prettier wilderness anywhere than is to be found along several choice sections of this river. The trip is best begun at the quarries near Maysville. Starting here, you will avoid many of the downed trees and snags encountered when starting upriver at the Hwy. 17 bridge. The quarries are not well known and somewhat difficult to find, however. Coming south on U.S. 17 from New Bern, you come to the town of Maysville. Just before you get to the bridge at the end of town you will see Maysville Milling on your right and a rusted, metal sign advertising "Lake Fishing" on your left. Turn left at the sign and follow the private dirt road a short distance past a gate to the stand where a launching fee must be paid. The gate is locked at evening and during the day in winter, as well. The phone number on the gate will put you in touch with the person in charge. After about 8/10ths of a mile past the gate, you come to a dead end at a dirt parking lot and a small boat-ramp leading down to the first pond of the trip. Unlike many other rivers in the east, the shoreline of the White Oak as seen from the water is untouched by agricultural and residential development along the entire length of this trip. There is nothing to see but lovely hardwood, pine, and cypress forest. The best time to make this trip is mid to late November, as the bugs are gone and the changing leaves offer a stunning show.

The first part of this trip takes you through a delightful series of deep quarry-ponds, seven in number, which are connected by narrow inlets. As you leave the boat ramp, head for open water on the first pond. The inlet to the second pond appears quickly on your right. Stay to the right bank and bear right toward the wide inlet to the third pond. Upon entering here, the outlet to the fourth pond is immediately visible, straight ahead. Halfway down the left bank of the fourth pond is the outlet to the fifth pond. The fifth pond is very small and immediately outlets into the sixth pond. In the sixth pond you may notice a stream of clean water rushing in through the woods on the left bank. This is treated water being pumped from another quarry operation and flows at certain times daily. Across the pond directly opposite this stream is the narrow, brushy outlet to the seventh pond. Stay generally to the right as you head across the middle of the seventh pond until you pass under a narrow, concrete bridge, where you return to the main river-channel.

Beavers are busy on the river. There are usually one or two impassable obstructions, so be prepared to portage a few yards if necessary.

Looking at the USFS map, you will see that there are two patches of federal land along the left bank of the river, where primitive camping is allowed. These are well marked on trees painted with a single, red band and marked with USFS signs. After about two hours of casual paddling, the first patch of federal land begins where Black Swamp Creek comes in on the left. A landing area among the cypress knees, here lies at the foot of a knoll overlooking the creek and a deep pool in the river. This high ground has a wide, flat area large enough to accommodate several tents. There is ample downed-wood for fires, as well.

Once I had set camp on this hill, a group of paddlers headed down the river for the day pulled over for a chat. One gentleman in a beautiful cypress-strip canoe asked me if I had seen any beaver yet. I had not. He explained that if I heard a noise that night that sounded like someone tossing a watermelon in the water, I ought not to be afraid. "It's just the beavers around here," he said. As we chatted about the river, he further explained that Black Swamp Creek had been a favorite hiding place for moonshine stills during Prohibition. Suitably briefed, I set about the usual routine of building a fire and baking the evening meal.

Nightfall comes at about six in the evening in late November, and by eight o'clock that night our little beagle "Jingles" was well curled up under my chair by the campfire. An onion and a potato were on their way to succulent perfection in the reflector oven, and nothing disturbed the silence but the trill of waterfalls in the creek below. Suddenly I heard a noise that clearly called to mind the image of someone standing on shore and tossing a watermelon on a high arc into the water. With this Jingles leapt into the air, in full song, and went off howling into the woods—certain that the Croatoan were at the gate, no doubt. The beaver were momentarily subdued by this response, only to begin again in earnest a half-hour later. This time, the plunges just kept coming one after another, not unlike a gang of kids trying to rock the deep end of the pool. I have heard beaver slap their tails before, but this was decidedly different. I counted thirty-nine cannonballs off the high dive that evening, with number forty coming just as I was nodding off to sleep.

The visitor in the cypress-strip canoe that afternoon had so perfectly and confidently predicted this phenomenon that it must be as reliable as Old Faithful in these woods. It later occurred to me that one could spin a marvelous campfire tale, here, about ill-fated moonshiners who hurriedly tossed jugs of the good stuff into the creek to evade the law—only to be caught and killed, or some such horror—and whose ghosts now return to the creek each evening in a fruitless, eternal effort to finish dumping the evidence and escape their terrible fate, etc., etc. It would be entertaining to see the looks on little faces as the beaver delivered their eerie denouement.

Departing this noisy but otherwise charming patch of woods the next morning, a sluice over a beaver dam provided a pleasing sleigh ride, and I was once again gliding along in still, deep water. The national forest continues along the left bank for about a half-mile or so, where there is good high ground for camping—some of it the prettiest of the trip. The end of the forest lands is again marked on a tree, but the character of the river does not change.

As one heads downriver from this point, there are areas where the channel becomes less well defined. By watching the slow movement of the current, the true channel will be apparent. At the next patch of forest service land, a wide channel leads briefly off to the left beside trees marked with the USFS sign and a red band. Avoid this channel and stay to the right, where the river's true course is quickly visible. It is from here downriver that one can expect to encounter some headwinds through beautiful marsh grasses and winding bends on the way to Haywood Landing.

Haywood Landing offers another place to camp. This is a cleared area with a gravel road that sees a fair amount of trailer-boat traffic and tenters on weekends but which has no improved facilities. To get there, turn right onto Hwy. 58 from U.S. 17-south in Maysville, before the left turn into the quarries. It is roughly seven miles from the turn-off at U.S. 17 to the small brown sign on the right of Hwy. 58 that marks the road to the landing.

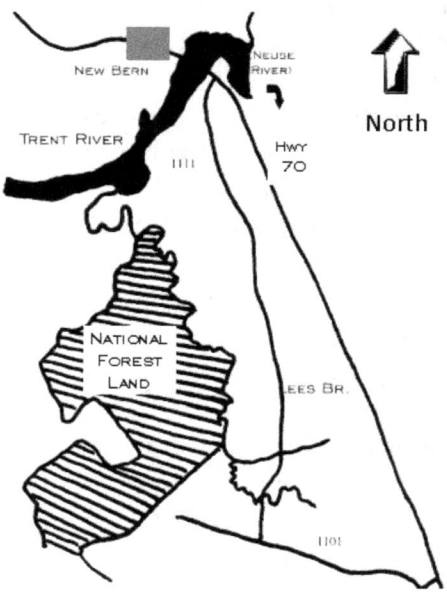

BRICE CREEK

In the winter issue we looked at a popular trip down the White Oak River through Eastern North Carolina's Croatan National Forest. Like the White Oak, the trip down Brice Creek covered in this issue floats by national-forest-owned lands on which primitive camping is widely permitted.

A Brice Creek float trip can be done easily in a day,

but there are several good bluffs overlooking the river that make excellent campsites. Because the paddling time before taking out and setting up camp is not more than two to three hours, this seems to be a good trip for getting young paddlers started. In fact, when my five-year-old son and I made the trip we were pleased to meet by chance another father and son who had come to camp and search for chain pickerel.

The float trip begins at the bridge on forest-road 1111, also named "Old Airport Road." As you leave New Bern going East on Highway 70, look for the Texaco station on the right, where you'll turn right onto Thurman Road. Go a short distance to the junction with 1111 and turn left. Rt. 1111 quickly becomes a gravel road. It crosses the bridge over Brice Creek, 1.4 miles from the juncture of Rt. 1111 and Thurman Road. On the south (far) side of the bridge there is a wide spot in the road to pull over and park. This side of the creek is also easiest for launching the canoe.

Brice Creek starts the trip as a dark-colored but clean river flowing out of the Croatan wilderness areas. The water is too naturally acidic in most spots far upriver to support game fish, but the fishing improves as one moves downstream. Bass and crappie are regularly caught in lower Brice Creek.

The take-out for this trip is at the Brice Creek Recreation Site of the National Forest, a distance of about five river miles from the put-in. The forest service allows camping at the Brice Creek Recreation Site, but it is often well-occupied. From the put-in, the second and third series of high bluffs that you see on the left bank are more secluded for camping and have plenty of downed wood for fires.

The USGS primary map for the "New Bern" quadrangle, 1:24,000 scale, is recommended for this trip. We couldn't find the large, false channel leading off to the right as shown on the map half-way through the trip. It may be overgrown with brush. In any event the clearly apparent channel was always the correct channel when the stream diverged. Slowing down and watching the drift of the current will also solve any directional problems in the upper reaches.

Farther downstream, by about four miles, the creek widens into a large river with only a slightly perceptible current. Here it was on one Spring afternoon a few years ago that I rounded a bend to find a whitetail with a full rack of antlers swimming strongly across the river in front of me. Great blue herons and a wide variety of other birds and animals also frequent the river, which has seen fairly heavy residential development below the forest-service corridor.

To get from the put-in to the take out, head back the way you came, but do not turn back onto Thurman Road. Follow 1111 (Old Airport Road) all the way to where it joins Rt. 1004, about 5.2 miles from the bridge at the put-in. Turn left onto Rt. 1004 and go about two miles to the juncture of Rt. 1143 on the left at Merchant's Grocery, which also rents canoes. Turn left here and go 1.4 miles to the brown sign that marks the dirt road to the Brice Creek Recreation Site. Turn left here and follow this road down to the boat launch. There is a nice camping area here and a wooden dock on the creek.

LAKE MOOMAW & MERCHANT'S MILL POND

GEORGE WASHINGTON NATIONAL FOREST

MERCHANTS MILL POND STATE PARK

I love my wife. I also know her well enough to realize when she really is not enjoying herself. One of those moments occurred last October on Bear Island on the Carolina coast. She fought off sand fleas, mosquitoes, and tired, whining children to help me portage what seemed to be several tons of gear a half-mile through shifting sands to our campsite. We aborted one portage to race back like madmen and lather ourselves with bug spray against the hordes of no-see-ums. The regard for me on her face as she finally staggered into camp, dwarfed by the pack on her back piled high with gear, was familiar. I had seen it before, during the final throes of childbirth. That's one trip you won't find fondly recalled in the pages of this journal.

On the other hand, there have been more than a few golden moments. Nights spent listening to the local country radio station by a glowing fire, competing to see

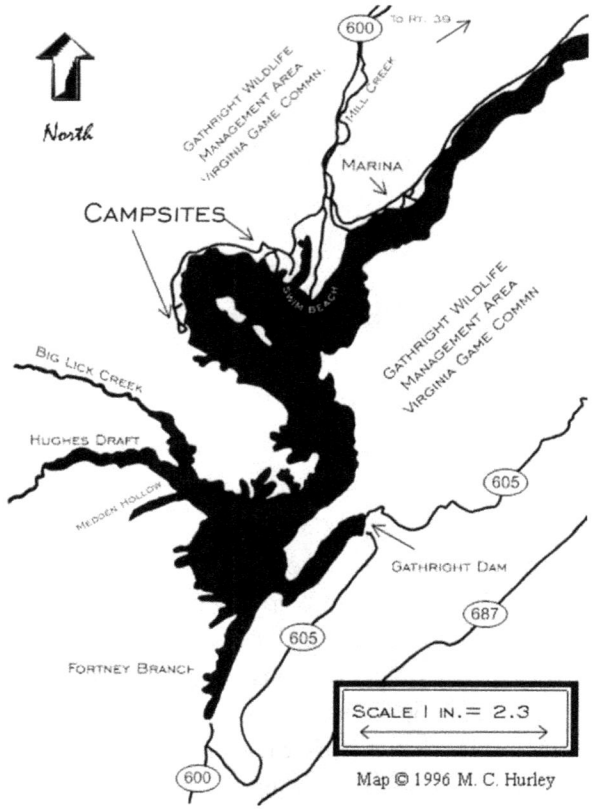

LAKE MOOMAW

who can roast the most consecutive, perfect marshmallows long after the kids have fallen asleep. Pulling steaks from the cooler when the fire's just right, talking over plans. Admittedly, wilderness canoe-tripping is not Julie's cup of tea, but rarely a week goes by when the kids don't ask when we're heading back to a lake somewhere, pitching the cabin tent, pulling out the lawn chairs, and making a home in the woods. Here are a couple of nice lakes where you can pull up your canoe and stay put.

Lake Moomaw is special because it is one of what seem to be a very few large, mountain lakes in the South whose shoreline has not been carved up into vacation homes and tourist resorts. This is apparently due to both U.S. Forest Service protection and the designation of the adjacent lands as Wildlife Management Areas by the Virginia Game Commission. As a result, when you look out from your campsite along the water's edge, you see only wooded mountains and sheer rock cliffs against the horizon.

The lake was formed by the construction of Gathright Dam on the Jackson and James Rivers. It lies nineteen miles north of Covington, Virginia, and straddles Bath and Allegheny Counties. It is co-managed by the Warm Springs and James River Ranger Districts of George Washington National Forest.

The lakeside campsites at Lake Moomaw are reserved for tenters, and you can pull your canoe right up into camp. Reservations must be made well in advance through the U. S. National Forest Service Reservation Center to secure one of these sites. The operator can help in determining which of the available sites is on the water. The forest service has been using a system of campsite "hosts"—private citizens who volunteer to supervise the camping area while they too are camped there—in lieu of tying up forest-service personnel with campground-duty. Our hosts were extremely efficient. They knew our name, where we were supposed to camp, kept others away from our pre-paid site until we arrived—late—and met us with a lantern to help us drive to our site.

As for the shower and restroom facilities, they were as clean as we had seen anywhere, with ample hot water for all. The forest service has also put in a small but nice sandy swimming beach with bath facilities at one end of the lake.

The lake is ponderously deep and gin-clear, with an average depth of eighty feet over rocky bottom. It has 2,530 acres of surface area and 43.5 miles of shoreline. Fishing is good. The kids caught no end of bluegills and pan-size largemouth bass on earthworms found below wet leaves. Small poppers cast at dusk and early morning back in the coves produced several nice fish.

Use Rt. 600 going into and out of the park and avoid Rt. 603, which becomes a dirt one-lane road. And finally, by all means tune in the little radio station in Clifton Forge that features a morning "swap shop," a little gospel wisdom, country music, and local folks you'll enjoy.

Merchant's Mill Pond

If you're looking for a weekend lake-trip with the wilderness feel of a canoe-in campsite, Merchants Millpond State Park offers an authentic backwoods experience. Nestled behind striking cypress trees and Spanish moss are two spacious canoe-in camping areas—one for family campers and one for groups. The campsites are dotted through the woods, uphill from the boggy shoreline of the pond.

As you enter the state park on the main east-west road,

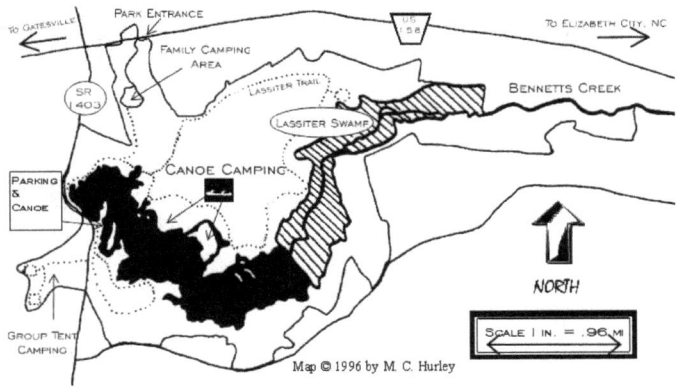

Merchants Mill Pond

the canoeing launch area is not apparent. The park entrance leads to the improved camping areas with the typical state-park facilities. To get to the canoe-in sites, follow the signs to the side road (see map, above) that runs by the canoe launch and parking area. The park service rents a large fleet of Old Town Discovery canoes at a concession stand, here. Most folks come out just to paddle around the pond for a day.

As you leave from the canoe launch, bear right and pick up the floating markers leading you through the cypress on one of two water trails. Maps are available from the park office. You should reach your reserved campsite at the other end of the pond in less than an hour of paddling. Pull up among the cypress knees on shore. From there it's a stone's throw to any of several, good campsites on high ground in a hardwood forest.

Rappahannock River

Kelly's Ford to Mott's Run

I was attracted to the Rappahannock by an earlier, delightful experience on another Virginia stream—the James River, covered in the Fall 1995 issue. The James will always be beloved for making me appear, in the presence of credible witnesses, a better smallmouth-bass fisherman than I am. The Rappahannock kept this happy fiction alive, while shattering all pretense to my competence as a whitewater paddler. That is to say, we and our gear got plenty wet. But more about that later.

The Rappahannock flows on a southeasterly course through central Virginia, north of the James, and offers very much the same geography. Long, winding stretches of flat water give way to rock gardens strewn across rapids that offer the beginning paddler an easy to moderate challenge at normal water-levels. The shoreline is almost entirely wooded, and numerous islands with adequate high ground for camping appear at convenient intervals throughout the trip.

This float trip is particularly popular among scout troops and fisherman for its widely available camping. Numerous small, cleared areas used as primitive campsites appear all along the river in this section. A local outfitter informed us that from Kelly's Ford to Mott's

Run all of the islands in the river are available for camping, and that the forested areas up to the high-water mark along both shores, except those posted "no trespassing," are owned by the City of Fredericksburg and open to campers. Much of the river in this section is also protected under the State Scenic River System.

This trip begins at the Route 620 bridge over the river at Kelly's Ford. Kelly's Ford is not a town but a place-name which appears on the map for this point in the river. The town nearest to the put-in is Culpeper, Virginia, where our party found a hotel for the night after a long drive from North Carolina.

The best way to manage this trip is to drive directly to the Rappahannock River Campground, located about ten miles downriver from Kelly's Ford, in Richardsville. Owners Steve and Sheila Stevens and their capable crew regularly shuttle gear, boats and paddlers to the put-in at Kelly's Ford and pick them up at a pre-arranged time at the take-out at Mott's Run. They have several large vehicles and trailers to handle parties of all sizes. They also have a nice selection of Old Town canoes and equipment for rent at reasonable rates.

En route to the put-in, our shuttle driver popped in a cassette-recorded narration about the river and the dangers of whitewater paddling, all to the disconcerting strains of the theme from "Deliverance." Thankfully the water hazards on this trip didn't even begin to measure up to the movie, although I would later regret not paying closer attention to the remarks about "strainers"— downed trees that block the path of the river.

At both Kelly's Ford and Mott's Run, wooden canoe slides and stairs to the water's edge have been constructed that make launching the boat and loading gear a breeze. At the put-in, a small island divides the river and provides the first, easy riffle of the trip, followed by a long stretch of flat water through woods and occasional pastures. If you're paddling in warm weather, don't waste your time casting for bass in this section—the fishing is better in the more highly oxygenated waters below riffles encountered farther downriver.

My son Kip and I were traveling in our 16-foot Old Town Camper, bumper-full of our gear and the shared equipment for our entire party of five. Because of the class-rating of the rapids on this trip, I had taken a few precautions not part of our typical flat-water routine. The first was to outfit Kip, age 6, with his bike helmet in addition to his PFD. While Kip had no occasion to test his helmet, a small child is less able to stay afoot in a current and more at risk to hit his head on the many small rocks adjacent to each series of rapids. The second precaution was to secure the gear beneath a cargo web (see gear-review, this issue) to keep it in the boat in the event of a capsize. Let it be said that what I lack in talent I generally make up for in preparation.

Our party made this float as a three-day, two-night trip. A distance of only 24 miles, it can certainly be done comfortably in two days and one night. If you are making a three-day trip or if you are unable to put more than eight or ten miles of water under the stern the first day, there are two options for camping on the first night. After gliding down the first set of small rapids in the trip at about mile 8 and coming upon "Snake Castle Rock" (shown in photos this page), I simply couldn't resist this charming, Tolkienian hideaway. We back-paddled and pulled our boats up right away.

Snake Castle Rock is a high, granite bluff rising from a small island. The campsite adjacent to Snake Castle Rock is a flat, sandy area shielded by a steep, wooded hillside. There was ample room for our three tents and a kitchen tarp. Local outfitters confirm that the land up to the high-water mark on this site is owned by the City of Fredericksburg and open to camping. Snake Castle Rock can be seen on the 7.5 minute series USGS map for the Richardsville quadrangle as the northernmost of two small, white islands, approximately 3.4 miles downriver from the point where the river enters this map-quadrangle.

The other site recommended for the first night's stay, and a must for scouts or other large groups, is the Rappahannock River Campground, mentioned earlier. It is located on the right bank of the river, about two miles below Snake Castle Rock, to the right of a large island. It is easy to miss the landing if you go to the left of this island, so the owners have placed a small, wooden sign along the river indicating the approach.

Rappahannock River Campground has thankfully preserved the beauty of the river and its own setting by keeping a buffer of trees between the camping area and the river. One wishes that more riverside campgrounds would resist the temptation to cut every last tree down to the bank. As you climb the wooden stairs leading from the river, you come upon a large grassy meadow with tent sites around the wooded perimeter. Aside from "warm" showers and immaculate privies, the facilities are pleasingly primitive. Pets and radios are not allowed. There is a freshwater pump at the head of this meadow, where the trail leads up to the campground office, store, and a stocked fishing pond. This is the only place along the trip to make a telephone call or purchase supplies. The owners and their staff obviously take a great deal of pride in the appearance of the campground, and they could not have been more helpful to our party.

"Rappahannock," we were warned, is an Indian word for "rapidly rising waters." Attention needs to be paid to the river gauges on both the Rappahannock and the Rapidan, which comes in on the left at about mile 16 of the trip. The easiest way to do this is to call Steve or Sheila at the campground. They monitor river gauges daily and can let you know if paddling conditions are unsuitable for beginners. You may also call the National Weather Service for a recorded message, updated daily, giving gauge levels on a number of area rivers. The Remington, Culpeper, and Fredericksburg gauges apply to this trip. As noted in the guidebook *Classic Virginia Rivers* by Ed Grove (Arlington, VA: Eddy Out Press, 1992), the maximum, runnable water levels for the Rappahannock are reflected at 5 feet on the Remington gauge, 2.5 feet on the Culpeper gauge, "pushing 5 feet" on the Fredericksburg gauge, and 2.5 feet on the U.S. Hwy. 1 gauge in Fredericksburg. Ed Grove's book offers considerable, helpful advice on this trip. It is available from The Great Outdoor Provision Co., 2023 Cameron Street, Raleigh, NC 27605.

Continuing past the campground, we soon encountered some of the more lively rapids of the trip, or so it seemed to our band of novice whitewater-paddlers. Even in our beamy, flat-bottomed Old Town Camper, loaded to the gunwales with heavy gear and with myself in the stern as the only paddler, we had surprisingly little difficulty negotiating the moderate riffles and rapids for most of this trip. The biggest nuisance was my inability to turn the boat quickly in an eddy or after gliding down the first series of rapids and finding a sharp turn necessary to reach the best path through the next series. On several occasions, this found us stuck ignominiously atop a shallow rock in the riffles, with Kip exhorting me to "scooch" us off. Just a couple of miles above the confluence with the Rapidan, however, I made a potentially more serious error.

We came upon a small ledge between two rocks. Aside from the fact that a large rock on the right partially obscured the view past the ledge, the drop was typical of many we had negotiated without difficulty. Taking what seemed to be the widest, clearest path at the entrance, I made the mistake of not looking past the rock, downriver, and to both sides of my course. Had I done so I would have seen that the water on my chosen route to the left was being forced through a small, downed tree whose branches descended well into the river—a "strainer." The two following boats took the clear path behind the rock to the right. The eddy swept our boat sideways to the current. Before I could recover, the branches caught us and the boat broadside. The pressure of the river on the upstream side of the hull dipped the gunwale slowly under the surface. We both tumbled from the boat into the warm, chest-high water. I grabbed Kip by his life vest and planted him on my back while I stood on the river bottom and horsed our swamped canoe, gear intact, to a nearby sandbar where our friends helped us regroup.

Any capable beginner could easily have avoided my mistake, as did the other two boats in our party and no doubt as do most boats making this trip. What made this mishap merely a nuisance instead of a crisis was the decision to float rivers of this type only in warm weather and at moderate water levels, to secure all gear with a cargo web, to pack all sleeping bags and clothing in a waterproof pack, and to go with others who were there to lend a hand.

After bailing out and changing Kip's clothes, we proceeded on to the confluence and our second night's camp at one of the large islands formed where these two rivers meet. Here, as at our first night's camp, we found an abundance of seasoned driftwood of all sizes. Bring your pack saw and you shall have a grand campfire for as long as you need one. In no time we were dry and huddled by the blaze, enjoying hot, buttered biscuits from the reflector oven and marinated chicken from the grill, while ruminating on the events of the day. After a leisurely sunset spent casting for bass in the riffles by our island, Kip was soon fast asleep in my lap beside by a crackling fire.

From the confluence to Mott's Run there are campsites galore, some of which are designated by the City of Fredericksburg. We lingered over coffee and breakfast the next morning before starting for Mott's Run at 10:00 a.m., completing the eight-miles well in time for our shuttle at 1:00. Mott's Run is first visible on the river-right as a mud bank leading up to a parking lot. Don't take out here, though. Paddle to the wooden steps and canoe slide located around the hill to the right.

Admittedly, no one will likely ever mistake me for a

whitewater paddler. But this was nonetheless a trip to be savored—not only for its beauty, but for the gentle lessons and valuable experience it gave us, as well. We will long remember the Rappahannock.

ALLAGASH WILDERNESS WATERWAY

NORTH MAINE WOODS

Every man infected with a passion for voyaging by canoe has at least three grand ambitions: to paddle and portage his way through the Boundary Waters of Minnesota, the Adirondacks of Upstate New York, and the Allagash River of the North Maine Woods. On July 20, 1996, in the face of a howling gale and breaking waves on Chamberlain Lake, we tested our ambition to paddle nearly a hundred miles along the Allagash Wilderness Waterway in seven days, through some of the most legendary and breathtaking scenery this country has to offer.

For years the literature sent to me by Gil Gilpatrick, a Master Maine Guide and author of the book *Allagash* reviewed in this issue, had languished in my tattered folder of places I hoped someday to see. This is not a region to be trifled with, nor is it a trip begun lightly or easily made with small children. But when a week opened up while my wife and her sisters packed our young children off to Florida, my brother-in-law Michael Rosenthal and I made plans for the Allagash.

The 98-mile route northward from Telos Lake to a point near Allagash Village, a few miles from the Canadian border, was designated as the Allagash

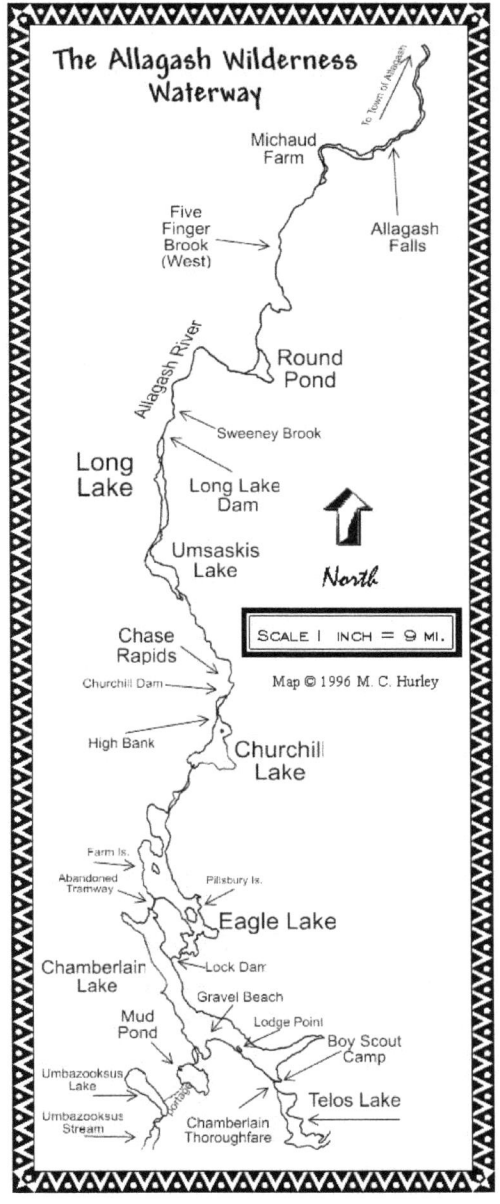

Wilderness Waterway by the Maine legislature in 1966. In 1970 the waterway became the first to gain protection under the National Wild and Scenic River System. Boats with motors are allowed on the waterway, but due to the number of portages, motorized traffic is rarely seen north of Eagle Lake.

The land along the waterway extending five hundred feet back from the high-water mark is owned and managed as wilderness by the State of Maine. It is protected from residential development, commercial timbering, and construction. Beyond this zone, the waterway sits amid two million acres of private forest owned by a federation of timber companies and individuals. The use of this private land is managed through an organization known as the North Maine Woods, which maintains a system of logging roads that are the only access to the waterway. Gated checkpoints are manned along these logging roads under specific hours of operation, and vehicles are required to register and pay a fee to pass. It bears noting that the logging road we took north from Greenville is a veritable "mooseway." After passing through Greenville near midnight, we encountered no fewer than fourteen moose on or along our route to Chamberlain Lake. Be ready to brake!

After arriving at Chamberlain Thoroughfare early on the morning of Saturday, July 20, we watched with some concern as the winds that had been howling outside our Jeep all night continued unabated well past sunrise. The ranger advised us that wind speeds were reaching thirty-five miles per hour, and this was apparent from the taller treetops whipping violently about. But no camping is allowed at the thoroughfare, and though it seemed the wind would blow strong all day, our only choice was to drive several hours back to town or load our canoe and try to make camp nearby on Chamberlain Lake. After taking the ranger up on a generous offer of fresh, hot coffee, we decided to set out.

We had allotted as much as eight days to complete this trip, while hoping to finish in seven. What we did not expect was that these cold, gale winds and high waves would persist for two full days. This was no passing thunderstorm but a full-fledged blue norther, sweeping down from the Canadian tundra. After a dinner of fried beefsteak, potatoes, and hot soup on that first night, we fully expected to wake the next day to calm waters and still air. Instead, the wind seemed to have gained strength. It was clear from the wave heights that we would be stuck in camp another day and that our itinerary might soon be in danger. It would be a mad dash for Allagash Village if we ever got started.

For a while as the wind continued, I wondered if the next morning would find us trudging back to our Jeep, having come all this way for naught. Near noon, however, we saw (or wanted to see, perhaps) a slight weakening in the wind and lessening in the wave heights. The decision to go was quickly made, the tarp doused, tent packed, and gear stowed in the canoe. The waves were still quite high, though, so for safety's sake we secured a cargo web over the boat.

We planned at first to cross directly to the northeast shore of Chamberlain Lake, where we hoped to find easier paddling in the lee, but soon after reaching open water we took a wave over the bow of the canoe and beat a hasty retreat to windward. There we continued to claw our way up the lake on a northwesterly course against strong wind and waves on our starboard bow.

Surprisingly, the navigation of this simple lake was somewhat confusing. Although we had ordered the complete series of USGS topographic maps for the waterway, the waterway map supplied to all visitors by the rangers seemed a more practical choice. As it covers the entire waterway, though, it is set on a large scale. When paddling hard into a headwind and strong waves it is easy to assume that you are making more progress on this map than you really are. After passing the Lodge Point campsite on the western shore of the lake (see map at left), we came to a large bay to the west that seemed clearly to me to be the one shown on the map behind the Gravel Beach campsite. We had not passed the campsites of Rocky Cove and Gravel Beach that precede the entrance to this western bay on the map, but I made the mariner's error of disregarding any information inconsistent with my assumed position. I figured that we had simply failed to see those sites due to the wind, the waves, or their position on shore. Not so. As we would soon learn, Chamberlain is a long and difficult lake in a headwind.

After three hours of slow, hard progress in wind and rain, we suddenly encountered breaking waves about twenty yards offshore. Our weeks' worth of cargo in a sixteen-foot canoe afforded us scant few inches of freeboard, and several waves boarded us amidships. Within seconds the canoe was swamped. We paddled with water to our knees until we reached the shallows, then hopped out and drug the boat ashore. After we removed the packs and inverted the boat to rid the water, Mike hiked up along shore to find us a better landing spot. To our considerable surprise, he encountered the Gravel Beach site just a few yards around the bend. We had made only five miles of progress from our last night's camp in more than three hours of paddling.

Mike came bounding back to the boat with two people who were already camped at Gravel Beach and who kindly helped bring our packs into camp. With an empty canoe, we skated around the bend and surfed a following sea right onto the beach.

One Mainer and his wife whom we found camped at Gravel Beach had been socked-in there for two days by the storm. With fishing all but impossible due to the wind and waves, the man had made good use of his time with an axe. He presented us upon our arrival—cold, wet and bedraggled on that gray afternoon—with the prettiest armload of seasoned, split firewood I have ever seen in the woods. In no time we had grilled chicken with sautéed onions, not to mention piping hot biscuits from the oven which I was pleased to offer in return of the favor.

Henry David Thoreau wrote of his travels here in 1857 in *The Maine Woods*. He and a companion began their trip at Moosehead Lake on the 24th of July in the company of an Indian guide. They arrived at Chamberlain Lake via Umbazookus Stream and Mud Pond on July 25. In his chapter on "the Allegash and East Branch," Thoreau describes landing at what today is the Gravel Beach campsite in a fashion not dissimilar from our own: "We had come out on a point extending into Apmoojenegamook, or Chamberlain Lake, west of the outlet of Mud Pond, where there was a broad, gravelly, and rocky shore, encumbered with bleached logs and trees. We were rejoiced to see such dry things in that part of the world . . . . After putting on such dry clothes as we had, and hanging the others to dry which the Indian arranged over the fire, we ate our supper, and lay down on the pebbly shore with our feet to the fire."

As was our fashion that week on the Allagash, we retired early at Gravel Beach. Drifting off to sleep with the waves crashing their rhythm on the lakeshore nearby, the mood was more reminiscent of the seacoast than the north woods. So common had that sound become in two days' time that the silence of the following morning startled us from our sleep at 4:30.

Not knowing whether the weather had merely abated temporarily or cleared altogether, we made quick preparations in the waning darkness to embark for the lee shore of Chamberlain Lake. This being the longest lake and the one most affected by wind, on the trip, we knew that crossing it to the portage at Lock Dam meant being able to continue indefinitely northward despite the weather, while missing the opportunity to cross could mean more idle time ashore if the wind suddenly returned.

By the time dawn broke in deep azure above the trees, we knew that our worries had been in vain. It would be a glorious day in Maine. A flotilla of émigrés from Gravel Beach crossed swiftly and silently on lake water that seemed incomprehensibly like glass, compared to the day before. Our progress was steady without the wind and waves to hold us back, and before we knew it we were at the earthen abutment of Lock Dam and its caretaker's cabin that marks the portage to the right.

The portage at Lock Dam is just a hop-over that leads to the stream inlet to Eagle Lake. This stream is strewn with rocks and requires wading for much of the way, but it soon disappears into the serene expanse of the lake. Keep your compass handy as you enter Eagle Lake, for though it is not possible to get lost, here, a compass course is helpful to avoid heading into the wrong bay en route to Pillsbury Island.

Pillsbury Island on Eagle Lake is where a campsite bears the name "Thoreau." This is a fine place to camp, with a wide, gradually sloping beach leading from the western shore of the island. We landed as did Thoreau and his party on the southeast side of the island, which Thoreau described as "rather elevated and densely wooded, with a rocky shore." Here Thoreau's Indian guide attempted to persuade him to continue north toward the St. John River—our intended route—where he advised, according to Thoreau, that "[t]here would be but one or two falls, with short carrying places, and we should go down the stream very fast, even a hundred miles a day, if the wind allowed." But this island would be the northern limit of Thoreau's 1857 journey, as he decided to turn east and south toward Telos Lake and the East Branch of the Penobscot River.

From his vantage at Pillsbury Island, Thoreau noticed "that there was another island visible toward the north end of the lake, with an elevated clearing on it . . . used as a pasture for cattle which summered in these woods." As we paddled north along this lake, we came upon the same island, aptly named Farm Island today, where a grassy clearing remains, and where a campsite is located. By this time of day a brisk wind had returned, and we were thankful for our purposeful paddling to cross the biggest water in the morning. We were approaching the narrows of Eagle Lake and the smaller lakes to the north, on which the winds shifting to the west and south would push us from the stern.

Eagle Lake flows into a small inlet bearing the name "Round Pond" that is so ubiquitous on the charts of these woods. A coterie of senior citizens in nine canoes, led by a guide, stopped on one bank of the logging-road bridge at Round Pond, we at the other. While munching our apples and ginger snaps, we watched as one of this group scrambled to the top of the bridge and nimbly did a back flip into the water some ten feet below.

Beyond the bridge one enters a weedy bay of drowned trees at the entrance to Churchill Lake, where we chanced to see our first moose from a canoe. She chewed water plants on the western shore quite deliberately with no apparent concern for us as we slipped slowly closer, snapping photos all the way. She dunked her head fully underwater to her withers for some fifteen seconds while snatching plants from the lake floor in her teeth, surfaced to reassess our position while munching steadily, then repeated the maneuver. We approached timidly with all the caution due a wild rhinoceros, but this animal just chewed on, lending credence to that old flattery, "cool as a moose."

Churchill Lake we roundly agreed was the prettiest lake of the trip, and there are several nice campsites here worthy of mention. Scofield Point appears as the second camp on the lake as you head north. It is situated on a long sandy beach which stretches for several hundred yards to the north, making an excellent place for children to run, play, and swim. It has tables and fire grates to accommodate up to three parties and tents separately. If you are traveling with a smaller group and are lucky as we were to arrive early, there is no finer campsite on the waterway than the High Bank site, located a little farther north on Churchill Lake. It will accommodate only one tent party and therefore affords a certain solitude. It sits well above the lake as per its name, where the view back toward the south and east is unmatched.

After finding a nice spot for the tent overlooking the lake and gathering the evening's supply of firewood, we set about some rest and reading. But as the sun waned behind the woods, my nap on the grass was soon interrupted. Mike came running up, whispering excitedly about a moose. I followed him down a short trail leading from the campsite to a small cove, where not fifteen yards away was another moose chewing her evening meal. She stood obediently by while I snapped nearly two dozen outstanding photographs of her, all the while blissfully unaware that the film in my ancient camera was not advancing. (There would be other moose, thankfully, of which you see less intimate pictures in this issue; but I have since resolved that an idiot should have an idiot's camera, which I purchased forthwith and now happily use in fully automatic mode.)

North of High Bank, we found ourselves in the Allagash River proper for most of the time. Full of anticipation for what Chase Rapids might throw at us, we rose before dawn and were the first party to make the rapids that morning. You will find the entrance to Chase Rapids marked by a dam and road at the far northern end of Heron Lake, separated by the narrows from Churchill

Lake. It is only a fifteen-minute paddle here from High Bank. Avoid staying at the camp at Churchill Dam, as its proximity to the road, the dam, and the ranger's station make it more crowded and less picturesque than other available spots.

Once at Churchill Dam you will land at a wooden dock to the left. Stepping onto the road from the dock you will see what appear to be barns on both sides of the river. Follow the road over the dam and head for the barn on the east side of the river, to your left. Continue past this barn to the ranger's cabin, where you may pay a ten dollar fee to have your gear hauled in the ranger's truck around Chase Rapids.

Take advantage of this service—it's cheap, and you can paddle the rapids without concern for capsizing with your gear. The ranger will also give you some free advice about how to run the rapids in the river, which as I recall went something like "take the first three rapids on the left and the last rapids on the right."

Now, I don't know what you might find when you paddle Chase Rapids, but when we went the river was a solid three feet above its normal water-level. Notwithstanding the good ranger's advice as to going left or right, my memory of Chase Rapids is of a huge funnel of water that sucked us into a series of head-high haystacks in mid-river from the get-go. Whether we were in the first series of rapids or the third I am clueless to say, as it all looked like a wall of whitewater to me. Had I not been too busy paddling to count, I would have said we were on about our eighth set of rapids when the ride abruptly ended across a large green rock hiding unfairly a few inches beneath the surface. My Old Town Camper made its now familiar half-gainer, and the two of us were in the water. I don't recall thinking about the temperature of this northern stream as we hit the waves, although Mike later mentioned that a moment or two passed before his breath returned. I do remember realizing that the worst might yet be ahead, as we were bumping steadily downstream at a fair clip in the continuing rapids. I shouted to Mike to get behind the canoe, and together we pushed it like a fender downstream until the river bottom returned to our feet. Quickly we sidestepped our way ashore a few feet ahead of yet another series of rapids. We shoved off again when it appeared that we were missing one paddle and a tackle bag full of fishing gear.

The remainder of the rapids, large and small, we negotiated successfully with white-knuckled determination. We recovered the lost paddle downriver, and a half hour after having given up my canvas tackle-bag for lost, it bobbed to the surface not five feet ahead of the boat. I took this as an omen and quickly stopped to cast for the trout that are reputed to lurk below the rapids, but the high water we later learned had made the ordinarily poor summer fishing all but pointless. We had all the chub we cared to catch, but no one found any trout on the river this week. The waterway is not reputed to be a fisherman's paradise once the summer weather returns. Even Thoreau found the fishing to be generally poor here in July. It is the scenery that most commends this voyage.

Some nine miles below Churchill Dam, beyond the rapids, a washed-out bridge abutment appears on the left. Here is where the ranger will have dropped off your gear and where it is most convenient to stop for lunch.

From Chase Rapids northward, on the waterway, more careful planning is needed as to when and where one plans to make camp for the night. The campsites on the waterway are listed and named on the waterway map published by the State Bureau of Parks and Recreation. Beside the campsite symbol for each site on the map is a number ranging from one to five. This number indicates how many sets of tables and fire grates exist at that site and, accordingly, how many separate parties may camp there. (The High Bank site does not have a number on the map, but it is a one-party site.) The tables are picnic-style with two or more upright wood poles to support a ridge pole that runs the length of the table and, usually, above the fire grate. The ridge pole allows you to suspend one rectangular tarp (12 x 9 feet is a good size) over the table, with another tarp covering the fire. This may be less primitive than some would prefer, but it provided a nice kitchen surface and ensured that a cooking fire could be protected in foul weather. If you're making stews, potatoes, breads, and other meals that require a long-term fire, you will appreciate this rustic convenience.

On the lakes that comprise the lower portion of the waterway there are many sites, and most of them allow for multiple parties. As you move into the river in the north, however, the campsites are more frequently single-party sites and, in some sections, appear in clusters several miles apart. If you get a slow start in the morning and are paddling into the late afternoon in the summer months, you may get to the last campsite within a given section of the river, find it taken, and wind up paddling five miles or more downriver to the next cluster of sites well into twilight. The way to avoid this is to plan approximately where on the river you want to stop for the day and plan to reach the first of the campsites, there, early. You can survey each site until you find one you like, and most likely it will not yet be taken. If it is, however, you will know it early enough in the day to reach the next available site on the river well before dark.

After coming through Chase Rapids one enters Umsaskis Lake, a well-known moose-sighting area. Here we saw two cow moose and one calf. The Ledges campsite on this lake was an attractive setting, and we stopped there briefly for lunch. At the northern end of Umsaskis Lake you will encounter another ranger's cabin and a logging-road bridge where some people choose to put in for a shorter trip north. Above this bridge lies Long Lake, which could be impassable in a north wind but which was a lark for us with the wind from the south. At the end of this lake on the right side, the Allagash River picks up again, not far from Long Lake Dam.

The ranger advises all canoeists to portage Long Lake Dam, which is washed out and appears runnable. Iron spikes that held together the timbers that once comprised the dam still protrude from logs underwater. They can puncture a boat. The spikes also pose a hazard to a paddler in the water from a capsize.

Avoid if you can the well-worn campsite at Long Lake Dam, which has been largely cleared and, being situated right in the middle of the portage, offers little sense of seclusion. The next two campsites, Cunliffe Island and Sweeney Brook, offer better surroundings. They are, however, the last two campsites on the river for another ten miles.

Even though we were traveling at the height of the

summer season, there were many campsites along the waterway that were empty. Where crowding was a problem, it was generally caused by an accident of planning rather than the numbers of paddlers on the river. One such example occurred after we had made camp at Sweeney Brook on the river by 4:00 p.m. on day four. This is a one-party site, but at six o'clock a weary troupe of six paddlers from New York called to us from the river, below, seeking space for their group which we were pleased to provide. Some minutes later six more friends from our camp of two nights ago at Gravel Beach arrived unexpectedly, and they too were welcomed—bringing our number to six tents and fourteen people at a one-party site! Remembering the warm reception we had received when nearly shipwrecked at Gravel Beach, we eagerly feted our guests to vegetable stew, hot tea, and buttermilk biscuits with peach jam. One of our guests from New York who inquired further of me upon hearing my last name turned out to be a reader of this journal, whereupon several others of the assembled guests enlisted to subscribe. The whole episode was a marketing triumph! The swapping of stories kept up well into the evening, and despite the crowded conditions we counted this as our most enjoyable night of the trip. Our destination for day five was the west-side site at Five Finger Brook, which we were happy to find unoccupied under threatening skies. Sitting atop a high bank overlooking fast water, this site was the best we found on the river. It was unoccupied perhaps because it is difficult to get to in high water, as the landing sits right behind a section of rapids. We made the landing only by sweeping downstream to the left and poling our way back along the western shore. This site has a delightful carpet of pine needles spreading out beneath a thinned forest, through which several trails lead. When heading through this section of the river, avoid the Hosea B campsite, which we found to offer little shade or downed firewood.

Day six brought us finally to the majesty of Allagash Falls. This forty-foot wonder will give you pause. Stop here with your fellow canoeists to take photographs and hear its thunder for a while. You will not see many like this one. When you stop at the Michaud Farm ranger station a few miles above the falls, as all paddlers are required to do, look in the ranger's office for a photograph of the falls. We forgot to check for this photo, but according to Gilpatrick in Allagash it shows a boat heading over the falls just when another paddler from Rhode Island happened to be taking pictures, there. Gilpatrick records the tale told by the ranger from Michaud Farm called upon to rescue these men, who suffered broken ribs in the experience and were taken out to a nearby hospital. (The brush around Michaud Farm, by the way, is also a place where you'll find wild blueberries growing for your morning pancakes.)

We camped at one of the four sites at Allagash Falls, which allowed us ample time to scramble up and around the various overlooks. While we were there, an experienced guide in one boat tried to put in at the first landing past the falls and paddle to the island that divides the falls. He wound up capsizing due to the strength of the eddies. There is a second landing farther down the trail around the falls, and here is where you want to put in to avoid the strong current.

Also mentioned in Gilpatrick's book is a small spring

in the bushes about twenty-five paces downriver from this second landing, where we filled our water bottles.

Due to the unusually high water conditions at the time of our trip, I know that many areas of the river that ordinarily might be difficult to navigate due to shallows and the number of rocks were not problematic for us. Despite comments in the literature as to the difficulty of the rapids at Twin Brook, just before the end of the waterway, we encountered no water here that was not easily negotiated with some attention by the bow paddler to fending off submerged rocks.

We paddled past the official end of the waterway and into Allagash Village, where our outfitter Bob O'Leary had driven our Jeep up from Chamberlain Thoroughfare. There are a number of outfitters in the area who offer such services.

As we loaded our gear into the Jeep, we felt a sense of disbelief that we had really come so far in the face of those early storms, when we thought that the end of this river was an unattainable goal. By Nature's leave, though, we had been permitted passage in ample time to meet our schedule.

The way south was spent indulging our taste for lobster and other perquisites of a Maine vacation. Sporting eight-day beards and smelling like a couple of moose, we sauntered among Polo-clad yuppies at L. L. Bean in Freeport, calling to mind actual uses for the cavernous stores of equipment offered there. I had explained the utility of Bean Boots for canoe trips to my brother-in-law Mike before we began our Allagash trek, but he had resisted, choosing instead to go with a colorful pair of suede boots that his wife had found for him. They had that contemporary, sporty look—and stayed waterlogged for the entire trip. Mike left Freeport with his first pair of Bean Boots. While the purchase was a little late for this trip, we both knew that a tradition had been rekindled on the Allagash that week. We would be back to tame Chase Rapids, to explore the secret ponds and coves we had passed by, to find at last the elusive brook trout, and to muddy our boots again in due time.

Pocomoke River

Maryland Eastern Shore
Snow Hill to Pocomoke City

Growing up in Maryland, I have memories of reading about float trips for bass on the Pocomoke River. It runs through the lower Eastern Shore, not far from the beach. Unlike other places in the state, the Pocomoke with its black waters and cypress trees seemed likely to offer the kind of big-bass haven associated with places farther south.

Well, judging from the numbers of souped-up bass boats frothing up the river during our trip there in early October, a few other folks have caught on to the idea. Yet no one we met, right down to the folks at the canoe livery in Snow Hill, seemed to have given much thought to the Pocomoke as a great place for canoe-camping. And aside from the happy few readers of this journal, here's hoping no one ever does. Because after the sun dipped low in the autumn sky, we had the woods and the water as much to ourselves as if we'd paddled a hundred miles into the Far North.

This trip begins in Snow Hill, a rural community that is no more than a half-hour's drive from the beach and the Virginia border. In the fourteen miles from here to Pocomoke City, the river runs deep, wide and slow through woods and wetlands that are only occasionally

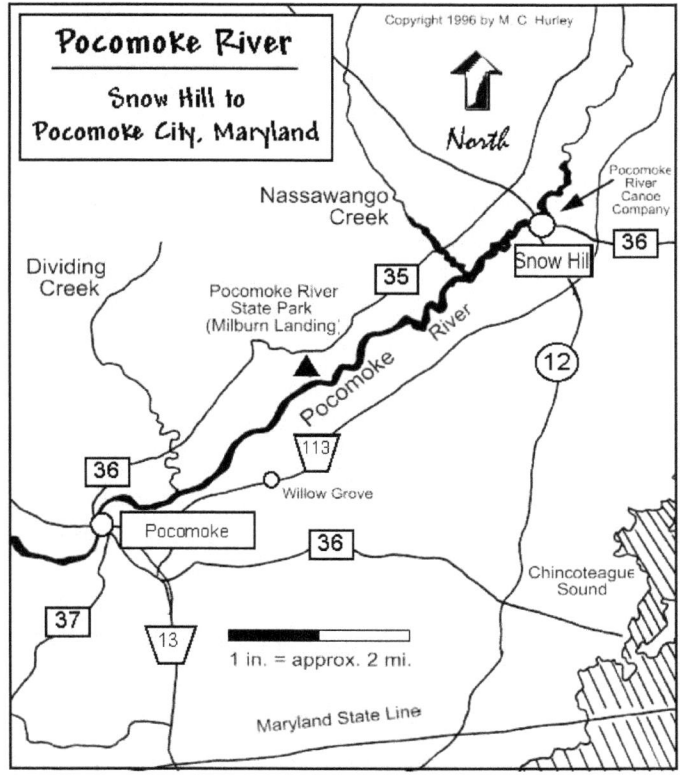

interrupted by farms.

The Pocomoke River Canoe Company in Snow Hill offers canoe & kayak rentals, parking, and a shuttle from the take-out in Pocomoke City. The business is owned and run by Barry Laws, whose forefathers were among the first settlers of the colony of Maryland. The livery sits right on the waterfront on the main street through town.

Once on the river from Barry Laws' store, you may have to duck under the low-water bridge. The scene here has a maritime flavor that is well suited to the Eastern

Shore. We glided by a beautiful small-scale reproduction of a skipjack on our way out of town. Soon enough, though, the woods crowd in, and the feeling is more remote.

The Pocomoke was designated the state's first Scenic and Wild River in 1971, under the management of the Maryland Department of Natural Resources. With this status came restrictions on new development along the river. Much of the section between Snow Hill and Pocomoke City enjoys further protection as part of the state system of Wildlands, which seeks to preserve these areas in their "natural condition." No doubt that is what Ed Gertler had in mind when he wrote in his book, *Maryland and Delaware Canoe Trails*, that this trip is "the best opportunity in the State for the beginning paddler to escape the civilized world."

The density of foliage along the river made for beautiful fall colors when we went in October, when the chilly evening brought forth a rousing campfire for steaks and baked potatoes. That's the kind of luxury—along with coolers of cold beverages—that can be afforded on a float trip like this one, with no portaging to interfere with the chef's imagination.

Not only did we pack enough food for an army, we brought the army with us: a patrol of six kids ranging in age from four to seven. Being a relatively short, two-day paddle with a spacious, riverside state park in between, this trip is a natural for kids. And because we went in October, we had the entire park literally to ourselves.

The Pocomoke River State Park is actually divided into two sections, or "landings," on opposite sides of the river. The first section is Shad Landing. It is hidden from view a few hundred yards inside Corkers Creek, which comes in on the left bank about 3.5 miles below Snow Hill. This is a large, commercial operation with a game room and grill, picnic area, and marina. Although I don't recommend you stop here unless it's to let the kids run around while you make lunch, there are campsites well off of the water at this location. The better place to camp, and the location where we stayed, is Milburn Landing, It is on the opposite shore, another 3.3 miles down the river.

Unlike Shad Landing, the Milburn Landing side of the state park offers no programs or concessions and no facilities other than running water and bathrooms with hot showers. There is access to Milburn Landing from S.R. 354 (see map, below) on an unimproved road, which remained open at night when we were there.

There is a well-constructed wooden pier and dock that comes into the river about a hundred yards below the canoe landing shown in the photo at right. This landing comes in at a thinned area of the forest, where fire-rings and picnic tables are located. This is where we pitched our tents.

It should be noted that the Milburn Landing side of the park is officially "closed" between Labor Day and Memorial Day, which seems a needless restriction on the use of state property. We didn't learn of this until after our arrival in Snow Hill. When we questioned the park staff at Shad Landing we got conflicting answers about whether Milburn Landing was actually "closed" to the public or just not actively managed (i.e., with nature talks and other interpretive programs) during this time of year.

No rangers could be found at either location, but

when we explained to employees at the park that we simply wanted to pull up our canoes at Milburn Landing and camp, they told us to go ahead. Only for purposes of this article did I press for a firm answer on whether or not it was closed. I finally got a reply to the effect that, yes, it is closed after Labor Day, but no, no one will bother you if you camp there in your tent. Figure that out for yourself and make your own decision.

I can tell you, though, that aside from one motorist who drove into camp looking for an astronomy club meeting under the starry sky (indicating that they apparently don't gate the road during the off-season), we saw not another soul in the woods that weekend. The kids had the enormous expanse of the park in which to run and play, where they could still be seen through the thinned forest at a good distance. The hot showers and the potable water were also still on in October.

Space does not permit me to recount the story of the ghost dog "Fang," which I told to our young charges by the campfire that evening. It was intended to keep them quiet in their tents for the night but had a powerfully opposite effect, and dawn came all too soon for the four dads on this trip. Perhaps a later issue will feature some of our "favorite" campfire tales.

The second day's paddle is a run of about six miles that seems a good deal shorter than the first day's leg. This section is also mostly wooded with a few scattered farms. The take-out is at the wooden dock at Winters Quarters Landing, on your left. There is a pay phone here for you to call your shuttle and a playground for the kids, to help them wind down the time well spent on this lovely river.

CROOKED LAKE CIRCUIT

BOUNDARY WATERS CANOE AREA

Regular readers of this journal will note that the Boundary Waters Canoe Area Wilderness of Northern Minnesota is out of our usual venue. Hurley's Journal is, after all, about "where to camp and fish by canoe in the East." But I don't expect they'll pause long over that thought, because there is not a wilderness canoeist in any state in the union who hasn't either been to the BWCA or is planning to go. It is without a doubt the "Mecca" of wilderness canoeing, and in the summer of 1996, a hearty group of pilgrims from New Bern, North Carolina had the privilege to journey there.

Coming from the airport at night in our outfitter's van, I didn't have a feel for the region. Hustling over the asphalt from store to store in Ely the day before we headed to the woods, the nature of the area was still not apparent to me. But when our canoe nosed out of the marsh into the cold, clear water of Fourtown Lake, the sense of this place was inescapable. The Blue North. The Great Wild. Whatever you name it, the Boundary Waters exudes that untouchable, unknowable essence we call "wilderness," and by which lesser woods are measured. Here, among thousands of shimmering lakes

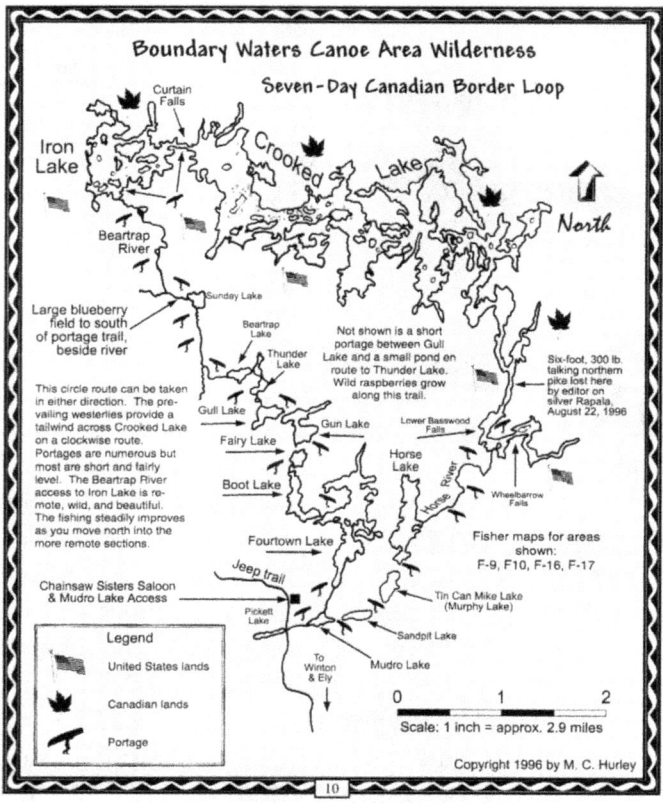

and the last, great virgin forest east of the Rockies, is the derivation for our collective image of the northern frontier.

We planned a route from Robert Beymer's book, *The Boundary Waters Canoe Area*, that would take us on a circular route from Mudro Lake, heading clockwise up through the Beartrap River basin, into Crooked Lake, and south via the Horse River back to Mudro Lake in seven days. Along the way we saw a good variety of water, from the tiniest beaver flows to majestic border lakes, with a sampling of rivers, waterfalls, and ponds in between. While I've had no other experience in the area by which to compare, anyone looking to travel to fairly remote regions, encounter a monstrous pike, and who is willing to pay the price in portages to do so would do well to follow us.

Our trip began at the Mudro Lake access, about a half-hour drive north of Ely. Entrance to the wilderness area is carefully regulated through a system of permits awarded by lottery to advance applicants on January 15 of each year, then on a first-come first-served basis to everyone else until the quota for each entry point is filled. A permit grants access to the canoe-only area on a given date through a given entry point.

The Mudro Lake access begins as a portage of thirty rods from the road. A rod is equal to 16.5 feet. It is the unit of measurement by which portages are identified on W. A. Fisher maps, which are standard for canoe trips in the area. There are 320 rods to a mile.

After negotiating a rock-strewn channel into Mudro Lake, we soon understood the recommendation from our guide-service to throw over our L. L. Bean boots for a pair of knee-high, all-rubber models. Although I can't say what they might have felt like on the bottom of the boat in the heat of noon, they would have kept us drier in the deeper water we had to wade to avoid the rocks, when coming ashore.

Unlike the Adirondacks and other areas, the portages in the Boundary Waters are not marked with man-made signs of any kind. This is a concession to the wild character of the area and makes careful attention to the map a necessity. Most portages are first spied as trodden areas of grass or dirt along shore in the vicinity where you are expecting a portage to be.

The first significant portage of the trip is 140 rods into Fourtown Lake. It was reputed to be the roughest carry of our route but earned only second place honors in our book. In fact, we had been advised to take our entire route in a counter-clockwise direction, just so the Chainsaw Sisters Saloon and a glass of cold Pig's Eye beer would not be far off after we completed this carry. On a clockwise route, this portage begins as a path along the left creek bank, then goes straight uphill. Watch for beaver swimming near the creek side of the portage.

We made an easy first day of it and camped at the first site we encountered on the left bank of Fourtown Lake. All of the campsites in the BWCA are first-come first-served. There is generally only one party to a site, given the wide variety of sites available in most areas.

The fishing in Fourtown Lake is reputed to be outstanding, but considering the time we had for casting on this lake, we did not do as well here as elsewhere. The pattern seemed to be that the more portages you made to the north, the better the fishing got. Undoubtedly the lakes more accessible to the entry points see greater fishing pressure than the more remote locations.

Not wanting to use our fuel unless foul weather made it a necessity to do so, we cooked breakfasts and dinners over an open fire, utilizing the forest-service grills, of course. These first mornings produced the welcome smells of bacon and eggs with coffee steeping by the fireside. If anyone's memory needed jarring for the reasons why we camp by canoe, the smell of woodsmoke, coffee and bacon wafting through the pines on a chilly morning in the wild surely sufficed.

The landing for the portage out of Fourtown Lake into Boot Lake was difficult to find. Once at the landing for the portage, do not follow the false trail to the right that leads along a stream. Take the portage trail from the left of the landing area to a sandy beach at the end of Boot Lake.

The short passages from Boot Lake to Fairy Lake, Gun Lake, and Gull Lake are straightforward, and the portage locations on such small lakes are easy to find. One soon realizes that anyone wishing to spend time investigating each lake could easily make a two-week voyage out of this one-week itinerary.

The best spread of raspberries we found was along the portage from Gull Lake into a little drop called Mudhole Pond. We stopped at the trail's end, here, to pick berries and have lunch. Our lunches that week consisted entirely of foods eaten out of hand, without preparation. These were most often apples, Power Bars, peanuts, and raisins.

As we floated the canoes in the shallows of Thunder Lake, at the end of the portage from Mudhole Pond, I nearly impaled the canoe on a submerged, abandoned dock from which several sharp, rusty nails protruded. Be careful, here, to avoid the same. This is a wilderness, but not one unknown to man.

Thunder Lake was a special stop on this trip. Not only was it here where the fishing started to get really good, but we had a gorgeous, wilderness lake of some considerable size all to ourselves in the height of summer, as well. And though we often hear of how crowded the BWCA can be, I sense that our solitude was not altogether rare even for this time of year. And so we treated ourselves to some gratuitous skinny dipping, to which our guest Becky kindly demurred. To her credit, though, she gathered, washed, and hung out to dry the dirty clothes of the astonished participants, whereupon it promptly poured down raining. As a result we had to carry our sodden underwear strewn atop the canoes like corpses for the next day or two before it all thoroughly dried.

A couple of hours of evening casting in Thunder Lake produced several nice pike. As a result of our success we enjoyed delicious filets for breakfast the next morning, and we would require the nourishment for the grueling distance to be covered that day.

If you camp on Thunder Lake as we did on the second day, you would do well to begin the next day's journey at dawn. From the campsite we selected—the second on the left bank coming in from Mudhole Pond—you may carry your gear through the woods to Beartrap Lake and avoid loading the canoes to paddle to the portage. The landing at the end of the trail from camp is also better suited for loading canoes than is the landing at the portage.

The portage from Beartrap Lake to the Beartrap River of some 200 rods, which is noted in Beymer's book, was not marked at all on the standard "F-series" Fisher map that we carried. It is, however, marked on the 1996 McKenzie no. 11 "Jackfish, Beartrap" map. This is a 1:31,680 scale map that covers a larger area than the F-series. It is available from local outfitters. We also noticed that this trail was very poorly defined in many areas—although the large bear that left tracks in the mud on this trail that morning obviously had no difficulty following it.

Several "R" markings on the map indicating the locations of rapids along the Beartrap River caused some needless worry. We were told that they simply did not rate rapids in this part of the country, because all of the rapids are either impassable or un-runnable. That turned out to be true. What were referred to as "rapids" were shallow riffles through impassable rock gardens, and around each of these was a carry. Those rapids that were not a foot deep and completely choked with small rocks were actually waterfalls, which were clearly not runnable.

The most important navigational pointers for this trip are to watch your course carefully in the upper reaches of the Beartrap River, where you will be surrounded by marsh, and on the expanse of Crooked Lake, where you'll be at risk of becoming disoriented amid the maze of islands and bays. After re-entering the Beartrap River at the end of the portage from Sunday Lake, you will (in the summer) paddle headlong into a problem noted in the front-page essay—a huge grass field that totally obscures the river's course. Check your map and you'll see that the river's bend to the north is flanked by high bluffs, as indicated by topographic lines. As you paddle, look to the right for these bluffs and cut toward the middle of them, where you'll regain the river's course north toward Iron Lake.

On Iron Lake we laid over for an extra day and enjoyed steady success while fishing, there. But a severe windstorm on the second night prompted us to get an early start and, to our regret as the storm later blew over, speed past much of Crooked Lake in search of more protected water. We did spend one night in the eerie rock-faced narrows on the east side Crooked Lake, however, camped on the U.S. side within twenty yards of Canada. There it was that I encountered something extraordinary: the Pike of Great Price.

Brad and I were out paddling toward evening, expecting to find more of the smallmouth bass we had caught the day before in similar spots on Iron Lake. I was not rigged with the steel leader and heavy rod we used for pike in the weeds, but with six-pound-test line on an ultralight spinning rig. After a half hour, I had given every nook and cranny of this narrow bend a good thrashing with a silver Rapala, to no avail. The absence of fish was so out of keeping with our experience thus far, I joked that there must be only one, huge fish down there that had eaten all the others.

Though it was nearly too dark to see and we were heading back to camp, I made one more cast too close to shore by a steep, rock ledge, and snagged the lure solidly. Brad kept paddling. He seemed not to notice my rod bending steadily backward toward the snag, and I quickly urged him to stop. Just then, the stuff of legend came caterwauling out of the deep attached to my 6-lb. line.

Due either to considerable skill on my part or a rather macabre sense of humor on the part of the fish, I managed despite the weakness of my line to bring him to the side of the canoe. What we could see of his back above the surface stretched a full three feet, and I soon appreciated Santiago's dilemma: it would break both rod and line to try to lift him in the boat.

In my mind's eye, when I remember the events of that evening, time is suspended as in a dream. My intelligence tells me what happened is that the line broke like a thread when I grabbed it to lift the fish. But I also remember as if it were hours the moment that fish lay at the end of the line; with only his head above the water by the canoe and a certain expression of contempt for the futility of my position. In my mind's eye, I recall that the fish spoke to me at that moment, and said: "You dummy, Hurley. You've waited for this trip since you were fourteen. You came all this way at great expense, and you didn't even have the good sense to pack a net."

I'm afraid my notes on the rest of the trip after Crooked Lake are a little halfhearted. The Horse River offered some striking scenery, and, thankfully, the remaining portion of the route was not difficult to follow. A portage here or there. Whatever. I don't really remember. I knew from that point forward that I was not so much finishing one voyage as beginning another—one that would take me and the biggest net science can create back to these Northlands, where I have some unfinished business with a rare, talking pike.

Cedar Creek Canoe Trail

Congaree National Forest

Coming to love canoeing in the coastal swamps of the South is a little like learning to love Cajun cuisine. Once you open up to the culture of the locale, a love for Boudin sausage and crawfish on a platter won't be far behind.

To be sure, there is little in a floodplain swamp that recalls the classic, sylvan beauty of the Adirondacks or the Quetico, but these swamps offer a unique ecosystem, a great variety of birdlife, and a very primal sense of wilderness all their own. That is owing no doubt to the natural impediment to their development posed by a high water table and frequently saturated ground. Perhaps this also explains why the Congaree Swamp in South Carolina can lay claim to a superlative we might more readily associate with the North Woods: the tallest trees east of the Mississippi River.

Congaree Swamp, which became a "monument," of the national park system in 1976, is located a short drive southeast of Columbia, near the center of the

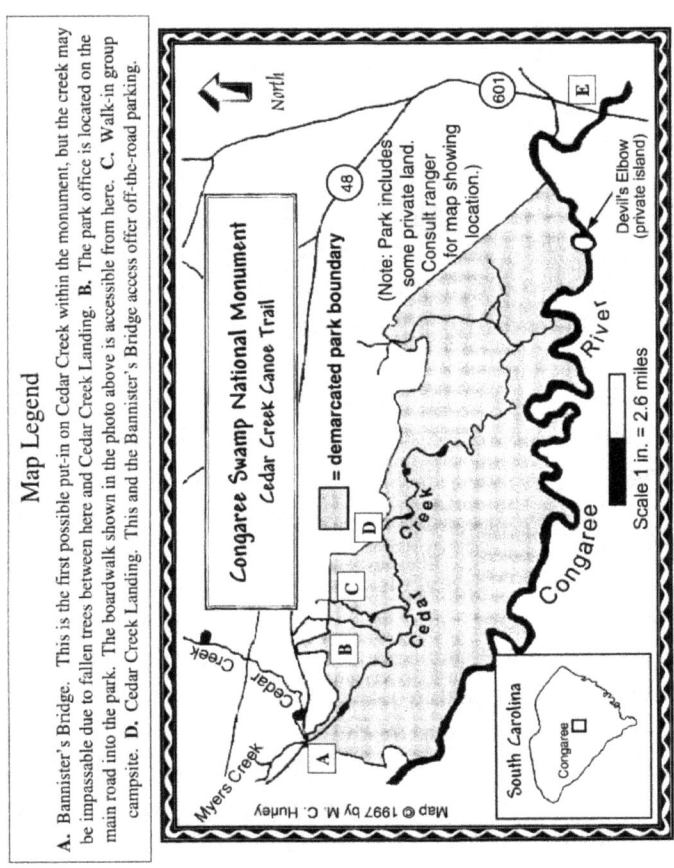

state. According to literature published by the Department of the Interior, here you will find the "last significant stand of old growth river-bottom hardwood forest" left in this country. The variety of tree species in the Congaree, which reportedly contains half the total number of tree species found throughout Europe, prompted the designation of the area as an International Biosphere Reserve. The most prevalent species along the water is the bald cypress, with a root system of distinctive "knees." The largest found in the Congaree has a circumference of 27-feet 5-inches, while some knees have measured 7-1/2 feet high. Other local records include a 162-foot Cherrybark Oak, a 145-foot Loblolly Pine, a 144-foot American Elm, and a 124-foot Water Tupelo.

The park service has designated and marked an easy canoe-trail through the swamp on Cedar Creek. No motorized craft are allowed on Cedar Creek, and it has a very wild feel for most of its length. There are three possible itineraries on the canoe trail. One is to put in at the farthest upstream point within the park at Bannister's Bridge and paddle 7 miles to Cedar Creek Landing. When we arrived at the park in February, however, we were told that this upstream section of the canoe trail was blocked in more than twenty places by fallen trees that would require a portage. The second option, and the one we took, is to put in seven miles down the creek at Cedar Creek Landing, establish a base camp several miles down the creek, and explore the creek upstream and down from that base. This is easy to do, because at normal water-levels Cedar Creek is a slow-moving stream with a current of only about 1 knot. We encountered no obstructions downstream of Cedar Creek Landing that required a portage. There were numerous logs submerged just below the surface and strainers in some locations, but given the slowness of the current these were all easily negotiated.

A third option is to camp in different locations along the creek as you make your way toward a take-out at the 601 bridge. Columbia outfitters Adventure Carolina and River Runners will shuttle you back to your vehicle from the 601 bridge. The charge quoted to me by River Runners for a shuttle from the 601 bridge to Bannister's Bridge was fifty dollars.

While we did not venture as far as the Congaree River on Cedar Creek, I did drive down to the 601 bridge. It is a slow, muddy river and not one that I would make a special effort to paddle given an opportunity to explore more of Cedar Creek. The creek by contrast is fairly clear, and the bass and bream fishing in warmer months is reportedly good.

Anyone putting in at Cedar Creek Landing should note that the concrete landing shown in the photo at right has some jagged rebar and steel tubing beneath the surface that will damage your canoe. Put in at the natural landing area just upstream, on the other side of the footbridge.

A backcountry-use permit is required for an overnight stay in the park. These are issued at no charge on a first-come first-served basis at the park ranger station. Camping is allowed anywhere on park land, but the park-service map points out the location of some isolated plots of private land to be avoided.

There was a surprising abundance of elevated, dry land suitable for camping adjacent to Cedar Creek at several locations. And while there is also an abundance of downed wood, campfires are prohibited by the park service due to the area's status as a biosphere reserve.

The USGS maps necessary for the entire length of the canoe trail are the Wateree and Gadsden quadrangles, which can be ordered by credit card from The Map Shop in Greenville, South Carolina. The ranger station will also mail a brochure on the monument and guide to the canoe trail to anyone who requests it. The park office may be reached from 8:30 to 5:00 p.m. by telephone every day except Christmas. You may also write to Congaree Swamp National Monument, Caroline Sims Rd., Hopkins, SC 29061.

Nottaway River

Peters Bridge to Careys Bridge

For some time I had been meaning to travel to Virginia to take a look at the camping outfit of Tom Tompkins. Tom builds fine wood-canvas canoes and is also a devotee of traditional camping methods. Aware that he was fully equipped with the requisite Duluth packs, campfire tent, and other gear you see covered elsewhere in this issue, I asked if he would be kind enough to set it all up in his backyard for a photo shoot. Instead, Tom and his longtime canoeing pal Fred Ostrander invited me along on a trip down the Nottoway River to see the boats and gear in action. Tom referred to this section of the river as a well-kept secret, and it is our good fortune that he has consented to share it with the readers of this journal.

The section of the Nottoway we paddled is about ten miles long between public access landings at Route 631 and Route 653. In this stretch, the river moves at a steady pace of 2 knots but without any rock gardens, rapids, or significant obstructions beyond an occasional blow-down or brush dam.

At the time we went in January of this year, the river was very high. In the photographs you see with this story,

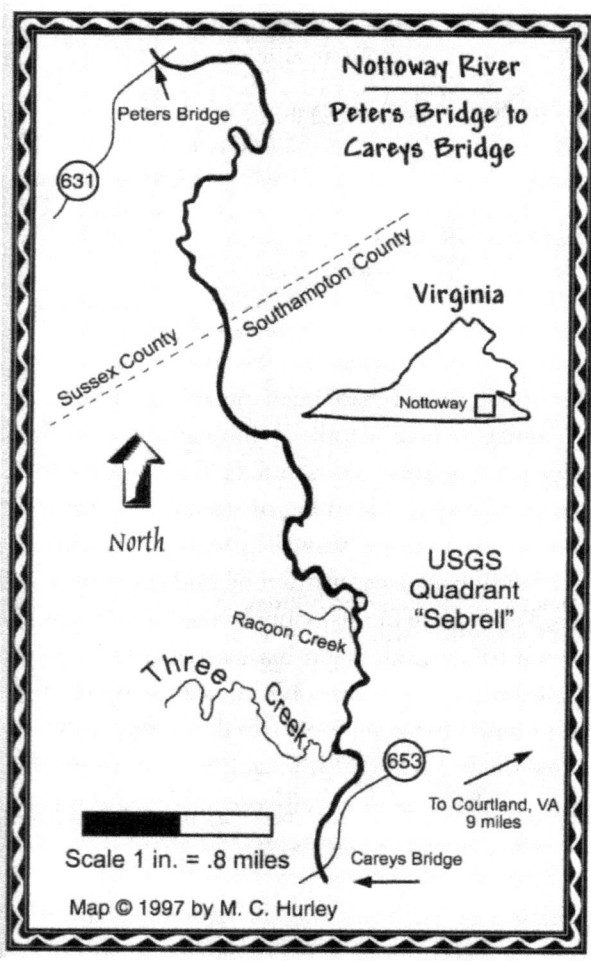

the water is several feet above normal. In fact, we had originally planned a two-night trip on a somewhat longer stretch of the river but shortened our stay when it appeared that high water had covered all of the sand bars usually available for camping. Although one would never guess it from looking at the pictures on these pages, Tom tells me that very often a trip down this same section of the Nottoway can be a drag-and-wade operation in spots.

Care must be taken along the Nottoway to avoid camping on private land. As I do with all river trips featured in the journal, I can convey to you what local authorities advise with respect to permission for camping and encourage you to use your own judgment and common sense. In the case of this section of the Nottoway, Tom sought out the advice of a local judge, who informed him that sand bars and other areas below the mean high water mark of the river are available for camping. Unfortunately, I am unable to show any of those areas in the photos with this story due to the water levels at the time of our trip. In our case, we camped on some higher ground for the use of which Tom had years ago secured permission from the landowner.

High water and cold weather are the bane of any fishing trip, and we had both in spades on this outing. I am assured, however, that the Nottoway is a fertile smallmouth stream—as are so many other great rivers in this state.

To find out how high the Nottoway is running, you can call and ask to speak to the Data Chief for the USGS office in Richmond. There is a river gauge just upstream of the Route 653 bridge that was damaged in Hurricane Fran, but it should soon be replaced.

This section of the Nottoway is different from other Virginia rivers. Because it flows through the coastal floodplain, its waters are not as clear as those of rivers which flow over rock beds farther west. The trees along the river also include a fair number of bald cypress, which aren't found on streams in the Virginia Piedmont.

Outfitted on this trip by Tom in one of his Cheemaun wood-canvas canoes, I had at last the chance to paddle what he and others had been telling me for some time was a fine, little boat for canoe camping. My experience with wood-canvas canoes goes back to summer camp in Maine, where we paddled heavy, eighteen-foot behemoths that required two people to lift into the water. The Cheemaun is a different proposition altogether. With Fred along in his 1939 Old Town Otca, and with the cold weather keeping us close by the biscuits and campfire, before long I had engaged both men in a rousing debate about the pros and cons of various designs of wood-canvas canoes. The upshot of that debate has been my decision to commission the construction of a Cheemaun for myself, the reasons for which I am pleased to share.

Both men seemed to agree that the traditional North Woods canoe, whose design best evokes the character of the breed, is the E.M. White "Guide" in the eighteen or twenty-foot models. This boat possesses long, gently recurved stems and a low-swept profile. First made in 1885, it has been the Maine guide's canoe of choice for many years. The eighteen-foot model, however, tips the scales at around eighty pounds. Having owned an eighty-pound and a sixty-pound boat, I can say that the difference in weight is a significant, limiting factor on the types of trips I can comfortably make as a man of average size and strength. Hoisting an eighty-pound canoe by yourself over portages of a third of a mile or more is drudgery, in my opinion.

It occurred to me that, while the day is not too far off when my six-year-old son will be tall and strong enough to help me carry an eighteen or twenty-foot guide canoe over a long portage, a smaller wooden boat could serve just as well as the second boat for a trip with a family of four. We already have a sixteen-foot Old Town Royalex Camper that is a good size for two people and a week's worth of gear. Now that our younger child Caroline is five and old enough to come on trips with her brother, however, there is no room for Mom in the canoe. We could solve that problem by purchasing a larger boat to carry all of us, such as the eighteen or twenty-foot models I mentioned, but the same concern about portaging weight would apply. The better plan seemed to call for a second boat, and because it is the second boat, it is not important that it be so large as to carry all of us and our outfit together. That's where the appeal of the Cheemaun comes in.

With the Cheemaun, I expect to be able to carry myself and most of the gear required for extended trips with our family, while Julie and one or both of the children take the other canoe. On those trips I make alone, while the kids are in school or when weather advises against their coming along, the Cheemaun will serve ably as a solo expedition canoe.

I should add that the boats Tom makes are more than just functional craft. They are stunning, family heirlooms. Tom's wife Gail hand canes the seats, their son Cort helps steam bend the ribs and stretch the canvas, and attention to details that affect the strength and appearance of the boat is everywhere apparent. In the next issue of the journal, you will see a photo essay of the Cheemaun under construction, with an explanation of the design and construction decisions to be made at each stage. In this way, I hope to educate myself and provide the many readers who regularly write with questions about what type of canoe to buy with a better understanding of aspects of traditional canoe design.

If you'd like to talk to Tom about the Cheemaun or other questions on wood-canvas canoes, you can write to him at 2204 Shingle Wood Way, Virginia Beach, VA 23456-4052. He teaches civics at a middle school in Virginia Beach and runs the canoe shop in his spare time. He is licensed by The Northwoods Canoe Company to build both the Cheemaun and the 17-foot Atkinson Traveler. Other information about wood-canvas canoes is available through the Wooden Canoe Heritage Association, which publishes Wooden Canoe magazine. You can write the WCHA at P. O. Box 255, Paul Smiths, NY 12970-0255. They have an extensive web-site on the Internet at www.wcha.org, with a table of contents that will refer you to web pages, addresses and phone numbers of various builders of wood-canvas, birch bark, and cedar-strip designs, books about wooden canoe construction and heritage, and activities planned by local chapters. They also have a members' classified advertising section where a number of new and used wooden boats in various stages of repair are listed for sale. The WCHA holds its Annual Assembly at Paul Smith's College in the Adirondacks each year in July, offering displays of various aspects of canoecraft.

Bog River / Oswegatchie Traverse

Adirondack Park

It can no longer be said that the Adirondacks are the impenetrable realm of mystery first perceived by the Algonquin tribes, who named these woods "Couxsachrage"—the dismal wilderness. A telephone call to any office of the State Department of Environmental Conservation (DEC) will fetch to your doorstep, in two-days' time, a lovely color "Canoe Map" on which most of the mystery of the trails and camps, here, are unfolded for the casual visitor. But there is a place in the Adirondacks which does not yet appear on the standard canoe map nor which is readily known to the casual wanderer. Owing to its remoteness from other areas and to the state's recent acquisition of 10,000 acres of watershed from a century of private ownership, it invokes a feeling of time gone by. This forty-mile journey through the Bog River flow and across Low's Lake, over the Five Ponds Wilderness and down the Oswegatchie River to Inlet, retains something of that raw character which one nineteenth century explorer summed up as a feeling of "indescribable loneliness."

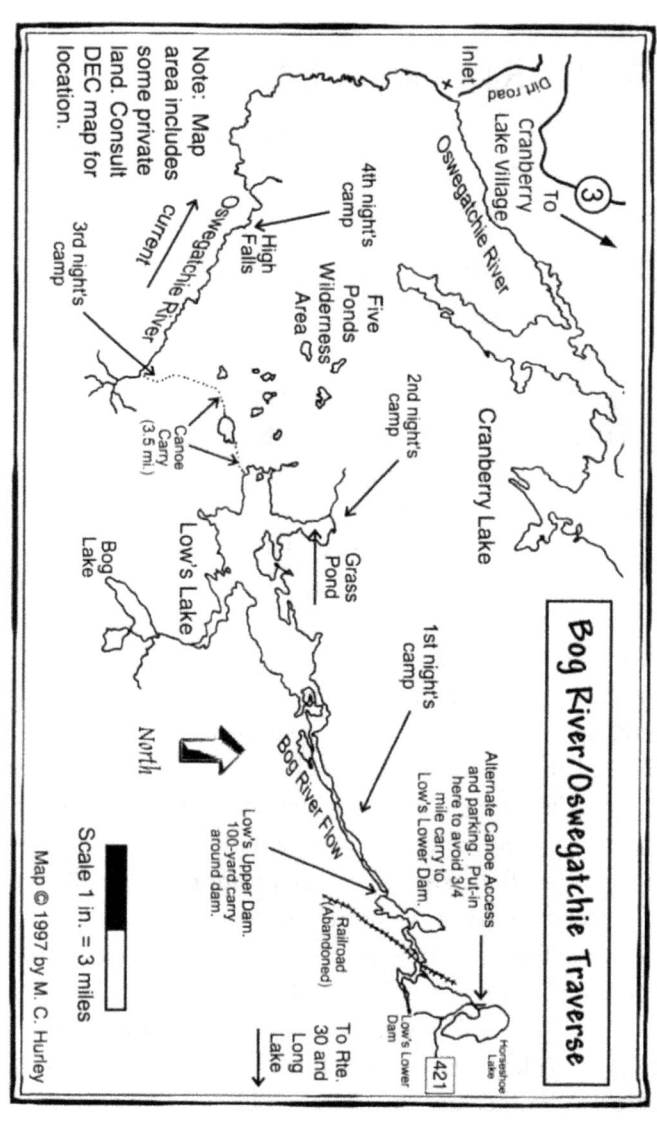

Our trip began in the more familiar and hospitable environs of the elegant Adirondack Hotel in the Hamlet of Long Lake, about a two-hour drive north of Utica, New York. Late in the evening after a wearying trip from North Carolina, we arrived at the Northern Born grocery in Long Lake, whose very helpful owner opened his doors long after closing time to allow us to purchase our supplies of fresh meat, eggs, butter, juice, and cheese. After two days behind the wheel of a Jeep I was grateful, as well, for the short walk across the street from the grocery to the hotel.

The grand, old Adirondack Hotel is not just the most convenient staging area for this expedition. It is perhaps the last, best example of the class of sporting lodges common to the Gilded Age of the last century. The original structure was destroyed with the rest of the town in the great fire of 1908 and was rebuilt shortly thereafter. Entering the lobby from its wooden porch you are greeted by black bear trophies mounted full-size and upright, an image you will surely recall as you hoist your food pack a little higher than usual in the days ahead. Over the clerk's counter rests the ponderous head of a moose, whose progeny have recently regained a small foothold in the Adirondacks in the areas to be encountered on this trip. The upstairs rooms overlooking the lake still evoke a nineteenth-century charm at affordable rates, and the restaurant is first class.

I make special mention of this hotel for two reasons: First, as you would likely be traveling to this area from some distance, you will need a place to freeze ice bags and fresh meat to keep cool in the food pack in the days ahead. The kitchen staff was more than happy to oblige us for this purpose. Secondly, the trip on which you are about to embark is arduous enough that you well deserve whatever small comforts you can afford before your departure.

Heading north from Long Lake on Route 30 toward Tupper Lake, you will see a DEC sign at Route 421 to your left, leading to the Bog River Access. It soon becomes a dirt road. Do not park at the first canoe-access sign that marks a 3/4-mile carry to a put-in at Low's Lower Dam. Drive a short distance farther on the same road to the spot marked as the "Alternate Canoe Access" point on the map, right below the outlet of Horseshoe Pond. Just below the road, here, a narrow stream winds through a bog. Unload your gear on the pine boards offered as a makeshift landing beside the stream, and park your vehicle in one of the marked areas in the woods a few yards farther down the road. I had mailed an extra key ahead of time to Dave Cilley at nearby St. Regis Canoe Outfitters. For $195.00 he sent a driver to find my Jeep at the put-in and deliver it that week to our take-out at Inlet.

Once on the outlet stream from Horseshoe Pond, you will wend your way through tight turns in the bog for a mile or so before coming upon a wide pool, shown in the photo below, created by a beaver dam. There is no place to carry around the dam. If the dam has not been breached in one spot to allow a canoe to float over, run the bow of the canoe up on top of a low spot on the dam, step out of the canoe onto the top of the dam (they are surprisingly sturdy), and while crouched on the dam bring the canoe hand-over-hand across. This will be a familiar drill by the end of the trip.

Shortly after the first beaver dam the stream widens into a pond. This is part of the Bog River Flow created by Low's Lower Dam. On the point to your left is the end of the 3/4-mile portage trail from the first canoe access you passed on the way in, and farther down to your left is the lower dam. Heading across the pond and to your right, you pass under a bridge of an abandoned railroad. The railroad and its builder are part of an interesting history of this area which has been chronicled by Michael Wilson in the Fall/Winter 1995 issue of the *Adirondack Journal of Environmental Studies*, published at nearby Paul Smith's College.

Low's Lake is named after Abbot Augustus Low, a wealthy industrialist from Brooklyn. Low was a copious inventor—only Thomas Edison claimed more patents. By 1896 he had bought up most of the acreage along the Bog River to apply his genius in a vast lumbering and maple syrup operation. A map from an 1873 survey shows that at the time Low bought the property, the Bog River flowed directly out of tiny Mud Lake, at the western edge of the area now submerged by the dams which created Low's Lake. Grass Pond, which retains its name but is now just a cove contiguous to the shoreline of Low's Lake, was then a pond much smaller in size and connected to Mud Lake only by an outlet stream. Low built the upper and lower dams to enable him to float more timber from the shores of his property around Mud Lake. He built the railroad to provide personal transportation to the area for his family and employees. However, fires in clear-cut areas strewn with timber debris were a constant risk in this age of coal-fired locomotives. When much of the standing timber on

Low's 46,000 acres was destroyed in the great Long Lake fire of 1908, he folded his operations in the area, and the property was gradually sold by his heirs over several decades. All that remains now are the dams—since upgraded by the state—some crumbling foundations, and an abandoned boarding house standing to the right of the canoe carry around the upper dam.

The state acquired the remaining 10,000 acres of Low's original holdings in 1985, opening portions of the Bog River Flow, Low's Lake, and access thereby to the Oswegatchie to the public for the first time in over 100 years. The DEC scouted, blazed, and marked the 3.5 mile carry from Low's Lake to the Oswegatchie sometime in 1987 after considering a number of routes.

One local guide considers the area penetrated on this trip the most remote region of the Adirondacks: "You're as far away from anything as you're going to get, up here." It has apparently always been thus. In his first report to the New York legislature in 1873, young surveyor Verplanck Colvin referred to Mud Lake as a "lonely, doleful water." Earlier explorers found the Bog River area teeming with insects and called it the "gloomiest sheet the wilderness contains." That it is one of the deepest recesses of the forest is evident in the fact that the elusive "last moose" in the Adirondacks was reported killed here "many times" in the mid-1800's by hunters eager to claim that distinction, as noted by Jamieson and Morris in their excellent guide, *Adirondack Canoe Waters, North Flow* (1987), published by the Adirondack Mountain Club.

Low's Lake has, of course, changed this area dramatically, and whether that is for the better or worse is a matter of perspective. The modern canoeist will find Low's Lake and the surrounding mountains quite as enchanting as any natural lake in the area, if not more so by reason of their remoteness.

Shortly after floating under the trestle of Mr. Low's abandoned railroad on the first day, we stopped on the northern bank of the flow for a break. There, while casting a no. 1 silver Mepps rooster tail spinner baited with a piece of worm, I caught first a small yellow perch, then the nice smallmouth bass. Considering that we began this trip on May 11, just one week after ice-out, I had rather expected to find some trout in the lake. Given the presence of bass and perch there, however, it is likely that brook trout are not much in evidence in Low's Lake. Still, the bass fishing was as good as any I've had in the area.

We chose to make our first camp at a fine location—DEC site no. 10—on the right bank of the Bog River Flow. All of the campsites on this entire traverse are numbered and marked on one of two DEC publications, entitled "Bog River Flow" and "Trails in the Cranberry Lake Region." Both are essential guides. You may measure your progress by the position on these maps of the consecutively numbered campsites as you pass them. Canoe campsite numbers appear on small signs nailed to trees by DEC and are usually visible from the water.

The Bog River Flow and Low's Lake are designated a "primitive area" (one grade below "wilderness"). Camping is allowed (but not encouraged) at non-numbered sites on state land, here. Parts of the land around the Bog River Flow and Low's Lake are still privately owned, however. The DEC pamphlet warns that if you choose to camp in a non-designated site, you are responsible for "knowing that you are on State lands and not trespassing on private lands," setting your camp back at least 150 feet from any road, trail, or water, and leaving no trace. To avoid unnecessary impact on the environment from fires and tent sites, no one should camp anywhere but a designated site except in an emergency.

We woke to a chilling, wind-driven rain on day two and opted to forego cooking breakfast to get a jump on the Low's Lake crossing. All of the literature on Low's Lake speaks of the persistent waves and headwinds that greet the paddler attempting to cross. We encountered the same. Keeping to the north shore, we were able to make fair progress but were cold, wet, and well worn by the time we reached Grass Pond for the second night's camp.

Grass Pond is a beautiful spot bordered on all sides by high ground and to the east by a granite-faced mountain. We had hoped to camp beside the unnamed brook that feeds into the northwest corner of the pond, but site no. 33 at that location was filled with trash—a completely new experience for me at a DEC site, all of which I've found to be nearly immaculate. Site no. 32 nearby, shown in the photo at the top of page 7, is not nearly as scenic as sites 29, 30, and 31 on the pond, due to its proximity to a jeep trail. When our bedraggled crew arrived late on a rainy afternoon, however, we were more interested in the large stack of split firewood here. We soon had a crackling blaze beneath our campfire tarp and dinner of marinated, grilled chicken, fried onions and green peppers, hot coffee, and, of course, biscuits from the reflector oven.

When a ray of bright sun broke through the clouds and lit up the pond just before dusk, two of us jumped in the Cheemaun and paddled to the flooded timber in the northeastern corner of the pond. There, my old standby—a three-inch silver floating Rapala minnow, scarred with teeth marks from various Minnesota pike—proved irresistible to a four-pound largemouth bass. Largemouth are not nearly as common as smallmouth bass in the Adirondacks, but Grass Pond on Low's Lake seemed to have them in spades. Another bass of about the same size took the same lure in another area of flooded timber the next day, but it managed to wrap the line around the bow of the canoe and snap it when it went tail-walking across the surface.

Our party of three carried on this trip the full complement of gear from the "Ultimate List" as well as two canoes. By the morning of the third day, the brutal reality of the 3.5 mile Low's Lake carry was upon us. Crossing over from Grass Pond to the south shore of Low's Lake and continuing toward the west end in search of the carry, you will first see an unmarked trail that comes down to the lakeshore on your left and appears to be the head of the carry, but is not. The head of the carry is farther to the west, marked with a standard DEC park sign (painted brown with yellow letters) and a sign-in box. Such boxes appear at each end of the carry and at the take-out at Inlet. Signing your name, address, length of stay, and intended destination will help the DEC find you if you are lost or injured in the woods.

What you will encounter along the entire length of the Low's Lake carry is a scene of vast and utterly astonishing devastation caused by the most violent windstorm to hit the Adirondacks in recorded history. A "microburst"—a sudden windstorm of maximum hurricane force—hit this area in July 1995. Toppling trees in its path almost as efficiently as if the entire forest had been clear-cut, it cut a swath some ten miles wide and thousands of acres long through what had been the last, great stand of "virgin" forest in the Adirondacks. Only a small percentage of the old-growth white-pine that had escaped the extensive logging of the last century survived this storm, some of it having already been cleared out in another devastating blow-down in 1950. No doubt it was partly the magnificence of this old growth that prompted DEC officer Thomas Brown, as quoted in the Adirondack Mountain Club guide, to call the Bog River/Oswegatchie traverse "one of the most exciting and adventurous canoe treks in the entire Adirondacks, if not in the Northeast." If one keeps in mind that the acres of graying timber are the result of a natural force no less impressive than the height these trees had once attained, it is still one of the most exciting trips one can make in the Adirondacks.

The Low's Lake canoe carry, unlike some other trails in the Five Ponds Wilderness, is not marked on any of the USGS maps for this area. The DEC publication "Trails in the Cranberry Lake Region" is, again, the best guide. This and all designated portages are marked by yellow DEC discs labeled with the words "canoe carry."

Starting up the carry, you soon encounter a marked DEC campsite just off the trail to your left. You are now in a designated "wilderness area" for the remainder of the trip. All campsites in this area are primitive with the exception of a few lean-tos on the river. The carry continues on a fairly level grade. Other trails branch off to ponds in the mountains, but at the time of our trip, two years after the big storm, all of these trails were still posted as closed due to heavy blowdown.

The carry appears to continue around Big Deer Pond, which comes in at 7/10ths of a mile; but do not follow it past the lone campsite on the pond at the northwestern shore. Drop your first load here and go back for the rest of your gear. The carry picks up on the other side of the pond, which is about a half-mile across. Paddling down and along the right shore of the pond, you will see the familiar brown and yellow DEC sign that marks the resumption of the carry, now 2.2 miles from the Oswegatchie River.

After leaving Big Deer Pond on the carry you will come to a large, well-established beaver dam grown over with grass. The carry trail passes right over the top of the dam with the pond to the left. Near this part of the trail, we had the good fortune to meet up with Dick and Roger Rether, two brothers from Upstate New York, now retired, who have been coming to camp, fish, and hunt the wilderness around the Oswegatchie in the spring and fall since the 1960's. They explained that it was on this beaver pond that a DEC helicopter established a fuel and supply base to support the Herculean task of clearing the carry of blowdown from the July 1995 storm. Along the carry there are narrow passes cut through downed trees that are stacked right where they fell. In some places the trees fell five or six deep, one on top of the other. Where the carry passes some giant white pine that has been sawn in two, you can count the rings back to your great, great grandparents. But according to the Rether brothers, the

New York State record white pine escaped damage in the big storm and can still be found a short distance down the outlet of the beaver dam crossed on the carry.

Once past Big Deer Pond, the best way to accomplish the carry is in stages. This makes for more walking and a longer day but with less exhaustion, to the extent that is possible on a 3.5 mile carry. Most of the carry is fairly wide and level, but at one point roughly two-thirds of the way to the end, you come to the top of a ridge on which the DEC in its mercy has installed two benches. Rest here if not sooner, then go back and fetch the rest of your gear this far. It was our outstanding good luck that after passing us, the Rether brothers, in a perfect act of kindness, went to the head of the carry at Big Deer Pond, found one of our more leaden packs, and brought it along with some other items of gear across the entire carry. Southern hospitality surely has its counterpart in the North Woods.

Having begun our odyssey on the western shore of Low's Lake at nine o'clock that morning, we finally pitched camp at six in the evening. We chose the site on the river just a short distance from the end of the carry, but if heartier souls have the strength to load their canoe and paddle about a mile downstream, they will find a charming site marked by ten wooden steps leading up from the river. This is where we later observed the Rethers' canvas wall-tent with a woodstove pipe jutting warmly though its side.

Sportsmen like the Rethers and many others have a special reverence for the Oswegatchie. Naturalist Peter O'Shea writes, in Dennis Aprill's *Good Fishing in the Adirondacks* (Woodstock, VT: Backcountry Publications,

1992), that "one of the most cherished adventures of early twentieth century sportsmen [was] a canoe trek up the legendary Oswegatchie." What they were after was trout—big, fat, falls-leaping, native brook trout by the droves. The usual trip began at the location known as "the Inlet," which is still the only place to put in or take out on the river. The name "Inlet" does not refer to any present or former village, here; it refers to the place where the Oswegatchie River comes into, or the "inlet" of the river at, Cranberry Lake. (Unnavigable rapids in the short section of the river remaining between Inlet and the lake impede a trip all the way down the river.)

From a rustic hotel that once stood at Inlet, sporting parties early in this century would embark in canoes paddled and poled by guides over the 15 miles upriver to High Falls, against the slow current. The famous Dobson Sporting Camps were located right on High Falls, where it is said that large brook trout could often be seen leaping upriver in the fray. According to the Adirondack Mountain Club guide by Jamieson and Morris, the Rich Lumber Company spared much of the old growth along the river from logging in the early 1900's out of deference to local guides, whose customers came here to see a virgin wilderness. The few remaining examples of these ancient white pines are quite conspicuous by their size.

At all designated brook trout waters in the Adirondacks, of which the Oswegatchie is one, the DEC has posted signs prohibiting the use of minnows as bait. This is due to the unintended spread of suckers—grown up minnows dumped from fishermen's bait buckets—and the resulting decline in trout population. This effect, combined with the introduction of yellow perch to

Cranberry Lake and, others say, a long history of overfishing on the Oswegatchie, has greatly reduced the output of trout from the river. Nonetheless the trout are there. I watched one patient fisherman camped at a lean-to on High Falls land a ten-incher just below the falls. The best bait in early spring seems to be a small trout worm or part of a nightcrawler (not the whole worm—too spooky for trout) on a hook and leader assembly trailing about twelve inches behind a gold spinner. These rigs were available in local tackle shops under the brand name "Adirondack Hooker," as were "trout worms." Cast the spinner and worm combination downstream into an eddy below the riffles or a deep pool, let it sink to about mid-depth, and retrieve it very slowly. The current will keep the spinner turning even on a slow retrieve. When you feel the quick tap-tap-tap of a trout taking the worm, let the line go slack for a three-count, then set the hook.

The river above the falls is reportedly navigable for another five to seven miles depending on the water level, though our party did not venture upstream from the point at which the Low's Lake carry comes in. On the morning of the fourth day, we pushed the canoes for the first time into the exceptionally clear, clean, and very cold water of the Oswegatchie. From the end of the Low's Lake carry to High Falls is a two to three-hour paddle, depending on the water level and number of beaver dams. If the water is too high, you will find it impossible to duck under the trees that stretch across the river in places. If the water is too low, you will have to carry over or around beaver dams you might otherwise have floated past. At moderate to high water, when we made the trip, we had to carry only once and step out onto a beaver dam to get across another time. The same trip could have posed five or six short carries at much lower or higher water levels.

The approach to High Falls is not marked by any sign and can be treacherous if one isn't paying attention. I was happy to have received guidance on what to do from the Rether brothers the day before. Their instruction is to keep to the right bank as soon as you see the small concrete blocks atop the falls which first appear around a corner to your left. The blocks are the remains of an old footbridge. The right bank opens up to an eddy above the falls, where there is a grassy landing. Take out here and follow the portage trail up the hill and down around the falls.

The photo at lower left shows a canoeist who has paddled over the first sluice of the falls (where the concrete blocks are) and taken out on steep granite ledges just to the right of the point at which a loss of control would put you on a fatal course over the falls. For safety, and because the carry around the falls is so short, anyway, I strongly recommend against this maneuver.

Today there are two lean-tos at High Falls, one on each side of the falls. We used the one on the north bank, just above the carry. Ours had a wooden floor; the one across the river reportedly has a dirt floor. True to the tradition of trappers' caches in the North Woods (but probably not to the liking of many wilderness-seekers), we found the lean-to at High Falls to be well-stocked with various useful paraphernalia purposefully left there by earlier voyagers. There was a pot, pan, utensils, a plate, two cans of sardines, a bag of soup (recently gnawed open by mice), a carton of live nightcrawlers without which I would have never caught the first trout, and, tucked carefully away in the rafters, a half-empty fifth of Canadian whiskey. Interestingly, there was also a journal left in a plastic case with a pen inviting others to record their tales, including a number of complaints about the black flies. Juvenile black-flies had just hatched when we were in the woods—identified for us by the Rether brothers as the little gnats flying about our heads—but apparently do not get their "teeth" for about another week. When that happens, everyone assured us, even the hardiest souls get out of the woods until about July 4. While I have camped in the Adirondacks in mid-June without finding the biting black-flies a nuisance, they are doubtless more prevalent in the deep woods of the Oswegatchie than in less remote areas.

After a dinner of too much canoe stew, and, from the reflector oven, a loaf of beer-bread and a double-crust apple pie, I decided to "rough it" like the old days by laying out my bedroll directly on the lean-to floor before a sparkling fire. (To be sure, everyone who has ever camped in the Adirondacks could build campfires there every night for a hundred years and not exhaust the supply of firewood on the forest floor from the storm of 1995.) Soon the fire was down, the moon appeared through a break in the clouds like a light bulb switched on in the sky, and all was right with the world—until there came the "scritch, scritch, scritch" of what I thought were likely mice somewhere in the lean-to. Because lean-tos provide excellent cover in the rain and allow standing headroom, they are often used for cooking. Meals are spilled on the wood floor and food scraps fall here and there, attracting mice and—it occurred to me as I nodded off—bears. For this reason, I would suggest using the lean-to by all means but setting up your tent somewhere else.

On the fifth day of our trip we had estimated the paddle from High Falls to Inlet to take us about seven hours and planned to stop somewhere to camp about half-way. As it turned out our estimate was wrong, and, without the DEC map at hand to measure our progress past the numbered campsites, we made the entire trip in about three-and-a-half hours. With a storm blowing in as we arrived at Inlet, we decided to take out that day. Were I making the trip again, I would opt to stay at the second lean-to below High Falls—site no. 38. Nestled beneath a beautiful stand of pine overlooking a long, deep pool, it seemed a place where some of the secrets of this river might be hiding—along with, I will bet you, friend, at least one great, unbeaten trout to rival any of those that once were the legends of the Oswegatchie.

South Fork of the Shenandoah River

Luray to Bentonville

That the South Fork of the Shenandoah River is a nice place to go canoeing will come as a surprise to no one living around Washington, D.C. Whenever a group of college kids in the area has a wild hare to go tubing or canoeing, the Shenandoah is usually the river of choice. Despite growing up in Maryland and going to school at College Park, though, I had never paddled the south fork until I made the trip this summer with Tom Tompkins—the wood-canvas wizard who built my Cheemaun. And while I am surely glad that I left the wood-canvas canoe at home on this rock-scraping adventure, the south fork turned out to be a crowded but otherwise delightful camping and fishing trip. Owing to its central location on the East Coast, it is also a trip which many readers of this journal can reach in less than a day's drive and finish in a weekend.

Most folks who grew up on the East Coast are also familiar with Virginia's Luray Caverns—a fixture of family car-vacations and class trips for generations. Not far from this location is the put-in for the most popular

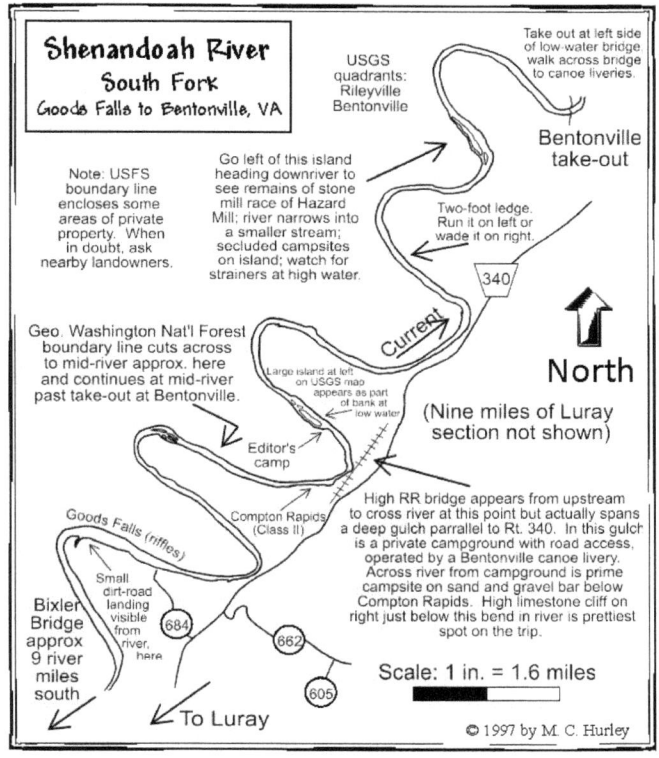

section on the south fork—from Bixler Ferry Road to Bentonville. Coming into the town of Luray on Route 211, one arrives at Mechanic Street (Route 675) just before the town's main intersection. Turning right onto Route 675 will take you across a small bridge and up a hill on your way out of town, where Mechanic Street becomes Bixler Ferry Road. In about three miles you come to a country store on your left, followed immediately thereafter by the bridge over the south fork, known locally as Bixler Bridge. Make a sharp right turn after the bridge to reach the parking area for the put-in. Make a wider right turn, and seven miles later you will come to Shenandoah River Outfitters. This outfitter does not shuttle canoeists back from Bentonville but does sell fishing licenses ($6.50 for non-residents for two days) and basic camping supplies.

At least two USGS maps are essential for this trip, those being the Rileyville and Bentonville quadrangles. The river cuts back and forth across these two quadrangles several times, but if you fold-in the edges and tape the two maps together, you will have an easily readable map of the entire river for the last 18 miles of this trip. The Luray quadrangle covers the first nine miles or so but was not in stock at the Virginia Division of Mineral Resources at the time of our trip nor at this writing. To order maps from this agency, you must either mail a check made payable to the Virginia Division of Mineral Resources with your order in advance or fax a purchase order on "company letterhead." The maps you need for river trips are the 1:24,000-scale series, also called 7.5 minute maps. For a map which divides the entire state into named quadrangles, call the agency to request the "Index to Topographic and Other Map Coverage."

There is reportedly a short section of the George Washington National Forest which comes in on the left bank a few miles below Bixler Bridge, but we needed to make more distance than that on the first day. The next national forest land does not come in until just above Compton Rapids, as shown on the map.

The caliber of land within the national forest boundary along the river might not be what one usually associates with national forests. While paddling through what the map indicated was land within the national forest boundary, we saw all manner of development. Parts of it were a real eyesore, I'm sorry to say. Other sections were pastures and farming developments. Several sections seemed almost pristine. The variation is due to the difference between property that is simply within the demarcated boundary-line of the national forest—much of which might be posted as private property—and land which is posted as United States Forest Service property. The latter type of land is open to public camping; the former type is not. When in doubt, look for the yellow USFS markers on trees along shore or ask for permission.

Tom, who like me had never paddled the Shenandoah, was bound and determined to bring one of his beautiful wood-canvas canoes on this trip. At the last minute, he was persuaded by a local outfitter not to do so. After passing the first mile on this river, Tom and I agreed that any wooden boat trying to navigate this river at summer water-levels would be torn to shreds. The rock formations at the bottom of this river are shale. The ledges point upriver at a 45 degree angle in a series of sharp, thin plates. My Royaflex Old Town was thoroughly shaved by the end of this trip. Wear a good pair of rubber sandals, as you'll spend a lot of time in the water helping your boat over these ledges.

It is possible for low-water levels to make this section of the river too much work for anyone to enjoy. At the time we made the trip, the Front Royal gauge was reported at 1.33, just barely above the 1.2 reading which Ed Grove, in his guidebook *Classic Virginia Rivers*, reports as the minimum runnable level. (A reading of 3.5 at the

Front Royal gauge is suggested as the maximum.) A recorded statement of the Front Royal gauge-level that is updated daily is available by telephone. Ed Grove's book is also an excellent reference to have along on this trip. Copies can be purchased by phone from The Great Outdoor Provision Company in Raleigh.

The fishing on this trip was some of the best I've encountered on Virginia rivers. This was somewhat surprising given the fact that we made our trip well into the season and were accompanied along the entire length of the river by a fair complement of float fishermen. Most of the smallmouth we caught were under one pound, and only two or three out of the couple dozen or more we landed that weekend even came close to the one-pound mark. Scrappy ten-inch fighters were in abundance, though, and Beetlespins were again the weapon of choice. By the time we reached our campsite on the evening of the first day, we had an ample stringer for a fish fry. It is amazing how well fed one can be from the filets of just a few, small fish.

If you choose not to make the entire twenty-eight miles of the trip from Bixler Bridge to Bentonville, a shorter trip to the take-out at Goods Falls is a good choice. We did not explore the take-out, here, but it is reportedly private property made available to boaters as a landing for a small fee.

This trip definitely gets prettier, and the landscape more striking, the farther downriver one gets. If you get on the river by 9:00 a.m., with the aid of the moderate current you should have no trouble in reaching the campsites below Compton Rapids by mid-afternoon with an hour lunch-stop in between. If it had not been an unusually busy, summer weekend when we made this trip, we would have been delighted to camp on the gravel bar shown in the top, right photograph on this page, just below Compton Rapids. When we arrived at the pool below the Rapids, however, both sides of the river were already staked out by a large youth group. These kids were having great fun splashing around next to the rapids above their campsite. Were it not so late in the day, I would have been glad to join them, as this truly is a beautiful spot beneath high, limestone cliffs on the right bank.

No section of the river poses any significant challenge to the novice canoeist except perhaps Compton Rapids. Paddling the river at very low-water levels as we did, I suspect that these rapids were more picky for us than they would be for most. At higher water levels less maneuvering would likely be necessary. When we made the run, we found the best route to be to start in the middle of the river and head to the right. This took us through standing whitewater that offered clear passage and some brief excitement. If you do take on a little water over the gunwales, you'll glide ride up to a sandy beach at the foot of the rapids where you can regain your composure.

After you round the bend below Compton Rapids, you'll see forest service markers posting public land on the left bank. We were looking for the large island that is marked on the USGS quadrant in this area of the river. Figuring that we had either passed it or not yet made it that far, we chose to land on a wide, gravel beach about a mile below Compton Rapids, on the left bank. Getting out to explore the beach for a campsite, we found a cleared tent-site in the woods just above the beach. Although we did not realize it until the following morning, the gravel beach where we landed is actually part of the island shown on the map; the river level was so low that the channel on the left side of the island had simply gone dry. We had this site all to ourselves and enjoyed, beside a campfire of driftwood, one of the best fish fries I can recall. Although one outfitter alone had over seventy-five canoes rented on the river that day, most of these folks had cleared out by the time the cool evening settled on the river. With the lowering dusk this place became a wilderness, again. The intense heat of the day banished all bugs from the evening air, as well, and a more peaceful seat was not to be had anywhere else in the Old Dominion that night.

Alas, the scenery that had become steadily more wild throughout the first day's paddling returned to an eclectic mix of development in several sections the next day. I wish I could report that the defenders of this river have secured at least what remains from further development, but the bulldozers were hard at work even as we paddled by. I would nonetheless encourage anyone to make this trip, as there is a great deal of wild and beautiful land still there to be encountered, and the river itself is a delight to paddle. I don't have any specific information about water quality, but the river was remarkably clear when we paddled it.

There is one section of water worthy of caution on the leg of this trip below Compton Rapids. At the approximate location noted on the map, there is a ledge with a two-foot drop. When we ran this ledge on the left at very low water, we took a good dunking over our bow.

At low water levels, I suspect that it would be very easy to bury the bow of a heavily loaded canoe going over this ledge. There is calm water on both sides of the ledge, and it is not technically difficult, but if you do not wish to risk a capsize you should run this ledge on the right side next to the bank, where it becomes a more gradual riffle.

After this two-foot ledge, the south fork changes to a wider, slower river on average for the remainder of the trip to Bentonville. There are long sections of deep water, including one in which we encountered a father, to the cheers of his two sons, attempting unsuccessfully to land an enormous channel catfish which he had somehow managed to snag in the back with a Rapala. In this section, as well, you'll encounter fleets of tubers on short trips upriver from canoe liveries in Bentonville.

We made arrangements with Downriver Outfitters of Bentonville to shuttle us, our canoe, and our gear back to the Bixler Bridge. They perform this service for thirty dollars for the first boat and ten dollars for each boat thereafter. The trip back to Bixler Bridge is surprisingly quick, owing to the winding course of this river over a short distance as the crow flies.

There is a brief detour that you want to be sure not to miss, about two miles above Bentonville. It is a channel running to the left of a large island which appears shortly after you pass the USFS Hazard Mill Recreation Area. Taking Ed Grove's advice to head down this channel, we encountered the mill race that he mentions in his guidebook. It is a stone wall high on the left bank of the river, below where a large house is now set back in the woods. A channel runs to the left of this island above the point where the mill race is located. If you are willing to drag your canoe across the several shallow bars encountered in this channel you will see a number of lovely sites for camping, including the one Tom is headed for in the photograph at the bottom of page 12. We spent a good hour wandering around back here and noticed that very few of the hordes of paddlers came down this narrow channel. Most of them seemed to prefer the wide and easy way. Float this river and take this "path less traveled," friend. Here you will find, while it lasts, a little wilderness all to yourself.

Potomac River

Paw Paw to Little Orleans

It seems painful to admit that it has been probably twenty-five years since I first saw this river. I cannot recall exactly how old I was, but fourteen is my best guess when Troop 35 of Baltimore brought a gang of scouts and a couple dozen canoes to put in on the Potomac at the little town of Paw Paw, West Virginia. It was the first canoe trip I ever made. My dim memory of that trip—squads of Grumman canoes sliding and banging over riffles and ledges—was happily re-kindled this summer with my seven-year-old son Kip, his cousin Bennett, and Bennett's dad Michael.

The section of the Potomac River from Paw Paw to Little Orleans is something of a rite of passage for Boy Scouts in the Maryland, West Virginia, and Virginia areas. Spanning about 22 miles through beautiful, limestone gorges in the Allegheny Highlands, it promises the kind of marathon day-trip in moving water that scouts need to test their skills, but without any dangerous rapids. Locals recognize that it offers excellent smallmouth bass fishing, as well, and camping in near-wilderness surroundings.

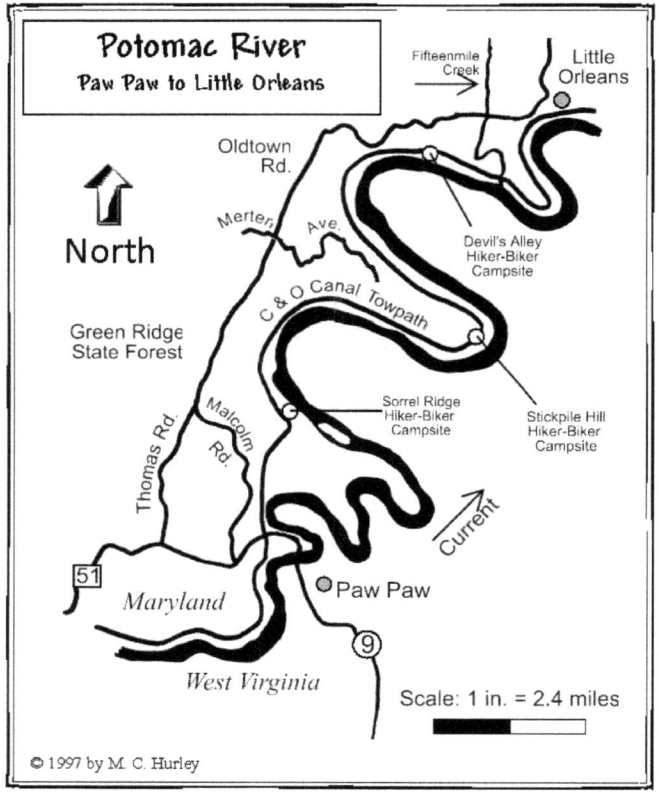

At the start of this trip, you will need to leave a car outside the national park campground at Little Orleans. Neither my computer mapping-program nor the one I accessed on the Internet was able to show any street-level detail for Little Orleans, so make note of these hard-won directions: Take the exit for Little Orleans Road off of Interstate 68, about eighteen miles west of Hancock, Maryland. Heading south on Little Orleans Road, follow the signs for the canal and a private campground. Just before Little Orleans Road makes a sharp right turn to become Oldtown Road, the tavern at Little Orleans appears to the left. Turn left here, continue down the hill past the tavern, and you will come to the Little Orleans Campground along the C & O Canal. There are parking spaces at the gate across the tow path, just outside the campground. It is a short walk from this parking area to the boat-launching area on the river. (The public campground at Little Orleans was not particularly inviting, and I would not advise camping there unless you arrive late and need to spend the night.)

The drive from Little Orleans to Paw Paw takes about 25 minutes via Oldtown Road. Shuttle service can also be arranged in advance though Pathfinders, a canoe livery at 125 West Main in Hancock.

The "official" campsites along this section of the river are not canoeing sites at all but rather "hiker-biker" sites established beside the tow path of the C & O Canal National Historic Park. Millions have hiked some portion of the tow path that stretches 185 miles from Cumberland, Maryland to the mouth of Rock Creek in Georgetown. The canal roughly parallels the Potomac River. Campsites adjacent to the tow path are available on a first-come first-served basis to canoeists willing to portage their boats and gear up the banks of the river and a short distance through the woods. There are three such sites along this section. We found, however, that there were many boaters camped on small islands in the river. We had initially planned to camp at the Sorrel Ridge site (see map), but because I did not appreciate how far back from the river the canal campsites are set, we wound up overshooting the Sorrel Ridge site and finding a lovely gravel bar all to ourselves.

If you choose to camp at Sorrel Ridge, note that its location is marked by the ruins of a concrete-block house visible up on the left bank through the trees. However, there are no official markers visible from the river to signal the location of any canal campsites.

The river conditions on this section of the Potomac should not tax the ability of the beginner at normal water levels. At the time the photographs shown with this story were taken, the river at the Paw Paw gauge was 3.62. In his guidebook, *Maryland and Delaware Canoe Trails* (Silver Spring, MD: The Seneca Press, 1979-1993), Ed Gertler notes that a reading of 3.3 at the Paw Paw gauge represents the minimum runnable level. At 3.62 we had to do only a minor amount of dragging. We encountered several ledges of the kind shown in the lower-right photo on this page.

The fishing even in the heat of summer was very good. Pan-size smallmouth bass were in abundance. A number of john-boat fishermen were using live bait, but the lure of choice as always was a Beetlespin cast in moving water below riffles and ledges as well as the deep pools. The preponderance of railroad bridges also made for good fishing around the pilings.

An interesting bit of history attached to the canal and the river is a letter written by Justice William O. Douglas to The Washington Post in 1954. Responding to an editorial proposing to convert the tow path to a scenic motor-parkway, he challenged the writer to hike the tow path with him and discover the surrounding beauty. The Post responded in an editorial entitled "We Accept," stating "we should not want it to be supposed that we are insensitive to the call of a warbler, the blush of buds in late winter, the crunch of autumn leaves under hiking boots, or the drip of water from canoe paddles." The hike took place over eight days in March of that year, after which the Post came out in support of saving the tow path. In 1971, President Nixon established the 20,000 acre C & O Canal National Historic Park, which was dedicated in 1977 to Justice Douglas. The park stretches along the left bank for most of the section between Paw Paw and Little Orleans.

If you choose to camp on gravel bars instead of along the tow path, the island where we camped is about one half-mile below the take-out for the Sorrel Ridge site. There is also a large island shown on the map just above Sorrel Ridge where we saw a number of tenters who had apparently boated in. If you prefer to camp for two nights, there is another nice island against the left bank about 300 yards upstream from the take-out at Little Orleans. Go left of this island and you'll come to a pleasant chute of water at the other end, where a point of land makes a small but attractive tent site.

The luck of the Irish seems often to influence our weather on these river trips with the boys, and as we are wont to do on such cloudless evenings, we pitched our tent along a riffles. There Kip and Bennett were drawn by the sound of running water to the swimming, rock-skipping, and lizard hunts that make for rare entertainment. This evening, however, as the stars began slowly bursting out across the cloudless June sky, the fates promised something out of the ordinary.

Now, I need to preface this story by stating that my son managed long ago to deflate any air of expertise that had come to me from thirty years of hard effort at the sport of fishing. There is something in the haphazard, unpracticed inefficiency of his technique that fish find irresistible. As best I have been able to divine through hours of careful study, the key features of his technique are two: First, it is important to cast your lure with utter disregard for the location where self-important "experts" assure you the fish are hiding. Secondly, once you have made your cast and the first few cranks of the reel, you must periodically be distracted to interrupt your retrieve for some reason—reaching for a passing butterfly or attending to a sudden itch are two familiar examples. On those occasions when this method does not result in a hopeless snag, it seems to impart a confused and frantic demeanor to the lure beneath the surface that far outperforms more conventional methods. And on this summer evening on the Potomac, Kip proved beyond all question his mastery of the hoodoo retrieve.

I didn't bother to tell Kip that he wouldn't catch any fish in the two-foot deep riffles filled with grass near our campsite. I was too busy attending the cleanup from dinner around the campfire in the waning hours of daylight when he told me that he was going to make a few casts. Of course I thought he'd probably get snagged in that part of the river, and I would have told him that it was too shallow for anything but baitfish, but it was good enough to keep him occupied while I was busy with the dishes. Not much time passed thereafter before the whooping and hollering caught my attention. I looked over and there was Kip, ankle-deep in the riffles, unable to make any progress shoreward against the weight of the fish. It was a smallmouth bass weighing between 3 and 4 pounds—larger and longer than any smallmouth I have ever caught in many more years of trying. He needed two hands to hold it and could barely keep it aloft long enough for me to take a picture.

I haven't given up hope that Kip's dad might one day be able to catch the really big ones. No doubt it is a simple matter of remembering how to think like a child—to worry less and leave more room for serendipity in one's life. Ah, but I am fortunate to have a willing teacher. I am learning to reach for butterflies at the critical time and hope soon to have my own hoodoo together.

Broad River

Rt. 108 Bridge to Hwy. 221A Bridge

On Labor Day weekend in 1997, two families set off in search of cool, flowing water for swimming and shaded places in the woods for summer's last stand. Among the gentle foothills west of Charlotte, close to the South Carolina border, we found just such a mixture hidden within the Broad River Greenway.

What protection the "greenway" designation affords this pleasant stream I am not sure. The term first appeared to me from a tourism poster of two canoes on the river that was tacked to the wall of a nearby hamburger stand. But green it surely is, as forests border the river for nearly the entire 24-mile length we paddled west of Cliffside, North Carolina.

The Broad River is perhaps better known for the section that flows just above and into South Carolina, as featured in Bob Benner's book, *Carolina Whitewater* (Birmingham, Alabama: Menasha Ridge Press, 1981, 1987). He writes in an introduction to the area that the river is popular with scout troops looking for canoe camping on long trips of as much as fifty miles. The only section on which he specifically notes the availability of

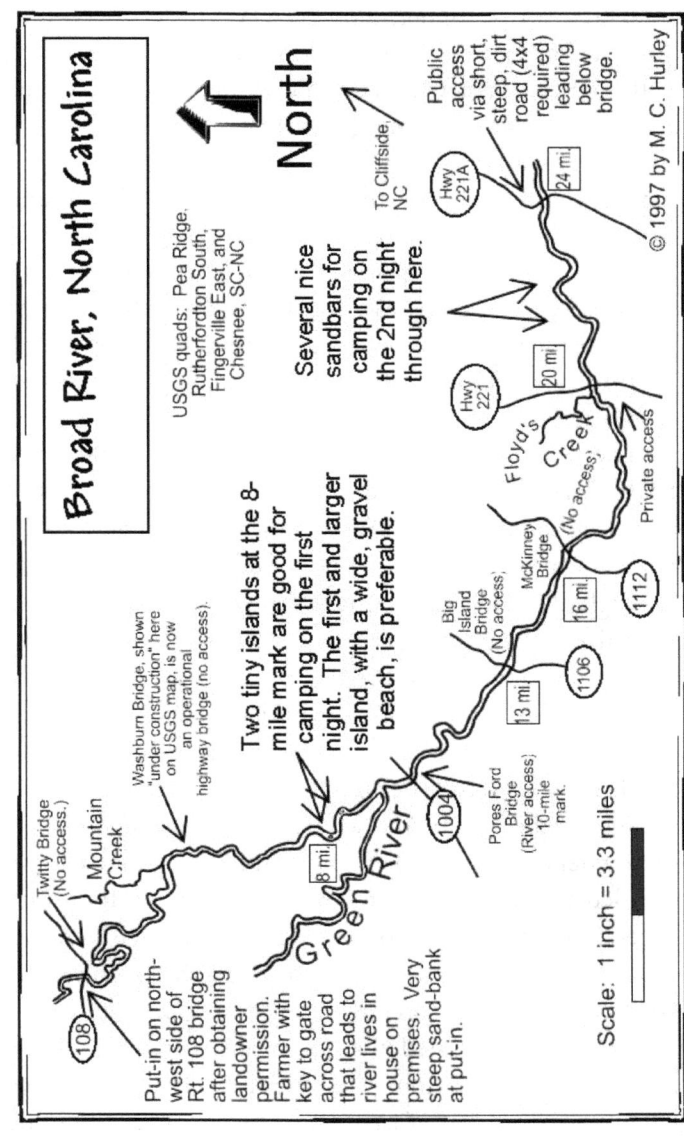

sandbars for camping, however, is an eighteen-mile stretch near Gaffney, South Carolina. As I was traveling with novice paddlers and several young children, I took to heart Benner's warnings about two hundred yards' worth of "shoals" that he advises should be approached "rather cautiously," current behind a dam that might catch a canoe not hugging the bank and carry it over the top, and a 700-yard portage around the dam in this section. We opted instead for a stretch farther upriver where the USGS map revealed at least one good island, no portages, and nothing more threatening than a two-foot ledge.

The section we ran begins at the North Carolina 108 bridge west of Rutherfordton. For the first two miles of this section, the Broad River is a contradiction of its name, winding beneath low overhanging trees and through tight deadfalls. Importantly, though, this is a river that remains navigable in almost any dry spell—and we'd had a long one before this trip.

The put-in at the NC 108 bridge happens to be on private land, which was not noted in the guidebook and produced some alarm upon our arrival. A local family was fishing on the bank when we arrived and assured us that the owners would allow us to put in if we wished, but we decided to look further for public access. We found no access on either side of the "Twitty Bridge" shown downriver on the map. A detour to find a put-in on the adjoining Green River, which flows into the Broad farther down, revealed that river much too low to be navigable. On returning to the NC 108 bridge we encountered a party of kayakers arriving to use the same put-in. Having been instructed by the fishing party to check at the farmhouse nearby, we found a gentleman there who cheerfully welcomed us. He produced a key and walked down to the cow gate to let us drive our vehicles right to the bank. Anyone who wishes to do the same and requests permission will likely be met with the same courtesy.

A cliff of soft, white sand has been trucked in to stabilize the river bank at the put-in. While the gradient is nearly 45-degrees, our feet sank up to our ankles in the sand, giving us steady footing on the descent. We offloaded the vehicles on level ground right above the bank, drove them outside the farmer's gate when we were through, and parked them beside his dirt driveway for the weekend.

Getting underway, we expected the river to be much slower and more predictable than, happily, it was. While in many places it has the look and feel of a sluggish, southern stream, around the next bend an exciting chute or ledge will betray its mountain heritage. None of the riffles should be especially challenging to the average J-stroker, although the two mothers on our trip showed a curious penchant for descending them backwards and sideways. By the second day, however, they were zipping along front-first and in good form.

Within a couple of miles of the put-in you will encounter a huge deadfall that will require a lift-over at almost any water level. This presents a simple task of pulling the canoes up on the bank, unloading each boat, lifting it over the log, stationing a paddler on the other side of the log, and handing gear over into the waiting canoe. With two boats this lift-over added about a half-hour to our itinerary.

Leaving the put-in at about eleven o'clock in the morning, and stopping for about an hour-and-a-half to rest, eat, and complete the one lift-over along the way, we arrived at our first camp on the sandbar shown in the photo at left between four and five o'clock in the afternoon. This sandbar is adjacent to the first of two tiny islands shown on the "Rutherfordton South, NC" USGS quadrant. The islands are about a half-mile apart.

It is important to note that a small sandbar which is not marked on the map appears shortly before the first island. This sandbar—which we were tempted to mistake for the first island—is low and weedy, has a very narrow beach, and is not ideally suited for camping. What distinguishes the first island from this sandbar is a well-defined elevation in the middle of the island that corresponds to the contour line drawn on the island on the map. For the Rutherfordton USGS quadrangle, the contour interval (given in the map legend) is twenty feet. The one contour interval drawn on the first island on the map tells you to look for an island with an elevation of roughly twenty feet above the river. (There is no elevation line drawn on the second island on the map.) Keep going until you see an island with that topography, and you will find our first camp.

The first island has a high, cleared area at the upstream end, but at normal water levels with no threat of heavy rain, the better spot for camping is on the sandbar to the north of the island. The main channel of the river bends right around this island and winds through some beautiful overhanging trees beside a pool at the downstream end. The children donned life-jackets and floated the current through this pool, walking back along the sandbar dozens of times to float it again.

The land above the sandbar is pasture, and this section of the river is accessible by a dirt road shown on the map. The tire marks on the sand showed it to be recently used by dirt bikes or ATVs coming in over this road.

The scenery along the river is pleasing to see in this age where so much of the natural beauty along southern waterways is giving way to new homes and golf courses. While some parts of the river are bordered by pasture, in all but a few spots a thick buffer of trees has wisely been preserved both to fend off erosion and maintain a feeling of wilderness. We saw no residential development to speak of along this section of the river. The several bridges were generally the only evidence of human habitation. Firewood is ample.

On the second day, we paddled for almost the entire day beside a thickly forested shoreline without seeing a single island or sandbar for camping. I had almost given up hope when we spotted a beautiful, shaded spot hidden back on tiny Floyd's Creek, just a few yards above its confluence with the Broad near the 20-mile bridge. Had we gone one or two miles farther, we would have found two nice, large sandbars on the north shore that we passed the next day and which I would recommend for the second night's camp.

A word of caution to drivers at the take-out: The short gravel road leading beneath the Rt. 221-A bridge is extremely steep, and the soft dirt requires four-wheel drive. Perhaps that's why we found this section of the river such a lonely, special place. With a little planning, your buddy's Jeep, and a minimum of sweat and effort, you can surely find the same.

Lake Opeongo

Algonquin Provincial Park

When one is first initiated into the culture of North Woods voyaging, the North Maine Woods, the Adirondacks of New York, and the Boundary Waters Canoe Area Wilderness of Minnesota loom large on the roster of classic destinations—and rightly so. As the initiation proceeds, however, one soon discovers that our northern neighbors in Canada are literally awash in spectacular, wilderness lakes and rivers with canoe-only areas and a user-permit system to preserve their wilderness character. One such area is Algonquin Provincial Park, in Southeastern Ontario. Situated only three hours by car from Toronto, its proximity to the Northeastern United States has made this a perennial favorite of Yankees who come here by the thousands each year seeking an authentic, Canadian-wilderness experience.

For the uninitiated American, planning a trip in Algonquin Park is not as easy as one would hope. There is no toll-free number—or any number, for that matter—

MICHAEL HURLEY

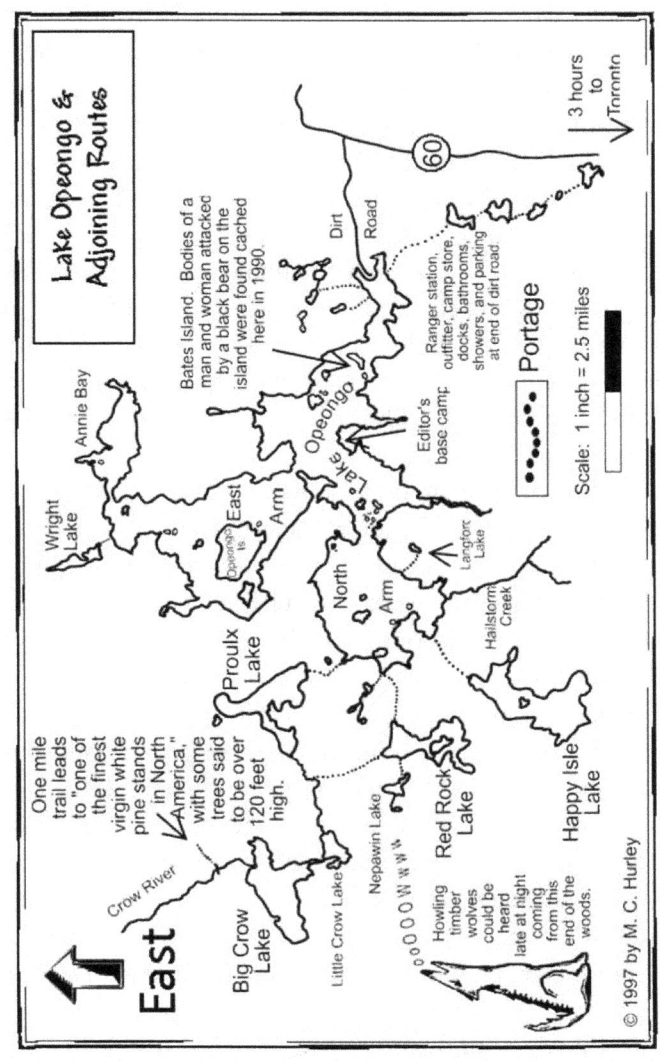

to call to request published, official information. Inquirers must first send a letter to a nonprofit group, "Friends of Algonquin Park" to request the publication list from which mail orders can be made. Their address is P. O. Box 248, Whitney, Ontario KOJ 2MO.

The "Canoe Routes" map which I obtained from the Friends contains a thorough explanation of park regulations, procedure for obtaining camping permits once one has picked a route, the history of the park, and even a primer on canoe camping. The map contains no elevation data but is the only map that someone who plans to follow any of the several, major canoe-routes is likely to need.

The many portage trails shown on the map for some of the more popular routes make it apparent that it is impossible to plan an itinerary of any distance without multiple carries. Because our group consisted of two men traveling in two canoes with two seven-year-old boys who are not yet capable of carrying packs across a portage, we looked for a base-camp that would afford us the option of day trips (sans much of our gear) to outlying lakes and rivers. Lake Opeongo filled the bill nicely.

Although it is situated in a "nature reserve" area just outside the designated "wilderness" zone of the park and may be traveled by motorboats of unlimited horsepower, Lake Opeongo is completely free of residential development. The forested shoreline of Opeongo stands in contrast to other area lakes, such as the popular Canoe Lake, on which motors of more than 20 horsepower are banned but where I am informed there is a good deal of cottage development. Being the largest lake in the park, Opeongo's sheer size keeps the presence of motorboats from being an intrusion. The motored craft we saw were generally run by outfitters taking parties of canoeists up to the North Arm or by the occasional lake-trout fisherman. In the peak of the summer season we saw no water-skiers or "personal watercraft" to clash with the area's wild appearance.

We arrived at the ranger station at Lake Opeongo early on a morning in July, obtained the permit that we had reserved in advance by telephone, and purchased some fresh supplies at the camp store on the premises. This store offers a fine selection of frozen beef steaks individually vacuum-sealed in plastic as well as eggs, milk, juice, jerky, cheese, and a complete selection of freeze-dried meals and trail food. The store also sold fishing worms and tackle along with a wide variety of camping equipment and souvenirs. It is operated by Algonquin Outfitters out of Dwight, Ontario. Canoes and complete trip-outfitting services are available on site. This group also runs motorboat shuttles to the North and East Arm for time-pressed (or just plain lazy) trippers who don't want to face the waves and wind often present on Lake Opeongo.

After loading up and leaving our Jeep in the long-term parking area up the hill from the lake, we shoved off into the clear water of Opeongo and began working our way up the narrow channel leading from the put-in to the main portion of the South Arm. The term "Opeongo" derives from the Indian words for "sandy at the narrows" and is one of the few remaining Indian names for lakes in the park. We encountered a sandy shoal, in fact, at the western end of Bates Island—a beautiful spot for swimming with a picturesque campsite in the trees atop its western point. The island has five campsites in all. As with many islands on the lake, the forest floor had been picked clean of all usable firewood. We decided to press on to a site, shown on the map, that is closer to the North and East Arms. From here, we were able to fish Opeongo to our hearts' content, leave a base camp set up all week, and travel with a light pack in one canoe on day trips to several outlying lakes. The plan worked perfectly for a party with small children, affording us time to take in roughly the same territory of a longer trip without the drudgery of tripling every portage.

We checked out a number of campsites around Lake Opeongo during our week, there, and agreed that the camp we selected was the best among them. Its proximity to the North and East Arms allowed us fairly quick access to and from the lee shores of islands on those days (most of the time) when the waves were whipped up by the northeast wind. From this base, we explored the North Arm across to Happy Isle Lake, Hailstorm Creek, Langford Lake, the East Arm and Wright Lake. The wind kept us in camp on only one full day, which we happily occupied with firewood-chopping and mussel-diving contests.

Another reason for choosing Lake Opeongo as a base camp is that, according to the booklet "Fishing in Algonquin Park" published by the Ontario Ministry of Natural Resources, it is one of relatively few lakes with a population of smallmouth bass. A great number of lakes in the park are populated by lake and brook trout, but fewer lakes contain bass and a very, very few are reported to contain any pike or walleye. This condition is attributed to the geologic history of the region. Glaciers a mile-and-a-half thick melted back from what is now Algonquin Park only 11,000 years ago, and the waters left by the melting glaciers were too cold to support warmer-water fish like bass, pike, and walleye. When the area eventually warmed up enough to support these species, the flow of glacier-fed streams leading to many lakes had slackened so as to become impassable to migrating fish. Smallmouth bass were artificially introduced for sport fishing in Opeongo and other lakes back around the turn of the century. We found the Ontario Ministry guide to be somewhat inaccurate as to the range and number of bass in the area, but because trout are so much more difficult to catch deep in lakes in the summer without electronic fish-finders, lead-core line, and heavy tackle, camping on Lake Opeongo assured us that we would at least have something to fish for.

Aside from the abundance of firewood in the surrounding woods, our base camp was well chosen for the shape and configuration of the point of land on which it sits. Anyone seeking to use this same site can easily reach it by reference to its location on the map, above, and the distinct appearance of the trees on an outcropping of rock. This point makes for something of a front porch from which one can survey the many canoeing parties that pass close by in the summer, headed for the North Arm and all other points north in the interior of the park. It also is one of the very few if not the only campsite on this side of the lake which offers a gradually sloping, sandy bottom. This entrance, on the north side of the point, is useful for swimming, hunting mussels, and loading or off-loading canoes.

Dawn came quietly on the third day, and we rose early

to take advantage of calm water for the crossing to the North Arm and Happy Isle Lake. A wide, sandy beach and wooden pier sit at the head of the portage to Happy Isle. The portage is about 1.25 miles long and mostly level. Timber braces have been erected between trees as rest stops along the trail. These allow you to remove the weight of the canoe from your shoulders while keeping the canoe inverted.

The first thing we noticed at Happy Isle Lake is the exceptional clarity and turquoise color of the water, reminiscent of a Caribbean beach. Having read in our handy guide that Happy Isle is the home of a number of cheerful brook trout (but no bass), we rigged up with earthworms trailing a foot behind small gold spinners and attempted to troll in fifteen to thirty feet of water. The wind had returned by the time we put in, so trolling was difficult. No trout appeared, but while trolling we caught two nice smallmouth bass.

Returning across the portage to Lake Opeongo we found the lake again in a frothy state. We managed nervously to surf our way home, but herein lies an important consideration for anyone making day trips from a base camp: When traveling for the day from a lake like Opeongo, you may find that wind and waves unexpectedly preclude your return crossing after you have traveled to some far-flung pond. In that case, if you have failed to pack the essentials for a chilly night in the woods—matches, rain gear, tarp, rope, bedroll, water, axe, saw, and a meal—you may have a rough go of it. Take along one large pack with these items. You need not carry it with you over a lengthy portage—just hang it from a tree at the take-out. If you find the lake impassable due to high waves upon your return, you'll have the gear you need to stay put rather than risk a dangerous crossing.

On the fourth day we struck out in a different direction, to the East Arm. While the bass fishing on Lake Opeongo thus far had been only so-so, here it picked up in earnest. Fishing with large Rapala floating minnows in five to fifteen feet of water in the morning, we hooked many fat fish and landed two of them. We had hoped for a fish dinner and tied our catch to a bush along shore, but we returned at the end of the day to find that the fish had snapped the frayed, plastic stringer and freed themselves. As it turned out we had more than enough mussels to eat, anyway.

At the far eastern end of the East Arm is a wide, flat area of thinned, pine forest and several nice tent-sites. The short portage-trail to Wright Lake begins here, just beyond a white, stone pyramid (part of the remains of a cabin) that is visible from several hundred yards out in the lake. Don't land at the east end of Lake Opeongo in this vicinity and head down the first trail you see, assuming it leads to Wright Lake. You might find yourself on the five-mile cart trail to Dickson Lake by mistake. Both portages are marked by signs at the trail heads.

Wright Lake is a quiet pond sheltered by a thick rim of fir trees. Here we felt confident to let young Kip and Bennett take a turn in the canoe by themselves. With Kip as his guide to steer, no sooner had Bennett wet a line than he had a flopping bass of nearly two pounds. Watching both boys shouting orders, with Kip trying to maneuver the canoe and Bennett hoisting the heavy fish first to one side of the boat and then the other, was a Keystone Cops moment that will be long remembered.

On the fifth day we resolved to venture into lonely Hailstorm Creek in search of the many moose reported to feed there every morning and evening. We were too early in the afternoon for moose, but we paddled anyway into the creek's twists and turns through flooded timber and eel grass for a mile or two of desolate beauty, far from the usual canoe routes. On our return we decided to search the banks of Opeongo for the head of the portage to Langford Lake.

Though it is marked as a "cart trail" on the map—meaning a path wider and more level than the typical portage—the portage to Langford Lake is in fact narrow and strewn with rocks and trees. We even sent one man back to make sure we hadn't taken a deer trail by mistake. Michael and his son Bennett got ahead of us on the trail, but it wasn't long before Kip and I met them coming back across the portage in the opposite direction at a determined pace. Asking whether they had already made it to the lake, I got one of those signals from Michael that my wife gives when the question is one I clearly should have known better than to ask. It turned out that Bennett had stumbled upon a rather large pile of fresh poop in the trail up ahead, left there by an animal that clearly was a member of the big-eater's club. With the recent bear attacks in mind, Michael had decided to beat a hasty retreat to the canoes. I paused and elected instead to apply a principle which I hold in ready reserve for just such situations in life: Act like you know what you're doing, and the world will follow. I examined the suspicious doo-doo carefully. After a suitable interval, I confidently remarked that the strands of vegetation in this dung ("not unlike horse manure") revealed it was produced by a grass-eating animal—a moose. Being "pretty sure" about such things is like diving in when you're pretty sure you can swim, but I was doggoned if we were going to walk all that way without seeing this lake. The scene as we marched on recalled Dorothy, the tin man, and the cowardly lion in the haunted forest. Finally, after crossing a waist-deep bog, we sloshed into the shallows of Langford Lake. There, spread before our eyes, was the stuff of a voyageur's dream—untouched, uninhabited, and stunningly pretty. The journey was a metaphor for our entire trip: A little effort and gumption had brought us to a land of wonders that was no place like home.

Sequatchie River
Tennessee River Valley

Taft Highway to Condra Switch Road

There is a soft spot in my heart for rural, Tennessee streams. In the inaugural issue of this journal in 1995, I told the story of my Great Uncle Jeff, the trapper, farmer, and storyteller who, this year, celebrated his ninety-seventh birthday on the Tennessee farm where he was born. The summers I spent on that farm often found me knee deep in tiny creeks like Shoal and Richland—little ribbons of shade meandering through cow pastures and past churchyards. The deeper holes in summer were pretty good bets for smallmouth and rock bass when they weren't otherwise occupied with preachers baptizing the faithful.

On our way back to North Carolina after a reunion with Uncle Jeff and the family last Thanksgiving, my son Kip and I stopped off to cruise and camp the Sequatchie, a river in the foothills of Middle Tennessee that calls to mind the little farm streams I knew in Giles County. It is well worth the time of anyone who happens to be in this part of the country.

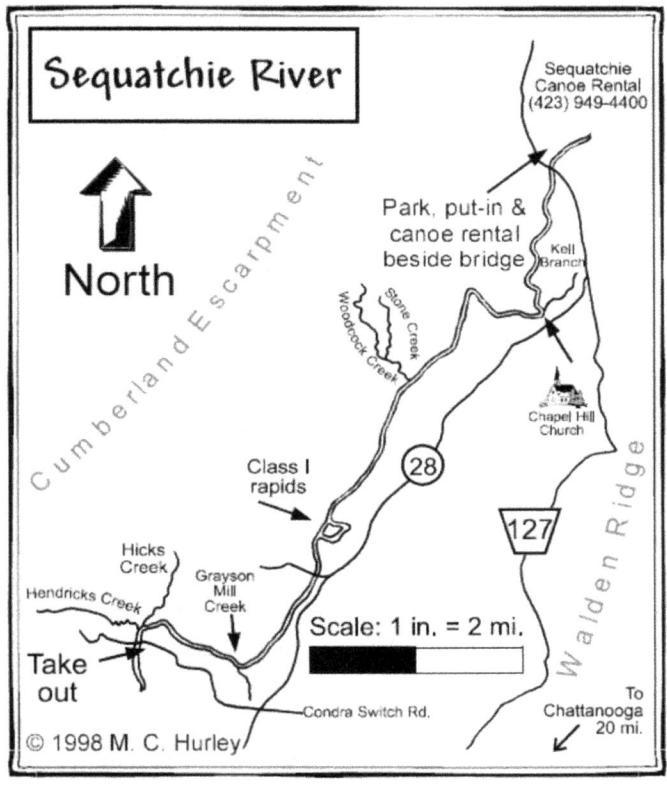

As noted in Holly Sherwin's helpful reference, *Canoeing in Tennessee* (Franklin, Tenn: Cool Springs Press, 1996), the Sequatchie Valley through which the river flows is a geologically rare formation between parallel faults, known as a rift valley—one of only two in the world. The ridges must produce an updraft, as the area is considered the hang-glider capital of the country. Varying margins of maple, oak and bottomland hardwoods protect much of the riverbank, but the valley beyond spreads out in pasture. The river flows at 700 feet above sea level, and the ridges in the distance rise to elevations of 2,000 feet.

The section we paddled and camped runs for nine miles between Highway 127 (William Howard Taft Highway) and Condra Switch Road, about 20 miles north of Chattanooga and twelve miles north of famous Signal Mountain. With the unfortunate exception of one improbable Swiss chalet sighted shortly after the put-in, there is currently no residential development along this part of the river. Because of the high banks, the pasture lands just beyond the woods at the river's edge are often not visible to the paddler, lending a feeling of wilderness to much of the trip

This is a clear, cold and seemingly clean river that flows at a steady, gentle pace of one knot in most spots. Sparse, class-I riffles should pose no challenge to the novice. Sandbars dry enough for camping are available but not in abundance. The entire trip takes three hours, which can be evenly divided for overnight camping.

At the put-in, the river is some twenty-yards across and widens only slightly throughout the trip. The clearly-visible bottom is rock and sand. The river is subject to flash flooding, as indicated by the high-water line and accompanying erosion some ten feet up on the bank in areas. Downed wood carried by floodwater is readily available for campfires.

In the first half-mile, strainers are encountered that are easily avoided. At 1.4 miles, lovely Chapel Hill Church is visible across the pasture above the left bank. Here, a small creek comes in on the left and the river turns right and widens into a deep hole. Rock ledges along the bank make this an ideal spot for swimming. At mile two, where a cow pasture ends on the right, the banks become more wooded and steep. There are a few areas suitable for camping below the high-water mark for the next half-mile or so in this section, depending on your tolerance for tight spaces. You will see many sections where flood waters have created a ledge of level ground below the high-water mark. We camped at a fairly level and wide spot in here, a few hundred yards upstream of a power line that crosses the river.

Once past our campsite on the following morning, after the steep woods leveled off again, we admired a beautiful stand of mature pine trees, some 100-feet tall, stretching for a mile or so along the river about 100 yards back from the left bank. At this point the river becomes a long, deep and slow pool. The first bridge since the put-in shortly comes into view, here, at mile four. It is possible to take out at this point if you wish. A narrow set of stone steps can be seen leading up the left bank on the upstream side of the bridge into a dirt parking lot.

A little more than a mile below the four-mile bridge, one comes to the first set of honest-to-goodness riffles next to where the river appears to detour around an island (see map, above). We kept to river-right. The riffles in this section were easily run without need of much attention. This was also the best mid-river camping spot, as there is a large sandbar where the riffles end. During summertime, children would find this section of the river a welcome place to cool off.

The fishing was slow when we went in the cold and drear of late fall, but this looked like the "fishiest" water of the trip. There are some rather large catfish in these Tennessee creeks in addition to the usual fare of bass and bream, and anyone who has the time and patience to go after them with a good stink or blood bait can catch a fish or two any time of year.

In the fall season we found the river alive with squirrels, and I pined for a shotgun to bring us some Brunswick Stew. Consigned to watch, we encountered a healthy population of all manner of small game, including a magnificent fox, geese, and ducks of all stripes. Two paddlers coming down the river at night, as they passed our campfire, told of the many raccoons they had spotted prowling along the banks.

At mile six there is another bridge where there again is access to a road. Between the point where Grayson Mill Creek comes in at mile seven and the take-out bridge, there are several good sandbars for camping—many of which we would have preferred to the camp I chose the night before. But the need for such lessons is why Uncle Jeff spun his stories by the woodstove; the telling of them is why Hurley has a journal; and the reading of them is why you, dear friend, have a fine trip ahead of you on the Sequatchie.

BATSTO RIVER

NEW JERSEY PINE BARRENS

On a black, winter night more than a century ago, on a rutted and treacherous road driven with rain, lightning and gales, legend tells of a stagecoach party that hurtled blindly through these woods. They were headed for Quaker Bridge over the Batsto River, unaware that the bridge had been washed out by the storm. No canoeists or weekend pleasure-seekers plied these pines then, mind you.

The barrens were an impenetrable and foreboding realm of mystery, a forlorn and nearly trackless thicket. They were filled with secrets and said to be guarded by men—desperate men—who aimed to keep them. It was a good place to get behind you in a hurry, and that was the intention of these uneasy travelers that night. As the story goes, just before the stagecoach reached the precipice of the rain-swollen river, a gleaming, white stag shot from the woods into their path. Lightning flashed around them and seemed to linger on the animal, which suddenly vanished. The startled driver veered into a ditch, only to realize moments later that the phantom stag's appearance had saved them from certain death.

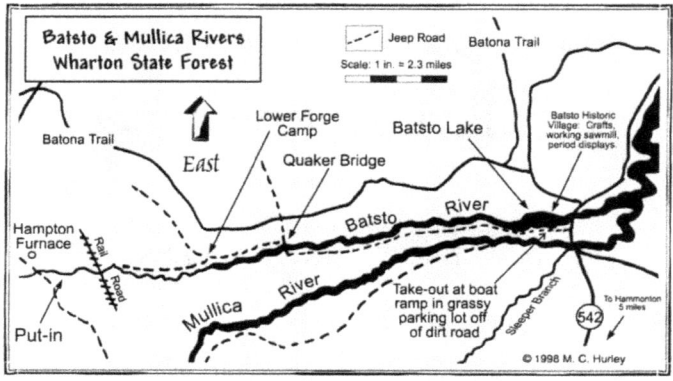

As we began our trip down the Batsto in the fall of 1997, we headed on a course that would take us not over but under the now repaired Quaker Bridge. The weather and the mood gave nothing to fear, but I warn you, friend: In these woods the vapors of those mysteries remain. Some still tell the story of a strange beast that was born in this area in 1735 to the unfortunate Mrs. Leeds, who in a moment of guile during the expectancy of her thirteenth child had wished the devil upon him. A devil he turned out to be. He is said to have leapt from the womb fully grown and flown to these woods, from whence he has made mischief to our very day. New Jersey historians record in all sobriety that, in the early 1800's, Commodore Stephen Decatur of the U.S. Navy shot the Jersey Devil clean through with a cannonball, but, apparently unaffected by the gaping hole, the beast "flew casually away." The last sighting on record occurred in 1987.

We grown men and our seven-year-old sons of course had no time for such nonsense as we shoved our canoes into the thin, tea-colored headwaters of the Batsto under an azure, fall sky. Still, there were the pines—one upon another fading before us into a dense curtain that the river bade us open, without revealing what lay hidden, there. The woods keeps its secrets well.

I have come to expect wilderness in unlikely places in the northeast, and this is one of them. Only two hours from Manhattan, the Pine Barrens has a familiar look. The pine ridges and its sandy floors that pass quietly underfoot call quickly to mind the idylls of American camp life. It is one of the premier canoe-cruising venues of the Atlantic seaboard.

In his invaluable reference, *Canoeing the Jersey Pine Barrens* (Old Saybrook, CT: Globe Pequot Press, 1978-1994), Robert Parnes provides a surprisingly thorough summary of the geologic and social history of the region. A thick, top layer of sand throughout the land was discovered early on to be too poor for farming, as it failed to trap sufficient nutrients for most crops—hence the name "barrens." This sandy layer percolates into an enormous underground reservoir known as the Kirkwood-Cahansey Aquifer, which contains some seventeen trillion gallons of water. The woods above it are shot through with more than a dozen canoeable rivers and streams.

While not well-suited to most food crops, the barrens produced vast stands of pitch pine that for decades provided valuable commodities in lumber and charcoal production. The discovery of iron ore in the region led to the early prevalence of ironworks such as Hampton Furnace, the ruins of which remain visible at the start of the trip down the Batsto. Cranberries and blueberries, which are among the few crops that thrive in acidic soil, grow naturally along the rivers of the barrens and in cultivated fields, but we found none for the picking on the Batsto when we made our trip in early October. The lack of arable land for non-acidic crops best explains the barrens' escape from the urban sprawl that characterizes the rest of the immediate region.

The Batsto River begins and ends its course entirely within New Jersey's Wharton State Forest. Robert Parnes writes that the Batsto "probably has more variety than any other river in the Pine Barrens." Due to the lack of road access along most of its length, it is popular among wilderness seekers. Solitude is less easy to find here; but the camaraderie of canoeists has its own rewards.

After arriving in Hammonton the night before, we drove north on Route 206 just past the Atsion Lake Recreation Area to a small cinder-block ranger station on the right side of the road. The office here opens at 8:30 a.m. on weekends for sale of campsite permits. It is best to call the office some weeks in advance to request a permit application by mail. The form needed is entitled "Application for Overnight Group Reservation," but the seven-person minimum party-size listed on the form does not apply to the one canoe-in site, named "Lower Forge," on the Batsto. The ranger's policy at the time was to reserve up to half of the fifty-person capacity of Lower Forge by mail and save the rest for same-day, walk-in permit requests at the ranger station. I understand that quite a line forms outside the station in the morning on summer weekends.

The ranger station is worth a little of your time to check out the interesting taxidermy displays of local fauna. It also has copies of the free state-park map, which is all that anyone planning to stick to the river should need for navigation.

Leaving the station, to reach the put-in you drive approximately a hundred yards farther on Route 206 to a dirt road on the right. This road has a number of large mud-filled ruts and holes that were no problem for the Jeep but very nearly swallowed a Mazda that ran them only by revving up to a series of punishing leaps.

Shortly before the dirt road crosses the Batsto near the ruins of Hampton Furnace, a large field appears on the left, and a small spur road leads thirty yards to the right. Take this spur to the river's edge to offload your boats and gear, then park your car in the field. Some warn of vandalism, here, but the rangers said that problems rarely occur. There is some tall grass in the adjoining field in which to hide a vehicle, provided it has the traction to get out. For those without four-wheel drive, an outfitter is the best way to avoid unplanned car-camping. Adams Canoe Rentals at 1005 Atsion Road in Vincentown offers shuttles to its rental customers as well as those bringing their own canoes.

Another much-loved stream in the Barrens that parallels the Batsto is the Mullica River. The Mullica is not navigable (or easily so) in extended periods of dry weather, while the Batsto is usually still a good choice at those times. Most people running the Batsto do not put in where we did, at Hampton Furnace. By starting there, one will encounter many narrow turns but also some of the prettiest and loneliest sections of the river. For those wishing an easier trip, a Jeep trail that leads through the woods just behind Lower Forge campsite meets the river at a put-in about one-mile farther downstream. The river even in the upper section is mostly clear of obstructions. Numerous stumps are encountered just below the surface, but these did no damage to our wood-canvas canoe. The forest closes in tightly in the upper reaches, giving a "deep woods" feel to the journey.

From our put-in, the one and only "must carry" we encountered is a tree, which we came to in the first hour. To get past it, we bushwhacked a trail over the right bank to carry our gear. Then, each man pulled his canoe alongside the sunken tree, stepped out on the trunk, and, while crouching on the tree, pulled the boat across hand-over-hand. A word of caution: There is a mud sink-hole among the palmettos on this carry that could immobilize a heavy man in all but the driest of weather. At 170 pounds I sank up to my butt and was very nearly in trouble. Carry your paddle with you on shore at all times for a brace.

Lower Forge campsite has no potable water. We drank and cooked with filtered river-water for the entire trip and had no trouble. Though clean, however, the river is naturally very acidic. There appeared to be no gamefish in the river proper. In fact, we did not even see a minnow. We carried our poles but had no luck until arriving at Batsto Lake, where we took a small pickerel on a Mepps spinner in the lilies and saw one fisherman land a nice largemouth bass on a crankbait.

A railroad trestle is the first and one of few signs of civilization encountered on the trip. There is a grassy spot on the right bank on the downstream side of the trestle that makes a nice landing at which to stop for lunch and explore the bridge. Be careful with children: There are wide gaps in between the rails on the bridge through which a child could easily fall.

As you get close to Lower Forge camp, the right shore begins to rise and fall in high, sand banks that call out "climb me" to seven-year-old boys. Had the weather been warm enough, they would also have answered the call of the Batsto's many, ideal swimming-holes. The water is clear, and the bottom in most spots is firm sand.

A few hundred yards before the Lower Forge camp, a false fork in the river leads off to the right. Stay left, and you will shortly see the sign on the river marking the landing for the camp on the left shore. The landing is wide and sandy and leads up a high bank to a cleared area in the woods.

Lower Forge has no fire rings or designated tent sites, but the entire area is well cleared. A thinned pine forest containing very little downed firewood recedes behind the campground. With a good saw and axe we found dead wood deep in the forest and had all we needed for a campfire, but anyone looking to pick up enough wood by hand to cook dinner will be disappointed.

There was a large beehive inside a tree at the far, downriver end of the campsite that should be easily recognizable by its cleft trunk. A local trail-riding group came in on horseback while we were there to post a temporary sign on the tree warning passersby. This also explained the prevalence of horse manure in the camp and the vocal disappointment of a fellow who discovered too late that he'd pitched his tent in one pony's favorite spot.

The rules applicable to wilderness campsites were followed by campers at Lower Forge, for the most part. Open campfires are prohibited before 6:00 p.m. No motor vehicles are allowed in the campsite, although you may see some on the Jeep trail behind Lower Forge on their way to the put-in upriver. Alcoholic beverages are prohibited, as are pets. Only six non family-members are allowed to camp together.

At Lower Forge Camp we met some members of the Philadelphia Canoe Club that had paddled upriver from Quaker Bridge to spend the night. After our small crew had eaten as much as we could of a prodigious dinner, I walked over to the neighboring camp fire and offered a pot of leftover "Canoe Stew." It was so named in the recipe first published in the Spring 1997 issue of this journal. The name "Canoe Stew" apparently betrayed me as the editor, and two subscribers stepped forward to introduce themselves. I was flabbergasted and honored to meet them both. As "goodnights" began to be heard around camp and the flames of our campfire flickered steadily down, slowly so did the eyelids of little Kip Hurley. He has his father's ability to sleep anywhere and, if need be, through the most conspicuous emergencies. Soon he was a lump on the floor of the tent. But contrary to habit, his wide-eyed cousin Bennett did not join him.

Bennett's father made gestures of encouragement toward the tent, but Bennett was unmoved. It soon was clear that Bennett sensed there were spirits in these woods. Lions and tigers, no—but who was to say not a Jersey Devil or a Phantom Stag? He calculated well enough that Kip would never wake to save him should the hideous beast show its face, and none could fault young Bennett for a strong instinct of self-preservation. Soon he prevailed upon his father to retire early, and they left me alone beside the fire.

The pines swayed in the night and breathed a long, deep "swwissh" with each passing gust. Darkness fell darker still, and I pulled my collar up against a chill that seemed suddenly about. The flames just barely did cast shadows on the curtain of pines at the edge of camp. As I stared at the shadows, I felt a compelling unease at what lay hidden, there. Yes, the woods keeps its secrets well. What would these pines tell us? What battles had been fought on this sand? What honor tested? What spirits remained? Slowly the flames flickered and fell down to ruby embers in the dust, and my eyes grew accustomed to the darkness. "Sww-iiii-ssshaahh" the pines sung impatiently, and the stars in the black-diamond sky seemed to flutter with the breeze.

Just then a great horned owl called and—from close in the darkness—came a rustle of leaves. The hairs on my neck stood up. I blinked and looked hard. Did something in the woods just move, I wondered, or was heat from the embers playing tricks on my eyes? Without thinking I rose and walked toward the black curtain of pines but slowed, and then—stopped. I stood beside the tent where Bennett lay sleeping. A smart boy that Bennett, I thought. A sensible boy, I said to myself. Let the pines keep their secrets. It was getting rather late, and high time I went to bed.

Roanoke River

Long Island to Brookneal

It is one of the unexpected perks of this journaling business to receive kind invitations from readers all over the country to come sample their favorite streams. For reasons of time, expense, and distance I cannot accept as often as I'd like; but on a crisp weekend last November I was pleased to join members of Virginia's oldest and largest canoeing club (or the oldest and largest members of Virginia's newest club—they couldn't recall which), on a rollicking run down a delightful, island-studded stream. Depending on which local you ask, it is known in this part of the Old Dominion as either the Staunton or Roanoke River.

The section we ran, between the towns of Long Island and Brookneal, is outlined in Ed Grove's dependable guide, *Classic Virginia Rivers* (Arlington, VA: Eddy Out Press, 1995). It is located in the south-central part of the state, just above the Carolina border, and bears the gently tumbling, rock-strewn character of all water making its way across the Piedmont. At normal water levels there are no dangerous or particularly difficult rapids. Even in the fast sections, there was usually a slower course to be taken beside the bank.

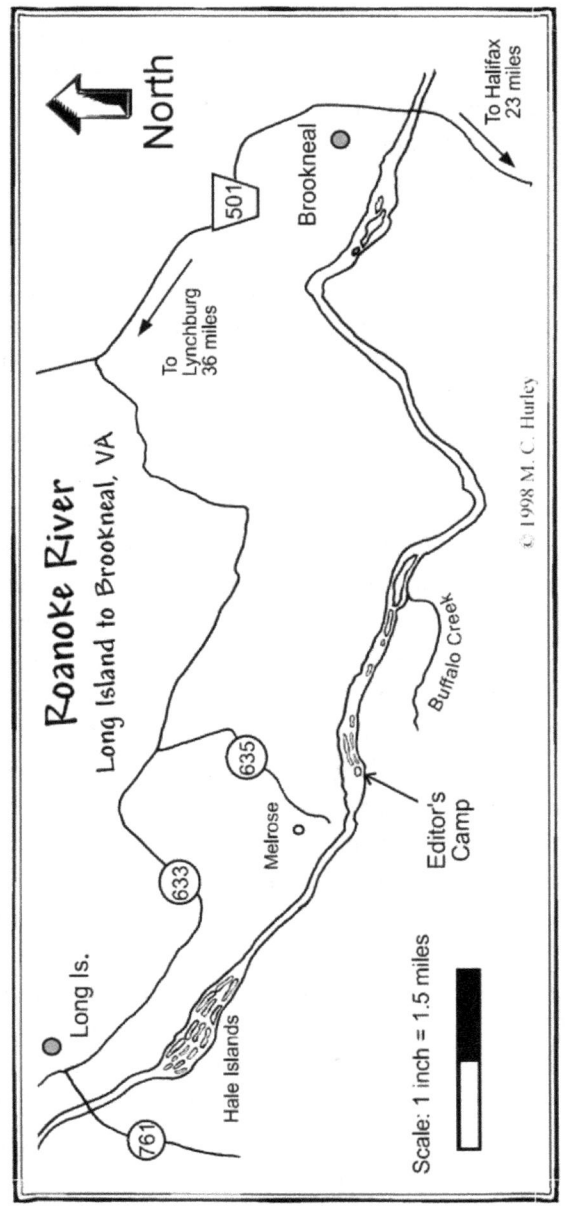

The dam-controlled water level is reportedly always dependable. In my wood-canvas Cheemaun I suffered no more than my usual share of scrapes, so you should expect to find enough water to float most boats and gear without damage in summer.

This trip has a near-wilderness feel for most of its length—including some beautiful, wooded islands and wide sandbars—marred only by a small park near the end of the trip, on the south shore, where the land has been deforested down to the bank. A working railroad that snakes behind the trees, high above much of the north shore, adds a little charm of its own. A few, distant houses are occasionally visible from the river.

The river begins this trip wide and flat, just beneath the Route 761 bridge leading into Long Island. The water here is a cloudy, light green with three-feet of visibility, and the current chugs at less than two knots. No sooner had we begun the trip than my brother-in-law Eric—who as a teenager pretended to listen to my fishing tips while he quietly caught most of the bass—quietly caught another: a two-pound largemouth and the bigger of only two, unexpected fish taken in the cold weather. This looks very much like a smallmouth stream and presumably is, but the fish population is also influenced by what spills through the dam upstream at Smith Mountain Lake.

A half mile from the put-in, one encounters the first of the Hale Islands, which are marked on the Long Island USGS 7.5 minute map, and the first rapids. This would be an excellent place to camp if you needed or were willing to stop early on the first day. There is an easy Class II drop on the right side of the islands, where there seemed to be more water and easier going than on the left. Class I riffles continue for most of the half-mile length of Hale Islands, then empty into a long pool. This section offers many good spots for swimming in the summer.

About two miles from the put-in one comes to a large, stone abutment on the right, a pile of rocks in the middle, and a pile of rocks and trees on the left that are the remains of a bridge. Deeper water is on the left. A short distance farther a wide, cleared area of thinned forest appears on the right bank, with picnic tables. This seems like a good tenting location, but the map shows it to be accessible by a dirt road and, therefore, it is not recommended.

Some houses appear well back from the left side of the river about three-and-a-half miles from the put-in, near where the town of Melrose is marked on the map. Note that the Long Island USGS quadrangle has not been revised since it was made from 1966 aerial photos, so it does not depict more recent development.

A railroad track comes close to the river, here, which now is about 150 yards across. A large rock garden and several more islands also appear. This is where we found a large island with a good campsite. There is plenty of driftwood for campfires, and the only drawback is that wide, flat tenting locations are few. To camp here, stay to the far right of the river as soon as you see the houses through the trees on the left bank at Melrose. Otherwise, you'll have to fight your way as we did back upriver through the left channel, which offers no suitable campsites.

Our afternoon and evening in camp were spent

experimenting with ways to keep a self-loading fire going in front of the lean-to, according to a concept suggested in somebody's copy of Canoe & Kayak. Wright Ellis, a high school English teacher from Richmond and editor of his canoe club newsletter, conceived the idea of positioning our campfire tripod irons like an artist's easel, with two legs spread out in front and leaning back, braced by the third leg.

We stacked evenly cut logs across the two facing tripod legs, with the bottom log sitting in the fire. The idea was that as the bottom log burned up, the next log would drop down by gravity—sort of like a drink-can dispenser. It didn't work as planned in this effort, but I succeeded on later trips to keep a fire going in front of the lean-to by this method for four hours or more. The trick is to use logs small enough to burn easily and round enough to roll down. Needless to say, never bed down when a large fire is still going in front of your lean-to or if there is any wind that might cause sparks to fly.

Efforts were also applied around the campfire at bread baking and stew, though we suffered a shortage of stewing vegetables through the editor's weak mathematics skills. A word must also be said for posterity about Wright Ellis' pernicious whiskey-cake, which felled us all in a vain search for the "cake" portion of the recipe. And finally, were reasons to prefer an open camp not already self-evident, we enjoyed not only the glow of the campfire from our beds but a live, late-night concert accompanied by a guitar packed along on the trip. There are benefits such as these to running rivers without portages.

The second day dawned amid the best intentions for

an early start, but pancakes and the unexpected warmth of the sunshine on our little island-home made dawdlers of us. Getting underway from our camp just below Melrose, some of us took the channel through the islands on the far right bank, which presented some rocky and narrow going in spots. The clearer channel leads to the left. In short order we passed several islands with sandy spots that were quite suitable for camping and a bit larger than our first choice. Take your pick. One of the nicest is a gravel bar at the upstream end of an island about one mile below Melrose, with plenty of firewood on hand. Another good spot is half a mile from where the railroad track wanders from the left bank into the woods for the last time. Here we could see the remains of a fish dam dating to Indian times. These dams were built by piling rocks in the river in a vee-shape facing into the current. This location is also marked by the remains of two wooden bridges that crop out of the right bank. On the opposite shore a large sandbar facing downriver offers the widest, most open, and flattest spot for camping on the river.

Shortly below the fish dam we came to the grassy park mentioned earlier, with a tin-roof pavilion and a boat ramp. Though it appears to be a municipal park, we could find no sign inviting us to land. On the downriver side the area was posted as private property. From here the river begins a two to two-and-a-half-mile section of flat, deep water followed by series of easy ledges—probably the biggest drops of the trip. It is best to run them near the left bank, where you'll see a large rock-face. When passing this rock you may take some water over the bow, but the course is a straight shot. The take-out appears a half mile below this short set of rapids. My novice brother-in-law, who on the first day of the trip had been making halting progress through the rocks and riffles, was by day two gliding along with a smile and shouting advice to me on his merry way. It would have been a stellar finish for him had he not come to realize he'd left the keys to the take-out vehicle at the put-in. But soon enough he had purchased the kindness of a local man for a ride back. We could not have feigned disappointment much longer, anyway. It would take more than this to mar the pleasant memory of a Roanoke run.

THE MOOSE RIVER BOW TRIP

It was the recommendation of fellow paddlers Bill and Anne Zeller, who own the Country Canoeist in Dunbarton, New Hampshire, that first led me to the Moose River in Western Maine. They had stopped by my office in New Bern, North Carolina on a southern tour one winter, and we were swapping "been there" stories. It is comforting to know that for all the paddling I do, more often than not I haven't "been there" or "done that" when readers regale me with stories of their favorite places. Lord willing, I shall be a very old man and quite the editor emeritus before I am dotty enough to believe otherwise.

The "bow trip" was only one of several in Bill's and Anne's repertoire that were mentioned, but the funny name stuck in my mind. I could find nothing about it until the name popped out at me months later from the "Canoe Trips" section of DeLorme's Maine Atlas. As it turns out, quite a few people—from the crustiest veterans to squads of elementary schoolers—have the Moose River Bow under their belts, and to no surprise. It is a perfect taste of what Maine canoeing, fishing, and woodlands are all about, packed into four easy days of

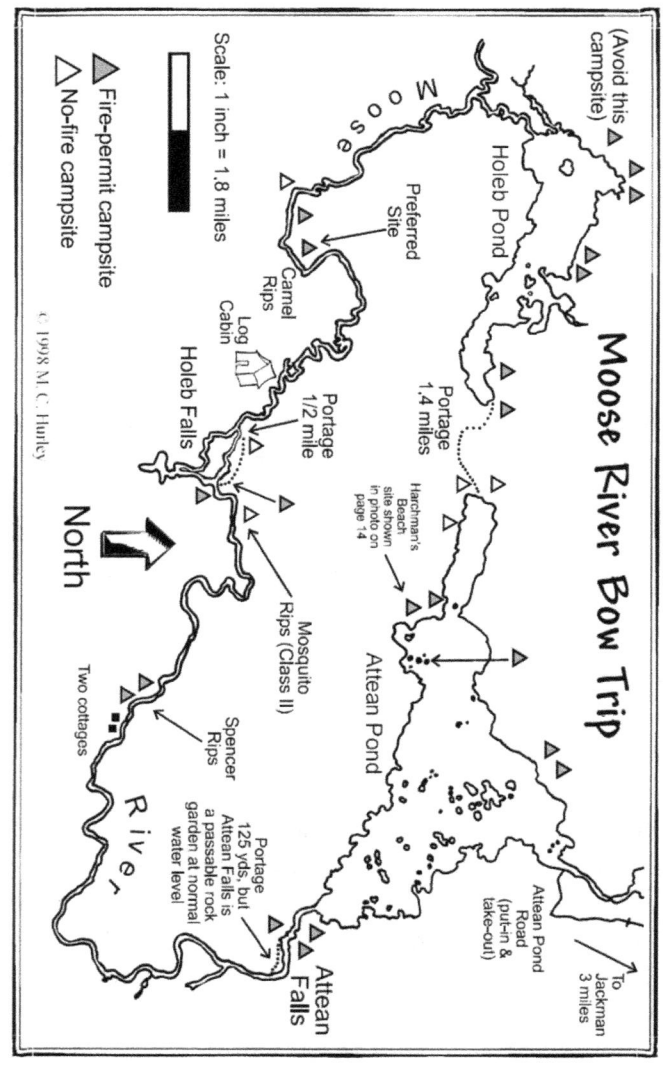

paddling through as lovely a stretch of country as I have seen anywhere. Go to Maine, friends, and take this trip before you take another.

The "bow" which the Moose River makes is by virtue of its connection to the outlet of Holeb Pond and the inlet of Attean Pond, as shown on the map. The river pulls back from these ponds and behind the mountains like an archer's string.

This is not considered a whitewater trip even though it offers one Class II ledge and several exciting, smaller runs. The trip begins and ends on two "ponds" that most folks outside Maine would recognize as lakes of respectable size. On the river, the fast sections are brief drops and in each case can be fairly easily avoided by lifting boats and gear a short distance over wide, flat rocks along shore. Some of the chutes look too temptingly easy to pass up, though, and many rank novices pass through unscathed.

The trip begins at the eastern shore of lovely Attean Pond, which remains undeveloped except for a dirt parking lot at the put-in and a few well-hidden cottages on a cluster of islands in the middle. Here you are close to the town of Jackman, "where even the moose are friendly." Attean Pond Road veers off to the left of Route 201 just after the Jackman Trading Post on the right side of the highway. The put-in appears at the end of a winding, pitted, dirt road that offered yet another affirmation of our investment in a used Jeep a few years back.

Anyone headed up this way would do well to acquire the topo maps for the trip in advance. The Holeb, Attean Pond, and Catheart Mountain USGS quadrangles are needed. Relying on L. L. Bean's usual infallibility, I was perturbed to find them out of all three maps. The Delorme Map Store nearby had all but the Attean Pond quadrangle. Leave it to "Bait, Bolts & Bullets"—an old timey sporting goods and hardware shop off of Route 201 in the town of Solon—to be the only place in the state with an ample supply of all three maps, along with some prescient advice from owner Gary Rogers on the feeding habits of local brook trout. There are no liveries along the bow trip, but Cedar Ridge Outfitters in Jackman (run by a husband and wife registered-guide team) advertises canoe rentals and guided trips.

From the boat ramp at Attean Landing one paddles west through a narrow inlet to the main expanse of the pond. Here the cluster of islands in the middle comes into view. To the right of these on the north shore is a wide, sandy beach that will serve as the first night's camp for most folks getting a late start. This is what is known as a "fire permit site" in the confusing classification system of campsites loosely managed by the overworked, underpaid state forest service. Use of these and other Maine forest lands, most of which are still privately owned by paper companies and individuals, is leased to the state forest service for camping. Only those who have obtained a "permit" from the forest service may have a campfire, and then only at "Fire Permit Sites" identified as such by yellow signs on trees. Not every site is a fire permit site, and on the river, in particular, you might find yourself camping on a site where fires are prohibited. To obtain a permit, simply call forest service headquarters in Greenville, tell them you're taking the "bow trip" and the nights you'll be camping, and they will read you a six-digit number over the telephone. That's your "permit." You get no piece of paper and are expected simply to recite this number to the ranger if asked.

Make sure you bring a camp stove for those unlucky nights when all of the fire-permit sites are taken. Planning, early morning starts, and paddling weekdays are the keys to enjoying this usually crowded trip. Once in camp for the first night, you will either enjoy or begrudge the luxury of a picnic table and the privy supplied at many sites—depending on your passion for roughing it. These amenities remind you that civilization is not far at bay, but without them the sites would probably look a lot worse for the wear.

The first site encountered on the north shore of Attean Pond is a two-party site with a table in each camping area. The sites are widely spaced in the woods just behind a long, sandy beach.

The dawn of the second day broke to a deceptive calm that lured me onto the lake and then gave way to strong, westerly winds. Paddling through driving waves, it was hours before I reached the portage to Holeb Pond. I nearly turned back several times to sit it out. On the way, I spied a jewel of a campsite on the beach of the near-western shore, noted on the map on the facing page. If you have the time to paddle all the way across the lake to this site on the first night, you will find all that you desire in a North Woods lake-camp, here.

Once on the portage to Holeb Pond, I caught up with a group of middle schoolers coming through the woods in the company of a very patient, older guide and two of his young crew. They went through with all the subtlety of a traveling circus, but lest we judge, remember that to such as these the future of the North Woods belongs. Years from now when their elders are fading and gone from these shores, may they remember fondly their time in the woods and find something here worthy of saving.

The portage from Attean briefly doglegs across a railroad track—which is actively in use and not a place to tarry—then down a rock strewn path. Here the west winds renewed their battle for the bow of my canoe as I hugged the shoreline. As a result, I have little to report about the character of Holeb Pond except my happiness in reaching the other side of it. I did see that the campsite on the north shore at the western end of Holeb is best avoided. It is accessible from a dirt road and seemed overused. Two other campsites which I could not see are reported to be near this one, as are two sites at the eastern end of this pond. The only site on Holeb Pond marked on the USGS map printed in 1989, and the only one I noticed by casual observation, is the westernmost site marked on the map. The new, state forest service brochure on the bow trip marks the location of all the campsites but does not tell where fires are allowed.

Both Attean and Holeb ponds are noted for their salmon and brook trout fishery and clean, clear water. On Attean Pond, especially, the big trout down deep draw a fair number of serious fishermen in motor boats. Recalling my disappointment at the trout on the Allagash the year before, I fully expected the offseason brook-trout fishing in the Moose River to be lackluster, but I was pleasantly surprised. The trout in the river were of pan size and fairly eager for small, gold spinners with an equally small piece of earthworm attached, tossed into the eddies below fast water and retrieved steadily. I would say

I hooked a dozen trout in a total of three hours of fishing and landed half that number. (One sizable brookie did throw the hook below Attean Falls—honest.)

The outlet to the Moose River from Holeb Pond is something of a maze. Several paths open through the marsh at the western end of the pond. To find the right one, hug the southern shore coming from the east, and choose the first well-defined outlet stream through the marsh. Match the bends in the river to those shown on the USGS Holeb Pond map, and if you fail to pass under a railroad trestle within the distance shown on the map after leaving the pond, you will know to turn back and try again.

The Moose River is a beautiful thoroughfare through the kind of scenery that comes to mind when people speak of classic Maine wilderness. Beaver are plentiful and active, here. The river runs deep and slow in most spots as it winds past low bluffs, alder rushes, and bogs. Due to the spacing and relative scarcity of campsites along the river, especially fire-permitted sites, some forethought is necessary to ensure that one finds a suitable place to camp this first night on the river. My advice is to rise early, put your shoulder down, paddle straight through, and make camp at Camel Rips. Though Camel Rips is marked on the USGS map, the campsite on the north bank by the rips is not. It is, nonetheless, the prettiest of the first three campsites you will pass on the river. Fires are allowed at the Camel Rips site. This site is also located at the top of the first "falls" encountered on the river, so you may easily turn and head the short distance back to one of the two sites upriver should the Camel Rips site be full.

The first ledge at Camel Rips is bordered by wide, granite boulders on each side that make a great spot for sunning and fishing from the bank. Assuming that the rips had been fished out by campers at this site, I had only a casual interest in casting here until I promptly landed a scrappy trout. That there were still any fish to be caught near Camel Rips and other well-trodden sites underscores the little-noted importance of timing. Where trout are concerned, the key to success at all times other than the early fishing season (when the black flies are out and most canoeists are home), is to fish just below fast water at dusk and dawn. Unless you can wait to fish during these periods, you might as well keep paddling. Don't waste your time with a big lure selection, either. Carry a box full of tiny gold spinners and earthworms, and the fish will find you.

If you go farther than Camel Rips on your first night on the river, you will not only be rushing past some pretty country—you'll have a long paddle ahead of you. It's nearly six miles and a portage to the next campsite, which is below Holeb Falls. Make camp early to avoid having to bivouac on the river at night.

Shortly after you leave the Camel Rips campsite, a quick dogleg to the left with another, short section of easy, fast water marks the end of these rips. From here until Holeb Falls the river becomes winding, deep, and mostly flat with impressive mountain views to the east. If you keep an eye to the right bank you will soon see a vacant log cabin. It is privately owned, but signs posted to the exterior indicate that it has been leased to the forest service. The guide showing the troupe of middle schoolers down the river took them in for a tour, and I followed suit. The inside is furnished with bunk beds and bare mattresses as well as a table and wood stove. I don't recommend that anyone "camp" here, but the only access is by canoe, and it had obviously seen recent and frequent use.

After leaving the log cabin, it is time to be on the lookout for the portage around Holeb Falls. Mistakenly going far past the channel from which the portage leads could make for a nasty hike back along the bank. Just before the channel appears on the left, a large mountain in the distance with a radio tower on top will enter your view from the river. The approach to the channel was marked by a forest service sign when I was there, but the folks at Bean's say the sign is missing on occasion. After entering this channel one takes a narrower channel immediately on the right to reach the head of the short portage. If you cut through the woods at the top of the portage you can get a good view of the near side of the falls.

Only the lower reaches of the falls are visible from the pool at the other end of the portage. There is a campsite where the portage ends, but this is a busy spot. A better site is just across the river, below the falls, on the south shore. One guide's "secret" to finding excellent fishing on the river is to backtrack to Holeb Falls along the trail that leads from this campsite. Carry your canoe the short distance on this trail and you can paddle right up to the base of the falls. The area is accessible only by canoe, and given the surprising number of canoeists I meet who have no interest in fishing, you may find a bonanza, here.

About a half a mile below Holeb Falls, the river arrives at the only rapids, known locally as Mosquito Rips. The name fits this narrow, Class II passage with a pinning rock in the middle. It is easy to carry the ten yards over this section as I did on adjacent ledges. One man I met on the river later that weekend had nosed in and capsized, here, but others did fine.

The last runnable rapids of the trip is Spencer Rips, located about 5 miles below Holeb Falls. These rips occur beside the ruins of a bridge. A homemade sign 200 feet ahead still warns of the low bridge and offers directions to the portage. The portage remains but the bridge is gone, allowing paddlers to test some easy whitewater. The character of the river changes after Spencer Rips, seeming to age and slow down awhile among the alders. Its last hurrah before returning you to the pond where you began is Attean Falls, a passable rock garden marked by a portage on the left. The best campsite of the trip is beyond this portage and across the river, beneath an ancient, white pine. Atop this bluff you can pitch camp and gaze back at the Moose River, reflecting that you have now "been there" and done that," while hoping not to depart this life before the chance comes to do it all again.

The Allegheny River Islands Wilderness

Kinzua Dam to Oil City

As a boy I looked upon Pennsylvania as the Great White North. Growing up in Baltimore, I would listen to the school closings on snowy mornings and hear that counties near the Pennsylvania border were inundated with huge drifts—schools closed for days— while we "southerners" couldn't muster more than a two-hour delay. As a boy scout, I recall our troop arriving after a long drive at the Susquehanna River, which had frozen solid, and skating it as fast as we could in a straight line for miles on end. But unlike its neighbor states to the north, Pennsylvania is not known for long-distance canoe-camping. The Allegheny River in the western part of the state, flowing through the national forest of the same name, is one exception to that reputation.

There was a time, as the driver of our shuttle van explained, when taking a dip in the Allegheny River meant coming out with an oil slick on your skin. Those days happily are gone. The Allegheny like many other American rivers has seen a dramatic recovery in the last

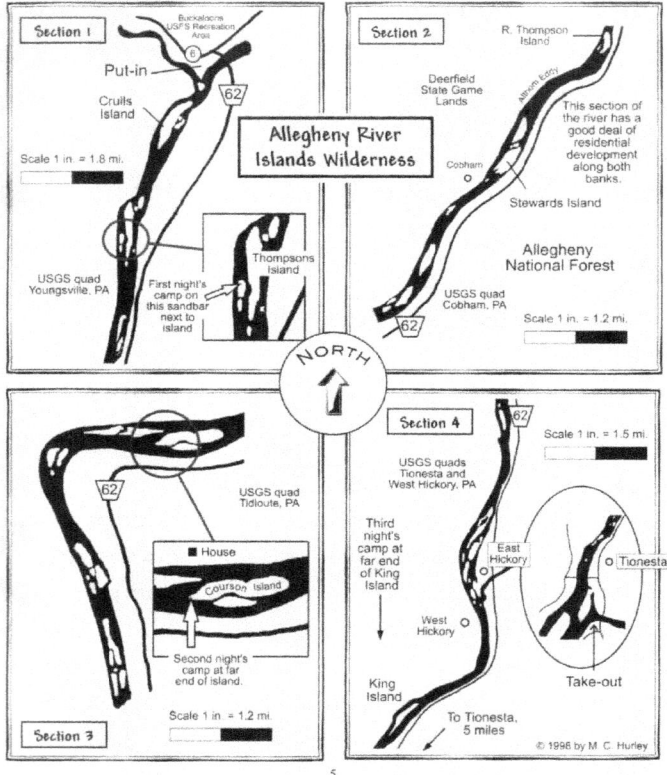

twenty years. On April 2, 1992, the eighty-five-mile section from Kinzua Dam at the Allegheny Reservoir in Warren to the section where the refineries begin at Oil City was designated a "Recreation Waterway" under the federal Wild and Scenic Rivers Act. Locals have long referred to the surrounding mountains as the "Big Woods," and understandably so. These hills are impressive in size and range and for the most part are densely forested. It is such a haven for wildlife, in fact, that the deer population has exploded into something of a nuisance.

The first thing to understand about a trip to the Allegheny River Islands Wilderness is the syntax of the name. The "wilderness" is contained within each of the seven islands designated by Congress officially as wilderness in 1984. The river corridor in which the islands are located, however, is not a "wilderness" by the usual definition of the term. A state highway cuts into the mountain above the eastern shore of the river and parallels most of its course. Several sections of the river we paddled were developed with cottages, grassy lawns and bulkheads abutting the shore. Not all of the residential development was tasteful and pleasing to the eye, either. Still, the water is clean, the fishing is good, and the river itself is an impressive body of water to behold. There is also enough woods along most of the trip to please the wilderness canoeist and casual paddler alike.

The fishing on this trip is primarily for trout and bass. Though the trout fishing is said to taper off as one floats farther from the dam, we witnessed a fisherman wading from shore at Althom Eddy, ten miles downriver, catch a trophy brown trout on an earthworm. For our part, we were luckless until we captured a live hellgrammite from beneath a rock at our first camp. These hard-shelled worms with beetle-like heads and pincers are a favorite food of smallmouth bass and a prized bait. Once the first bass was aboard and we realized the worm's attractive power, we managed to keep it on the hook until we had two more fish and a fine mess for dinner. The hard-working little hellgrammite was well missed for the rest of the trip. Though the boys found and carefully transported several crayfish along the way, they apparently did not have nearly the same appeal.

A trip down the Allegheny can begin and end at any number of sections, including great distances inside or outside the national forest. A brochure offered by Allegheny Outfitters features river trips ranging from eight to forty-five miles. Because the river is dam-fed, the water level is always adequate. Although there are riffles and eddies in some sections, there are no rocks to avoid, and navigation is easy. Nothing we encountered would rate above a Class I in difficulty, in my opinion.

"Buckaloons" is the name of the national forest recreation area where we put in just outside Warren. The distance from this point to the ramp where we ended our trip, in the charming town of Tionesta, is thirty river-miles. We made the trip comfortably in four days and three nights. The more popular (but not necessarily more scenic) trip is a thirteen-mile section from Buckaloons to the state fisheries boat-ramp in Tidioute (pronounced "Tih-dee-YOOT").

The forest service publishes a two-page guide to natural features along the river as well as a fold-out map showing the location of the seven, designated wilderness-islands between Buckaloons and Tionesta. Private islands are also marked on the map. Despite this help, the forest service literature for the most part offers little guidance on finding campsites. Their map does not feature locations on the islands that have been cleared for camping, and on some islands we could find no suitable areas. Generally speaking, cleared, dry and level sites for camping were rare amid the dense trees and brush on the high banks of the islands. We spent a good deal of time each afternoon scouting for a place to camp.

The forest service advises that "camping is permissible on any national forest island unless otherwise posted." A USFS brochure counts twenty-nine "national forest islands" in all between Kinzua Dam and Tionesta, including the seven, designated wilderness-islands. Only five groups of islands in the section below Buckaloons are marked on the USFS map as privately owned.

Although our outfitter estimated that on a given weekend in season there might be more than 150 canoes on the river above Tionesta, only twenty-five or so will camp on the river, he said. I would guess the number is even smaller. Until the third night of the trip we encountered only one other group of campers and few canoeists during a sunny weekend in late May. We were more likely to encounter power boaters plying the river, including one fellow who whirred by us in an improbable, homemade airboat with all the subtlety of a helicopter gunship.

According to Allegheny Outfitters owner Fred Mendenhall, the flow-rate of water released through the dam at times can make the river too swift to run safely. This does not happen suddenly, but he advises paddlers to check with him before making the trip, to be sure the river is runnable. We made the trip in the photos shown with this article when the flow-rate was 5,000 cubic feet per second.

From Buckaloons downstream, the river is mostly wide and flat. Gentle eddies occasionally boil up above rocks that are well submerged. Crulls Island, the first of the wilderness islands, is encountered quickly after pushing off from Buckaloons. However, there is a good deal of unsightly, riverside development in the vicinity of this island that makes this an unsuitable spot for overnight camping. For our first night's camp, we headed to Thompson Island.

The main body of Thompson Island is sixty-seven acres. According to USFS literature, this was the site of the only Revolutionary War battle in the northwest area of the state. Taking the channel to the right of the island, one soon comes to a small, sandy landing. One river house is still in view, looking back upriver from this point. On the bank above this landing we found the first campsite. There are at least two other campsites farther down the right bank of the main island. Young Sam Heller and Kip Hurley stood for a moment at this first site, and, when asked to imagine how many redcoats died there in battle or camped there for the last night of their lives, inexplicably decided to move on.

If you choose to camp on the main body of Thompsons Island, you will find the interior filled with verdant grass-fields that are quite pristine and lovely. There is not much firewood, though, and the shaded campsites here were quite muddy when we arrived. We chose instead to camp on a clean, dry gravel bar that the river has cut away from the right bank of the island at the downstream end. Here we found dry, seasoned driftwood galore and good fishing for smallmouth in the eddy at the end of the bar. The river makes a nice pool for swimming between the island and this sandbar.

Below Thompsons Island, there are two, private islands on which no camping is permitted. Some swift but easily navigated water is encountered, here. Good walleye fishing is reported in this area through Althom Eddy.

After Althom Eddy one comes to Stewards Island,

where there is a nice, grassy campsite half-way down on the right side. Another campsite—probably the most picturesque of the trip—looks downriver from the southernmost point of the island. Mosquitoes had the better part of it when we arrived there, so we kept going.

Fuelhart Island is not shown on the map in the USFS brochure but appears to be privately owned. A cottage is visible on the island from the right channel. Shortly after this island a public boat ramp marked by a brown sign on the left bank appears. A take-out here completes the trip to Tidioute. Canoes taking out at state fisheries boat-ramps such as this one must be marked with registration numbers either from Pennsylvania or another state. A stiff fine awaits violators, and the wardens patrol aggressively.

After you pass the state boat-ramp at Tidioute, it will be getting about time to choose a campsite. The next wilderness-island you will come to is Courson. Despite its size, Courson Island offers only one good place to camp, located at the downstream tip of the main island, beneath a large shade tree. It is not directly visible from the water, but going ashore one will see it readily. We did not discover it until we were getting underway the following morning. Instead, we camped on a small gravel-bar that is not shown on the map but which has recently been cut away from the main island. By camping on the main island, you will avoid the view of houses along the right bank that offer the only distraction from the otherwise wooded setting.

The third and final night of the trip provided the best campsite of all and the only one at which we had any company. This was King Island, one mile past the town of West Hickory. The downriver side flattens out into a thin stand of trees, with plenty of good tent-space. From here it is a pleasant trip of only five miles to the take-out on the left bank just after the bridge at Tionesta. This section contains some of the "fishiest" looking water of the trip in several swift sections. The river narrows briefly above the bridge at Tionesta and whips up into a bit of a chop, offering a thrilling but easy send-off to paddlers upon this lovely river reborn.

"Highway" of the Adirondacks

Fulton Chain to Tupper Lake

The Adirondacks have that reliable, familiar feel of a woods we have grown up with. Even the farthest-flung sections of Adirondack Park lack the edgy, "out there" aura of raw wilderness that permeates just about any place on the Canadian shield. Perhaps it's because the canoe camps here were first hacked out of the woods so very long ago. Many of the sites cleared by pre-historic Indians in the pine and spruce forests still dot the shores of water-trails in this part of New York State. Over time, these routes became as familiar to the succession of trappers, guides and sportsmen who crossed them in canoes as a family vacation in a Buick down Route 66—with the location of each camp along the way marked and measured as surely as any Holiday Inn.

Among the avenues available to canoeists paddling for sport or sustenance through the myriad ponds, lakes and streams in this region, one stood out as the naturally most efficient and direct route. Beginning in Old Forge, New York, it leads some ninety miles east and north

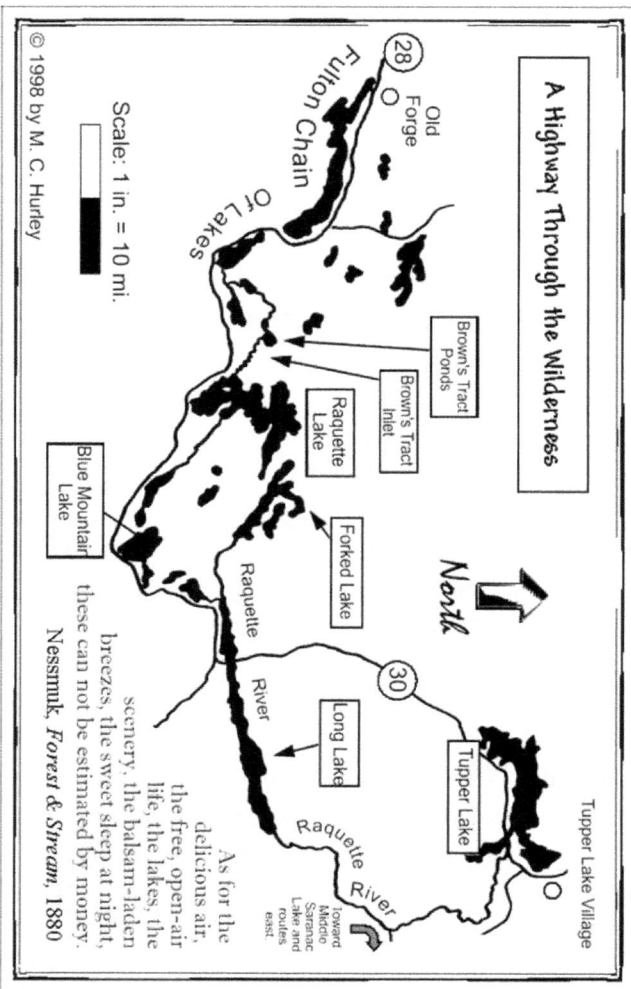

through a series of lakes beginning with the "Fulton Chain"—named after an early surveyor of the region and not the famed inventor whose steam engines powered passenger ferries, here. Today the route is known as the "Highway of the Adirondacks," though its ultimate destination is a matter of one's personal preference and itinerary.

The man most responsible for popularizing this highway as a distinct route for canoes was George Washington Sears a/k/a "Nessmuk." He diaried his travels, largely between Old Forge and Paul Smith's Hotel (now the town of Paul Smiths), in eighteen "letters" to Forest & Stream magazine between 1880 and 1883. Describing the route that over the years tested the mettle of many wilderness wannabees, he wrote in July 1880: "From the Forge House, foot of the Fulton Chain, on the west, to Paul Smith's, Lower St. Regis Lake, on the east, is ninety-two miles. About five of this distance is covered by carries [writers seem uniformly obliged to mention that one does not say "portage" in the Adirondacks]; the longest carry of this route is about one mile; the shortest, a few rods . . . The tired, overworked man of business who gets away from the hot, dusty city for a few days or weeks cannot do better than to come to this land of lake, river and mountain and hire a guide."

Heedless of this advice, many sought to imitate Nessmuk's skill in "going through alone" by canoe, and a tradition of self-reliant voyaging for sport was born. Today, that tradition is celebrated each fall in the Adirondack Canoe Classic, a "friendly race" which starts as Nessmuk did in Old Forge but diverts from his route to end ninety miles and three days later at the Village of Saranac Lake. Others, including the hordes of boy scouts who make the trip every summer, consider the legendary highway to lead principally to Tupper Lake and the Raquette River beyond, as shown on the map. As for myself, I have followed the throng of racers into Saranac

Lake Village but have also paddled variations of the trip in different legs and directions, with and without young children (literally) in tow.

The forest and lakes along the "Highway of the Adirondacks" seem something of a grande dame, today—a gray old lady still beautiful and proud but not the temptress she once was. Even by Nessmuk's day many of the lakes had already been dammed, and development was gobbling up the forest. "A very clear and beautiful sheet of water is Blue Mountain Lake," he wrote. "It has often been called the gem of the wilderness. But its days of natural wildness are gone forever. There are three large hotels on its banks filled to overflowing with guests. Lines of stages leave daily for different points to the eastward . . . Besides the hotels there are private boarding-houses, while many families have private residences on the preferred sites on the lake, which they are pleased to call camps."

It has gotten somewhat worse. The town of Old Forge where Nessmuk embarked is now a veritable Coney Island of tourist amusements, and the shores of most lakes in the Fulton Chain are, with welcome but sparse exception, built up in cottages. Yet at the bottom of a concrete ramp in the parking lot of the Old Forge town hall, overlooking a man-made beach on Forge Pond, a sign proudly marks this place as the impetus of the "Highway of the Adirondacks."

To complete this trip one needs only a single map—known simply as the "Canoe Map"—sold everywhere in the park. The official state brochure entitled "Adirondack Canoe Routes" provides an excellent, narrative guide to navigation on this and other trips. You may obtain this free guide from the Department of Environmental Conservation. For guiding, maps, outfitting, canoe rentals and shuttles, contact Adirondack Canoes & Kayaks, owned by Harry and Martha Spetla, a husband and wife guide-team out of Tupper Lake. I can personally vouch for their dependable, friendly service.

Despite the development, choosing Old Forge as an historical place to begin a ninety-mile camping trip is not without merit. The forest does its best to hide many of the buildings that would otherwise be visible from shore, leaving views for the traveler in the Fulton Chain that are still worth seeing.

If you choose to begin in Old Forge, you will wind your way along a narrow channel for about a mile to the inlet of First Lake. Should you get a late start and need to make camp soon, nearby DeCamps Island on First Lake is state land. There is a small, gravel landing on the northeast shore that leads uphill to a level overlook. I spent a sleepless night alone here through one of the most violent electrical storms I have ever experienced. The rangers allow primitive camping but not fires on this island. You will also likely have company, as this is a favorite spot of day parties for lunch and exploring.

If possible, it is best to continue on at least through Second and Third Lakes to the state-owned lean-tos on Alger Island at Fourth Lake. I have not camped here, but I understand they are available on a first-come first-served basis for a fee and fill up quickly on weekends. A caretaker is on the island in season.

As you pass through the narrow inlet that separates Third and Fourth Lakes, take time to admire the giant pines (assuming, as I greatly hope, that they survived the wind storms which devastated other parts of the forest since I last paddled the Fulton Chain). I would guess that some of these were already big trees at the time of Nessmuk's journeys. They make a cathedral-like sanctuary of the deep, still water through this passage.

The fishing for trout in the lakes of the Fulton Chain is said to be quite good, with the emphasis on "said to be." Luckless souls may take comfort in knowing it wasn't much better in Nessmuk's day: "Those coming out of the woods do not, as a rule, claim notable success with the trout," he reported. "Many of them would eat salt pork oftener than boiled trout were it not for the guides." The fishing experts at the Moose River Company, located on Highway 28 in Old Forge, can sell you the right tackle and teach you the rudiments of fishing the "Lake Clear Wobbler." This is a giant spoon used to attract attention to a trout fly at the end of a leader 18 inches below. It is trolled slowly from a drifting canoe in deep water in summer. I had no success with it, but I have seen this method work for others. The Moose River Company also offers guided fishing trips, and judging from the photos of trophy trout on their walls, they are well up to the task.

Those who have gotten an early start and who choose not to camp on Alger Island will have to continue on to Seventh Lake to find a place to stay. Toward the end of Fourth Lake, stick to the south shore where you will see the beach and docks of a summer camp. Shortly afterward the inlet leading to Fifth Lake and the town of Inlet appears. Fifth Lake is just a tiny pond right off of the highway, but its small size gives you a better chance at least to annoy a trout, here, than on the other lakes of the Fulton Chain.

The carry to Sixth Lake leads up a hill and along the highway for a short distance before crossing traffic and turning left. If you or your clothes need washing, take advantage of the coin-operated laundry and hot showers which you pass on this carry. My son Kip and I made extravagant use of both on our trip together this summer. The facilities are clean and the hot water is dispensed generously.

At the end of the carry to Sixth Lake you will notice a dam from which water flows west to the lake you have just left. When Nessmuk crossed this carry in the summer of 1880, he wrote of "a dam being built at the foot of Sixth [Lake], where there is a sixty foot fall or thereabouts." As Nessmuk noted at the time, the construction of many other dams was already planned or underway in the region.

The desire to control and enhance the water table in the Adirondacks is, paradoxically, the very reason why so much forested land has been preserved, here. In his 1994 book, *Forever Wild*, Professor Philip G. Terrie explains that Adirondack Park was formed by the New York Legislature in 1892 not principally to preserve wilderness but rather to protect the watershed of the Hudson River. It was feared that the rapacious logging common to that era would affect rainfall in the region and, ultimately, the navigability of commercial waterways in the state. This fear, Terrie says, was a driving force behind the constitutional amendment adopted in 1894, which required that state land within the park be kept "forever wild" and prohibited the removal of timber. Since then, state and private groups have worked actively to add parcels of land to the state's holdings in the area, even while development on private and municipal lands within the park boundaries continues to grow. Conflict between those who seek to bring more growth to the park and those who wish to see it restored and preserved as wilderness remains a thorny political issue, but every legislative referendum to soften the constitutional mandate over the last hundred years has failed.

You should have a brief, easy paddle across Sixth Lake, but Seventh Lake with its long and narrow fetch may show you a bit of wind and chop. The north shore is undeveloped and offers a number of good campsites. If you prefer a state park with hot showers, the Eighth Lake Campground straddles the portage between Seventh and Eighth Lakes and is a very clean and attractive facility. Most of the campsites there are not on either lake, however.

There is reported to be a navigable channel to the left between Seventh and Eighth Lake that allows one to avoid part of the mile-long carry in periods of high water, but I found it to be impassable some years ago. The carry follows a paved road for most of the way through the campground. This is the carry that Nessmuk wrote would leave the "sport" of his day (a term used to describe greenhorns who hired guides for outings in the woods) "in a limp and exhausted state, and with a firm resolve never to carry that load again."

Eighth Lake is entirely wild but not terribly remote, by reason of the highway that can be seen and heard along the east shore. Still, this is a clean, forested lake with a beautiful island in the middle. The Adirondack Museum at Blue Mountain Lake displays a photo of a rather large cabin that once stood on this island, which has since resorted to its wild state (save the presence of one lean-to). There are primitive campsites here and two other lean-tos on the west and north shores of the lake.

Unless you arrive at Eighth Lake before noon, I recommend that you camp here or out on Seventh Lake and get some rest. The carry from Eighth Lake to Brown's Tract Inlet is long and buggy anytime, but it gets longer and buggier when one is tired and the sun is setting. Nessmuk clearly wrote from experience when he warned of "claw[ing] madly at punkies and black flies," at the end of this carry, and it is uncanny how accurate his description of the place remains today, more than 100 years hence. Get an early start across the carry in the morning.

Brown's Tract Inlet is a beautiful, serpentine trough through a marsh and seems much longer to the paddler than it appears on the map. You will pass over a beaver dam or two. The route is clear, but a solid hour or more is needed to get through it all.

Unless you are very early in the season or near the mouth, it is not worth your time to fish Brown's Tract Inlet. Raquette Lake, however, is a different story no matter when you're there. Shortly after you cross under a bridge that crosses the inlet, the deep blue waters of the lake appear. If you have the poor planning to arrive at this point between mid-morning and nightfall, you will likely find the lake in a froth. Its reputation for rough water is long-standing and well-deserved, as Nessmuk's quoted remarks on the next page suggest. Turning left, you will follow Raquette Lake for nearly seven miles to the next carry, but there are many lovely campsites in between that you won't want to miss.

Many people choose to begin their trip at Bird's Marine off of Route 28 on Raquette Lake to avoid the jet skis and crowds that populate the Fulton Chain in the height of summer. Our whole family did just that in late June 1997. Julie and I embarked with kids, beagle and baggage in two canoes from Bird's, where we paid ten dollars to park our Jeep for the week. Before we knew it, the strong afternoon breeze had pinned Julie on a lee shore, but it was no trouble to bring her boat the short distance to Big Island under my tow. Little did we know that in two days' time we would both be wind bound for hours on another lee shore of this lake after getting started too late in the day.

Big Island has three permanent lean-tos, but the best camping is in tents away from these dirty barns. A wide, lovely site overlooks a high bank on the west side of the island. Here we spent two relaxing nights. The island is quite large as its name suggests and has plenty of firewood. There are several DEC campsites around the perimeter of the island in addition to the three lean-tos, but part of the island is privately owned. A cottage stands on the northwestern end. We found the jawbone of a deer in the brush and spotted a doe with her fawn in the marsh on the east side of the island.

On the morning of the second day I had planned to rouse the family for an early start across the lake, but the sun was streaming gloriously through the pines, the winds were gentle, and it just seemed the sort of day to linger over coffee and pancakes. That was a mistake.

By the time we shoved off from camp and were past the wind shadow of the island, a quartering breeze was already rolling the canoe uncomfortably. Even so, were it not for my mistake of running down the wrong bay looking for the outlet to Forked Lake, we would have made it just fine. It wasn't until we had to turn and face the wind in Boulder Bay to regain our course that our troubles really began.

Against the building wind, we were forced to hole-up for several hours behind a tiny, no-name island in Boulder Bay, near the north end of Raquette Lake. Conditions were too strong for Julie to make any headway by herself and too strong for me to tow a second canoe into the waves. Each time the whitecaps seemed to subside for a moment we would dash out from our hiding place, only to be blown back again and be left more exhausted for the effort. Finally, we sideswiped our way to the other side of the cove and made camp at Tioga Point in a lean-to, just before dark. A campfire and dinner of stew and biscuits partly restored us before we collapsed in the tent, which we had set up inside the lean-to to keep our gear dry.

The black flies were still a nuisance in late June and even more so, it seemed, here on Tioga Point. We broke camp quickly the next morning and had no desire to remain there any longer than necessary—that is, not until we discovered that our beagle had mutinied and disappeared into the surrounding hills.

It was unlike Jingles to be gone long—beagles are gluttons for attention and can't stand to be away from the action—but the hours went by. It was a low, cloudy morning, the bugs were already up and flying in formation along shore, and the wind was building again on the lake.

We searched for that little dog all morning, up and down the wooded trails of Tioga Point. In my considered opinion at the time, she had either met up with the business end of a raccoon, found her way to a road, or gotten badly lost in the woods. Having the children sit idle in a buggy, low-lying camp while brooding on her failure to return seemed a poor option. I decided instead to move on and explained to the children that notifying the ranger at our next camp, on Forked Lake, offered the best chance to find her. The ranger could put out an alert to all points and bring her in, but neither Julie nor I held out much hope of that. She had always checked back in with us periodically before, if only to see what else might have fallen to the ground to eat. Her long absence now seemed rather ominous. Jingles was gone.

Kip, the extrovert, began a wailing competition with the loons, while stoic, little Caroline cried quietly to herself. We were a pitiable sight as we pushed our canoes off from the lean-to camp where Jingles had slept with us the night before. I felt bad for the little digger but much worse for the children, imagining how all this would play out in their memory: "We went canoe camping, got blown off course in a storm and eaten by bugs until even our dog—Man's Best Friend—decided to throw in the towel and take her chances on the road."

The far end of Raquette Lake extends east and north into Outlet Bay to become the Raquette River again for one mile before entering Forked Lake. This section of the river is reportedly impassable due to rocks, so we took the carry that leads off from the left. We saw several good campsites in Outlet Bay but were too downhearted to explore them.

The landing of the carry to Forked Lake abuts a private residence, and care should be taken not to trespass in the owner's yard. From here the carry follows a well-cleared road up a steep hill and across the highway, where there is a payphone on the shoulder should you need to call for supplies, a new dog, or what-have-you. From there it descends a dirt road to a covered boathouse on the shore of Forked Lake, altogether a distance of one-half mile.

If I were asked to name the five best lakes in the Adirondacks, Forked Lake would be at or near the top of the list. It has been largely preserved from any development, is surrounded by picturesque mountains, and has more than its share of postcard-pretty campsites. Add to this the most dependable fishing for both largemouth and smallmouth bass I have found on any Adirondack Lake, and I scarcely know what more one could ask.

The procedure for making camp on Forked Lake is to paddle all the way to the east end where the ranger cabin sits and purchase a permit on a first-come first-served basis for a specific site. The ranger provides a map showing the location of each site by number. The fee is nine dollars per night. We chose site no. 40—in my opinion the best one on the lake. There are also some nice sites on the islands, but firewood there is harder to come by. The road-accessible sites on the eastern end are generally much less attractive.

We made our missing-dog report to the ranger and braced to keep a stiff upper lip for three days on Forked Lake. That night around the campfire was spent in silent, grim imagination of where Jingles might be and what hardships she faced. Even my wife—widely known for her wistful reminiscence of life before dog hairs and carpet stains—shed a tear.

The next morning we were going about our usual chores in camp when the low, distant murmur of an outboard motor grew close. Looking out on the lake, we saw Ranger John Rayome heading slowly for us in a DEC jonboat. We could not help but notice that there was no sign of a small, black-and-tan beagle anywhere aboard. He obviously had some news, but I wasn't sure we wanted to hear it.

The expression on the ranger's face as he neared our camp in a motorboat gave no hint of his purpose. We could only hope that he had some news of the lost beagle we had reported the day before. We had last seen her a long day's paddle and one portage ago, however, and the mood by now was grim. Forked Lake being an established, public campground, many tent sites around the lake have tiny docks such as ours did, where the ranger came alongside.

"We think we might have found your dog," came the hopeful news.

In a moment I was happy to be flying along with Ranger John on a plane of blue water no mere canoe could create, while my children stood waiting like tiny sentinels on the shore that fast disappeared behind us. The internal combustion engine has its virtues.

During the ride to the end of Forked Lake, I explained to Ranger John that I publish a canoeing journal, which I often find produces the same expression in people as comments like, "I'm a consultant" or "Yes, honey, I own this bar." John was polite enough to show interest in seeing a copy, and it is a pleasure to tip my hat in these pages to the hardworking folks at the DEC. The Adirondacks would be a much poorer place today without them.

Coming ashore at the foot of the carry leading back to Raquette Lake, I started up the hill at a livelier pace than I had managed coming in the other direction, the day before. At the other end of the half-mile carry, the resident Raquette Lake ranger was waiting in another DEC jonboat to meet me. As far out on the prow of his boat as she could reach without falling in was the weary prodigal—the very one which the American Kennel Club and Santa Claus had entrusted to our family two years before, now squirming with the promise to sin no more.

Of the happiness and rejoicing that attended my return to camp, that day, I can say nothing that is not already familiar to your own experience or imagination. The lesson of the moment was not lost on me, however. No more will I fear the day that I overhear my wife cursing me under her breath or wishing that the neighbors would claim me for their own. I have only to spend one night lost in the Adirondacks, and all will be forgiven.

After this happy reunion we decided to end our itinerary on Forked Lake, where the excellent bass fishing offered an added incentive to linger. This gave us time to explore the dirt-road carry between Forked and Long Lakes. In this distance, the Raquette River briefly resumes its identity and gives us legendary Buttermilk Falls.

Due to the rocks and rapids that punctuate the river's exit from Forked Lake, one must carry along the road for 1.6 miles, where a trail leads off to a lean-to campsite beside the river. Those walking the carry from Forked Lake will put in, here, and paddle 1.5 miles of flat water to the next carry around Buttermilk Falls. If you catch the Forked Lake rangers at a convenient time, they can provide you with a "truck carry" down this road for a small fee, about ten dollars when I last heard. When my son Kip and I resumed this leg of the trip in the Summer of 1998, we put in below Buttermilk Falls. From this point on the river, there are no more carries for twenty miles.

The Raquette River is a place of some renown. In 1869 William H. H. Murray, a Boston minister, published the book which began the public's fascination with the Adirondacks. *Adventures in the Wilderness* collected a series of essays extolling the sporting life in these woods, newly accessible by train and stagecoach to those who could afford the price of a guide. One chapter tells the story of an Indian princess who loses her life on the falls of a river in despair over a lost love.

The story recounts the nightly appearance of her spirit in a ghostly white canoe that emerges from the river, headed for "phantom falls." Murray and his guide decide to lie in wait for the ghost one night and, after unexpectedly breaking a paddle (natch), find themselves sucked into the fray. They successfully negotiate the falls with a steely grit that is ubiquitous among heroes in the genre of wilderness travelogues.

Murray never gives away the name of the falls, but he does clue the reader "to believe no more" of his story "than you see fit." Nonetheless, his context, the description of a drop of "twenty-five feet," and "water churned into foam" strongly suggest Buttermilk Falls, where he was known to have traveled. Is this the eternal abode of Adirondack Murray's famous ghost? Let your imagination follow her down the river, but keep your feet and your canoe safely upon the carry!

The view of the falls along the carry is quite good. When we embarked upon the river from the lean-to below the falls last summer, we paddled upstream for another look. Be careful not to paddle too close below the falls either, lest you, like Adirondack Murray, get sucked in by its beauty and the powerful reverse hydraulic!

Though it looks every inch the trout haven, I have caught nothing but smallmouth bass from the Raquette River between Forked and Long Lakes. Downriver from Buttermilk Falls the Raquette is flat and slow as it quickly widens into Long Lake. This section of the lake, resplendent with lily pads and eel grass, is well known for its northern pike fishing.

The locally preferred method for pike is a gold "Red Eye" spoon on a wire leader, tossed in shallow, weedy bays and retrieved at a fast clip. Bass are usually skeptical of wire leaders. You may use a three-inch floating Rapala minnow without a leader to fish for bass and pike at the same time, but you will lose a certain number of pike.

On arriving in Long Lake, my son Kip and I found the water level exceedingly high due to heavy rains early that summer. This is why August is the preferred month for canoe trips in the Adirondacks. High water means lots of bugs and natural fish-food in the water, which invariably spoils the fishing until the water recedes. Not to worry, though—the abundance of blueberries made hunters of us instead.

We were fortunate to find a campsite thick in the middle of them on Long Lake. Our Long Lake camp was the group site marked on the Canoe Map (put out by the DEC) between Caitlin Bay and Round Island. In the middle of July we had this lovely site all to ourselves. Campsites were widely available on Long Lake during the week. No fee is charged for these sites, but they may not be reserved in advance.

It was a much-anticipated luxury during William H. H. Murray's day to stop at one of several established "camps"—actually hotels—located along the northward routes leading from Old Forge. These camps ranged from rustic to lavish but were all built to separate city slickers coming to the Adirondacks in increasing numbers (known as "Murray's Fools") from their cash. Even Nessmuk, that pioneer of solo voyaging by canoe, never missed an opportunity to stay at these "camps" and wrote affectionately of his time, there.

If you care to treat yourself to a little elegance as you make your way up Long Lake, spend a night at the Adirondack Hotel. Aptly named, the Adirondack is a well preserved example of the great camps of the gilded age. It sits not more than thirty yards from shore in the Town of Long Lake. Though it was rebuilt in its present form at the turn of this century after a fire, it retains much of the classic charm of a bygone era-complete with a moose head above the reservation desk and a trophy black bear, standing with arms grasping outward, at the entrance. There is a formal dining room suitable for robber barons and a knotty-pine bar where Nessmuk might have held court for the guiding class. The rooms are small and simply furnished, with shared or private baths.

Long Lake is a body of water lovely as can be but with very much the air of a summer resort, not a wilderness. Sea-plane rides take off from the lake beside the Route 30 bridge, where the town operates a public beach with swim docks in the summer. Cottages dot the entire length of the lake until it disappears north into the Raquette River.

If you have paddled the Allagash in Northern Maine, the Raquette River above Long Lake has very much the same classic beauty—wild, remote, and rimmed in pines and firs. Shortly after one re-enters the river at the end of Long Lake, a lean-to appears on the left. Just past this point a huge boulder at midstream marks the mouth of Cold River, coming in on the right. Several miles above the point where this officially designated "wild river" becomes impassable, the famous Adirondack hermit Noah John Rondeau lived. His life and times are now featured at the Adirondack Museum in Blue Mountain Lake. It is a distance of nearly five miles from the first lean-to on the right bank, at the entrance to the Raquette River, to the carry for Raquette Falls. I first crossed this carry in the Adirondack Classic canoe race in 1993, under the crushing weight of an eighty-pound fishing boat and a yoke of two paddles lashed together.

The carry begins by going straight up and continues along an arduous path for 1.25 miles. So tired and disgusted was I near the end of this trek in 1993 that I could do little more than drag my old battle-axe through the woods by a rope. Even the racers in lightweight boats dreaded it.

Connecticut-Yankee and fellow devotee of the former way of things, Robin Lauer, accompanied me on a return trip to the Raquette River in December 1998. It was December 11 and 12, to be exact, and if you check the ranger's logbook for the names of people crazy enough to be paddling the river in December, you will find that ours stand alone—a testament to the stubborn refusal of two fools to accept the reality of winter.

Robin is one of those fellows we remember from our childhood who was always ready, at a moment's notice, to drop everything and light out for parts unknown. Lured by unseasonably warm temperatures in late November, we planned this trip on the QT, only to see winter tighten its grip as our departure-date approached. Neither one dared be the first to call to cancel, and sure enough, we found ourselves in fifteen-degree weather and an inch of snow, headed for Raquette Falls.

At one point I lost all feeling in the toes of one foot and had to stop, remove my boot and sock, and revive the flow of blood. Between the ice edging in around the river and the time we took to admire the outcroppings of granite and pine, we made slow progress toward the falls. Arriving at the head of the carry near darkness, we decided to leave our canoes and carry only our packs to make camp that night at the other end.

The approach to the carry is marked by a sign on a rock in the river warning of the falls. Rangers have fastened the torn section of an aluminum canoe to a sign on shore at the head of the carry to give pause to anyone contemplating the Class V run. The written sign incorrectly advises that it is 1.75 miles to the Raquette Falls lean-to. The entire carry is only 1.25 miles, and a lean-to appears to the right of the carry after only about a mile. We made camp here.

The DEC has erected a ranger cabin in a clearing not far from this lean-to. A trail leading from the campsite will take you there. It was shuttered for the winter when we arrived. The Raquette Falls lean-to is furnished with a narrow, rustic table on one side that came in handy for the preparation of meals. There is a stone fireplace in front of the lean-to and ample tent space all around. A bear-pole for hanging food packs at night is set high between two trees just outside camp.

There is plenty of downed wood here for a campfire, and in the bitter cold we fried potatoes, onions, and summer sausage for dinner. All of our drinking water froze solid overnight, requiring delicate work to thaw the plastic water-bottles by the fire.

I regretted not taking time to look at the falls when I crossed these woods during the 1993 canoe race. On this trip, we found them brilliant with ice and snow. A narrow, brush-strewn trail leading off near the end of the carry takes you to the falls. You can walk right out on the rocks, which we found to be slick with ice and mist. The pool beneath the falls is said to offer good trout fishing with a spinner and an earthworm, but all of the trout were in a deep sleep when we were there. This is an enchanting place in the Adirondacks, worthy of the time and effort needed to reach it.

By the time we needed to replace our drinking water, the pump on my water filter had frozen shut. Though I don't recommend drinking unfiltered water, by necessity I found the Raquette River below the falls to be delicious and clean. In fact, by the time we got back across the carry to pick up our canoes we were thirsty enough to bend down like two deer and drink directly from a spring that crossed our trail. This is still a Good Earth.

From the falls northward, you have your choice of a number of possible destinations. About five miles from the end of the carry around the falls, a sign on the right bank marks the entrance to Stony Creek. This creek heads east about two miles through two ponds to the landing where "Indian Carry" provides access to Upper Saranac Lake. The Summer 1996 issue of this journal featured the three Saranac Lakes, which are replete with campsites and trip possibilities too numerous to cover in this story.

Just a few yards beyond the sign for Stony Creek, Axton Landing appears along a channel cut to the right. There is a parking lot here where one may leave a car.

It is approximately five miles by river from Axton Landing to the next possible take-out at Trombley Landing, marked by two lean-tos—one straight ahead and one far to your right at a bend in the river. Exactly one mile past Trombley Landing, the state has installed an official "fishing access" site on the river, right off of Route 30. This is as far as the scenery on the river makes it worthwhile to go, unless you plan to camp on Tupper Lake.

Those headed to Tupper Lake should take the cut-off channel located upriver from the fishing access site. This channel comes in on the left, about a half mile past Trombley Landing. It avoids a mile of uninteresting paddling on the river beside Route 30.

Tupper Lake is well regarded for its beauty and fishing, and I have taken bass and pike there. Like Long Lake to the south it has a well-established municipality on its shores, but most of the opposite shoreline of Tupper

Lake remains undeveloped. The Raquette River as it leads into Tupper Lake, however, has not been so lucky. After it turns west at the state fishing access, the river flows past homes where the trees have been cut to the water's edge and the banks have been beautified with lawns, patio furniture, barbecue grills and other improvements. As we passed this sad scene in the growing cold of the evening, Robin and I quickened our pace and bore down for Tupper Lake.

Soon we could discern our course through the darkness only by the faint reflection of starlight on the water and the occasional crack of breaking ice, telling us that us that we had lost the river and strayed into a blind channel. (Through this method we learned that where the river forks beside a wooden boathouse, one should pick the channel to the left, not the right.) But despite these brief forays into error, at length we glimpsed the dim lights of Tupper Lake Village, found the cut-off channel to the left that leads to the lake, and arrived at the Route 30 bridge.

Wind and fatigue persuaded us to land among the rocks, here, rather than continue around the bend to the public boat-launch on the lake. The bite in the air told us it was December, after all. The ice would soon have its way with the river. This is a summer place, and a canoe is a summer thing. It was time for two of Murray's Fools to retreat again into the city and let the ghosts of a thousand Adirondack campfires walk these winter woods in peace.

Tyger River

Sumter National Forest

Experience has taught me that, with patience and a little tenderness, every girl will eventually come around. And so after a dry season of no camping with Daddy following two outings last summer that turned out to be less enchanting than we had hoped, six-year-old Caroline Claire Hurley resolved to give it another go. She joined her big brother Kip and a group of friends on the lovely Tyger River in the South Carolina Piedmont.

Warm, blue skies and cool, starry nights kindly did not breach a father's promise that all would be bliss. Our voyage began and ended within the dense woods of Sumter National Forest, a sprawling, 360,000-acre tract named after a South Carolina Revolutionary War hero. Brigadier General Thomas Sumter was actually a Virginian whose most famous namesake is the fort at Charleston where the Civil War was ignited. That war ended less nobly for South Carolina than it began, with

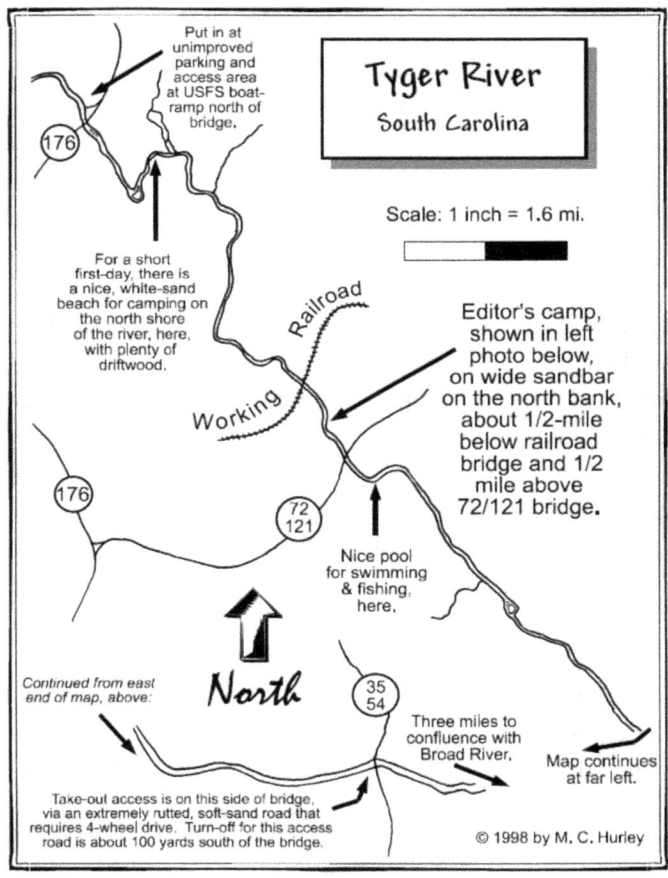

Sherman burning the nearby city of Columbia and most of the large plantations on his way there. Reconstruction saw the return of smaller farms in these midlands—an area of the state which remains very sparsely populated to this day. Tourists may have discovered South Carolina's mountains and beaches, but it is still possible to be quite literally alone in the woods of the central part of the state. On this beautiful river, on the last weekend of the summer, we saw absolutely no one for three-days and thirteen miles. Not one boat. Not one passerby. The cannons of war have long been silent in these ancient hunting grounds of the Cherokee and Catawba, where the forest is resurgent and the Tyger flows notably clearer, faster and cooler than the blackwater streams to the east. The river bottom is a clean, coarse sand that does not stick to the skin and offers a welcome massage to wading feet. The shorelines are thick in bottomland hardwoods and grasses. Camping is available on a few, soft sandbars of ample size along the river, within national forest boundaries.

Be sure to note that there are two separate tracts of land known as Sumter National Forest in South Carolina. One is near Union, while the other is twenty-five miles to the south near Augusta. The Tyger River runs through the northern tract. The southern tract contains the Chattooga River of whitewater fame. The section of the Tyger that we paddled is ideal for a one or two-night trip. It begins where Highway 176 crosses the river about fifteen miles south of the town of Union. Here the Tyger is no more than fifteen yards wide, moving at a slow to moderate current, with relatively few obstructions. The put-in is at an unimproved USFS boat-ramp on the north, upriver side of the bridge, where a dirt parking lot is provided.

Within a mile of the put-in, one comes to a tight bend to the left around an island. There are a number of deadfalls blocking the river at this point, but no portages are necessary if one takes the right-side channel. There are no rapids in the entire trip, though some tight spots and obstructions will test your steering ability. The water ranges in average depth from two to six feet, with a few deeper holes. After we encountered the island at one mile, a lovely sandbar unusually white in color appeared on the left bank. Having gotten a late start, we were tempted to set up camp here but decided instead to put a little more distance behind us. There was a wealth of seasoned driftwood at this location, and I would recommend it to anyone looking to camp for two nights in different places.

While the Tyger is not crystal clear like the streams of the mountains to the west, the visibility at the time of our trip—about a week after the last heavy rain—was some three feet, and the color of the water was a pale green. This cleanliness is no doubt owing to the straining effect of a solid buffer of vegetation along almost the entire river and no housing development along the section that we traveled. We did not hesitate to go swimming, and we used filtered river-water for all of our drinking and cooking.

The fishing in the Tyger is not its brightest feature. Despite giving every eddy and riffle a thorough thrashing with that proven nemesis of smallmouth bass and bream, the Beetlespin, we had only one small perch and a bluegill to show for our efforts by the end of the trip. Through some further reading afterward, I discovered that catfish, not bass, are the prime quarry here. We might have done much better drifting a gob of worms through the deeper holes, and I would recommend that approach to anyone looking to do some serious fishing.

On the upper leg of this trip, you will pass a cow pasture posted as private property that briefly intrudes behind a thinned area of trees on the right bank, followed shortly thereafter by a railroad bridge. This is a working railroad trafficked several times a day by freight trains. About one-half mile below the railroad bridge, as shown in the map on the next page, we camped on a large sandbar on the left bank. The location is approximately three hundred yards upriver from the 77/121 bridge, well out of earshot of the modest amount of road traffic. This is the last good spot for camping along the river for the next two miles. Our camp is shown in the photo directly above and at the lower left of page 6. It abuts a long pool with no obstructions, and a gradually sloping, sandy bottom makes it well suited for swimming and wading.

There was very little downed wood for campfires at this particular site, but we made do by using canoes to ferry loads of wood sawn from snags in the river. The sand on this bar was also extremely soft, requiring that the tarp be secured by "dead men." For those of you not used to camping on sand, this means tying the guylines to a log and burying the log. (Regular tent stakes will pull right up through soft sand.) If there aren't enough logs for this purpose, another method that works well is to bury a regular-size tent-stake sideways in the sand. The deeper the hole, the more tension the stake will hold. We chose to camp for two nights at one site, given that we were traveling in "kitchen-sink" mode and not with our usual lighter, portage-able assortment of gear. That didn't keep us from exploring the river on our layover day. With the river running in normal water at between one and two knots, it is fairly easy to paddle against the current—making it possible to jump in the boats, paddle upriver or down for a look-see, and then return to camp.

The trees along the river are largely deciduous,

including some truly enormous sycamores. In the late summer and fall of the year leaves of many different shapes dot the smooth surface of the water. As the cover sketch depicts, Caroline made great sport of retrieving the prettiest ones for closer inspection.

Some sections of the land along the river, though within the national-forest boundary, are clearly posted as private property and must be avoided. Primitive camping is allowed everywhere else on national-forest land, provided that one obtains a permit from the ranger. The main office for the U.S. Forest Service in the region is at 4931 Broad River Road, Columbia SC 29210-4021. We found no canoe liveries or other means for arranging a shuttle in this area. Instead, we left a vehicle at the take-out by the Highway 35/54 bridge. The steep, sandy road leading approximately one hundred yards to the landing below this bridge, where we left our Jeep, requires four-wheel drive. There is however a grassy shoulder at the top of this road where cars may be left. By the end of this trip I had found some redemption with young Caroline, who had taken a gleeful step closer toward a sense of the woods as a sheltering place to play and explore. I heartily recommend it to any grownups in search of the same experience.

Lac LaCroix Circuit

Boundary Waters Canoe Area

At a rather young age, I began to dream of the Boundary Waters. The photographs in the back of fishing magazines would show some fellow holding a muskie or a pike longer than himself, standing alone beside Great Bear Lake of the Can't-Get-There-From-Here Woods or some such place, and I would imagine myself in his shoes. *Wouldn't that just be something,* I would think—and then head to the city reservoir, where the banks were worn to dust from fishermen's feet and a one-pound bass was a considerable trophy. Wouldn't that be something, indeed. I still dream that dream.

One year my scout troop in Baltimore announced plans for a two-week canoe trip in the North Woods for the coming summer. The germ of this idea had been planted by our scoutmaster, Dr. Carl A. Zapffe, the brilliant metallurgist, author and historian from Brainerd, Minnesota. A man of towering energy then in his sixties with an improbable mane of snow-white hair, he would preside over our meetings from a rocking chair of twigs

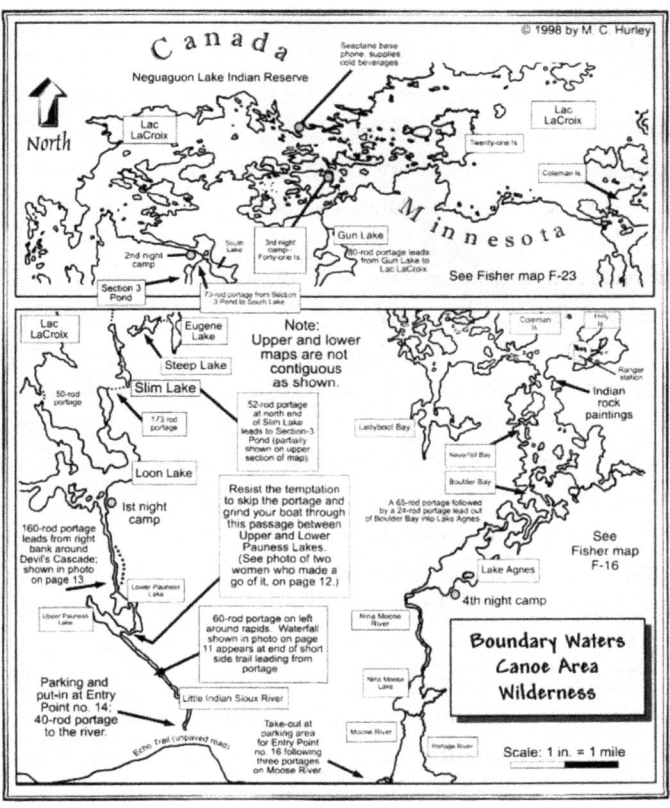

lashed with twine, wearing a buckskin-fringe coat. The father of seven daughters but only one son, he reveled in our boyish zeal and we in his aura as a Man of the North.

A campaign was begun to drum up interest in a trip to the Minnesota Boundary Waters. One night in the church hall, the troop saw an 8-milimeter black-and-white documentary, narrated but with no live sound, of two teenage boys voyaging through Canada by canoe. It seemed a remarkable concept to me at the time: no need for a car that I didn't own or have a license to drive to get from lake to lake; the ability to go under your own power to places where there were no fishermen crowding you out for casting space; a vessel able to carry more food for long expeditions than one could ever store in a backpack; fish for the taking in places so far off and inaccessible to the hordes that you could catch your dinner at will. *Wouldn't it just be something*, I thought, to journey through the woods in such a fashion.

A moment later a loud "cr-r-r-aack!" came, as a shower of hard candy hit us and the hardwood floor of the church hall in which we were seated in the dark. Bedlam ensued. It was a favorite trick of Dr. Zapffe's to wait until just such a moment, while we were all still and in rapt attention, to break the mood. I don't know what happened in the rest of the movie, but I'm quite sure that the first pages of this journal were already written that night.

The scouts who signed up for the trip got a big sendoff at the troop banquet, complete with a mock-up of a North Woods canoe-camp on the dais, with a yellow spotlight to make a full moon and cricket sounds on a tape loop. As it turned out I was unable to come up with the money for the trip (about $1200 in those days), but with this kind of build-up there was no question in my mind that I would get there someday.

This past summer marked my second trip to the North Woods mecca officially known as the Boundary Waters Canoe Area Wilderness—more than a million acres of forest on the Minnesota-Canada border interspersed with rivers and thousands of lakes closed to motorized traffic. My first trip (covered in the Winter 1996 issue of this journal) had been a rugged, challenging expedition with three other people, traveling over a sixty-eight-mile route with nearly thirty portages. As I would be going through alone this time, I looked for a way to get well into the backcountry mostly by water routes, with a minimum of portaging, and see a variety of terrain at the same time. Staring up at me from the large-scale Fisher map of the entire park was the answer: Lac LaCroix at 34,000 acres is easily the largest lake in the park. It straddles the boundary with Canada and is riddled with islands and bays. Leading to and from this majestic lake is an inviting loop of smaller lakes and rivers offering good fishing and a variety of scenery.

It is easy to forget when planning a Boundary Waters voyage that the forces of wind and weather can interfere dramatically with the itinerary. It is always best to have contingent routes available to avoid these situations, and therein lies the beauty of this particular trip—especially for the solo paddler who cannot count as much on brute strength to propel him against waves and wind. The route shown on the map allows for changes of course in a variety of directions after getting underway, depending on the strength of the wind, one's stamina, how well the fish are biting, or what-have-you. I found it to be rather sparsely traveled in the height of summer—owing, I suppose, to the fact that it crosses some areas of the park to which there is motorized access from Canada and which canoeists consequently plan to avoid.

The trip begins at the Little Indian Sioux River (entry point no. 14), just off the Echo Trail—a motor-vehicle road that leads from Ely. From here the river flows a winding course of barely open water through a typical northern bog of eel grass, with the forest shores keeping their distance to either side. On the way north and west to Upper Pauness (pronounced "Pawnee") Lake, a sixty-rod portage comes in on the left at about 1.7 miles from the put-in. (A rod is 16-1/2 feet.)

The river is briefly impassable due to rocks and a falls beyond this point. This portage carries you above the gorge on the right through which the river continues its course. Half-way down the portage, a narrow side-trail leads to a waterfall. A mossy ledge at the end of this path makes a scenic spot for lunch, if you happen to be there at that time of the day. On the other side of the portage the marsh closes back in but widens, gradually, as one nears the end of the remaining 1.3 mile leg to Upper Pauness Lake. On the Pauness Lakes there are a number of good campsites, but here one is still too close to the put-in to want to stop. When you enter Upper Pauness Lake you will be floating on the pool of eel grass, at which point it is necessary to take a hard right and paddle back nearly in the direction from which you came to reach the connection to Lower Pauness Lake. Given the scrapes and soggy boots you will endure getting through the shallow, rocky passage, it is best to walk across the eight-rod portage, here.

The portage to return to the Little Indian Sioux River leads north out of Lower Pauness Lake just before the point where lake waters plunge into Devil's Cascade. The trail begins from the right bank. After fifty yards or so, several faint trails lead through the brush to overlooks of the cascade. Devil's Cascade is formed where the river narrows briefly in a tight passage of rocks.

After Lower Pauness Lake the Little Indian Sioux

River widens considerably to become the southern arm of Loon Lake. I made camp at the first site on the right shore of the lake, which offers great views and plenty of solitude. Like many sites in the BWCA, this one sits high above a wide, flat, rock ledge convenient for landing and loading canoes. All USFS sites have pit toilets set back in the woods.

The campsites in the Boundary Waters reflect the government's keen interest in avoiding the forest fires that have plagued this area for centuries. Archaeologists reportedly have uncovered increasing evidence that large-scale fires were commonplace in the region long before the arrival of Europeans. Author Grace Lee Nute, in her book Rainy River Country, cites a letter by a Jesuit missionary to his family in France in 1735, describing the journey from Lake Superior to Lake of the Woods (a distance of some two hundred miles) "through fire and thick stifling smokes" that altogether obscured the sun.

According to the forest service, open fires were not allowed at all in the Boundary Waters prior to 1980, when fire grates installed at all USFS campsites became available for use by campers. These grates are wisely built very low to the ground, inhibiting the wasteful and dangerous practice of bonfires. They are also usually fixed into granite outcroppings well out on the lakeshore, away from trees. These open locations offer little means of securing a tarp in wet weather. Consequently, when in the BWCA one should carry a small backpacking-stove to handle the cooking on those days when rain interferes with a campfire.

The fishing in the evening on Loon Lake was not all that I had hoped. Some considerable effort on my part yielded only two average bass and a small walleye. Of these I made a stuffing meal by moistening each filet and breading it in instant potato flakes before frying in light oil—a simple recipe from the *Campsite to Kitchen Cookbook* by the Outdoor Writers Association of America. These fish were all taken on a three-inch silver Rapala floating minnow, cast near shore and retrieved at moderate speed. I surmise that motorized access to Loon Lake from Canada has put considerable pressure on the fishery in these waters. Although the summertime canoeist will see relatively few boats of any kind, motorized or otherwise, after the long northern winter, the first few weeks after ice-out no doubt bring a sizeable contingent of fishermen in motorboats to these shores. The better fishing awaits elsewhere.

At Loon Lake one is faced with the first of several routing options. Here it is possible to cross a short portage (only the fifth of the trip so far) and pass directly into the western end of Lac LaCroix. This choice avoids any other portaging for the next three days or so, as you make your way north and eastward. The two factors that will control this decision are wind speed and wind direction. If the prevailing westerly winds are strong, your progress will be stopped by boarding waves when trying initially to go west and north to get out onto Lac LaCroix, where the wide expanses of water can make for sloppy going. The beauty of this trip is that an inland route in the same clockwise direction is readily available to deal with this contingency.

As shown on the map, the eastern arm of Loon Lake leads through a narrow passage to a 173-rod portage to Slim Lake. Along this route you will be sheltered by the forest from strong westerly winds, and waves on these mailer lakes will pose no hazard. The trade-off is the portages necessary to cover the same distance and direction that one would simply paddle on Lac LaCroix. You can depend on the fishing in any given lake in the Boundary Waters to improve in linear correlation to the length of the portage one must travel to get there. Slim Lake is proof of this theorem. After putting in at its southern end amid a driving rainstorm, I had little enthusiasm to stop and cast. Instead, I baited-up with a one-inch "Countdown" Rapala that had been recommended to me by Robin Lauer—a subscriber who shares my addiction to the rod and reel. Robin claims to catch most of his fish by trolling one of these lures behind his Chestnut canoe while underway. After testing his method on Slim Lake, I can say without hesitation that it was an utter failure: No one can possibly make any meaningful progress while having constantly to put down the paddle, pick up the rod, and disengage one fish after another attempting to drag the boat backwards. In the length of Slim Lake—making no special effort—I caught and released seven outstanding smallmouth bass.

Lest you think it was all just fish and solitude on this trip, I cannot fail to tell the story of the young couple camped on "Section-3 Pond"—the oddest name for a body of water that I ever did hear. One comes to this pond after a fifty-two-rod portage from the north end of Slim Lake. Section-3 Pond is just the very sort of place where a man might honestly assure his wife that they are unlikely to encounter another soul and where, after eight hours of solid rain, a wife might honestly believe him. For starters, it lies the considerable distance of one river, five lakes, and six portages away from the nearest road to the south. Add to that the fact that there is only one campsite on the entire pond—that being smack in the middle—and you have the setting for unfettered romance. And so it was understandable that the young lady in question did not expect to see the likes of me coming slowly up the lake just as the rain broke on that summer day.

She emerged from a shuttered tent only a few yards away as I glided along shore and, from my lateral view, appeared to be wearing a tee-shirt over an exceedingly high-cut swimsuit; but then, as she turned toward me, it was obvious that I had given her too much the benefit of the doubt. Now, I have been told that I have an unusually quiet paddling stroke, and whether that is true or not I am sure I don't know. But without a doubt this woman had either misplaced her glasses or never heard me coming, for the realization of my presence came over her rather abruptly. When she whirled around and bent over to fumble with the zipper of her tent—clearly eager to return within—the reason for her alarm was broadly apparent. I looked away, wondering to myself how many moons will pass before that particular moon finds the confidence to shine again in the light of day.

By the time I made it across the portage (another fifty-two rods) west from Section-3 Pond to South Lake, my new rain suit had long since given up the battle and joined forces with the enemy. I made camp on South Lake at the site closest to the outlet to Lac LaCroix, dried out, and planned to enter the big lake the following morning. Fishing that night on South Lake produced a couple of small northern-pike from the shallows.

When ready to head west out into Lac LaCroix the

next morning, I encountered a twenty-five-knot headwind that refused to allow me any progress through the inlet. That was no cause for concern, however. The other option at this point in the journey is to portage south (and up in elevation) to Steep Lake, then on to Eugene Lake and Gun Lake. From Gun Lake another portage puts one at last onto Lac LaCroix, in the lee of several islands and on an easterly course. This way is more grueling, but at least one is not resigned to sit in camp for what could be several days of waiting for favorable weather. Steep, Eugene, and Gun Lakes, which lie just behind the southern shore of Lac LaCroix, are reportedly all "trout water." Coming through as I was in the heat of summer, I had no success with the fishing, there. Despite its size, Steep Lake provides only one lovely campsite, located just beyond the landing of the portage from South Lake. This was occupied by a couple that had strung his-and-hers hammocks from the trees and were enjoying a morning of peaceful reading. All of the camps on Eugene and Gun Lakes were empty when I passed. Gun Lake, I would have to say, is the loveliest body of water I encountered on the entire voyage.

Judging from the condition of the portage, few people pass from Gun Lake into Lac LaCroix. Upon reaching the end of that portage, however, it is clear that you have come upon a lake that is in a league apart from those you have passed thus far. The large, ragged boulders hint at the destructive power of the glaciers that once clawed their way north from these shores. The waves are bigger, the fish are bigger, the water is strikingly clear and deep, and the sheer expanse of the lake itself is a marvel. It is more than twice as large as Basswood, the next largest lake in the BWCA.

By all means, make camp as I did on the eastern end of Forty-one Island in Lac LaCroix. From your campfire, here, you can look out over a nice view, and the size of the island affords an ample supply of downed firewood. The occasional sound of seaplanes taking off from the fishing outpost on the Canadian side should prove to be the only distraction. It is a one-mile paddle from Forty-one Island to this base, where a phone and supplies are available if needed.

The international boundary line which divides Lac LaCroix also separates the canoes from the motorboats. Motorized traffic is allowed on the Canadian side but not on the U.S. side, which is part of the B WCA. One or two motorboats came along in Canadian waters, but I never saw one canoe north of Coleman Island on either side of the boundary.

I left Forty-one Island at 5:30 in the morning to ensure that I would make it across the lake before the wind increased. Past Twenty-one Island there is a long fetch of open water to the east, but as long as the wind blows from the west or south as it usually does, this route poses no threat of high waves.

On Lac LaCroix there are so many islands, so close together, that there is a real danger of losing awareness of one's position in relation to the map. One island looks very much like the rest, and the beginnings and endings of islands can overlap in the distance to look like a solid shoreline and obscure a passage. The best technique to avoid getting lost and heading miles down the wrong bay is to draw a "dead-reckoning line" from the point where you begin the day's journey. Vigilantly mark your course by extending the line on the map as you recognize and pass each island. That way, you will always have a line on the chart to help you recall the most recent "fix" of your position. A compass is also helpful for staying on course across large bays that contain no nearby islands to use as reference points.

Some of the loneliest territory I have seen is below Coleman Island on Lac LaCroix. The islands and cliffs in this section are high and windblown, and the boulder strewn passages give a raw and untamed appearance to the world, here. In this section of the lake the fishing reportedly improves further due to lack of access, but in poor weather I did little more than troll, and that without success.

Coming into Boulder Bay, at the southern end of Lac LaCroix, I encountered several youth-groups and scouting parties making their way to and from the Moose River entry-point. This increased level of traffic always forebodes poor fishing, and such was the case on most of the water south of here. The scenery, however, remains outstanding.

Two short portages from Lac LaCroix returned me to the comparatively peaceful world of smaller lakes, and I made camp at the last site on the left bank of Lake Agnes. The campsites were almost all spoken for, here, and one would be wise to arrive early. Some people come in to set up a base camp on Lake Agnes from which to explore points farther north on Lac LaCroix.

After Lake Agnes, the route returns to a serpentine riverscape that recalls the beginning of the trip. The Nina Moose River runs into Nina Moose Lake from the north but becomes merely the Moose River as it leaves to the south. Be careful to leave Nina Moose Lake by the correct outlet for the Moose River. The outlet to the aptly named Portage River is close by and leads a long way to nowhere.

The trails near the end of this journey become more worn, other canoeists are encountered more frequently, and the signs of civilization intrude; but the dream that first brought you to this wilderness is by now written indelibly in your memory. After a series of short portages on the Moose River (exactly one more than is marked on the Fisher map) you will arrive at the parking lot for entry point no. 16. From here you can meet your outfitter's shuttle van, walk an easy seven miles on the Echo Trail back to the put-in, or do as I did and hitch a ride to the put-in with one of the many carloads of paddlers passing by. It is possible, of course, to portage one's way back to the original entry point by a series of other lakes instead of coming out by the Moose River, but I will leave that to younger readers to discover. For me, this modest journey would suffice to quiet for a while the small, distant voice of a boy who thrilled to ask, "Wouldn't it just be something to be there?"

"Way Down..."

THE SUWANNEE RIVER IN FLORIDA

Let me not waste too many words on hyperbole. Simply said, the namesake of Stephen Foster's famous tune is the most intriguing river I have ever paddled. When I paddle a better one I will let you know, but until now, of all the rivers, lakes, and streams I have crossed at the back of a canoe—and there have been a few—none has captivated me so well as the Suwannee. That is not to say that this river is a flaxen-haired enchantress who brooks no rivals for sheer beauty. No, she has her scars—too many of them—and one can clearly see she has known too few champions to defend her through the years. It would be unfair to compare these woods to Quetico or the Allagash, but who would want to? There is something about the place that recalls the girl you always knew but never noticed until, one day, you could notice no one and nothing else. And though it feels as if I am about to give out my own sweetheart's phone number, it wouldn't be fair to keep this river from you any longer.

The Suwannee pours out of the Okeefenokee Swamp in Georgia, but its swampy beginnings are mostly a memory by the time it crosses the Florida State line at

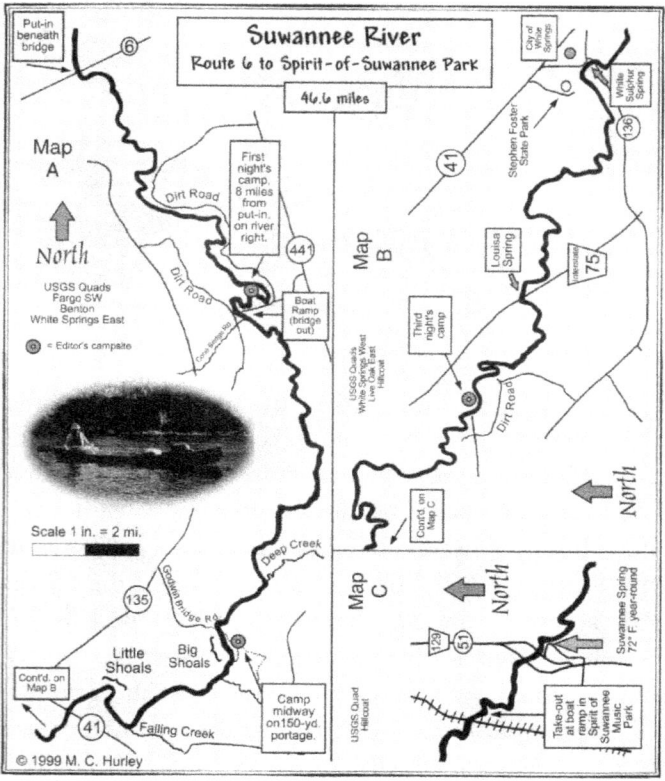

Fargo. Moving west from the north central part of the state, through an area known to archaeologists as the Hammock Belt, the river spreads its banks in sugar-white clouds of sand as soft and pure as those of any beach on the Florida coast. By the time it reaches the bridge at Highway 6 near Jasper, where I put in, the terrain has become charmingly unpredictable—lifting up to ridges of dense forests at one bend, descending through thickets of palmetto to wide expanses of white powder at the next. The river itself is equally eclectic. Long, sand-rimmed pools that recall a tropical lagoon give way below the fall line to periodic riffles, drops and rocks such as can be found anywhere in the Virginia piedmont.

The water of the Suwannee is clean, though stained a tea color from the vegetation that uniformly guards her shores. Sandbars and beaches appear regularly, but elsewhere the banks are locked in place by limestone ledges or the exposed, tightly intertwined roots of the Ogeechee tupelo. This squat, spreading hardwood imparts an air of Tolkienian fantasy to the place, such that the emergence of trolls and gnomes from the forest would hardly seem out of order.

The tupelo compete for the waterfront with bald cypress of considerable size, draped in Spanish moss, and with the beaches. One warm, sunny beach after another that beckons you to give up your foolish paddling and collapse like Robinson Crusoe with utter disregard for whether you have or don't have or forgot you have a tent, a sleeping bag, or a care in the world.

Though I came in the week between Christmas and New Year's Day, when one would assume a good chunk of humanity might be headed to the Sunshine State, I found here an enclave of virtual solitude. Perhaps that is because in the dead of winter, one is still too far north in this part of Florida to find water warm enough for swimming (except for the hot springs—more on those later). This season on the Suwannee can chill you to the bone, with overnight temperatures commonly in the thirties and dipping into the twenties on occasion.

Upon the arrival of warmer weather and vacation days in May, the lower reaches of this river will be abuzz in jet skis, bass boats, and teenage revelers. Anyone coming here then I'm sure would think I was quite daft to call this river a wilderness. Remember that I knew her in quieter moments.

The river empties into the sea on Florida's western coast, near the town of Suwannee, after spanning more than two hundred miles. The trip covered in this issue accounts for only about forty-six miles of that distance. It also includes only one of the six hot-springs along the river which maintain year-round temperatures of seventy degrees or greater.

You cannot take the full measure of the various geology, flora, and fauna that the Suwannee offers in a matter of four days, which was the time available to me. This journal, therefore, is not a definitive guide to the Suwannee though a good one, I submit, to its wilder reaches.

The forty-six-mile trip from Route 6 ends at the Spirit of Suwannee Music Park near Live Oak. This is a private campground with tent and trailer sites and an amphitheater where big-name country music stars perform in the summer. The Suwannee Canoe Outpost, on the grounds of the park, rents and shuttles canoes at reasonable rates. Their office is located a short distance from the river beside a boat ramp and a private parking lot where you may leave your car.

A canoe map is offered by the state through the Suwannee River Management District, but it is too large in scale and lacks sufficient detail to be of much use to the camper. You are better off ordering the USGS quads. (The names of the six quadrangles needed for this trip are listed on the map.) These and all other USGS maps are available by mail from Timely Discount Topos in

Colorado. Armed with these maps as well as up-to-date information from the outfitter about the water level, you are ready for a trip down the river.

If you are getting a start any time before noon, I would suggest that you paddle to my first night's campsite shown on the map, a distance of eight miles. It is impractical and unnecessary to go farther than that on the first day. This lovely site is one of the finest on the river and lies less than two miles above Cone Bridge Road. If you come to a huge tupelo on the left bank, about thirty yards upstream from a bald cypress in the middle of the river, you have just passed this site.

Throughout the distance between the put-in and Big Shoals, literally dozens of sandbars and beaches suitable for camping regularly appear, particularly above Cone Bridge Road. In addition to the first site where I camped, there is a beautiful site on an island about three miles below Cone Bridge Road. When I saw it a beaver dam spanned the entire length of the river at the upstream end of the island, making a lovely lagoon. What you will see in addition to an abundance of campsites—particularly if you make the trip at low water as I did—are feeder streams and waterfalls leading from springs of which I completely lost count. These springs are the lifeblood of the Suwannee. They add millions of gallons of crystal clean, pure water to what the river brings south from the Georgia swamps, giving the Suwannee a freshness uncommon among southern streams. When the water is high they seem to boil up at the river's edge. At low water, they pour over the bank into the river like a mill race. Were it not for the knowledge that this is Florida, one would be tempted to throw a Parmachene Belle in after a fat brook trout on these tiny creeks.

One particular reason not to rush on the first day is that you will undoubtedly want to camp at Big Shoals for the second night. Big Shoals is a moderate two-days' paddle from Route 6. These shoals are impassable to all but the extremely foolish, due to the sharp rocks that lay hidden beneath the surface. Liveries tired of dealing with the damage will require you to portage. In my wood-canvas Cheemaun, it wasn't even an issue. Besides, the portage and campsite at Big Shoals are its finest features.

The portage begins at river-left just a few yards before the first riffles appear at the head of the shoals. About fifteen minutes before you reach the portage, you will see a yellow hazard-sign posted on a private dock on the right bank warning you not to attempt the shoals. The portage follows a wide, easy path for a short distance to an idyllic campsite on an overlook, high above the river. The trees have been thinned to make a campsite on a carpet of pine needles worthy of any North Woods venue. Downed, dead wood was scarce at this location, but I picked up an adequate supply for a small "Indian" fire, which is all a solo camper needs.

The portage does not lead completely around Big shoals. It puts you back in the river just ahead of the last eddies and riffles. These are easily navigated, but use caution in getting down the slippery slope at the end of the portage. You will find that the exposed roots of a tree at the farthest launching spot come in handy as a foothold when descending the bank.

In the thirty miles between Big Shoals and the take-out, the face of the Suwannee changes yet again. Hardwood trees become more predominant among the pines and the banks much higher and more steeply inclined. From this point until well past Highway 75, fewer sandy beaches appear than before, giving way to limestone ledges both on shore and in the riverbed. In this section the Suwannee takes on the look of a northern, woodland stream for a while, with occasional riffles. Highway 75, then more noticeable as one gets closer to the take-out. To those involved in local efforts to preserve the Suwannee from further development, I urge you to pursue this cause vigorously.

About three miles below Big Shoals, Little Shoals appears—a Class I rapid. The best course is straight through the small haystack of whitewater in the middle. A second, smaller rips appears about five-hundred yards past the first, and this is best run on the left side. If the water is low, there are some nice eddies and sandbars around Little Shoals that make a good lunch spot.

One would hate to return to this river in twenty years and find that it has become just another rich man's view. Speaking of preservation, you might encounter during your Suwannee adventure one of Florida's great preservation success stories: the American alligator. Though it seemed that every log up ahead might be a lurking leviathan, as the song says "it was just my imagination"—except once. About three miles above Big Shoals, a five-footer was floating on top of the water, facing downstream. From fifteen yards away it reacted to the soft "snap" of the latch as I opened my camera case. Instantly it dove beneath the surface with a "thawhoosh!" Don't expect me to tell you that your fear of alligators is a lot of nonsense—it isn't. On average a half-dozen people are attacked—that is to say, bitten—by alligators every year in Florida. The overwhelming majority of these casualties are the result of reckless, human behavior or occur in areas where alligators have lost their natural fear of humans. Alligators on the Suwannee, by contrast, are wild and exceedingly shy. Don't let small children swim in deep pools or play alone on the bank. There are plenty of shallow riffles where little kids can swim. Alligators feed between dusk and dawn. No one should swim at those times. If you see an alligator, keep your distance, don't harass it, and do not throw food. It takes just a little common sense to be safe.

By the middle of the second day of this trip you will pass White Springs, recognizable by the large white pavilion and concrete bulkhead that has been built where the spring enters the river, next to the Route 41 bridge. Within fifteen minutes of passing White Springs, one comes to the boat dock and pavilion of Stephen Foster State Park. Though it will dispel the aura of "wilderness" you have enjoyed thus far, this place is worth a look for the curious. On the hour, a large bell tower at the park plays tunes by Stephen Foster, who was a prolific composer. "Babes in Toyland" was playing as I came up the hill. Near the pavilion, a pole dramatically marks the high-water levels from several of the big floods of the century, the highest of which was some forty feet above the place where my canoe was floating. A placard here tells visitors that the origin of the name "Suwannee" is a mystery, coming possibly from a Spanish mission located on the river in the 1700s named San Juan de Guacara, or from the Creek word "Suwani," meaning "echo."

After the boat dock at Stephen Foster State Park, signs on trees marking the park boundary continue along the river for another mile or two. The dense woods and steep banks block the view of campsites set back in the park. Not as many springs and creeks enter the river now as did above Big Shoals. Between the state park and Highway 75, I saw only two good campsites due to the predominance of rocks and the steep incline of the banks.

Just before Highway 75 one comes to lovely Louisa Spring on the right. You will find something special here—a sparkling, clear stream that tumbles out of a limestone canyon. So pure was the water that, despite the strong flow, it scarcely left a bubble on the surface where it dropped into the Suwannee. In warmer weather it would be worth exploring this creek all the way to the pond that is shown on the USGS map just north of the river, here.

Contrary to the advice in one guidebook, you cannot cover the distance between Highway 75 and the take-out in two hours. It will take you a solid four hours of paddling. Take your time. In this section the plenitude of spacious, sandy beaches characteristic of the upper river returns. For the third night I found a small site about three miles below the Highway 75 bridge, but I discovered that better sites lay just two or three miles farther. Suwannee Springs is a treat that awaits you near the end of your journey. The stone walls that supported a hotel over the spring more than a century ago still stand, now as part of a public park with road access. Walking up to the spring after four days in the wild without a bath or a shave, I would have been a queer sight to any tourist who happened by, but no one was there. When I stooped to touch the water, it seemed from the reflection of moss below the surface to be tinged an emerald hue. As promised, it flowed eternally seventy-two degrees and felt deliciously warm on that cold January day. Per usual I had no swimsuit in my possession. The photograph you see on the first page of this story is of me at this very point in the trip, trying to decide whether to take the plunge in this very public place. I carne close but ultimately decided against the chance to write this installment of the journal from the Suwannee County jail. Still, I must imagine that when Hernando de Soto realized he would never find the fabled treasure of the lost tribes of the Tirnucuan in these woods, he settled for his share of golden moments, here basking in the warmth of springs like this one and lying upon the sand until the reason for the day was all but forgotten. May God grant me the grace to return, one day, and claim the unworldly treasure of this magnificent river.

Fontana Lake to Hazel Creek

Great Smoky Mountains National Park

The Great Smoky Mountains of North Carolina and Tennessee harbor memories for nearly all of us. It is the most visited national park in America. Some nine million folks pass through each year. There is scarcely anyone living on the East Coast who cannot tell you of a vacation he took here at some point in his life.

As if God were trying to tell me something, I was repeatedly drawn to the State of North Carolina and the Smokies in particular, during my youth. What struck me at first was bow many schemers and fast-buck artists were making a living marketing a roadside, made-in-Taiwan version of the Great Smokies wilderness experience, where, just a few steps down the trail, the real deal was busting out all over.

It was my intention to peek behind the carnival tent, as it were, that first drove me to venture beyond the tourist traps of Gatlinburg and Cherokee into the woods, here. As a young boy, I was given an enormous, elk-handled Bowie knife by a relative in Nashville who hunted black bear in these mountains. I imagined the size

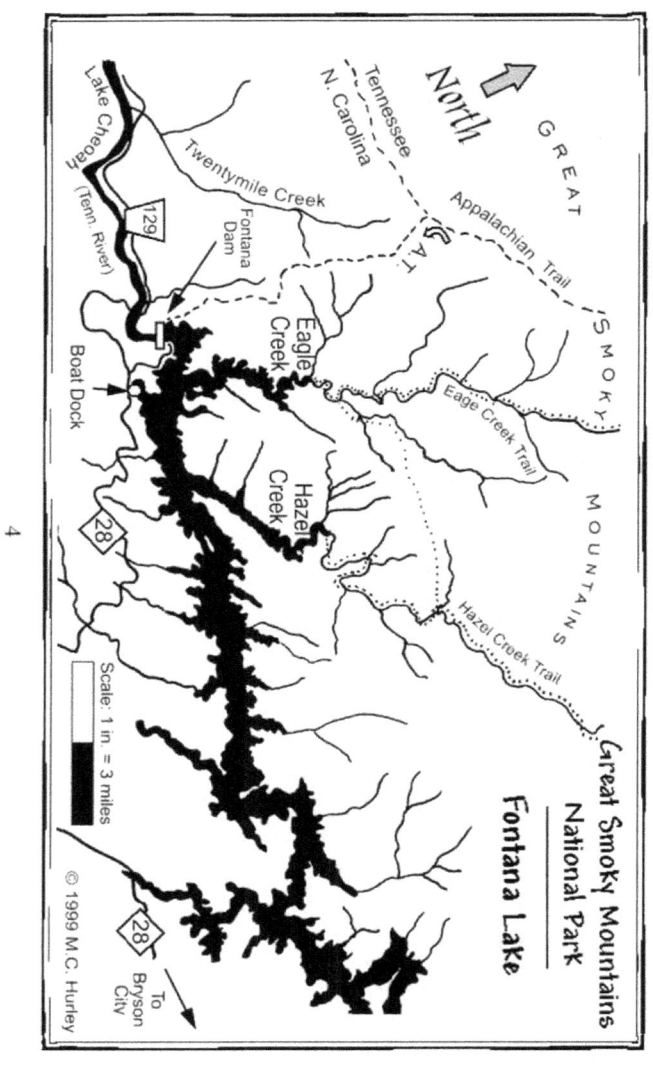

of a creature that would require such a ponderous knife for skinning. I listened intently to stories of men who fell through the snow into "crevices" (pronounced, for reasons not clear to me, "cra-vaá-ses) deep in the Smokies, never to be seen again. This was a foreboding place, with an irresistible temptation to be explored.

My first trips into the Carolina mountains were tentative, made from the safety of the resort village of Fontana Lake on family vacations in the early 1970s. I ventured out onto the lake with a guide known to me only as Mr. Griggs. Though not more than three hours passed between us in a boat on Fontana Lake, I remember the man's name to this day because he produced more large fish in the course of an hour than I had seen in one place in a lifetime. After this performance, the stage was set for the ill-fated scout trip I would lead up Hazel Creek in 1973.

My sister Sherry and a local basketball coach volunteered to drive a half-dozen of us scouts down from Baltimore to hike the Hazel Creek trail from its origin on the shores of Fontana Lake. We had set aside spring break to cover the thirty-six-mile distance up Hazel Creek, down Welch's Ridge, and over the Forney Creek trail to Noland Creek, where we'd left our car. My experience making that journey on foot more than twenty-six years ago is the reason why I am telling you, today, to come with your canoe.

The mouth of Hazel Creek is a little less than six miles from the boat dock at the Fontana Village Resort, on the North Carolina side of the national park. By canoe it is a good two-hour paddle, but we made the trip in no time back in 1973 with our gear piled high across a motorboat taxi. As we stepped off the boat into the woods, the wild side of the Smokies spread before us in greater glory than

I had imagined. With the lake at low water, Hazel Creek tumbled from the mountains like a picture-postcard into shimmering pools of clear blue. The sun was shining, the air was warm and sweet, and every back was rested. We set out on the wide, level trail with a spring in our step.

The trail followed Hazel Creek up the mountain on a fairly wide and gentle grade for the first day, switching back and forth across the stream just often enough to wet our boots and socks thoroughly. In the warm weather, we didn't mind. A wild boar snorted off into the woods after we surprised it beside the trail, and everywhere there was an excess of birds, wildflowers, and beauty to behold.

After about mile ten, the trail narrowed and climbed, and the temperature dropped. A cold rain fell, and spirits sank. Our group quarreled and split in two. The farther we fought our way up the steep mountainside toward Welch's Ridge, the fainter and more varied the trail became. Tearing through thickets of rhododendron, I would follow one spur until it disappeared, then another. My sister and I grew tired and took more frequent breaks to relieve the weight of our packs. Though in looking back I realize the challenge was as much mental as physical, I recall having then at the age of sixteen the very real notion that we were lost and might not survive long enough to make it out alive. It began to snow.

I learned a good deal about group dynamics on that trip. I watched people react to stress and deteriorating conditions. Some handled it better than others.

Somehow, though, we made it to the top of Welch's Ridge. Due to the worsening weather and difficulty in discerning the smaller trails, we decided to head west for the clearly discernible Appalachian Trail and the nearest road at Clingman's Dome.

If you have never hiked in the Smoky Mountains, you might not appreciate the experience of walking literally above the clouds—the mists that settle upon the hills and hollows and from which the park takes its name. Clingman's Dome, where we were headed, is at 6,643 feet the pinnacle not only of this park but of the entire Eastern seaboard of North America.

Toward evening of the third day, we finally reached the Appalachian Trail where it meets Welch's Ridge and pressed eastward toward the Double Springs Gap shelter, which sits at 5,590 feet. Arriving there, we found the shelter nearly full of other spring-breakers stranded by the weather. The shelter had a chain-link fence to keep out bears and two tiers of wooden bunks where we hunkered down for the night. On the dirt floor of the shelter, amid the chaos of boots and packs and gear, I tinkered with a backpacking stove and heated a precariously perched pot of water.

Straight from the "it can't get any worse than this" department, my plastic pouch of freeze-dried beef stroganoff buckled and spilled its steaming contents all over the shelter floor. In its stead I stuck a chaw of fruit pemmican in my mouth and hit the rack. That night, as the temperature dropped and the wind howled, some impetuous members of our party struck out in the snow for the road at Clingman's Dome, leaving just four of us behind. They made it in spite of their poor judgment, and so did we the following day. Despite the ordeal of that night, the beauty of the next morning as we hiked in snowy silence above the clouds toward Clingman's Dome would forever transfigure these woods in my memory.

That is why, I suppose, I had to come back, and why I have the audacity to urge you to do the same—not fighting your way up Welch's Ridge, and not anytime when snow threatens, but according to the gentler prerogatives of the canoe.

Canoe up Hazel Creek, you say? Nuts! Now that would be a marathon. No, the trip I made in 1996 and the one I recommend offers the best of both worlds. Starting out from the boat dock at Fontana Village Resort, where you may leave your car and purchase licenses, fishing tackle, and gobs of bait (illegal on Hazel Creek but okay for the lake), head due east. Take your time paddling the six miles of lovely lakeshore on your way. The channel narrows and turns as you get closer to the head of the creek, until one of several small landings appears on the right bank. How far you go and which landing you take will depend on the lake level, which can fluctuate as much as thirty feet. Above the landing is the Hazel Creek trail—an old jeep-road that crosses the site where the logging town of Proctor once stood, about one mile in.

There are a number of idyllic, streamside campsites just above the point where the creek enters the lake. You can set up a base camp and portage your canoe, carry it back down when you want to fish the lake, and hike up the creek when your tastes run to trout. The Hazel Creek trail is wide and gradual for as far as you'd ever want to go from a base camp, and there are many little spots through which to duck into the creek and cast. The farther up you go, the better the fishing gets. In these days of high-tech camping as an endurance sport, you almost never see a backpacker carrying a fishing rod, much less taking the time to use it. That means that if you're willing to hump it a little farther upstream than most, there are still some dream-sized trout waiting to be fooled.

Fontana Lake was formed in 1943 when the TVA dammed the Little Tennessee River for hydroelectric power. The dam flooded the bed of Hazel Creek about five miles up the side of the mountain, ruining that much of a great trout stream but making ideal habitat for smallmouth bass and walleye. In the spring, small minnows fished on the bottom of rocky points, with a split-shot for weight, will produce handsome stringers of fish.

I'm not sure what the park-service rules are on picking the odd sassafras plant (I can just about guess), but the mountains are thick with them. Boiling the tender roots makes a fine tea to go with honey. In 1996, as summer breezes wafted through these woods and the water went laughing by my feet, I had a steaming kettle-full to reminisce by. The creek was as lively and bright as when I first saw her, which is more than she could say of me if she were talking. I had returned to Hazel Creek once before in my college days, but never again to try for Welch's Ridge. I'll stick to the low going, thank you. Perhaps the hordes who've climbed this trail in twenty-six years have beaten it into a thoroughfare. I doubt I'll ever know. I've come to treat these hills with the caution rightly accorded any old flame who invites us to relive the temptations of our youth.

NEW RIVER

New River State Park
Wagoner Road Access to VA Line

Although the tributaries of many rivers flow northward, and some rivers flow north for a part of their journeys, you may be surprised to learn that there are only two river systems in the entire world that flow primarily south to north. They are also the two oldest rivers in the world. Sixty-five million years ago, your choices for river trips on Planet Earth would have been limited to the Nile, in Egypt, and its slightly younger cousin, the New River, which begins in the mountains of North Carolina. Frankly, though, if fir-crested vistas and smallmouth bass are what you're after, the New River beats the Nile hands down.

It's no wonder, then, that the New River was among the first rivers in the nation (along with the Allagash in Maine and the Wolf River in Wisconsin), to be protected under the federal Wild and Scenic Rivers Act of 1968. In 1976, Congress designated "that segment of the New River in North Carolina extending from its confluence with Dog Creek downstream approximately 26.5 miles to the Virginia State line" as part of the national wild and

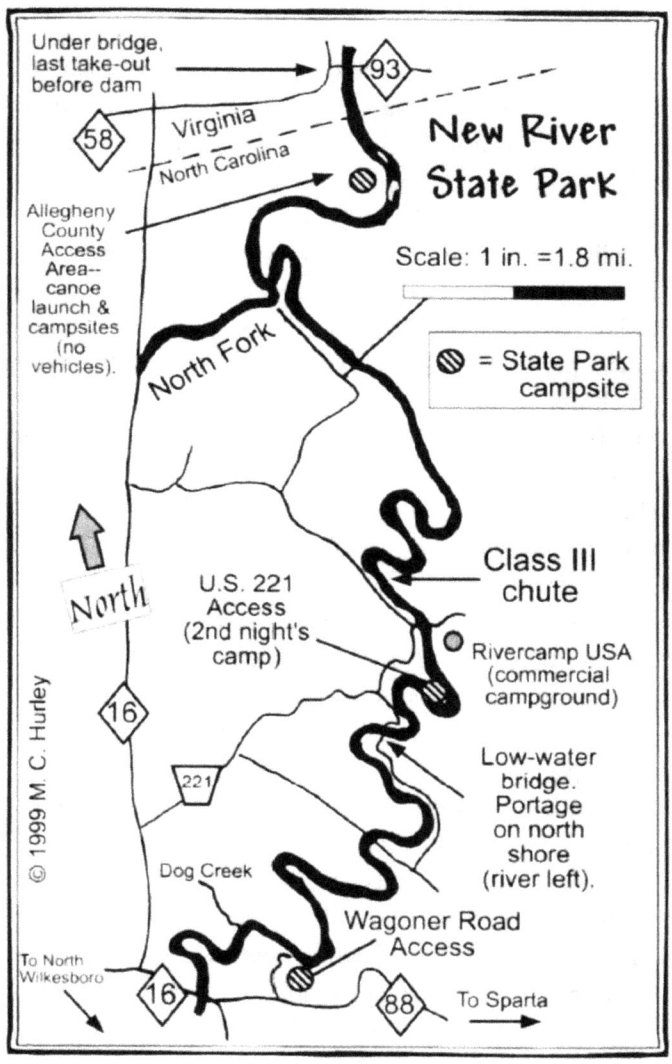

scenic rivers system. It merits only a "scenic" classification, given that much of its watershed was cleared long ago for farms and roads.

Those seeking pure "wilderness" will be disappointed, but the vacation-home development that once threatened to overtake the river has been checked. The designated section now comprises the New River State Park. Within the park are three campsites, known as "access areas," planned with canoe-camping in mind.

Still far from the whitewater tantrums that characterize its more northern reaches in West Virginia, the New River in North Carolina is a local favorite for scout trips, tubers, those seeking to learn on gentle rapids, and church groups. Ask anyone almost anywhere in the state, from the mountains to Cape Hatteras, and chances are he's taken a canoe down the New River at some point in his youth. Zaloo's and New River Outfitters are two of the better-known liveries that rent mostly canoes. Zaloo's is located five miles upriver from the Wagoner Road access area, where the state park begins and where the first campground is located. New River Outfitters operates out of an historic general store located on the river at the Rt. 221 bridge. Both liveries run shuttles to various points on the river all the way down to the town of "Mouth of Wilson" on the Virginia border, where a dam forces paddlers to take out.

I have paddled this river twice, covering the designated scenic-portion in its entirety on my first trip in 1994 and taking out farther upstream, at Rivercamp USA (a commercial campground), on a trip here in 1998. The best way to begin the trip is to drive into the state park access-area farthest upriver at Wagoner Road. Here you will find paved parking, showers and restrooms. A concrete ramp leads to the river from the parking lot, but most folks portage their canoes and gear the hundred-yard distance across an open, grassy field that separates the parking lot from the campsites beside the river. Campsites may not be reserved. The ranger walks through the campsites here at evening to collect a small fee. If you are planning to camp the next night at either the Rt. 221 or Allegheny access areas, the ranger will collect the fee in advance and give you a permit.

The campsites at Wagoner and the Rt. 221 access have, regrettably, been mostly cleared of large trees and planted in grass. Each comes with a picnic table and a fire ring and is set off from neighboring sites by brush. With a little effort, you can find enough kindling in the surrounding forests for a small fire. To reduce destructive cutting, the rangers periodically distribute small quantities of split wood to each campsite. At each access area, canoe landings with wooden steps leading to the water's edge have been installed. This provides an easy way to put in and also marks the location of the campground from the river.

Due to its old age, the New River flows wide and shallow from its birthplace near Boone, North Carolina until it drops into the New River Gorge of West Virginia, where I hear its fame for whitewater is richly deserved. The biggest factor in planning a trip in the North Carolina section is making sure there is enough water flow for canoes. I have made the trip smack in the middle of summer without difficulty, but during dry-spells that won't be possible. The best paddling runs through June and picks up again in the fall.

The rapids in the state park are for the most part pretty pedestrian. The greatest challenge is to avoid getting stuck on rocks in the shallower stretches. This will test your ability to "read" rocky water, and you'll come out a better paddler for it.

The rapids get only slightly tougher below Rivercamp. A hundred yards downstream from the campground, one comes to a fairly easy Class II-III chute that even I managed to run upright—which should be reassuring to everyone. A short distance farther, the North Fork comes in, and the river seems to take on a wilder character. Boulders and eddies are more frequent, and the fishing gets better. I took one small bass here, but the fellows who were really slaying them were tossing hellgrammites and nightcrawlers without weights into fast water above pools, then letting the bait drift down. Inside the store at Rivercamp, you'll see some trophy examples of the muskellunge—yes, muskies—that swim this river in the 15 to 20-pound weight-class. I've never caught a muskie. I lost all interest in ever doing so when, as a boy, I read that it takes an average of 10,000 casts to catch just one. I figured that any fish or girl that played that hard to get wasn't worth chasing. What I've learned since about women and fish is that chasing them is the fun part. Now, with my dating days long behind me, the muskie are starting to look better and better. So here's hoping you spot me on the New—I'll be the guy with the big fish and the tired arms.

BIG SOUTH FORK OF THE CUMBERLAND RIVER

BIG SOUTH FORK NATIONAL RIVER & RECREATION AREA

They say that these rugged mountains and verdant foothills, seeming to ripple out in folds and valleys as far as the eye can see, are the country of Daniel Boone. This is a gritty, rugged place of breathtaking beauty. On this my first foray into the hills of Kentucky, I feel a sense of gladness to know that this place is here for me and for my children, still free and wild—almost untamed.

You see, I remember Dan. Daniel Boone was a man— "Yes, a bi-ig man. With an eye like an eagle and as tall as a mountain was he. . ." If you hear a melody with those words, you probably were stationed where I was every Sunday evening in the 1960s, when Fess Parker played the part of America's legendary frontiersman alongside an Indian sidekick known as Mingo. I remember that they invariably wound up around a bedding down beside a campfire in a little pine-needled alcove of the woods— the kind that only exists on a Hollywood set but which remains to this day the prototypical campsite for millions

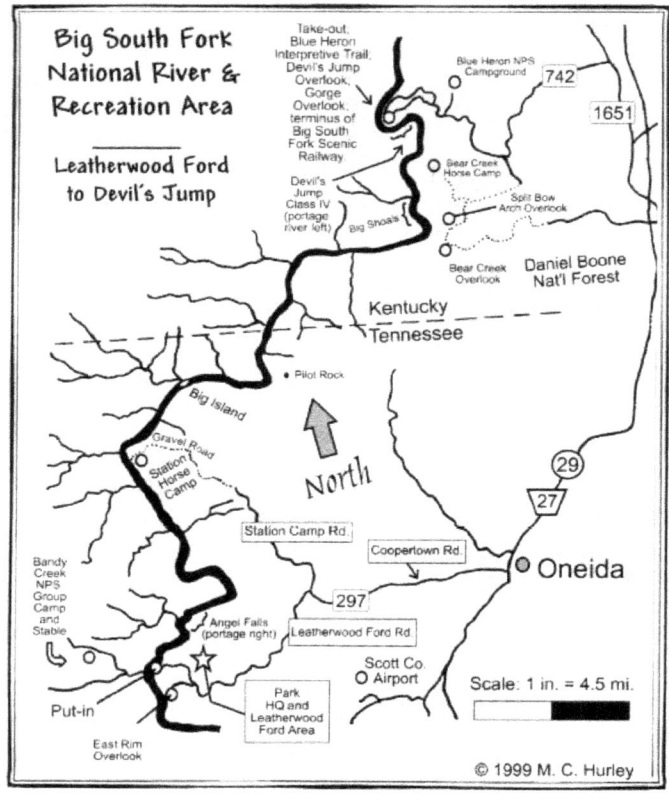

of aging Baby Boomers. I keep waiting for reruns of that show, Mutual of Omaha's Wild Kingdom, and other staples of television in once-upon-a-time America. Alas, I suppose stories of hunting with flintlock rifles and Indians who speak broken English have sunk into the bogs of political correctness, never to rise again. No matter. Turn off your TV, and pack your buckskin coat. Daniel Boone has left Hollywood and lives on in the Big South Fork of the Cumberland River.

Our trip on the Big South Fork covered what author

Bob Sehlinger described in *A Canoeing and Kayaking Guide to the Streams of Kentucky* (Hillsborough, NC: Menasha Ridge Press, 1978), as "one of the most popular canoe-camping runs in the southeastern United States"—twenty-seven miles from Leatherwood Ford to the old Blue Heron Mine. This section of the river is located partly in northeastern Tennessee, about fifty miles from Knoxville, and partly in southeastern Kentucky, about 100 miles south of Lexington.

Since Sehlinger wrote his book in 1978, the river has acquired the additional cache of national park status. An act of Congress passed on March 4, 1974 gave the Army Corps of Engineers power to begin acquiring land around the Big South Fork and $156 million with which to do it. On November 15, 1990, control of the Big South Fork National River and Recreation Area officially passed from the Corps of Engineers to the U.S. Department of the Interior.

By federal law, no motorized craft is allowed anywhere upstream of Devil's Jump—a Class IV rapid that marks the end of the traditional, twenty-seven-mile canoe trip from Leatherwood Ford. The logging and strip mining operations that once denuded the mountains surrounding the river gorge are now banned, and strict limitations on road construction have been enacted. It is an area of striking beauty and remoteness. The ridges of steep mountains and sheer cliffs that line the river gorge establish the boundary of the protected area—a distance that spans anywhere from two to fifteen miles across, depending on the topography surrounding the river.

Primitive camping is possible anywhere along the Big South Fork, but high, dry sites are few and far between above Big Island. The National Park Service maintains two large campgrounds (Blue Heron and Bandy Creek) that have restrooms and showers, three horse campgrounds with improvements, one primitive site, and a backcountry lodge. All of these facilities are remote from the river, which has been preserved from signs of man.

My wife Julie and I, our seven-year-old daughter Caroline, and our son Kip—a few days shy of his ninth birthday—arrived here at the start of Memorial Day weekend, this year. After catching a few short winks at the Parkland Motel near Whitley City, Kentucky, we met our shuttle at the Blue Heron campground at 6:00 a.m. We left our Jeep at the take-out, there, and Sheltowee Trace Outfitters shuttled the four of us, our two canoes, and gear to the put-in for forty dollars. The outfitter fills up well in advance of most summer weekends, and reservations are required. Shuttles run at various times, but the 6:00 a.m. shuttle is recommended if you plan to get far enough to make camp on the river for the night.

After an hour's drive back across the Tennessee line, the shuttle arrived at the put-in. Leatherwood Ford is near the park headquarters and is improved with a parking lot, wooden steps to the river, a small pavilion, and restrooms. The NPS keeps an ample supply of its "Official Map and Guide" to the river in a rack in the pavilion, here, or you may request one by mail from the Visitor Center. This map is all one really needs for canoeing the river. Too many USGS 7.5 quadrants are necessary to track the river's course, and they don't provide much more detail. With the free shareware version of Acrobat Reader, you can download a PDF file version of the park map from the park service web page.

The put-in at Leatherwood Ford begins on a gravel bar just below the parking lot. Almost immediately, the river provides a taste of what for the next twenty-seven miles will be a steady diet of Class I-II rapids followed by beautiful pools. Water level plays a big factor here, and you'll quickly notice that it occupies a lot of discussion among paddlers. At low water levels, you must pick your way carefully to avoid running up on rocks. Wear river sandals or old sneakers for stepping out of the boat and shoving it free. The NPS website noted above offers a link to information on current stream-gauge conditions, published by the U. S. Geologic Survey. According to Sehlinger's book, a reading at the Leatherwood Ford gauge of 350 cubic feet per second (cfs) is the minimum runnable level. Those seeking whitewater sport would agree with that, but canoe-campers can get by with less. The photos with this story show the river at about 220 cfs. We had to hop out and push off of rocks now and then, but only when we chose the wrong route. The river is probably canoeable down to 150 cfs at the Leatherwood gauge. The park service considers anything between 500 and 1,000 cfs to be "ideal" for canoes, and Sehlinger puts the maximum level for open boats at 1300 cfs. Sheltowee Trace Outfitters keeps track of the river level for its customers, or you may contact the U.S. Geological Survey office in Nashville to request the current reading on the Leatherwood gauge.

Within two miles of the put-in, one encounters Angel Falls (Class III-IV). Though some said they saw a sign marking the approach to the falls, I did not. Had we not backed up to some boats taking out on the bank, we might have gone past the portage. You won't miss it if you remember that Angel Falls is the first rapids you hear after you see a high rock-bluff some 800 feet above the river in the distance. The portage, which also is not marked, leads up the right bank for about a quarter mile around the falls. The water here is an amazingly clear, pale green. A pool at the other end of this portage makes a lovely spot for a swim.

Between Angel Falls and Big Island we encountered a long section of deep, mostly flat water. Only one good campsite—a high, sandy beach on the river left—presented itself in this entire section. In fact, despite the reputation of this river for canoe-camping, we noticed almost no good campsites at all above Big Island. Finding high ground (10 feet or more above the river level) is necessary due to the reputation of this river to rise high, fast, and without warning. We did not explore Big Island on shore, but it rose thirty feet above the river level on our trip, and there are likely some campsites on the island for those willing to beat the brush to find them.

Below Big Island the park service horse camp known as Station Camp appears on the right. This was the only section of the river where road noise was briefly heard. If you're not bothered by the noise or by horses sloshing across the river, the downstream end of a small island at Station Camp would make a nice camp.

It was our good fortune to meet up with a group from the Elkhorn Paddling Club of Shelbyville, Kentucky. They offered to share their campsite and generously assisted us with our packs and canoes. The club comes here every year, and members prefer to camp at a spot near the second of two creeks that enter the river below

Big Island. The first creek is Crooked Branch, which comes in on the right and is not marked on the park map. The second is larger and shown on the park map as Williams Creek., next to Pilot Rock (elev. 1200 ft.). Wade your canoe about 100 yards up the cold, clean water of Williams Creek until you come to a landing on the left, formed by trail riders coming to water their horses. The trail leads up another fifty yards into the woods to a clearing used as a horse camp. In summer there is no view of the river at this site, but there is no risk of flooding.

Those not wishing to climb the trail to the Williams Creek horse camp can paddle down to one of several campsites on the riverbank that we discovered the next day, less than three miles downriver. Unless rain is in the forecast, these sites are preferable to the one back in the woods on Williams Creek.

The fishing on the Big South Fork was not particularly fruitful, with only two small rock bass to show for our efforts. Others, however, had better luck with live minnows and small Rapalas. We saw several fishermen with one or two nice smallmouth and one fellow with a pretty good walleye. I spotted some nice trout in the clear water of deep pools, too. The feeder streams are popular with fly fishermen.

The second day of this trip offers more challenging if not more frequent rapids. None of these may be portaged except Devil's Jump, but the path through each is fairly straightforward. Big Shoals—a series of rock gardens that are picky at low water—sounds worse than it is. On the entire second day, we encountered perhaps three good ledges of two feet or more. It is easy to take enough water over the gunwales on these ledges to swamp a canoe, even if one finds the clear path through. Kip and I did just that on "Mabel's Bump"—the last rapid above Devil's Jump. Having split the apron of smooth water dead-on for our trip over this ledge, we were preparing for the obligatory "yahoo" yell when the nose of our little wood-canvas Cheemaun went under and stayed there. The water poured in, and Kip and I poured out. The photographs in this issue are a testament to the waterproofing of Pelican camera-cases, which I happily endorse. With help from others, we gathered all of our gear (save a rod and reel) and made it ashore. Julie and Caroline eyed our performance and opted to sneak down Mabel's Bump on foot, leaving us to catch their empty boat.

After we bailed water, Devils Jump loomed. It is aptly named. At least one life is lost there each year, and a fair complement was vying for the honor when we arrived. A steep portage, unmarked, leads up the left bank. The take-out lies just a half-mile of paddling from the other side. I was moping about dumping my boat until a man tried to take his brand new Old Town through Devil's Jump. He broached, and his canoe was folded in half against a rock. He escaped alive, but there is a lesson here for all of us. I'll bet you even Daniel Boone and Mingo carried around the big ones. You do the same, and you'll live to tell your tales, bedded down in a perfect spot somewhere in a piney woods, where the campfire glows.

St. Croix River

Vanceboro to Loon Bay

The waters I have known in Maine, no matter how urban or remote, and however swift or serene, all seem to exude that rocky, rugged character that well represents this state and her people. The St. Croix, outlining Maine's northeastern coast and the boundary between the United States and New Brunswick, is cast in that mold.

The St. Croix fits into that much-sought-after class of rivers that is often referred to as "easy whitewater." No lazy slough, it tumbles and turns its way through a fairly steady succession of Class II rapids, but none that even the most novice reader of this journal has reason to fear on a warm, summer day. And for your efforts, you will find surprisingly good fishing, an abundance of postcard-pretty campsites, and unexpected solitude in a most picturesque woods. It would be trite to say that some of the best camping in this nation can be found here, because the entire State of Maine offers no less.

The St. Croix has played an interesting role in our nation's history and was long a source of international controversy. For more than a hundred years in the

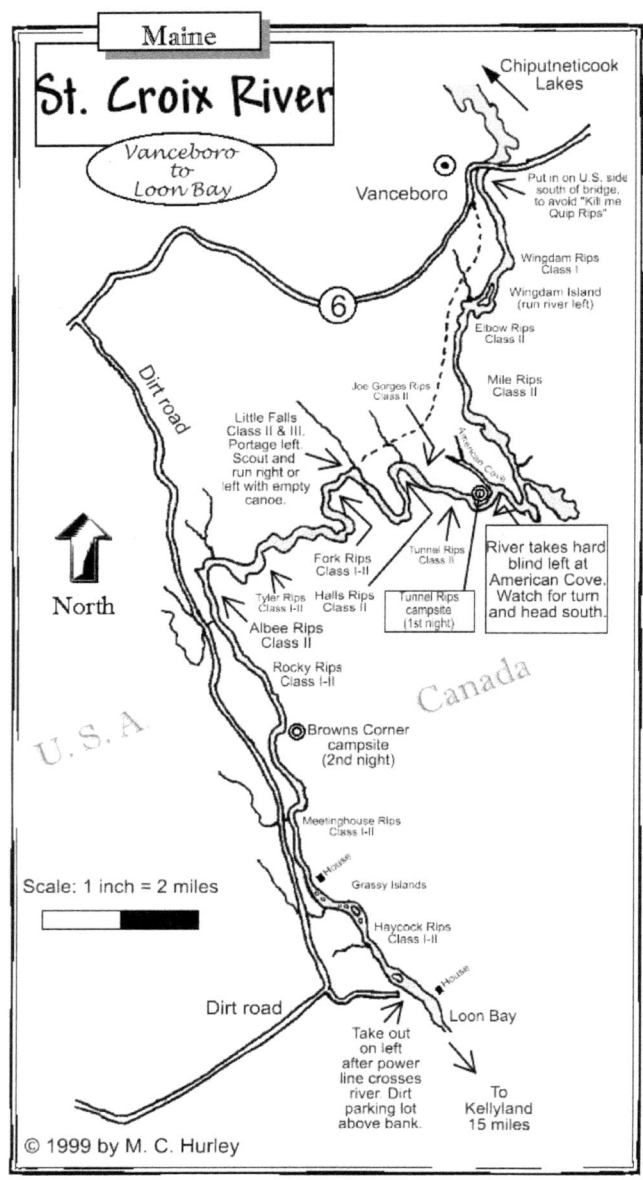

1600s and 1700s, it was the front line in bloody fighting among the English, the French, and Passamaquoddy Indians over territorial boundaries. The Treaty of Paris, which officially ended the American Revolution in 1783, attempted to fix the boundary between United States and British lands in Eastern Canada along the middle of the St. Croix River to its "source." Difficulty in defining that source kept the boundary in dispute, culminating in a tense but bloodless standoff in 1838 between 10,000 volunteers of the Maine Militia and British troops of New Brunswick, known as the Aroostook War. You can thank Daniel Webster, America's Secretary of State, for finally putting the controversy to rest in 1842 in a treaty with the British that fixed the northeastern boundary of the United States as we know it today, right smack in the middle of the St. Croix River.

As depicted by the small patch of white on the map, the area comprising this trip takes some getting to. It is close to nothing, which is really the point, and located in the poorest county in a state known for its hardscrabble way of life. Timber and seasonal work—blueberry picking in summer and wreath making in fall and winter—are mainstays of the inland economy, here, while tourists generally stick to the coast. Washington County is the first place in the continental United States on which the sun's rays fall each morning, hence the name taken by Sunrise County Canoe Expeditions. They outfitted me for this trip as they have thousands of others since 1973.

The SCCE base is tucked behind the trees on the shores of Cathance (pronounced Cát-ance) Lake about halfway between the towns of Calais and East Machias. If you fly here or drive by way of Bangor, don't count on finding a motel on short notice along the road—there are virtually none—or a vacancy in any of the little coastal motels, which stay booked in the summertime. Your best bet is to rent one of the cabin tents that SCCE keeps pitched on its property for overnight use by its customers. Tell them when you're coming, and they'll have a campfire going outside your tent when you arrive. The shuttle leaves from this location.

The run recommended for a weekend trip and featured in this issue is roughly twenty miles, from Vanceboro to Loon Bay. Some prefer to travel thirteen miles farther downriver to the town of Kelly land. The truly adventurous could follow this river thirty-two miles past Kellyland to Robbinston, where it empties into Passamaquoddy Bay behind Deer Island and the Atlantic Ocean, but no established, public campsites lie below Kellyland.

Local outfitters and guidebook authors rate most of the rapids on the St. Croix, called "rips," at Class II. I don' t dispute that except to say that some of you will not recognize these Class II rapids as posing the same level difficulty found on a Class II stream in, say, Virginia. When you run a Class II rapid down South, you're likely going over and down something at an angle—usually a chute between two big rocks, where the safe course is clear but you've got a fair chance to dump your boat if you get off balance. The Class II rips on the St. Croix, on the other hand, tend to be prolonged rock gardens running down a more gradual incline. True to the textbook definition of a Class II, finding and steering the correct path through these rocks is moderately difficult, but choosing the wrong path more often means getting stuck on a rock and having to shove off—not nosing in the bow and capsizing. Aside from Little Falls, a true Class II-III where you'll want to portage your gear, the rapids in this section pose few technical challenges.

If you have time and are willing to pay the added fee, SCCE will follow you to drop your vehicle at the take-out in Loon Bay, then carry you and your gear in their van north to Vanceboro. The take-out is in the middle of nowhere. Leaving a vehicle in the dirt parking lot there is preferred over trying to time the conclusion of your trip to coincide with the arrival of a shuttle driver from base camp. Pay attention to the various turns on the dirt road leading into the take-out so that you can easily find your way out, on your own. A four-wheel-drive vehicle is not absolutely necessary, but you'll want to be driving something with high ground-clearance to negotiate the ruts and potholes.

The put-in that SCCE recommends is downriver of the bridge at Vanceboro. Others begin the trip upriver of this town and go through Kill-me-Quick Rips. Having not run that section I cannot tell you much about it, but unless you particularly want to add that rapids to your belt, it makes more sense to start this trip below the developed section of town.

Réserve Faunique La Vérendrye, Quebec

Circuit 78

It may be a guy-thing, but it is a well-known fact that, with the possible exception of french fries, there is an element of romance in all things French. It comes over you (not you ma'am, your husband) the first time a woman says bon jour to you in Quebec, no matter how far and faint a cry she may be from Bridgette Bardot or Catherine Deneuve, and no matter that her next, seductive gesture may be to take your order for ham and eggs.

The French mystique certainly cast its spell upon some of us as we arrived at the put-in on Grand Lac Victoria, in La Vérendrye Reserve, one sunny Saturday last August. There beside the lake was a man in the company of an auburn-haired woman who turned out to be his wife, both in their late forties I would guess, cheerfully unloading their canoe at the end of a week in the wilderness. My buddy and guide for this trip, Robin Lauer, asked the man and woman the usual questions about weather and bears and such, but what was unusual were the answers. They came to us in a lilting French

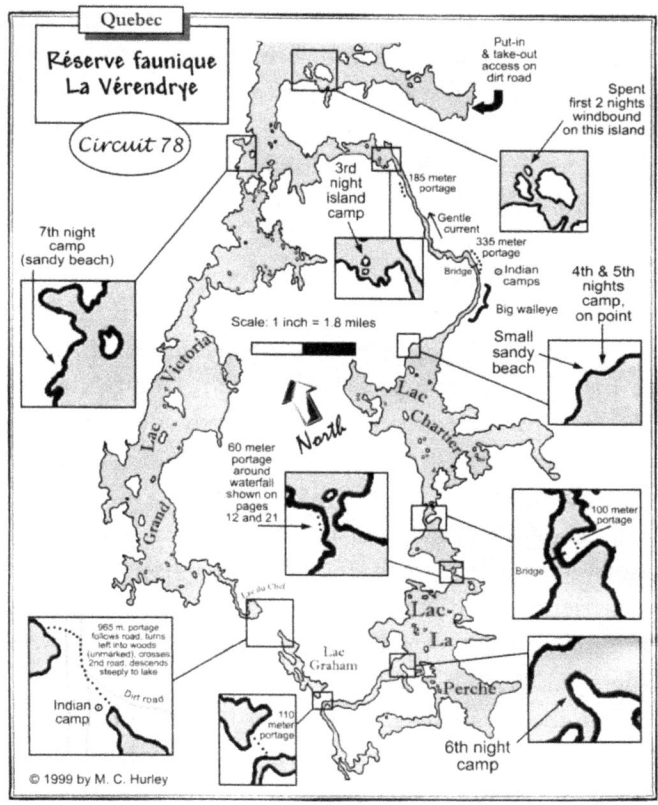

accent from the wife, not her husband. Stepping closer to listen, I noticed that, despite a week in the deep woods, there was nothing about her clothing or appearance that was the least bit unflattering, or her demeanor that gave any sign of fatigue. And in her hair, was it a hint of lilac?

In short order Robin pulled out our map, and the woman stood there beside him, looking on and correcting his pronunciation of French place-names that appeared along our route. "Laahhk Eyiee-nó" she said slowly and carefully, with Robin slowly and carefully repeating each word after her, butchering the French pronunciation like only a guy from Brooklyn can. His effort to impress her by passing me off as the editor of a prestigious journal drew a blank look, to my noticeable discomfort. Still, I saw no need to correct her references to me thereafter as the "ów-thur."

Yes, that's me all over—Papa Hemingway. Everyone says so. Though it went unspoken among us at the time, clearly the French-Canadian woman had left her mark on the men in our group, as every mention of "Laahhk Eyiee-nó" for the remainder of the trip made clear.

But I digress. You're reading this journal to find out about the fishing and camping and canoeing in Quebec's La Vérendrye Reserve, not fairy tales about uncommon beauty, love at first sight, and old men's hopes of glory. Well, friends, I am here to tell you that they are one and the same. Pack your French cologne and steel-wire leaders, and head north.

First, the essentials: La Vérendrye is a wildlife preserve ("réserve faunique") located about a six-hour drive northwest of Montreal, between the towns of Mont-Laurier and Val-d'Or. The park covers 5,256 square miles of territory, an area larger than the State of Connecticut. Within it lie more than 4,000 lakes and rivers connected by over 1300 miles of portages, many of them dating from ancient times. It is administered on behalf of the provincial government by the Quebec Canoe Camping Federation (Federation Quebecoise Du Canot-Camping, Inc.), a private company. The federation collects fees and issues permits for travel in the park from its offices in Montreal. Since 1993, it has also operated a base camp within the park at Le Domaine from May through September. Le Domaine is not a town in its own right, just a collection of rental cottages, a small restaurant and gas station, a convenience store, an outdoor clothing and equipment shop, and a small campground. From this base, the federation offers complete outfitting services, permits, fishing licenses, maps, hired guides, and shuttles. These services may be reserved in advance or purchased on-site. The federation has identified and assigned numbers and names to thirty-four circuit-routes within the park suitable for trips ranging from two to ten days. Brief navigational details for each of these circuits have been published in a free booklet, entitled "Canoe Routes." The federation sells a series of 22 x 25-inch maps depicting the routes for the circuits described in this booklet.

Given the difficulty in calculating the exchange-rate by mail, it is best to pay for the materials offered by the federation and any services you wish to reserve with a credit card by telephone. If needed, the mailing address is Federation Quebecoise Du Canot Camping, Inc., 4545 Ave. Pierre-DeCoubertin, C. P. 1000, Station M, Montreal (Quebec) HI V 3R2.

Campsites on water routes in the park are not numbered or named, but some are shown on the canoe maps with an indication of how many tents they will accommodate. Many of the nicest sites we saw, though, were not marked on the map, including our camps for the first and third nights. In fact, we rarely passed even a tiny island that did not have a clearing suitable for camping.

Robin Lauer, my brother-in-law Michael Rosenthal, Michael's son Bennett, my son Kip and I began this trip with ambitions to do a seven-day circuit but, due to inclement weather and Kip's unexpected illness, wound up paddling Circuit 78—typically a four-day route-in seven days' time. As it turned out, true to the advice given in the article on voyaging with kids in this issue, that was probably the better plan from the start.

The put-in for Circuit 78 is on Grand Lac Victoria, close to a two-hour drive north of Le Domaine. A large, folding map of the entire park available at Le Domaine shows the driving route. The distances in Canada can be deceiving. Flying into Ottawa or Montreal to go canoeing in Le Vérendrye, for example, is equivalent in terms of distance to flying into Washington. D.C. to go canoeing in New York City.

Grand Lac Victoria is a large, sprawling lake of many islands and bays. It is open to motorized traffic, which you will see on weekends. The fishing here is mainly for walleye and northern pike. There are no smallmouth bass in this or any of the other lakes we paddled on this trip.

We had paddled only a short distance from the put-in on Grand Lac Victoria before Robin Lauer had boated two pan-size walleye for dinner and thrown back a small pike. Soon thereafter it threatened to rain in earnest, which set the stage for the entire trip. The weather was uncommonly cold, wet and windy, but the fishing was uncommonly good—uncommon for me, that is. According to Robin, who had traveled much of this route, before, the fishing is usually even better than the results shown on these pages would suggest.

Out of concern to get the boys under shelter before the rain really set in, we opted not to cross Grand Lac Victoria to the northwestern shore before making camp that first afternoon. This was a mistake.

After spending our first night on the small island you see marked on the map, we woke to gray skies and a stiff wind the next morning. We had nearly packed up camp before noticing that the wind and waves were increasing. Two of us headed out in an empty canoe to see just how rough it was. Steering toward the north, we had not gone more than ten yards before the first wave came sloshing over the bow of Robin's Chestnut Prospector. We turned back, re-pitched our camp in the same spot, and hunkered down for the day.

Storm winds in the North Woods almost always blow from the west or north, rarely from the east. If you are headed north or west across big water, as we were that first day, it is best to make as much northing and westing a you can while the weather is calm. Had we done so, we could have paddled down Grand Lac Victoria under the lee of the northwestern shore and avoided an extra day in camp. Even so, the boys showed a lot of initiative in making their own fun on the island.

To pass the time, Kip recreated an Indian rock-pile sculpture we had seen at Le Domaine. This is an easy and fun project made by piling flat rocks side-by-side and upward, in a pagoda-like structure, using each rock to counter-balance another. The trick is to see how far you can extend the flat rocks sideways, adding tiny rocks a counter-weights to one side of the sculpture or the other a needed.

Late on that second, windbound night on the island, I heard Kip in a faint voice sound the alarm that his stomach didn't feel good. I have learned the hard way that when Kip bothers to mention how his stomach feels, I have only precious seconds before I get a graphic demonstration of exactly what he means. But, after a hard night, Kip looked much improved at breakfast and insisted he was fine. We set out in the cold, gray dawn for Lac Chartier. Not twenty yards into the first portage he was sick again, and I began to worry. We retreated a short distance along our course to the nearest island and made camp. Not seeing any sign of fever or chills, for the next twenty-four hours I fed Kip water and what few items in our food pack fit the BRAT diet recommended for kids having trouble keeping food down (bananas, rice, applesauce, and toast). By the next morning he seemed to be fully recovered, and we resumed our journey.

Turning south from our first camp, we entered the cove that opens to the east of the lake. The guide published by the federation advises that this route be run counterclockwise, but you may run it in either direction.

Running clockwise in mid-summer, we had little trouble paddling against a mild current in the stream that that flows out of Lac Chartier, which is officially named Riviere de La Baie. If you are heavily loaded, you will likely have to step out and pull the canoe up the riffles in a couple of spots.

The map notes the ruins of a bridge at the mouth of the river. Beaver have built onto the old log tresses of the bridge to make a dam that is passable going upstream. Avoid the campsite marked on the federation map, here, which we found to be weedy and damp.

The first portage is marked by a yellow sign, but many others, we found, were completely unmarked. Most were overgrown, due to a lack of traffic. Riviere de la Baie, on both ends of the 335-meter portage, yielded good-sized pike. But the winning monster of the trip was the four-pound walleye taken by Michael Rosenthal in the river above the portage, leading into Lac Chartier. Robin caught one in the same place that nearly matched it. Both made an excellent meal of filets, half dipped in Old Bay Batter and the other half rolled in instant potato flakes, and fried.

When the weather turned nasty again on the fourth day, the dads and boys stayed in camp to stoke the fire and take turns reading aloud from Where the Red Fern Grows-a classic boy-and-his-dog tale about coming of age that I would recommend to any boy under twelve. Undaunted, Robin headed out on the lake that day and returned with only one walleye for his efforts, but we gave his fish an exotic send-up in a creamy, garlic pesto recipe I promise to share in the next issue.

On Lac Chartier and some of the other interior lakes, you may encounter Indians traveling to and from cabins in motorboats. I have not looked at the legislation which controls this park, but we got the impression that restrictions on development have been relaxed for native peoples. I wish I could say this has worked out for the best. The poverty of the Indian has combined with an apparent lack of concern for preserving the wilderness character of their surroundings to make for some depressingly squalid scenes, in places. It calls to mind what Thoreau wrote about the Abenaki in Maine, as far back as 1846: "These were once a powerful tribe. Politics are all the rage with them now. I even thought that a row of wigwams . . . would be more respectable than this."

There is a moment in every trip when a paddler comes upon an unexpected vista that causes him to pause and give thanks that such a place remains untouched to enchant him. One such moment came at the pool beneath the falls that connect Lac La Perche to Lac Chartier, chosen for the opening photograph of this story. When this vision of paradise appeared around a bend as I was casting my way toward the portage, the idea that I would not immediately discard every scrap of clothing and vestige of earthly restraint to immerse myself in it suddenly became the most unthinkable heresy. My son and the other fugitive from motherly instruction who was in my charge needed no encouragement to join in the fray. We were only momentarily detained in our preparations by the arrival of a journal subscriber from Massachusetts. He called Kip by name and caught him completely off guard. It was our good fortune to meet this fellow, who directed us to the camp on Lac La Perche where he had left a pile of dry kindling.

Every canoe trip settles into its own, quiet rhythm once we loosen the ties that bind us to the modern world. At Lac La Perche the onslaught of vicious, northern pike kept up its steady pace. But, with our boys having been cut off from the mother's milk of fast food now for six straight days, I took pity and made a facsimile of cheeseburgers from biscuits, summer sausage, and sliced cheddar for dinner, instead of fish. We would get another chance to savor the fruit of these northern lakes on the final night, back on Grand Lac Victoria, with the impromptu creation of pike jambalaya.

There is always a surreal feeling about returning to civilization after a week in the woods. I felt it again as I stood in a store check-out line back at Le Domaine. Tired and only half aware of the world around me, I gazed in the general direction of a pretty girl behind the counter in French braids, while she waited on the customer ahead of me. I was not much to look at—what with a week's growth of beard, blackened hands, and covered in campfire soot, but then I realized that she was looking, right in my eyes, longer than any woman needed to look just to notice that I was there.

I looked back just long enough—maybe a little longer—to convince myself that it was me and not something stuck in my teeth she was studying. The last time a strange woman caught my eye across a crowded room was in a bar in Georgetown in 1978. I never found out who she was back then, and I didn't find out this time. Handing Kip a wad of Canadian bills, I said "You pay for your own tee-shirt, son," and stepped outside.

Lately I've been thinking that I could strike it rich by making a men's cologne that recaptures the essence of that week in the Quebec woods. "Old Smoke" seems like a catchy name, but results of pre-market testing have been mixed. Our CEO and head of motherly instruction, here, assures me that it's just a passing French thing.

Upper Pasquotank River

Albemarle Region Canoe Trail
Great Dismal Swamp

It was one of those gray December days, too warm to snow but pregnant with the threat of a cold rain. The air was not quite raw—just fresh enough that we would pull the corners of our sweaters and jackets around us a little closer when a breeze drifted by. The four of us knew the afternoon would be colder, and the night chillier still. It was not a morning that would have inspired anyone to load up the car and go canoeing and camping in the swamps of Eastern North Carolina, but it was the day that all of us had appointed to just such a plan.

This was 1996, and our friends the Pauls had just bought a shiny, new Old Town Penobscot. It appeared in our driveway, firmly lashed to the rack of their van and ready for the trip we had planned as a sort of christening—not only for the boat but for their family's introduction to canoe camping. The Pauls were good friends, with two girls close in age to our son and daughter. All four children tumbled and rolled and tossed inside their van like a litter of puppies in a cardboard box,

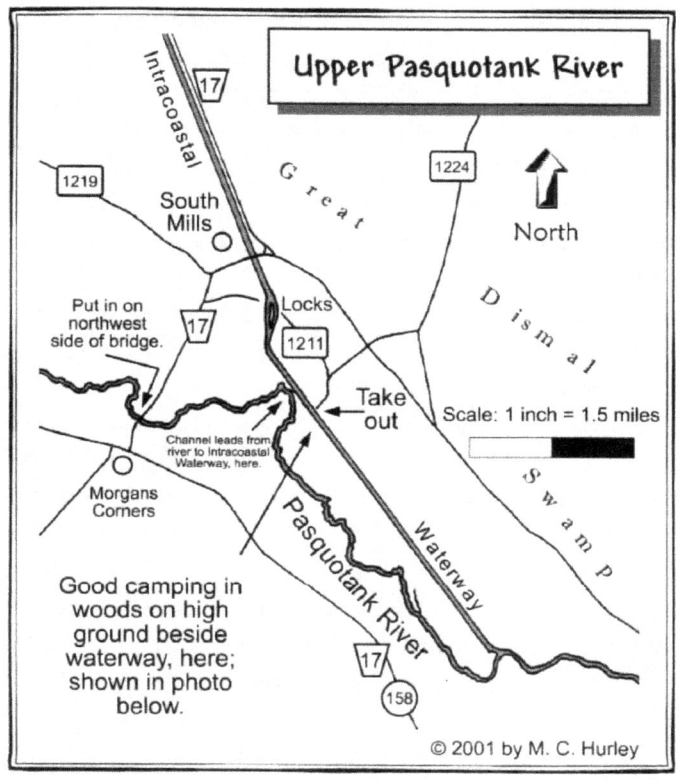

not sensing the rain in the air or the swamp that still lay hours up the road, north of Elizabeth City.

Most of us who spend more than an occasional weekend in the woods have introduced a couple to canoe camping. You meet them at a picnic or a school fair, and the subject of family vacations inevitably comes up, followed by the usual complaints as everyone nods knowingly about the interminable lines at the theme park, the high price of hotels, and where they (and everyone else) will go next year to avoid all of that. When it is your turn to speak, you summon all the nonchalance you can muster as you explain that your family spent a week last summer paddling through the Canadian forest, camping on beds of pine needles, the campfire flickering as the moon rose over rivers and lakes filled with fat walleye. "It was nice," you say, but you lie—it was better than nice, and you can't imagine trading that experience to stand on vast tarmacs of scorching asphalt, noshing on a cheese-fried heart attack as you and several thousand strangers wait in line for the "Voyageur of the North Woods" log-plume ride.

When the couple next to you describes that very vacation of your nightmares with sighs of fond remembrance, you lie again: "Sounds like fun," you say. "Can't wait till we can afford to go." But behind your painted smile you are thinking that if there is a God in heaven, you will never have the money or the time or the shortage of compelling, sudden emergencies to permit such an ordeal. Just then, one couple changes the subject back to your canoe trip. "About those lakes," they begin.

One question quickly follows another, and you talk for an hour, not realizing that everyone else has migrated back to the buffalo wings. The husband listens intently and asks questions about equipment. He tells you about the types of boats be has been looking at, and you realize that he is serious. You offer your advice. He asks more questions about systems for storing and carrying gear. Finally, when you've exhausted your store of knowledge, you embellish a little about how good the fishing was and how the black flies were "really no big deal." You leave the party promising to get together soon.

A week later he calls you—he's found a good deal on

a canoe. "What do you think?" he wants to know, and you share with him almost verbatim the speech someone gave you when you bought your first canoe, about every boat being a compromise. The one he's picked is as good as any, you say—and it is. He promises to let you try it out, and you promise to keep him posted on your trip plans.

As winter grinds on, there is a break in the weather and your schedule. The calendar says December, but the temperature says April. You call up your friend and, expecting the weather to hold, make plans for the following weekend. He and his wife and kids are excited to make their first trip. They order another two hundred dollars' worth of the dry bags and special gear you recommended and pack enough food for Lewis and Clark's entire outfit. Then, as the day approaches, the weather forecast grows discouraging, but you are resolute. Your reputation as a voyageur is at stake. Your friends don't call until late in the week, and when they do you confidently tell them the trip is on! Your enthusiasm is catching. They are too new at this to know better, and they have faith in you.

For my wife Julie, this December voyage with the Paul family wasn't a matter of faith at all. A veteran of many cold, wet vigils in the woods, she no longer needed faith—she had knowledge. And she wasn't going.

Kathy Paul's expression fell perceptibly but only briefly when Julie walked out onto our driveway dressed for shopping, not canoeing. Kathy is no shrinking violet. In the days before children and mortgages, she and Eric interrupted high-powered careers to buy a sailboat and take an extended, ocean cruise. We all stood there in the driveway that December day, laughed awhile at my wife's demurrer, and knew without saying so that there was no good reason for the rest of us not to go as planned.

It turned out that Julie was right as usual, though only partly so. We eventually came to appreciate a number of good reasons not to have made this trip, including the cold, the rain, and the unexpected requirement of a good topographic map for finding a suitable place to camp. Paddling around in the chilling drizzle and gathering darkness of the Great Dismal Swamp, any of us would have been hard-pressed to tell you what it was, exactly, that possessed us to go. The answer to that question did not come until later.

We began our trip at the corner of Southeastern Virginia and Northeastern North Carolina. About twelve miles north Elizabeth City, new Highway 17 crosses the Pasquotank River. Coming from the south, just after the bridge, we turned left onto old Highway 17, and continued two hundred yards or so to the old highway bridge. A state access-ramp and a small parking area have been installed on the northwest side of this bridge, between the towns of Morgans Corners and South Mills. We parked here and shuttled a vehicle through South Mills to the take-out on the Intracoastal Waterway, on Route 1211.

To get to the take-out, we continued north on Highway 17 to the first right, which is Main Street, then passed a grocery store and turned right onto 343. This took us through the town of South Mills and across a very salty-looking drawbridge over the canal. Immediately after the bridge we turned right onto State Road 1211, which runs along the canal. Continuing several miles on

1211 we eventually came to the state canoe-access, near a farmhouse. We pulled our van to the right side of the road, parked, and returned to the put-in to begin our adventure.

The driving directions may sound easy, but for us they were hard-won. We wasted a good hour of wandering in fits and starts along back roads before finding our way, and—after a late start—wound up back at the put-in with less daylight than we would need to make camp. Undeterred, we excitedly loaded the canoes with packs and our intrepid beagle, Jingles, and nosed the bows into the water.

I suspect that if Robert Frost had been born in the South he would have written that there is something that does not love a swamp. Swamps are no match for the pine-swept vistas of Maine or the clear, granite lakes of Canada. Even so, the Great Dismal Swamp is unfairly named. It is, in its own way, a hauntingly beautiful and serene place. The dense woods hide you quickly. And no matter what river it may be, no matter where—even in the deepest, most dismal swamp—there is always a little magic in that first paddle stroke that pushes you away from civilization and back among the voyageurs. I felt it again, here. We were off!

The Upper Pasquotank varies in width but is easily passable. It is one of several rivers in the inventory of the Albemarle Region Canoe and Small Boat Trails System. In the early 1990s, ten counties in northeastern North Carolina working together as the Albemarle Resource and Development Council started a program to identify and promote area waterways suitable for canoeing. A system of water trails marked with orange-and-white, numbered signs was installed. Each trail is mapped and described in a brochure available from the local council or the state division of parks and recreation. Also available is a guide, entitled "The Albemarle Canoe and Small Boat Trails System," containing a brief description of each trail and showing its location on a large-scale map of the entire region.

About two miles from the put-in, a channel leading north from the Pasquotank meets the Great Dismal Swamp Canal, now part of the Intracoastal Waterway. Three miles south of this point, the arrow-straight canal ends where it rejoins the river, which continues it winding course. Surveys for the canal were drawn by George Washington himself, and construction began in 1790.

The best camping on the river is on the canal. As advertised in the Albemarle Council brochure, the trail "offers an overnight canoeing experience on the banks of the Great Dismal Swamp Canal," which is government land. Those high campsites were nowhere to be seen as the rain intensified in the waning daylight. We paddled up and down the canal but we were confounded by a shoreline thick with trees and underbrush. We remembered seeing a clearing that seemed to rise up a little, back in the swamp, and—not willing to let the children languish much longer with bottoms grown wet and cold from rain—we paddled hard back into the bald cypress to find it. Around one bend and the next we went, as the misery index seemed to steadily increase with the darkness and fond thoughts of Disney World actually flashed in my mind.

Finally the tiny clearing appeared, unlovely though it was, and we made camp. There was room enough for only our largest tent, so we all bunked together. This suited the children just fine, though I'm sure it was a little startling to Kathy. A tarp went up. The temperature dropped further, but spirits rose as a fire slowly crackled to life, drawing in a ring of children beneath the shelter. Before long enough canoe stew to feed Washington's army was boiling cheerfully, and we felt that special sense of accomplishment and pride that comes from beating fear and discouragement. The rain gave up. Little eyes widened awhile at the hoot owls' ghostly serenade which, before long, became a gentle lullaby. The kids slept comfortably, even though I periodically sprang awake fearing that Caroline—a champion cover-kicker—had crawled out of her sleeping bag into the cold, night air.

The next morning we summoned our resolve under brisk, blue skies to build a breakfast fire, brew coffee, and flip pancakes. The children explored and climbed and swung through the surrounding swamp, less foreboding now in the daylight. Children never brood on life's little hardships but welcome each new dawn on its own merits, which is one of childhood's enduring values that we grownups too quickly forget.

Leaving camp, the swamp was lovely to us again, and we all remarked at what a pretty place it is to paddle. Re-entering the canal at its northern junction with the river, we turned south and, a few hundred yards past the take-out, discovered too late a high, dry bank of thinned forest perfect for camping, just as described in the guide. An ideal, overnight trip, provided one begins early enough in the day, would be to paddle down to the second confluence of the river and the canal and paddle back up toward the take-out, in a loop. On such a trip the good campsites would appear on the west bank of the canal, with the best locations readily identifiable by the high-elevation marks on the South Mills topographic map. If there was any lasting disappointment to this trip, it was not that we had gone but that we had not persevered to find this place and give the children more room to run—but no matter. Our struggles are your ease, dear reader. Come to this mystical, ancient place. You shall find it not so dismal, after all, and discover that there truly is something that loves a swamp.

Lake Lila Primitive Area

Adirondack Park

When I first heard of Lake Lila, I was in Tickner's Canoe Outfitters in Old Forge, New York. It was one of my first if not my very first trip to the Adirondacks, and I was looking for recommendations. The weather forecast had grown dreary, and the topic of conversation was the likelihood of high winds and rain for a Raquette Lake crossing as well as the mud expected on the carries. "You ought to try Lake Lila" piped up the fresh-faced, young, college student who was working the counter. "It's beautiful up there—lots of wide, sandy beaches, loads of campsites, and it's open only to canoes." I didn't know it then, but I would wish in a few days' time—somewhere in the middle of the carry to Brown's Tract Inlet—that I had taken his advice. It would be many years after that, however, before I would see this place.

I was reminded of Lake Lila again when a buddy of mine camped there on his way to a rendezvous of readers of this journal at Tupper Lake. In addition to the beauty of the area, which he confirmed, he reported good bass-fishing. His comments moved Lila up several notches on

HURLEY'S JOURNAL

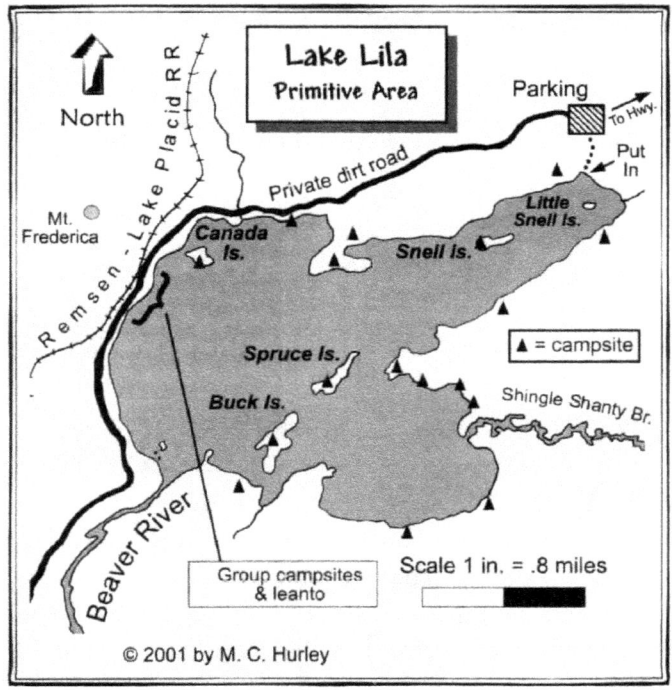

my mental list of "places I really ought to paddle someday." But the final decision came last year when, searching for a place to rendezvous with readers of this journal that would be remote and beautiful but accessible by car, lovely Lila came back to mind. I went digging through my boxes and folders looking for the park brochure as if it were a pretty girl's phone number I had always saved but never dialed.

For the few readers of this journal who are as yet uninitiated in the wondrous achievement of environmental policy that is Adirondack Park, this sprawling wilderness roughly the size of Connecticut that lies "within the blue line," as depicted in the image at right, is a creation of the New York State Constitution. The constitution mandates that the public lands in the park (roughly half the total area) be kept "forever wild." Roads and towns traverse the region but are limited in scope and character. The Adirondack Park Agency is the local governmental body charged with reconciling local zoning issues with the constitutional mandate. Much to the credit of this organization and many conservation-minded companies and individuals, private lands in the park that might otherwise have made prime locations for a lot of tacky, Swiss chalets are being added to the public side of the ledger. Only in January of this year, it was announced that the Adirondack chapter of the Nature Conservancy and the Adirondack Land Trust will purchase from International Paper approximately 26,500 acres of land in the Long Lake area, for $10.5 million. (Thanks to reader Kevin McCarthy for alerting me to the press release for this news, at www.tnc.org/press/press131.html.) One year earlier, in what a local paper described as "one of the largest land-conservation deals in the nation's history," New York State announced it was buying several other tracts of Champion International Paper lands totaling 139,000 acres in the northwest corner of the park. These land deals bring cheers from the hardworking corps of local activists, who dream of the day when the entire area might gain further protection and funding as a national park.

Acquired in 1979, the 7,215 acre Lake Lila Primitive Area became the key piece in a jigsaw puzzle of many later acquisitions. The adjacent William C. Whitney area, added in 1997, protects 15,000 acres around Little Tupper Lake and several nearby ponds from further development. After acquiring Lake Lila, the state removed the only residence on the lake—a lodge once owned by an heir of the Vanderbilt fortune—and restored the area to "essentially wilderness conditions." However, the area is still bordered to the south and west by private lands whose owners, I am told, are dead-serious about prosecuting trespassers. The private land that envelopes the Beaver River, about three-quarters of a mile south of the lake, is particularly well controlled, I understand.

A dirt road that parallels part of the western shore of the lake is barred by a gate at the end of the parking lot. The road sees infrequent but daily use by land owners who have a key to the lock.

Railroad tracks traveling the same direction showed signs of recent use, but I saw no activity during my trip. If you camp anywhere but on the western shore of the lake near the road, you will find nothing at all to remind you that you are actually still within the borders of the Town of Long Lake. In fact, I having unwisely decided to leave the two-dozen scheduled rendezvouers to find their own campsites, the entire group very nearly never found each other. A few who came enjoyed the scenery but never did track us down. This is a big place.

The brochure published by the Department of Environmental Conservation tells us that Lake Lila was once known as Smith's Lake and received its present name from William Seward Webb, the baron of the Adirondack Railroad who married the former Miss Lila Vanderbilt. No doubt he decided to give her name to this place while admiring the view from atop Mt. Frederica. A lovely woman she must have been. (That's Bill Jones in the cover drawing on Mt. Frederica. I met Bill at Lake Lila along with his faithful dog Capt. Hardy, the very model of a "canoe dog.")

The park brochure promises that visiting anglers will find brook and lake trout, salmon and smallmouth bass in the lake, but indefatigable honesty compels me to disagree. I gave Lila and a fair distance of her tributary Shingle Shanty Branch a long look at all the assorted temptations my tackle box had to offer. Only one juvenile smallmouth accepted my invitation to dinner, and I jilted him for a thin bowl of noodles, at that. I wish you luck on Lake Lila, but if there are swarms of fish here I found no evidence of them.

Although a fair percentage of the campers at the lake on this late August weekend were readers of this journal who had come for the rendezvous, I was struck by the popularity of the place. Word has definitely gotten out, and for the first time in my experience anywhere else in the Adirondacks, I would guess that every campsite on the entire lake was occupied. The asterisk to that unusual circumstance is that all of the people you will meet, here, are paddlers who value as much as you do the peace, quiet and cleanliness you have come to enjoy. Motors are not allowed on Lake Lila.

As I paddled the entire perimeter of the lake, I encountered a young DEC ranger who was checking in with campers. She was paddling a solo canoe straight for me, using a double-bladed paddle with a sure, well-practiced stroke. I was breathing at the time, which means of course that I was also fishing. Fearing she would ask to see the license I bad neglected to purchase and that I would thereafter be towed to the slammer, I decided to take the offensive and snap her picture. She responded with embarrassed surprise. Seizing the juxtaposition of the moment to engage her in polite conversation, I chit-chatted just long enough about the weather to make it too awkward for her to change both her direction of travel and the subject. She floated by and was gone. "You slippery fellow, Hurley," I thought, and kept paddling on my felonious way. (In truth, I have no idea whether DEC rangers have the slightest thing to do with fishing licenses.)

By the time I made it around the lake, every campsite other than the large, group sites on the western shore was taken. There I pitched my little bivouac in a row alongside eight other tents comprising two or three groups of people. A short distance farther north of this site is a lean-to which reader Walter Ilchuk had secured for our group's campfire.

Although I found no mention of this in any of the literature, I suspect, given the close proximity of the railroad tracks, that the group campsite is the same place where Lila Vanderbilt's lodge once stood. From this site, one follows the private road, across the railroad tracks and for another three-quarters of a mile until a foot-trail appears on the right, which leads to Mt. Frederica. If you do nothing else while you are camped on Lake Lila, take this trail. You will hike another three-quarters of a mile from the road to the top, but the path is easy to follow. The view from the top is spectacular, so be sure to take your camera.

Another attraction you ought not to miss, here, is an afternoon's paddle up Shingle Shanty Branch. The recently announced, 26,000-acre land-conservation deal which I mentioned, earlier, includes 15,000 acres along Shingle Shanty Branch that will now be protected. If it is wilderness you seek, here you will find it.

The entrance to the branch is camouflaged by a wide bay of marsh grass at the eastern end of the lake, bordered by long, sandy beaches on either side. Paddle the rim of the marsh until you find the channel leading in. The current is slow enough to make progress upstream not too difficult, even for a solo paddler. A band of us crossed the lake and met readers Denise Zembryki and Ronald Mamajek, who had chosen the excellent campsite just south of the entrance to Shingle Shanty Branch. In the stiffening breeze, we battled our way to the entrance of the creek and zoomed upstream on a tailwind. Our progress was slowed by my insistence on casting at every "trouty" looking undercut in the grassy banks, to no avail. Only small trout-worms will fool the wily brookies said to hide in these waters.

Shingle Shanty Branch switches and crosses back on itself several times, treating the persistent paddler to several, beautiful beaver dams along the way. Only once or twice was it necessary to step out and encourage the canoes over a log or a shallow spot. We continued for almost two hours without seeing any sign of the terminus of this charming little stream. What you will not find are many good places to land. The banks of Shingle Shanty Branch are almost uniformly lined in tall grass. Following the creek as it switched directions back and forth, we kept our eye on a large stand of white pines in the distance, but we never reached them. We eventually gave up and made a lunch-stop in some high grass well inshore from the creek. In the right photograph on the facing page, you can see the pines in the distance. I made my own trail through a hundred yards of grass and stood silently awhile in no particular place among these giants, wondering how many years (Centuries, perhaps?) it had been since another human being had done the same.

Bidding our friends goodbye on the eastern shore of the lake that afternoon, the west wind forced us to duck behind Buck Island and crawl our way along shore. The wind would keep several rendezvouers from joining us for our last night, here, but we sang that much the louder around the campfire. The next morning I rose before daylight to paddle out for the long drive south. My infallible Bean's alarm-watch chirped at 4:00 a.m., and the moon ducked behind the clouds. It was pitch-black on the water when I shoved off. An hour later, the crackle of sand startled me as the canoe ran ashore in the darkness, at the take-out. I had just met the lovely Miss Lila only to leave her again, but she was well worth the journey.

ANTIETAM CREEK

RT. 68 BRIDGE TO POTOMAC RIVER

I magine, as you slumber in these woods of oak and hickory and maple, that on September 17, 1862, a young Confederate soldier awoke from a fitful sleep in your campsite. He was far from home—perhaps a farm somewhere back in Georgia, where his family waited in vain for news of his well-being. But with Southern Pride swelling in his breast and a confidence shared with 40,000 Confederate troops led by General Robert E. Lee, he was resolute. Lee would march toward Antietam Creek, this day, on his first attempt to invade the North. Yet unbeknownst to the Southern general, the Northern army had intercepted a copy of his battle plan. Near the banks of this river, Lee's troops would meet an immovable obstacle in the form of 87,000 Union soldiers led by General George McClellan. McClellan had promised: "If I cannot whip Bobbie Lee, I will be willing to go home." It was a meeting that would turn the waters of Antietam Creek red with blood and enshrine this place to the memory of a sorrowful, young nation.

The Battle of Antietam claims a chilling statistic. It produced the largest number of casualties in a single day of any battle in the Civil War. On the Union side there

HURLEY'S JOURNAL

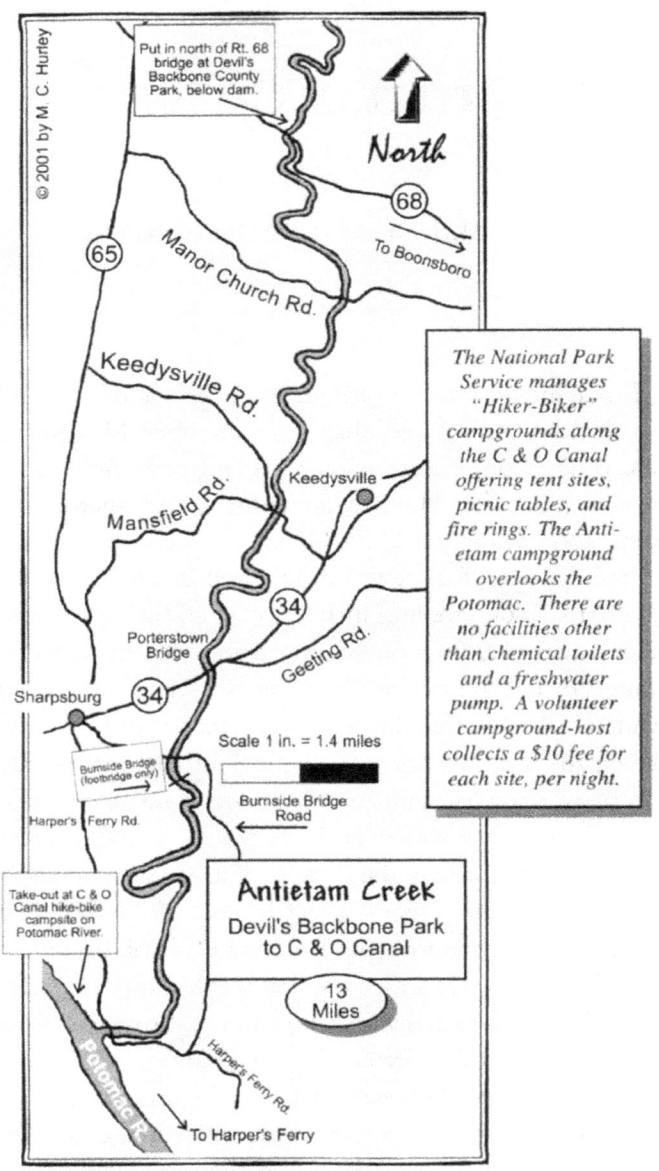

were over two thousand dead and twelve thousand wounded or missing. Nearly three thousand troops gave up their lives for the Confederacy, here, with about ten thousand wounded or missing. The Confederates—outnumbered two to one—sustained fewer casualties than the Union army, but the news of General Lee's retreat across the Potomac the next day emboldened President Lincoln. Five days later, he delivered his first proclamation freeing the slaves. The second Emancipation Proclamation of January 1, 1863 would lay the groundwork for the Thirteenth Amendment.

When the fighting ended in 1865, the Civil War had claimed over 600,000 American lives—more than World Wars I and II combined. The Antietam today is a much less daunting place. At the time of the war, the surrounding woods had largely been cut into cornfields and pasture, as you can see in an historic photograph taken of President Lincoln when he traveled to these fields, shortly after the battle. In the ensuing 140 years a beautiful forest has grown back around the banks of the river. With the exception of the National Historic Battlefield, which borders the Antietam for four miles, the banks are privately owned. There still are pastures, but scarcely any residential development. You will find this section of the river quite beautiful and remarkably wild, given its proximity to Washington, D.C.

The section of this river which I paddled on March 23 of this year stretches from the Route 68 bridge west of Boonsboro to the Potomac River. This section sees strong, weekend use from day-trippers and kayakers who come solely to surf the Class II rapids below Burnside Bridge. It remains relatively undiscovered by canoe campers. There are many ideal campsites where high water has cut a level ridge in the bank in this section of the river. Given the problem of private land-ownership, however, the safer choice is to paddle the entire thirteen miles in one day and camp at the National Historic Park at the C & 0 Canal, where the creek meets the Potomac.

The put-in is located at Devil's Backbone County Park, which is on the right as you travel west from Boonsboro, Maryland on Route 68, immediately after you cross the river. The "Devil's Backbone" is the name given to a one-mile section, just above the put-in, where the river doubles back on itself sharply beneath a high, steep ridge. Antietam Creek Canoes occupies a barn on the west side of the creek, below the Route 68 bridge. The outfitter is not without a sense of humor. His web page (antietamcreek.com) advises: "A few years back Gen. Jackson marched his troops across the neat old three arch stone bridge on our place to get on to capturing Harper's Ferry. That was a busy day I'll tell ya what." Parking is free at the county park, but be aware that the gate is locked shut every night.

There are bathroom facilities (but no phones) at the put-in. The first rapids of any significance appear just below the Route 68 bridge. I paddled directly into the large haystack at mid-river and sailed right through. Once past this point, the river turns west into a very pretty, hardwood forest. Herons led the way down the creek ahead of me. After two hours of paddling or about four miles, you will pass two tiny, riparian islands suitable for bivouac camping before you come to the abandoned, stone bridge. The bridge once crossed the river between Manor Church and Keedysville Roads. Neither the bridge pilings nor the islands are shown on the topographic maps for this trip, which include the Funkstown and Keedysville quadrangles.

The river moves at a steady pace with only occasional, easily navigated obstacles above Burnside Bridge. A sign prohibiting boats from landing for the next 1,000 feet appears on the right just before the famous bridge, which is easily recognized by its well-preserved stone arches. At midday during the Battle of Antietam, General Ambrose Burnside received orders to march 12,000 Union troops across this bridge, but the entire division was held at bay for more than an hour by a small band of Georgia sharpshooters hiding in the woods west of the creek.

As you pass here, look to your right to see the high, wooded bluffs where the rebels lay in wait for Burnside's men. So accurate were the Georgia riflemen in picking off Union soldiers, the General probably believed there were thousands of them. In actuality, there were only 450—outnumbered twenty-seven to one by Burnside's division—but each was deadly with a rifle. At one o'clock, two full regiments—more men than the sharpshooters had lead to kill—stormed the bridge under Burnside's orders and made it across.

When I passed Burnside Bridge, I got a much warmer welcome than the general. A lone woman crossing the bridge with her dog kindly warned me of the steep ledge just ahead. She watched from the bridge to make sure I made it safely through. Somewhat startled by her warning, I opted to carry around the ledge instead of running it. In the chilly water of March, I was glad I did. You can easily avoid the ledge by stepping out onto a rock on the right bank, just above the falls, and letting the loaded canoe float down while you hold the stern line. If you choose to run this section, the best route is at midriver, right through the long, vee-shaped wave.

I was still feeling pretty proud of my good judgment to carry around the falls below Burnside Bridge when the rapids they call "the Furnace" loomed ahead. (It gives me pause when someone has thought enough of a stretch of rapids to name it after an inferno.) Furnace Rapids lies immediately upriver from the bridge at Harper's Ferry Road, almost at the end of the trip. An island appears on the left bank at the head of the rapids. Unless you are braced for a swim, you'll want to take out on the island and carry past the big haystacks. If you want to run the Furnace but aren't looking for the biggest "yee-haw" you can find, the safest route appears to be close alongside the island. The big haystack in the middle can swamp your boat if you're not careful, but technical whitewater paddlers will find the Furnace not terribly challenging.

The most common take-out and shuttle-pickup location is at Harper's Ferry Road. I am told that there is a small area off the road, here, where the park service allows canoeists to make camp for the night. This is where kayakers congregate to surf Furnace Rapids. A group was heading that way to cut strainers from the creek and practice their strokes when I came through. To reach the park service campground, paddle another quarter of a mile past the bridge at Harper's Ferry Road, past the footbridge that carries the C & 0 Canal towpath over the Antietam, and on to the confluence of the Potomac. Entering the Potomac, you will paddle about two hundred yards upriver before you see yellow paint on a tree on the bank, which marks the landing. Come ashore, here.

A short walk up the hill from the landing will take you to the towpath. Turn left and continue another few yards, and you will see the park service sign and the campsites above the Potomac, on the left. On your right you will see a re-watered section of the old canal, and just above that, a country road leading to the town of Antietam. The area is beautiful and, in the early Spring, quite unpopulated. You will enjoy a much more pleasant journey and find a more peaceful night's sleep, here, than did those brave men of blue and gray.

LITTLE TUPPER LAKE

WILLIAM C. WHITNEY AREA
ADIRONDACK PARK

I have been coming to the Adirondacks on a regular basis for canoe-camping trips since 1993. Each time I leave I tell myself that I have finally seen the best that this region has to offer. Each time I return I discover that I was, again, pleasantly mistaken.

Little Tupper Lake and its surrounding network of wilderness ponds are some of the newer jewels in the Adirondack crown. In 1997, the State of New York agreed to purchase 15,000 acres of private forest owned by the Whitney family around the area of Little Tupper. Part of this purchase, since named the William C. Whitney Area, opened up lands around nearby Lake Lila, as featured in the Winter 2001 issue of the journal. Little Tupper is a similar lake, but one with easier access to remote ponds and trails.

Our trip north began in Maryland over the Fourth of July with a small memorial service for my mother, who passed away in May. It was a low-key affair attended by my brother and two sisters, under sail on the waters of Chesapeake Bay, just outside Annapolis, in the state where she and all of us were raised. Someday I will find

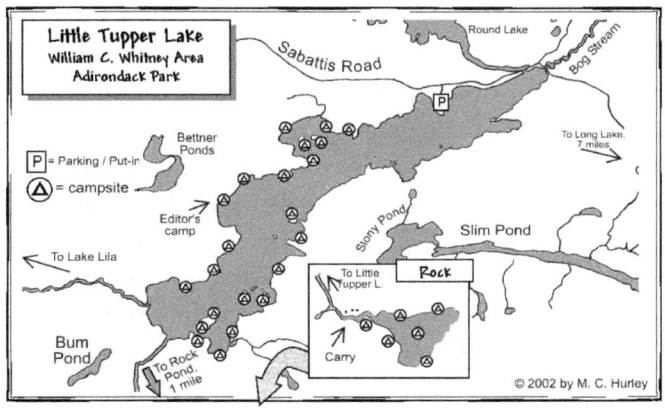

the words to give order, in my mind, to the complex sea of emotions and longings that was Joanne LaCroix Hurley, but for the time being those waters are still roiling in my memory. And so it was with disquieted thoughts that I traveled with my wife Julie and our children Kip and Caroline back to New York, in pursuit of the peace and stillness of Little Tupper Lake.

I had tarried more than usual in ordering topographic maps before leaving North Carolina for this trip. We especially needed maps for the journey down the Penobscot in Maine (Summer '02 issue) that would immediately follow our travels to Little Tupper Lake. To make sure I received them, I had my supplier mail them to the good folks at the historic Adirondack Hotel, in Long Lake, where I expected to pick them up on my way north. As we pulled up to the grand porch of that beautiful hotel, merely to pick up our delivery and drive on, Julie stayed in the car out of embarrassment. "You mean you just expect them to receive your mail for you?" she asked. I did, and without worry, because I had come to know the good folks of this hotel on a previous trip. Three of us had shared two of their endearingly small and quirky, turn-of-the century rooms and, on numerous other occasions, a fine meal in their elegant dining room. In the wee hours before dawn one year they had opened their kitchen to fetch the steaks they were keeping frozen for our food packs. Taking delivery of a few maps would be no trouble by comparison. Besides, I could not leave without seeing the campy growl on the face of the giant, stuffed bear standing in their lobby. Alas, they would not be open for brunch on Sunday, they told us, and we would miss a good meal on our take-out day.

Little Tupper Lake lies eleven miles by road to the north of Long Lake Village and sixteen miles south of the Village of Tupper Lake, in the northwestern quadrant of Adirondack Park. This area is 290 miles, or about a six-hour drive, from Manhattan.

Long-time readers will know that in each story I write about the Adirondacks, I cannot resist repeating the superlative that it comprises an area roughly the size of Connecticut, nor my disappointment that less than half of this area is public land. Local residents would be horrified to hear of my dream that one day all of the concrete within the blue line will be ripped up and the area returned to its primordial splendor. It is not that I have anything against modernity; I simply believe that there are parts of the world in which development is something akin to painting a moustache on the Mona Lisa. The Adirondacks is one such place. God gave us land enough for farms and factories and houses elsewhere, but places like these he tied up in a silver bow and made a gift to us as if to say, "Look at what I can do." Too often we have tried to improve on his handiwork.

The mandate of the New York Constitution that public lands within the demarcation of Adirondack Park be kept "forever wild" has, despite the tide of history and more than a few legislative assaults, preserved much of this area. Acquisitions of private land are slowly adding to the public domain. Timothy J. Burke, Executive Director of the Adirondack Council, remarked that the purchase of the Whitney tract "brings us one step closer to establishing a 400,000-acre wilderness in the west-central Adirondacks that would be the largest totally wild area east of the Mississippi River." Paul Jamieson, co-author of *Adirondack Canoe Waters* (Lake George, NY: Adirondack Mountain Club, 1994), wrote in his preface to the 1975 edition that the "[t]he Adirondack forest is, paradoxically, more beautiful today than it was a century ago." This is apparent, he observed, from historical photographs as well as the paintings of Winslow Homer. Thus, there is hope for the future. A trip to these woods will serve to remind you that it's a future worth fighting for.

We turned down Sabattis Road where it breaks off to the left, about seven miles north of Long Lake Village, and four miles later arrived at the parking lot near the lake. The boat house, docks, and buildings you will find at the north shore of the lake were built between 1923 and 1946 to support the Whitney family timbering operations, which date back to 1898 in this area. The DEC has preserved these structures for its own use as an office and residence for its rangers. All trips originating on Little Tupper Lake begin at this location.

After we parked our creaky old Jeep, laden with two canoes and all our gear, Caroline wasted no time in spotting a large pile of black "poop" in the grass beside us. Before my wife could even ask what it was, the helpful, young, DEC ranger who came to greet us mentioned that a bear had raided the cars in the parking lot the night before. The beast had actually torn the back window out of a car to get at the food left in the back seat by some unsuspecting paddler. He had not yet returned from his trip, and I almost wished we could stay to see the look on his face. The ranger warned us that there had been a bear "problem" in the area and suggested that we use a tree and a long rope to hang everything, including cosmetics, that might have an odor. Interestingly, she also asked us to participate in a poll asking campers whether they intended to have a campfire. When I asked her about the results, she reported that some campers had no intention of kindling a flame in the woods.

Well, the ranger's warning and the gathering storm clouds made for an auspicious beginning to our trip. To their credit, though, my intrepid family again followed Daddy on what clearly at the time seemed another ill-considered venture into the unknown. To quell their fears, I ran through the usual list of horrors—car accidents, lightning strikes, killer tornadoes—that they were far more likely to encounter than a bear attack. Notwithstanding these long odds, Julie insisted that we sleep with paddles at the ready with which to bludgeon any curious bruin that came our way. And, again, despite the dire warnings, we saw neither hide nor hair of a bear.

I spend several weeks each year in the wild woods of various places and, to this day, have never had a bear wander into my campsite—an errant moose, a porcupine, and all manner of squirrels and mice, yes, but no bears. I attribute this snubbing somewhat unscientifically to the fact that I also never make camp without a small cooking fire, come rain or shine. However, the absence of a campfire is the growing trend among modern campers. The Boy Scouts now routinely adhere to a policy against campfires in the wild. I find that most folks whose introduction to camping has come from the REI store at the mall know nothing about how to use an axe to split wood or how to arrange kindling for a fire. We are now three generations removed from those Americans for whom the long rifle, axe, and saw were familiar, essential tools for outdoor living. To the bears, we have become an army of picnic basketeers fetching great spreads of sweet smelling delights to their dens. Is it any wonder they are answering the dinner bell in increasing numbers?

Animals are instinctively terrified of the smell of a campfire—even an old one. It is the odor of destruction and unnatural to their daily world. The smell of nuts and berries and meat and sweets, on the other hand, is distinctively attractive. I surely hope, therefore, that the ranger's survey does not result in an ill-considered edict to ban all campfires in the region.

There are campsites aplenty on Little Tupper Lake, which is thriving and lush with shoreside vegetation. Like most other lakes in the region, the water here is clear as a bell. It is also reportedly the home of a unique, native strain of brook trout. The DEC brochure suggests, in fact, that this may be "the largest lake in the Eastern United States with its original strain of trout"—a status which they seek to preserve by banning all live bait. In other lakes, minnows used for bait have escaped from fishermen's bait buckets, resulting in the introduction of "predatory" species of fish. So far, that has not happened here. I did manage to capture (and quickly release) one brook trout on a teeny spinner-fly combination cast in the still water behind a beaver dam.

The park service map and brochure on the William C. Whitney Area features detailed drawings of the lake and surrounding trails and ponds. It is the only reference you will need, and it is available from the DEC by mail. Following this map, on a holiday weekend we had to travel to the ninth campsite along the western shore before finding one that was open for camping. As elsewhere in the Adirondacks, DEC approved campsites are designated by a yellow disk, nailed to a tree and usually visible from the water, printed with a tent symbol and the words "camp here." Many more campsites farther down the lake were also taken. You cannot reserve a site, here, but generally something will be available to anyone arriving early in the weekend.

Our campsite lay within a bowl shaped cove, above a small, sandy beach. The gradual drop-off makes it an excellent site for children, and it is far enough from other sites to offer privacy for swimming. In early July the mosquitoes were already somewhat daunting, but we overcame these easily enough with copious amounts of repellent. The campsite offered several large, cleared areas that accommodated our two tents and a tarp. There was enough space for four tents overall, and this seemed to be true of most campsites we saw.

Our plan was to keep a base camp for two nights and travel to outlying Rock Pond, on Saturday. We left all our gear in camp and took only a small daypack in one canoe with first aid, lunch, bottles of water, fishing gear and, of course, enough camera equipment and film to record the invasion at Normandy. The trip across the lake took us past many attractive campsites and other campers just rising for their morning coffee. Several, to our surprise, had made similar plans and were getting started for Rock Pond. One young couple featured in the photos on page 18 was making their way toward the inlet to Rock Pond, with us. The wife or girlfriend, dressed in a bandana and what to us seemed like trendy outdoor duds, conveyed the very image of a "woman of the wilderness." Seeing such women always invites comment by Julie, who harbors a smoldering ember of suspicion that there are no such things as women of the wilderness—only women who suppress their true selves to appear so, either in deference to their husbands or in pursuit of some hidden agenda measured in total carat weight. I thoroughly disagree, having met a goodly number of "women of the wilderness" in my travels, including some who would paddle and portage circles around most men. The debate lives on.

Rock Pond Outlet winds its way for about two miles between the pond and the lake. At the southern end, a carry to the pond comes in on the left. Where the carry crosses a dirt road, a bridge appears to the south. Don't turn on the dirt road; keep going straight across and into the woods, where you'll pick up the carry for a few more yards to the landing.

Rock Pond is a stunning, remote beauty. It is inaccessible to all but canoes, so it is extremely peaceful. However, the six campsites are frequently in use, so don't count on finding one unless you get here mid-week or early on a Friday. Although closed to the public, a jeep trail leads here from the DEC headquarters, so you may see a ranger or two.

Typical of outlets in this region, the one leading to Rock Pond runs through a network of marshes. Avoid the two campsites along the outlet. We went ashore at the northernmost one and found it to be little used, damp, full of bugs, and overgrown in poison ivy.

The outlet is "moosey" looking water, and moose reportedly have been making a comeback in the Adirondacks since the last one was shot, here, in the very early 1900's. I have yet to see a moose in New York, but the ubiquitous loon never disappoints us. These birds have an unpredictable repertoire of laughs, including one that is hair-raisingly suggestive of someone dying a slow and painful death. As we entered the outlet to Rock Pond, we spotted a nest of loon eggs. Three canoes stopped to admire them from a distance. Something about the unrealized potential of those eggs told us that the future of the Adirondacks lies in what we are willing to protect and preserve, and therein I find reason to hope.

LA COSTA ISLAND

CAYO COSTA STATE PARK

This was not to be the usual canoe trip. For one thing, I was making it sans canoe. This year's reader rendezvous was scheduled for a Monday and Tuesday in April to coincide with what would be my first two-week vacation since I have had a job to be taking vacations from. The appointed place was Cayo Costa State Park, which I discovered while perusing guidebooks in search of a location for a family sailing-trip. At seven miles long, Cayo Costa is Florida's largest, undeveloped barrier island. It protects the vast expanse of shallow water known as Pine Island Sound from wind and large waves, making it perfect for kayakers and, on all but the windiest days, canoeists as well.

Cayo Costa is the name of the state park that occupies La Costa Island. There is a house or two barely visible to the tourist on the northern end of the island. These I suppose were given a long term lease when the place became a state park, but otherwise the island likely appears as it did when the legendary (and some say fictitious) pirate Jose Gaspar plied these waters for Spanish gold in the eighteenth century.

Coming from North Carolina with our family's

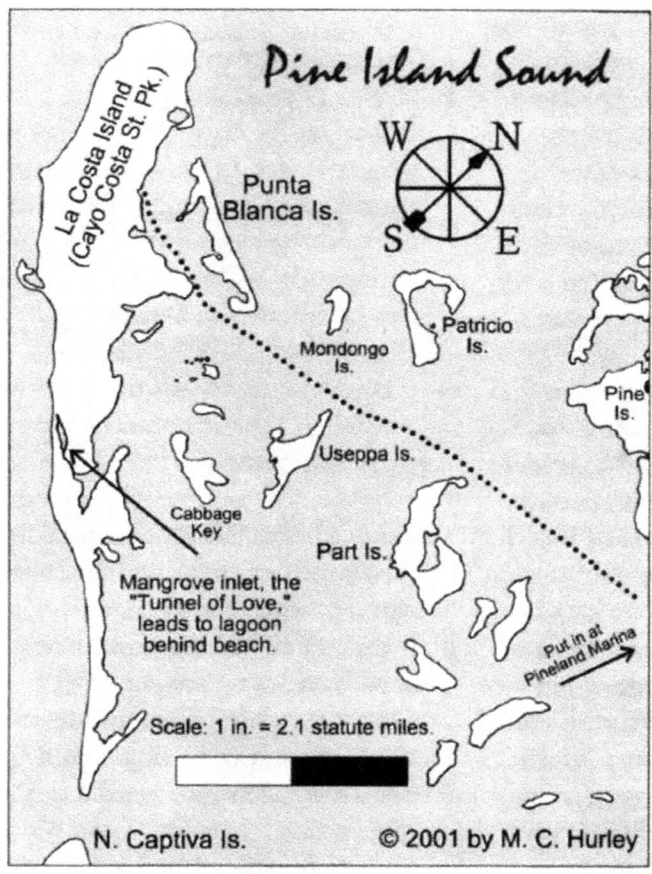

sixteen-foot sloop "Whisper" in tow, I was to meet the paddlers at this year's rendezvous in Matlacha, Florida, about 120 miles south of Tampa and just off Interstate 7 5. The rendezvous would run Monday to Wednesday, after which I would be "slumming" it aboard Whisper until my wife and children arrived at the Tampa airport the next Monday.

As the rendezvous approached, the dozen or so

attendees dwindled in number due to various, unforeseen emergencies. Finally, only three stalwarts—Jim Shaver and Dave Zamos from Philadelphia, and Mike Richard from Indiana, met me at the appointed time at Gulf Coast Kayaks, in Matlacha. The trio had paddled the Boundary Waters together, before. Dave Zamos brought his new sea kayak to try out. Jim and Mike planned to paddle a canoe. While spending nights aboard Whisper on the sound side of the island, I would enjoy their company, eat a great quantity of the food they packed, and paddle from the middle seat of their canoe during the day.

The first question of the trip—which is faster, a kayak or a sailboat—was answered decidedly in favor of the kayak on the breathless morning of the first day. The dearth of wind made for easy paddling across the six miles of water to La Costa Island.

We put in at Pineland Marina, which is located on Pine Island. Turning west from Interstate 75 onto Highway 78, you follow this road into the tiny fishing village of Matlacha. This is Old Florida: little pink cottages, kitschy tourist shops, local seafood restaurants, and mangroves. An eclectic mix of beach trinkets, bric-a-brac, weird art and stunning natural surroundings can be found in Matlacha. Crossing the bridge at Matlacha Pass onto Pine Island, you will turn right at the four-way stop to reach the put-in. After passing a vast palm-tree plantation, Pineland Road on your left leads to the marina.

It is quite expensive to park one's car for any length of time at Pineland Marina. The marina at Bookelia, father down the road, reportedly had better long-term rates. Pineland offers the most protected and direct route into Pine Island Sound, though, so I opted to start there.

The snappy and polite service at the marina—under new management—made the high prices easier to swallow.

Pine Island Sound is a picturesque collection of small islands, most of which are locked by the densely woven roots of the red mangrove around the entire perimeter. Only a few of the islands in the sound, notably Useppa (which is privately owned) and Punta Blanca (which is uninhabited), have any sandy beach to speak of. On the gulf side, however, La Costa and its adjacent islands—Gasparilla, North Captiva, Captiva, and Sanibel—are famous for pale, blue-green waters and gentle waves on pristine, sandy beaches. This is reportedly the shelling capital of the East Coast, and we brought home many specimens for our collection.

I had heard it said that you could walk many parts of Pine Island Sound at low tide, and that certainly is true. Mean low-water depths at the eastern end of the sound are regularly charted at one to two feet and just a half a foot in some spots. The sound deepens in the middle, where four to ten foot depths are more the norm. Oyster bars creep out at unexpected locations, but except for these well-recognizable spots, the bottom is entirely soft.

I have made a habit when arriving in strange waters to purchase whatever lure the locals cherish most. When no verifiable "locals" are able to tell you what that is, a foolproof method for choosing the right plug is to buy whatever is almost out-of-stock at tackle shops and gas stations in the area. On this trip, I bought the last two brown, plastic shrimp at the Pineland Marina store. While my rendezvous pals were paddling much faster than I could sail in the light wind of that first day, I took a speckled trout while trolling in shallow water. On the second day while trolling from a canoe, I took a somewhat larger trout on the same lure. Go with the brown plastic shrimp.

To reach the sound side of the state park, our group of paddlers had to cross the Intracoastal Waterway. The waterway is a marked channel that passes between Punta Blanca and Mondongo Islands, then between Cabbage Key and Useppa Island. As any of you who have been down this highway in the water before know, it is filled with large boats befitting their owners' egos. The skippers of these floating gin-palaces get less courteous to the small boater with each passing year, it seems. They rarely slow down enough to reduce their wake, which could easily swamp a canoe. For this reason, those paddling open boats may want to wait on the shore of Mondongo Island or, coming back, on Punta Blanca Island, until the coast is clear.

Arriving at the south end of Punta Blanca Island as shown on the chart, one paddles north and west to reach the state park entrance. The entrance appears at a small dock with a few public slips. The waters of this cove between La Costa and Punta Blanca Islands are almost always calm. A few folks take advantage of the kayaks the park service offers for rent at the marina. Many sailboats and cruisers anchor here on their way south, while others make the trip to this anchorage from nearby Punta Gorda for the weekend. Dolphins and manta rays are regularly seen in this cove, which is teeming with sea trout, snook, and saltwater catfish.

The park service runs a tram at scheduled times along the one-mile park road between the marina and the campsites, on La Costa Island. The camping area is situated in a beautiful clearing of tall, ancient pines just a few yards behind the low dunes of the beach. Tour boats regularly bring day trippers here to take the tram to the beach. Paddlers arriving with packs to portage will definitely want to call ahead to find out when the last tram leaves, to avoid the one-mile carry.

The campsites on the island are booked well in advance. There are several park service cabins for rent here, as well, and these are often booked a full year in advance. The facilities in the campground are sparse: cold, outdoor showers, flush toilets, and potable, fresh water. Each campsite has a fire ring, and all the sites are well cleared on soft ground covered with pine needles. Trails run throughout the island to various points of natural and historic interest. The campground contains an amphitheater for presentations by the ranger.

Several sites are available directly on the beach. The ranger can help you select a site, but personally I thought the sites in the woods were prettier. They are certainly much cooler due to the shade, on hot afternoons. The heat of the day and a dependable, afternoon breeze keep the mosquitoes and no-see-ums at bay, but you'll run for your tent when the wind dies at night.

In an age when news of declining catches seems to keep up a steady drumbeat, I am happy to report that Pine Island Sound has a plentiful supply of fish. You will often see bottlenose dolphins, here, following schools of terrified mullet. There are platoons of osprey on every channel marker, signaling a healthy population of fish for food. We caught and ate one sea trout that was delicious. Throw the saltwater catfish back, however—their meat is chewy and tough. Kids in camp came back after breakfast with stringers full of sea trout I suspect they caught in the surf on bait of live shrimp.

One morning as I weighed anchor, I was startled by the noise of a school of shiny fish that jumped from the still water suddenly and in unison. A second later and a few feet behind, a dolphin lazily broached the surface. The dolphin are everywhere. Manta rays grow to huge sizes, here, and can swim at surprisingly swift speeds. While sailing almost silently past the shallows at Cabbage Key one morning, I must have startled the granddaddy of them all. The water beside my boat suddenly erupted in a tremendous, boiling cauldron of water and sand some ten feet wide, as if someone had just pulled the plug on the sea floor. I suspect it was a manta ray, but whatever it was, it was quite large and not at all happy to see me that morning.

On Tuesday morning, our little band slathered on the sunblock and headed out by canoe and kayak in search of sea trout, the "tunnel of love," and a cheeseburger in paradise. The sea trout requires no explanation. I took one behind Punta Blanca Island on a rubber shrimp, and Mike Richard took another on live bait not long thereafter. As for the tunnel of love, that is something you don't want to miss, and not for any of the obvious reasons.

The "tunnel," as it is more simply known in these parts, is a place near the southern end of La Costa where the sound intrudes into the island through a narrow, mangrove-shrouded inlet. The inlet leads to a wide lagoon just behind the beach. It's all just a little too Gilligan's Island to be believed, but it is real and well worth the visit. To get there, we meandered our way down the sound side of La Costa Island into Murdock Bayou. Stay glued to the shore of the island on your right as you paddle south, and you can't miss it. What looks to be an abandoned fishing shanty appears on the right just as you enter the bayou. Farther down on your right you will see the mangroves part in a cathedral-like arch over an inlet. The depth of the inlet is less than a foot in most spots. The clear water is filled with saltwater catfish, crabs, and conch, but remember that live shelling is prohibited on La Costa. Wildlife is abundant. As I came out of the tunnel with my family a week after the rendezvous, I saw a herd of wild boar escaping through the mangrove swamps.

The tunnel empties into a lagoon. There surely are alligators, here, if they are anywhere. (A park service sign, in fact, warns of their rare—but not unheard of—appetite for swimming humans.) Bringing our canoe onto the beach, we saw a few of the picnicking couples who give the tunnel its proper name. More often than not, though, the area is simply deserted. You just can't get any more "away from it all" on a beach in Florida than in this spot. The arrays of driftwood the size of dinosaur skeletons along the beach tell you what most of Florida's coast probably looked like before the bulldozers and high rollers arrived.

After a hike on the beach and some photographs, we could no longer resist the siren call of that "cheeseburger in paradise," not far from here. Yes, the namesake of the Jimmy Buffett tune and his inspiration for the lyrics of the song lies an easy paddle less than a mile east of La Costa, on the island of Cabbage Key. I assured my fellow rendezvouers that if Nessmuk could paddle the

Adirondacks and still find reason to pull his canoe up at hotels along the way, we could allow ourselves a visit to Cabbage Key.

The first thing you will notice as you climb the hill to the quirky little inn, restaurant and bar is that you are climbing. At thirty-eight feet above sea level, it is one of the highest points on the west coast of the state. This height is owing in part to the appetite of the Calusa Indians, who spent their time shucking oysters, here, 4,000 years before Christ. They tossed the shells onto what is now the lush island of Cabbage Key.

I cannot leave this story without grateful mention of the food and fellowship offered to me by Jim Shaver, Mike Richard, and Dave Zamos. Discovering to their horror that I had planned a monastic, shipboard diet of noodles, canned chicken and smoked oysters, they refused to serve themselves before lavishing my plate with steak, grilled peppers, and fresh salad. That kind of food is but one of the benefits of an early spring trip on Florida's open waters. The park service tram makes it easy to bring along coolers of gourmet fare, and I certainly benefited from the largesse.

Walking the mile back along the park road to my waiting sailboat in the dark, carrying my guitar with me, I looked up at a sparkling, stunning, night sky. *Such beauty*, I thought. A shooting star scuttled briefly across the horizon. To the north, the waning lights of tiny Boca Grande could scarcely diminish the glory of a bright universe amid the blackness.

I said goodbye to my fast friends on a Wednesday morning. The wind they had feared would stymie their passage home was mild enough that my offer of an escort across the waterway seemed unnecessary. Two were headed back to the rain and cold of a late winter that had stubbornly held onto Philadelphia and all of the northeast. They were resolved to go, but their faces told the tale of what they were leaving behind.

In the days that followed, I sailed north to Gasparilla Island, South to Captiva, and all over Pine Island Sound. I anchored in the lee of Punta Blanca one afternoon with no purpose other than to watch a manta ray play in the shallows. I swam beneath my boat, played my guitar, and let the tide wash winter away. When my family arrived, we took off together by land and sea, on foot, via kayak and under sail. I showed them all the secret places I had found, and we re-discovered them together. If old Jose Gaspar came here looking only for gold, he missed one of Florida's greatest treasures, indeed.

GRASS RIVER

SOUTH BRANCH, TOOLEY POND TRACT
ADIRONDACK PARK

The banner headline in the January 1999 issue of Adirondack Explorer struck a tone of breathless excitement: "Historic land deal clinched. Champion deal opens up classic canoe rivers for the first time this century." Here in North Carolina, I received a copy of this issue from attorney and wilderness advocate Dan Luciano. Dan had been kind enough to keep me posted in years past about the ongoing litigation involving public rights of access along the Moose River in the Adirondacks, and he passed along the story of this latest advance in the conservation agenda for my interest. My interest, indeed. I was as excited and ready to go as a hungry pioneer reading the news of gold in California in 1849.

In a landmark conservation deal in 1999, New York purchased 139,000 acres of Adirondack lands formerly owned by Champion International Paper. Included in this purchase is an area known as the Tooley Pond Tract, through which flows the Grass River. On June 30, 2000, this wild river and its spectacular waterfalls were opened

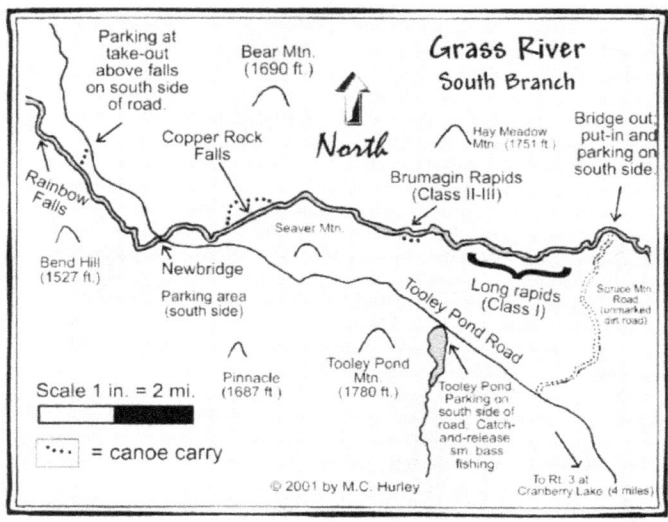

to the public for the first time in more than a century.

Anyone who has read the writings of Headley, Thoreau, and William Murray must long, as I do, for a glimpse of the nineteenth-century New England frontier. One imagines the frontier in that era as a distant land out west, but that term aptly describes much of Upstate New York at the time. There were places in the Adirondacks even as late as the Civil War that had not been mapped in any useful detail and that were unknown to few other than the Indians who still lived and hunted there. America's voracious appetite for timber, iron and recreation soon changed all that. By the time George Washington Sears first wrote under the pen name "Nessmuk" in 1881 about a novel means of wilderness exploration by canoe, industry of all kinds had made its way to this area. There were Fulton steamboats plying the chain of lakes that still bear the Fulton name, and hotels and camps were rising from the forest floor at a brisk pace. The timber companies that had already cleared so much of Maine's great wilderness found their way here, too.

If you have an interest in the history of this region, you could find no better use of your time than the hours you can spend touring the Adirondack Museum on Blue Mountain Lake. The enormity and scope of Adirondack timbering operations—as well as their staggering human cost—is difficult to imagine until one sees the giant murals of photographs of that era on display at the museum. Whole forests were cut to the ground, and waterways were so clogged with log drives that one wonders how

they ever made it to market. All but a few comparatively tiny parcels of this sprawling forest were timbered to some extent in the last two centuries. Much of the virgin forest was already gone by the time the New York legislature drew the "blue line" around six-million acres to establish the Adirondack Forest Preserve in 1885. In 1894, a constitutional mandate that public lands within the blue line be kept "forever wild" ensured the revival of the Adirondack wilderness. Many lakes and streams in the area are more wooded and wild, today, than they were a century ago. The thousands of acres already in private hands within the park, however—including large tracts locked away from public use by timber companies—remained just beyond the conservationists' grasp, like a glimmering jewel in Aladdin's cave. Those who dared venture there risked vigorous prosecution by private owners, many of whom came to resent the Adirondack Park Agency's controls on land use. So when a gem like the tract along the Grass River is sold back to the public after a century of private ownership, there is cause for celebration.

As for myself, the idea of venturing into a woods locked off to all but a few people since Nessmuk's day held more than a little fascination—and fantasy. The truth is that the lands donated by Champion Paper, now denominated the "Tooley Pond Tract" by the Department of Environmental Conservation, are not quite a pristine wilderness. Gun clubs have been operating on leases here, for decades. There are roads and towns nearby. Sadly, the Tooley Pond Road was built within eyesight of some of the more spectacular sections of the river below Rainbow Falls. The eight-mile section above Rainbow Falls that we paddled on the weekend after Labor Day, however, is easily one of the most wild and scenic waterways I have encountered in the Adirondacks.

The Tooley Pond Tract lies just a few miles north by northwest of the town of Cranberry Lake. We took Route 3 out of Tupper Lake and were told to look for Tooley Pond Road on the right, just after passing the bridge over Cranberry Lake. After one travels about four miles down Tooley Pond Road, an unmarked dirt road appears on the right. Turning here, you will know this is the Spruce Mountain Road by the mobile home that appears on the left, with a mailbox painted with the words "Deer Reports." No, this is not a wilderness—not yet. After two more miles, the road is barred by a gate at the bridge over the South Branch of the Grass River.

The view of the river as I first saw it was stunning—like catching the eye of a beautiful woman unexpectedly for the first time, in that moment when it is hard to look away. I lingered awhile and made a few casts before taking the Jeep on the shuttle. We were early, having shared the driving all night after meeting in Richmond. Now that we were here, there was no need to rush.

The put-in from Spruce Mountain Road is just above the aptly named Long Rapids. The entire trip is only eight miles to the carry at First Brook, above Rainbow Falls, but there is enough rough paddling and trekking in this section to take two days.

The DEC map and brochure are all one needs to navigate the river above Rainbow Falls. The DEC office for this area is at Potsdam. I had spoken to someone at the DEC to get information about this section of the river before our trip. I was told then that campsites were plentiful and that carries were well marked above Rainbow Falls but not below. That turned out to be only half true. The carries, though overgrown and poorly cleared, were easily spotted, but there were no designated campsites to be found. I called the DEC again after the trip and was informed that there is not a single, designated campsite in the entire eight-mile section of the river we paddled. I was also told that some folks have urged the DEC not to create any campsites, so as to force paddlers to camp in the brush more than 150 feet back from the river. I have a hard time believing that anyone pressing this point of view actually enjoys camping or intends to camp on the river. The underbrush is too dense or the banks are too steep in most spots to permit camping that far back. Expecting to find the designated sites promised us in the DEC brochure and described to me by the ranger, before our trip, we made do by camping on a little rock outcropping below Copper Rock Falls and on a tiny island just upriver from Rainbow Falls. I encourage readers to write to the DEC Bureau of Public Lands, 6739 U. S. Highway 11, Potsdam, NY 13676, to express support for designated campsites in this section.

The Grass is not a place where you'll want to bring your nicest boat. My buddy Wright Shields is mighty proud of his fiberglass canoe, but it took an impressive beating on this river. Before they bad made it past Long Rapids, Wright and his bow paddler Mike Avery had capsized, thoroughly watered down the food basket, managed to put a hole through the bottom of the boat, and cracked one of its ribs. Yet, this upper section is not so dangerous as it is shallow. I am foremost among river cowards and will gladly take a carry before I'll risk myself or my boat on anything better than a class II rapid. If you pick your path in this river with some prudence, you will have nothing to fear. I was paddling a Camper made of Old Town's proprietary "Oltonar" Royalex: the best design and the best material made for canoes, in my opinion. Because the river is often so shallow and consistently rocky, you'll want to leave your fiberglass, Kevlar, aluminum, and wooden canoes at home.

We repaired Wright's canoe by cutting two green sticks to use as a splint, placing them across the fractured rib, and securing them in place with duct tape. We also filled the hole in the hull with duct tape. She was dry and nearly good as new.

The flora and color of the Grass River resemble that of the Allagash of Northern Maine. Both rivers are fairly tannic and given to foaming up from the vegetation that lines the banks. Some mistake this for industrial pollution, but the Allagash runs for a hundred miles with no industry on its banks. The Grass is less isolated but similarly untouched by industrial waste. The streaks of foam you see are from the action of the rapids on the natural oils of vegetation that grow around the water.

Once done with our arduous course through Long Rapids, my partner Ed Childs and I turned the nose of the canoe back upriver to fish the eddies and wait for the other boat, not knowing it was capsized upriver. Ed quickly pulled two luminescent, native brook trout from the water on a spinner and sent them back again. The river is strictly catch-and-release, and natural bait is prohibited. It was surprising that the fishing was not better, though, as we did not see another soul on the water for these three days in September during perfect brookie-weather. Still, in a river as pretty as this, with so many likely looking eddies and pools to which to cast, the anticipation is almost reward enough.

You will be tempted as we were to run the hairpin turn at Brumagin Rapids and avoid the short carry on the left bank. We scouted and thought hard about taking the class III drop in the left channel of the turn. It looked like it might be exciting on a warm fall afternoon, but it flowed into a pinning rock with too little room in which to turn a sixteen foot canoe. On the right there is an easy class II drop that we took without problem. The fiberglass boat took the carry.

After leaving Brumagin Rapids at three o'clock, we began to look in earnest for one of the "many" designated campsites promised to us by the ranger, in this section. We came to another unnamed carry on the left bank, less than a mile above Copper Rock Falls. The trail was narrow and overgrown, but the DEC had nailed the familiar, yellow carry signs to small trees to guide us through. The river alongside this carry looks as if it might be navigable, but we tried it and found it too shallow. When we came at last to the thunderous and beautiful Copper Rock Falls, it was nearing nightfall. We expected to see a DEC campsite here but, finding none, decided to pitch camp for the night in the only clearing we could find, beside a pool just below the falls. With this gorgeous falls as a backdrop, we joked that this was the kind of picturesque campsite you never see anywhere but on labels for camping equipment. In fact, though, the roar of the falls was so loud we could scarcely carry on a conversation that night around the campfire!

You will still see "posted" signs along the river, but rest assured this is all state land. The state purchased outright a corridor of a half mile to two miles wide on each bank of the river for public use. Beyond this corridor, the state has a conservation easement that allows public use for a much wider area. However, in a temporary concession to local gun clubs, the public is not allowed on easement lands with hunting leases in force between June 30, 2000 and June 30, 2014, during the rifle season for whitetail deer.

I was uneasy as we approached the end of our trip at Rainbow Falls. Having taken a trail to see the falls before leaving my Jeep at the parking lot, I knew the power of the water rushing through that chasm. Even so, I had hoped to find at least one marked campsite near this spot, where we might spend our last night on the river.

As the take-out loomed closer, it seemed we might be disappointed. But when the carry appeared, I kept paddling-toward the falls. Ed looked nervously astern. "Just a little farther," I said, "not too close to the falls, and we'll turn around." Right about then, we saw a tiny island. It made a fine camp, a perfect ending to a wonderful trip, and a fitting place from which to savor the last light of summer.

THE LOBSTER TRIP

UPPER WEST BRANCH PENOBSCOT RIVER
NORTH MAINE WOODS

I discovered Henry David Thoreau in high school in the early 1970s. Those were the days of a renewed awareness of our heritage as a nation of rugged individualists. The Wilderness Act had recently been passed. Americans were canoeing and backpacking in record numbers, reading the Foxfire books about frontier living, watching The Waltons, and listening to Euell Gibbons tell us where to find edible food in the forest. Yes, Henry David Thoreau fit right in with the times. Aside from being a literary icon whom we were required to study in school, he seemed to possess all the qualities important to my self-searching adolescence: a love of solitude, a facility for language, and the ability to make a marriage of both in his reflections on nature. He wrote about Maine—a country as remote and inaccessible in my imagination as it had been to Thoreau when he first ventured there, in 1847.

In July of 2002, my family and I retraced Thoreau's famous voyage along the West Branch of the Penobscot River to Chesuncook Lake, in northern Maine. There I would reacquaint myself with this writer-philosopher

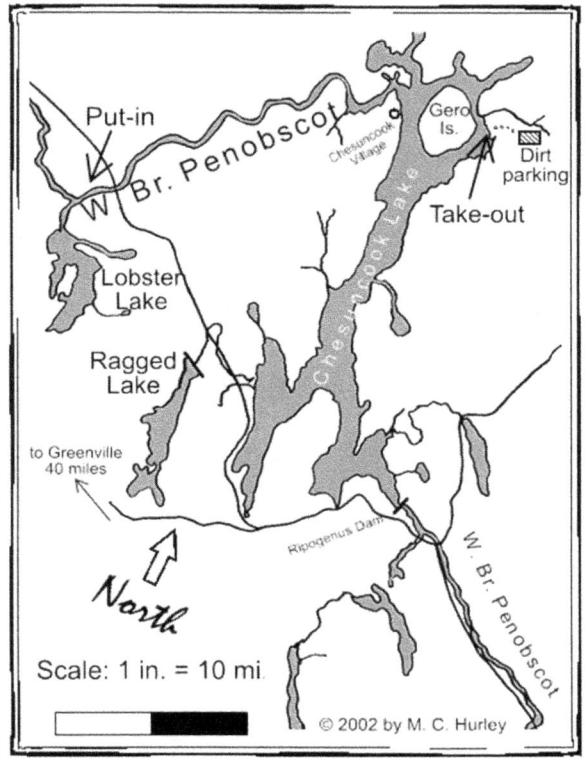

and, separated by 150 years of history, savor a beautiful waterway that is, astonishingly, almost unchanged from the days he spent there. By Thoreau's time, most of New England had been cleared for farming, causing him to react with wonderment, in Maine, at the uncommon sight of spruce trees: "[W]e had hardly got out of the streets of Bangor before I began to be exhilarated by the sight of the wild fir and spruce-tops, and those of other primitive evergreens, peering through the mist in the horizon. It was like the sight and odor of cake to a schoolboy . . . I had come all this distance partly to see where the white pine, the Eastern stuff of which our houses are built, grew."

Seeing so much natural beauty only lent a greater sense of urgency to Thoreau's expeditions to the Maine woods, which he feared would soon meet a similar fate. At the end of his journey on the Penobscot in 1853, he lamented that "Maine, perhaps, will soon be where Massachusetts is. A good part of her territory is already as bare and commonplace as much of our neighborhood, and her villages generally are not so well shaded as ours. We seem to think that the earth must go through the ordeal of sheep pasturage before it is habitable by man."

Thoreau's worry, thankfully, proved unfounded. Amid the clamor about global warming, the great, untold story of the last half of the 20th century is the reforestation of the Eastern seaboard. According to the Journal of Industrial Ecology, while the total land-area covered by forest in the United States has remained constant since about 1952, the number of trees has increased thirty percent to a point where America has more trees, today, than it did 100 years ago. What accounts for much of this change is that the pastureland of Thoreau's New England and the upper Great Lakes region is now densely forested. Nowhere is this more apparent than in a journey to northern Maine, where, even along the corridor of Interstate 95, a man can still get the sense of entering a vast—albeit well-charted—wilderness. Thoreau traveled less widely in Maine than some might think, making only three reported sorties into those woods which inspired some of his most timeless essays. Born the son of a poor pencil-salesman on July

12, 1817, he made his way to Harvard. From there he scaled not merely the mountains of his native New England but the far loftier heights of literary immortality. In that rarefied air he met the likes of Ralph Waldo Emerson and Walt Whitman. Together they became the standard bearers of an emerging, American philosophy of wilderness romanticism that prevails to this day.

The journey that Thoreau made on the Upper West Branch of the Penobscot is what Mainers today affectionately call "the Lobster trip." The name derives from nearby Lobster Lake. The point at which the inlet from Lobster Lake feeds into the West Branch is where we chose to begin a three-day, two-night voyage spanning twenty-three miles.

Having managed to get good and lost trying to find this place, I should mention at the outset the importance of a suitable map. Every gas station and coffee shop in the state seems to have a dog-eared copy of the "Maine Atlas" on hand. It is published by the Delorme Company of Freeport. If you don't have it, you'll need one to find your way along the network of unsigned, unpaved, private logging roads that are the only evidence of civilization for thousands of square miles.

To begin our trip on the West Branch from the south, we drove to the Allagash Gateway Campsite, which lies thirty-three miles west of Millinocket and forty-four miles northeast of Greenville. If you are coming up Interstate 95 at night, your best bet is to take the Medway exit and find a room. The Gateway Inn, just off of the interstate at exit 56 in Medway, provided us with very nice accommodations for about fifty-five dollars. I would advise anyone not familiar with this area against attempting to navigate logging roads at night. Flat tires are common. Help is far away. Rarely is there cell phone service. Your best chance is to hail a passing truck on CB channel 19, but the trucks don't run these roads at night.

We paid to have our Jeep brought to a take-out on the northern end of Chesuncook Lake. Most folks who make this trip paddle another seventeen miles down the length of the lake, which is the third largest in Maine. Stories abound of the high winds and steep waves that regularly bedevil canoeists trying to make their way with loaded canoes all the way to Ripogenus Dam at the southern end without capsizing. To avoid this excitement, we paid twice the usual shuttle fee of fifty-five dollars to get our Jeep brought to the end of a dirt logging road that comes within forty yards of the lake behind Gero Island. Allagash Gateway Campsite (allagashgateway.com) provided the shuttle. The driver accompanied us in our Jeep to the put-in, dropped us off with our canoes and gear, then brought the Jeep to the take-out for us.

Most of the wild land in northern Maine is owned by paper companies and private individuals. Together they formed an organization named North Maine Woods, Inc., to manage land use by the public. NME has put up gated checkpoints along access roads. One must stop to buy a camping permit and pay a hefty toll (in cash) for use of the roads. The gates are locked at night.

The Great Northern Paper Company, which owns the lands along the Penobscot River Corridor, granted the state a perpetual conservation easement in 1981. Pursuant to this easement, the Department of Conservation regulates camping along the river. They publish a brochure with a map of the river and campsite locations which is available at no charge at NME checkpoints.

As my children and I paddled down the West Branch, we passed the very creeks and islands that Thoreau described in a travelogue of his 1853 voyage on this river, entitled *The Maine Woods*. Julie dutifully read to us passages of that essay describing the plants, trees, and topography that Thoreau encountered as we encountered the same. Thoreau's description, 150 years later, was eerily accurate.

One imagines that the fir trees along shore must have been much larger and more dense, then, but Thoreau found them to be sixty-feet, on average, and interspersed with occasional marshes and meadows. That's exactly what you will see there, today. How many places can you go and find things largely as they were described a century-and-a-half ago?

Trying to see all things through Thoreau's eyes as we swept down the river, I had a short-lived but lovely daydream: Dare I suggest it, I thought? We are after all much the same, Thoreau and I. He was a writer; I am a writer. He loved the solitude and beauty of the North Woods, as do I. He wrote about his adventures for the education and entertainment of others, and I try to do the same. Yes, the shoe fit. Congratulating myself, I turned to my wife to say, " Honey, when you think about it, I really am sort of a modern-day Henry David Thoreau myself, come again in this age to exclaim the glory of the American Wilderness to a new generation!"

She let a moment pass, for dramatic effect. Then she turned her head slowly, like gun turrets on a destroyer, and looked at me from beneath a lowered brow as though to take aim. I could see that I was about to be blown out of the water. She carried a lethal ammunition of humility in one barrel and reality in the other. There was no escape, I knew, as I braced for the sting of impact. Instead, in a backward and unintended sort of way, she paid me this compliment: "No, Michael, you're not Henry David Thoreau. Oh, no," she said, chuckling sardonically. "He was a dandy who came to the woods in luxury, with an entourage of underlings who did his paddling, cooking, and dirty work for him. There's no one like you."

By these remarks, Julie reinforced a central theme of so much of her commentary, through the years, about my particular style of outdoor adventure, to wit: that my fondness for living for days out of a pack basket, cooking in the soot and smoke of wood fires, bathing au naturel and heeding Nature's Call with a trowel and a trench is uniquely Paleolithic and—well, uncivilized. This point of view persists despite twenty-one years of marriage. It owes much to the fact that "roughing it," in her family, meant landing a shot outside the fairway at the country club. And so, with occasional, editorial grumblings such as these coming from my rear flank, 1 made my way proudly in Mr. Thoreau's wake and imagined myself in his company, as Julie continued reading *The Maine Woods* out loud from her perch in the bow.

A word about the bugs: Our driver warned us that the put-in below Lobster Lake is the place where "every bug in Maine is born." Even in mid-July, when black flies have taken their leave of the Adirondacks, small swarms of them danced around our heads, in Maine, as we loaded the canoes. They stayed miserably with us for the first two or three miles until, as promised by our driver, we emerged from the swamps and they departed.

To reach the river, Thoreau had come north on Moosehead Lake by steamboat to Northeast Cove of the lake, where a carry leads to an area on the river known as Penobscot Farm. At the head of the carry, Thoreau's party met a man with an ox-drawn truck to take them and their belongings through the woods to a point on the river about two miles above Lobster Stream. There, they set out in birch-bark canoes with an Indian guide named Joe Aittean.

As to the origin of the name given to Lobster Lake, Thoreau dutifully retells the explanation given to him by his guide, that "it was so called from small freshwater lobsters found in it." The guide was either spoofing his often-condescending employer or didn't know. Modem texts explain that the lake is so named because it forms the distinct shape of a lobster claw.

Just as Thoreau wrote, "below the mouth of the Lobster we found quick water, and the river expanded to twenty or thirty rods in width." Indeed, the river travels at a steady but gentle pace of two to three miles per hour at most spots, allowing one to make ample distance with minimal effort.

Once on the river, we immediately encountered a small island. Getting out to explore, we discovered it to be a designated campsite marked with a sign: "Thoreau's Island." This is the location of the writer's first campsite on the river, where his guide cleared "a small space amid the dense spruce and fir trees." The campsite contains a clearing to this day, covered by grass that the rangers must, I assume, periodically mow. Each of the thirteen campsites between here and Chesuncook Lake is marked by a brown and white sign bearing a place name, not a number. Each site has a wooden picnic table, fire ring, and a ridgepole for suspending a tarp high above the table and the fire. Each site also has a wooden outhouse many yards behind the tenting areas, along a trail. We found these latrines to be exceptionally clean and in good condition.

All of the campsites along the river are visible from the water. It is pleasant, if the river is not crowded with other paddlers, to stop at one of these camps for lunch and a swim, as we did. The river can get quite crowded in late July and August. We were advised to pick a site early in the afternoon to avoid getting caught without a site near dark. All of the campsites are postcard pretty, but we found the Big Island South site particularly attractive.

Here the river drops a bit, creating a pleasant sound as the rips swirl around the end of the island. Those who camp here have a water view on three sides. The moving water, the breeze that sweeps this high, pine-needled point of land, and the absence of much underbrush seemed to suppress the bug population a bit.

The black flies and mosquitoes were much more daunting at the Big Ragmuff site, where Ragmuff Creek comes in on the river left. Thoreau camped there, and judging from his essay, it was a brushy site even when he found it. It was there that Thoreau's Indian guide left camp to explore the far reaches of Ragmuff Creek in search of moose. Thoreau thought him simpleminded for not taking a gun:

We stopped to fish for trout at the mouth of a small stream called

Ragmuff, which came in from the west, about two miles below the Moosehorn. Here were the ruins of an old lumbering-camp, and a small space, which had formerly been cleared and burned over, was now densely overgrown with the red cherry and raspberries. While we were trying for trout, Joe, Indian-like, wandered off up the Ragmuff on his own errands, and when we were ready to start was far beyond call. So we were compelled to make a fire and get our dinner here, not to lose time . . . Joe at length returned, after an hour and a half, and said that he had been two miles up the stream exploring, and had seen a moose, but, not having the gun, he did not get him. We made no complaint, but concluded to look out for Joe the next time.

As Julie and the children and I stooped and climbed our way over the impassable rocks and falls of Ragmuff Creek, it occurred to me—as no doubt it did to Joe—that if he had shot a moose two miles up the creek, Thoreau would have expected him to dress and drag the thousand-pound animal back to camp while Thoreau sat inspecting his flowers and insect boxes. Julie editorialized that poor Joe probably ran up Ragmuff Creek just to get a break from his pompous employers, making up the story about looking for moose as an excuse.

A party of canoeists whom we met at Big Island, seeing our children, recommended for our second night's camp the "Boom House" site. It lies eight miles distant from Big Island, on the right bank, just before the river enters Chesuncook Lake. There the river widens considerably, and the demon wind of the lake first makes its presence felt. They told us of a trail leading from this site to an old store at Chesuncook Village where we could have our fill of homemade fudge, root beer, ice cream and nothing else. I was keen to go ever since reading a sign about the place that had been put up on the wall inside the privy at Big Island. We found the trail (marked with an arrow and a sign reading "store") behind Boom House, as promised. The treats and scenery are well worth the hike, as the trail is not more than a half-mile long. Boom House is a grassy site with a gravel beach and a pleasant view of the mouth of the river. Those wanting more of a wilderness setting should try Pine Stream, just two miles upriver.

On the final day of our journey we awoke to a north wind whipping in the trees. Despite the relative protection of land, the wind and waves were strong enough to force us to shore on Gero Island, where we waited in the trees for a lull in the weather. The take-out is marked only by a few strips of red tape hanging from tree branches, where the trail comes in. Following this trail forty yards, we came to our mud-encrusted Jeep and found our way out along the logging roads. Soon we were on our way to hot showers and a place in Bar Harbor, where local folk would pamper us with steaming lobster and blueberry ice cream, leading me to wonder whether Henry and I are so very different, after all.

CALDERWOOD LAKE & THE SLICKROCK WILDERNESS

CHEROKEE NATIONAL FOREST

At 1,086 feet above sea-level, in the clouds of the Great Smoky Mountains and on the border between Tennessee and North Carolina, sits a shimmering, turquoise jewel named Calderwood Lake. Formed by two dams along the Little Tennessee River, it offers the canoeist easy access to Slickrock Creek and the wilderness area named after Joyce Kilmer. His famous poem declaring that there is nothing so lovely as a tree aptly describes these surroundings, where a last stand of virgin timber has been preserved in his memory.

Calderwood Lake seems an unlikely choice for a canoe-camping trip. The steep, thirty-degree incline of the mountains that plunge beneath its depths scarcely grants a foothold to the deer, much less space for pitching a tent. But where Slickrock Creek enters the lake a trail begins, on the North Carolina side, in the remains of a railroad grade. At the mouth of the creek and for many miles inland along this trail, primitive camping areas have been cleared that offer some of the most picturesque and remote sites anywhere in the region.

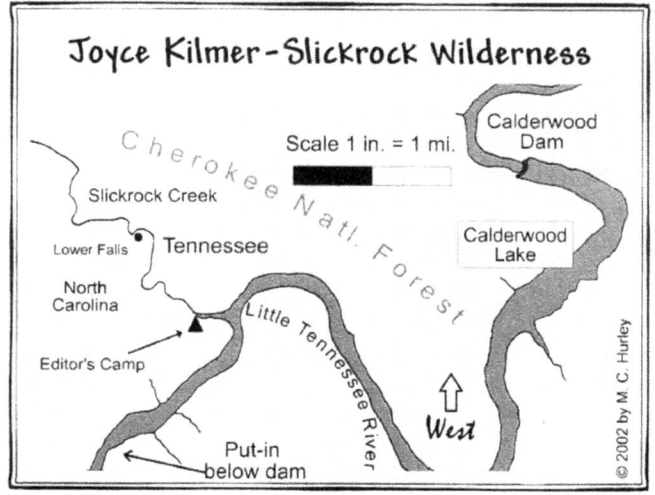

All of the land, here, belongs to the U.S. Forest Service. The creek forms the border between Tennessee and Cherokee National Forest, on one side, and North Carolina and Nantahala National Forest on the other. No permits or fees are required for camping. There are no improvements and, for the most part, no distractions from the primeval beauty of forest and stream.

To reach this Shangri-La we drove eight hours from Raleigh, stopping to pitch our tent for the night in the Cable Cove camp ground maintained by the forest service on Fontana Lake. Fontana Lake lies along the southern border of Great Smoky Mountains National Park and, like Calderwood, draws water from the Little Tennessee River. Fontana Dam backs up the Little "T" for thirty miles. The spillway below Fontana Dam flows into Cheoah Reservoir, a narrow ribbon of calm water that winds eight miles through the mountains before it meets Cheoah Dam. Cheoah Dam was the location for the scene in the movie, The Fugitive, in which Harrison Ford leaps from a dam presumably to his doom, but survives. Do not try this at home or at Cheoah. The spillway from Cheoah Dam creates Calderwood Lake. Those looking for a different method of access to the lake than a desperate leap can find it a half-mile below the dam at the Alcoa boat ramp. (Alcoa owns the Tallahassee Power Company, "Tapoco," which operates the dam.) At the boat ramp, public parking, potable water, and campsites are provided. The distance by canoe from the Alcoa boat ramp to the mouth of Slickrock Creek is no more than a mile.

This trip on Calderwood Lake was the realization of a promise I had made to myself at the age of fourteen, when my mother first brought me to the Smokies on a family vacation. Staying at Fontana Village, we drove the mountainside parkway along Cheoah Reservoir that leads to Deal's Gap, where the road bends 111 times in three miles. Looking down from the car as a young boy, I could see the calm surface of the blue-green water where it shot off into the distance, away from the road, between the steep, forested banks of the mountains. It seemed such a placid, wild and uninhabited place. The lake was so far below us that it appeared almost to be painted into the landscape. It looked like an ideal place for the silent meandering of a canoe. I imagined someday that I would return here, to explore.

Cheoah Reservoir is overlooked by a road, but Calderwood Lake and the surrounding forest offer hardly any sign of civilization once one is safely away from the ramp. It was not always so. After President Andrew Jackson signed the order for removal of six thousand

Cherokee Indians to Oklahoma in 1838, in what came to be known as the Trail of Tears, white men were allowed to bid on Cherokee lands. Small towns began to appear in the mid-1800s. Wide-scale, commercial logging came to the area around Fontana in 1890.

Work on Cheoah Dam began in 1916 and, in an unintended way, saved the surrounding forest from destruction. Construction of this dam flooded the railway that had been built along the banks of Slickrock Creek to haul logs down from the mountain. The loggers made a mad dash to complete their work but ran out of time to reach the higher elevations before the dam was completed and the rail tracks had to be removed.

The four-hundred-year-old yellow poplars that stand today in Joyce Kilmer Memorial Forest might still have been logged but for the decline in lumber prices during the Great Depression and the farsighted vision of the chief of the U.S. Forest Service. At his urging, in 1935 the government paid twenty-eight dollars per acre for 13,000 acres described as "some of the finest original growth in the Appalachians" and one of the "very few remaining tracts of virgin hardwood" in the East.

Today, you can see the Joyce Kilmer Memorial Forest on a loop trail that leads from a parking lot off of Highway 129. What you will see along the lower stretches of Slickrock Creek are not the 400-year-old denizens preserved in the nearby memorial forest but second growth which has not been timbered since about 1917.

After a leisurely, one-hour paddle from the boat ramp, we made camp beside the mouth of the creek where it became too shallow to paddle farther. Just ahead was a waterfall where the creek makes its final plunge into

Calderwood Lake.

The level of the lake fluctuated as much as two to three feet due to releases from the dam, and at one point the falls at the mouth were submerged. The water rose enough that we had to pull up the stakes on one tent and move it higher up on the trail.

We camped in the same location at Slickrock Creek for two nights, taking time on the second day to hike about three miles up the creek to the spectacular Lower Falls. The trail from the mouth of the creek leading to Lower Falls passes by several campsites which, depending on your interest in portaging, you may prefer to a camp at the mouth of the creek. These are backpackers' sites right on the water, with no facilities other than fire rings made of rocks.

As we hiked the trail on a week in mid-June, we saw no one other than two older gentlemen out for the day on a five-mile connecting trail that leads from Cheoah Dam to the creek. They caught us skinny-dipping and stopped to tell the tale of a cousin who had stolen another boy's clothes on a summer day, here, back in the thirties. A wrestling contest had then ensued—in a poison ivy patch. "That was back in the days before air conditioning," the men said, "and the bandages didn't come off those boys until September." We tiptoed gingerly thereafter.

The trilling waterfalls we had seen so far had more than satisfied us when, farther up the trail, we heard a distant, steady sound akin to static on a giant radio. By now we had crossed onto the Tennessee side of the creek. After climbing a steep ridge, the cool, clear pool of Lower Falls appeared through the trees. Above it, water rushed over wide, flat rocks some fifteen feet high in a milky foam that disappeared immediately beneath the surface. The boys swam out and reveled beside the spray more like a pair of otters than children. I, ever a model of right judgment, climbed high atop the rock and, getting ready to jump, slipped onto my fanny and tumbled in—unhurt but wiser. They didn't name it "Slickrock Creek" for nothing.

Later that summer I asked Kip, who at twelve has paddled more rivers than most men see in a lifetime, to list his top five trips. To my delight, Slickrock Creek made the cut, and he vowed to bring his own family here one day. A promise I made long ago had been kept and made again.

GREEN RIVER

MAMMOTH CAVE NATIONAL PARK

I have always been intrigued by caves. They are not unique to this country, by any means, but there is something uniquely American about them. Think of two boys encountering a wild cave by a river, and you have the very image of what Mark Twain tried to convey through the characters of Huckleberry Finn and Tom Sawyer. They would hesitate at the opening. "You go in." "No, you first."

In ancient times, man feared what lay deep beneath the earth almost as much as he longed for Heaven, above. In my own upbringing, caves meant a trip down the Blue Bridge Parkway into Luray and the Shenandoah Valley of Virginia. There would be little shops along the way, pungent with the smell of freshly sawn cedar from which all manner of boxes and placards had been made for souvenirs. These stores sold leather moccasins that you could stitch yourself, with yards of gimp, and the most improbable jellies and jams made from exotica like elderberries and turnips. Here, Southern spies posing as smiling women called me "Honey" and seemed so glad to meet me that I expect, with only modest encouragement, they would have taken me home and

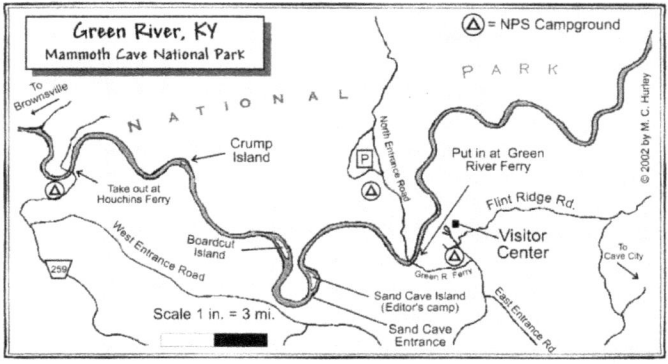

raised me to full grown. Attractions like these had been constructed at every little rest stop and gas pump, and they were an integral part of the vast, secret conspiracy to capture me for a son of the South. The plot succeeded, and so goes the old joke that the Confederacy may have lost the war, but they are still taking the Yankees prisoner, one by one.

Traveling over the North Carolina mountains into Tennessee and on to Kentucky, this summer, I had that familiar feeling of those road trips of yore. Kentucky proudly claims its Southern heritage, but its rural charm seems comparatively untouched by the suburban blight that has gobbled up so much of the New South. Not far north of Bowling Green, in Mammoth Cave National Park, where the Green River flows, there still are kitschy roadside stands offering pecan logs and exhortations to "Chew Red Man." Maybe some things really never do change.

I bad been looking for another Kentucky river to put under our belts ever since my introduction to paddling in this state in a glorious trip on the South Fork of the

Cumberland, a few years ago. There are rivers aplenty in Kentucky for camping, and Bob Sehlinger has written the premier guide to finding the one just right for your trip. His book, *A Canoeing & Kayaking Guide to the Streams of Kentucky*, was first published in 1978 by Menasha Ridge Press of Hillsborough, North Carolina. Though hard to find today in bookstores, it is available (along with every other book on the planet) at Amazon.com. Sehlinger describes the Green as "one of Kentucky's largest, longest, and most navigable rivers." In the extended drought of this past summer, we took his advice that the Green River is canoe-able year-round and set out for the Bluegrass State.

For an overnight trip, we chose the reportedly popular, twelve-mile run between the Green River Ferry and Houchins Ferry. These are not merely historical place-names but crossings where real, diesel ferries ply the river several times each day on an overhead cable. Cars pull up to a concrete ramp at either side of the river and wait for the ferryman to wave them aboard. It would seem a lot more efficient simply to build bridges at these locations, but perhaps not nearly as much fun.

Julie and I, traveling with our son Kip and his cousin Bennett, made the obligatory tourist stop at Mammoth Cave National Park before beginning this trip. The national park encloses the truly, well, *mammoth* cave in this area—the largest cave in the world, to be exact. There are over 350 miles of nooks, crannies, and passages below the surface. But if local flavor is what you seek, there are many mom and pop cave-tour operators that are less inhibited by park-service officialdom. The private owners of Crystal Onyx Cave (apparently not to be confused with nearby Onyx Cave), for example, claim to have unearthed Indian remains nearly 3,000 years old. Diamond Caverns, in Park City, boasts of being Kentucky's "most beautiful cave" since its discovery 140 years ago by a local slave who mistook its brilliant calcite formations for diamonds. Lost River Cave, in Bowling Green, touts its billing in Ripley's Believe It or Not (another staple of Southern culture) as the location of the "world's shortest and deepest river." It features boat tours on the river that runs through the cave. There are stories of outlaws and Civil War soldiers and assorted characters of all kinds who hid-out or died here, and it all just rings with the kind of Americana you can't get anywhere else but in the South. God love 'em, I hope there are always places like these. Generally once we have had our tourist fix, it is time to get out into the woods of these areas and encounter them in much more authentic ways. We did just that one balmy afternoon in June, just as the skies began to open up with rain.

There is scant room at the ferry landings for anything but the loading ramp of the ferry itself. We, in our boots and foul weather gear, pulled our two canoes to the side while casually dressed ferry goers studied our strange-looking canvas packs and loads of provisions. An authentic paddle-wheeler offers rides down and back on the Green for a few miles of the river, here. Watching the passengers watch us, as we drifted by in our wooden craft, I had a feeling we must have looked as curious as Indians on horseback beside a locomotive full of waving homesteaders.

Due to the recent, steady rains at the time of our trip, I cannot give a fair account of the water-clarity of the

Green. I would expect in drier days that it is a fairly clear stream with a tint of color suited to its name. When we went it was more opaque, though more green than the color of mud. The rains in preceding weeks had been so relentless that periodically we would hear a giant sycamore come crashing down the steep hillside with a noise that quite resembled a bomb exploding in the distance. It occurred frequently enough that we confined our paddling to mid-river so as not to be squashed by one of these tumbling behemoths.

The woods of this area recall the stories of Davy Crockett and Daniel Boone. They are dense, hardwood forests with thick underbrush, where pioneers no doubt found many suitable targets for their squirrel rifles. The river in this section splits the middle of Mammoth Cave National Park, and several maintained hiking trails come near to the right bank. Canoeists who prefer ultralight camping in the park backcountry can pick up these trails from the river and follow them north to backcountry campsites. The trails are well marked on the official map and guide, available for free at the park-service headquarters in the visitor center. This is where hordes of tourists congregate to ride park-service buses to the entrances of various cave tours. You must provide identification and an itinerary to receive a free backcountry permit that will allow you to camp at one of twelve, designated interior sites, or anywhere along the riverbank, or on islands in the river.

After receiving our backcountry permit, we took time for the "Frozen Niagara" cave tour, which had been recommended to us by one of the locals we had met in Cave City. We were not disappointed, and I would highly recommend any of these tours as part of your trip, here. There is even a "wild cave" tour available to skinny people over the age of sixteen. You will be given a miner's hat to go shinnying through tight cracks and crevices on your belly and back in pursuit of wonders not accessible along the guard-railed paths of conventional tours. The highlight of our tour came when the tour guide cut the lights after we were all deep inside the cave. The blackness is absolute. Try as you may, you cannot get a glimpse of your hand even an inch in front of your face.

I know of only two canoe liveries in this area. One is Mammoth Canoe & Kayak, located on Highway 70 a few miles west of Exit 53 off of Interstate 85, in Cave City. The other is the Green River Canoe Company, located in Brownsville, near the intersection of Highways 259 & 70. We hired Green River Canoe to drop off our Jeep at the take-out at Houchins Ferry, close to their store. They sell a variety of live bait and camping supplies, as well.

As we left the put-in, the current of the Green bore us gently westward beneath lush, overhanging greenery. The soaking rain which had imparted that "Why on Earth are we doing this?" expression to my wife 's face at the outset gradually gave way to dry, overcast skies and, with them, a much-to-be-preferred, "Hey, I can do this!" expression which endured happily thereafter.

In fairly short order, we came to the wide, sweeping gravel bar marked as Sand Island on the map. Joel Davis at Green River Canoe had told us to look for this island to find a cave nearby which is not marked on the map but, given the name of the island, I presume to be "Sand Cave." Joel spoke of a cave lying several yards distant from the left bank of the river in this area. The entrance, he said, was blocked by a deep pool of clear water. Paddling past the island, Julie and I could see the gaping, black maw of the cave in the distance. The bank was too muddy from the rain for us to camp there, so we paddled a few yards back upstream to the island.

Here we found clean gravel and ample space for our tents. A huge brush-pile of logs that had been swept downstream in high water provided firewood. The Green River is dam fed, but all reports are that it maintains a fairly steady and safe flow of water. Otherwise, I am sure it would swamp many of the ferries that cross downstream. Water levels fluctuated very little during our trip.

Interestingly enough, there are no black bears in the forests around Mammoth Cave. There are deer aplenty, but the black bear apparently were overhunted and have never made a comeback. But for my lack of foresight this would have been a welcome comfort to my wife, who, despite my lectures on the repellent effects of campfire smoke, lays awake at night and worries. Hoping to extinguish both her fears and any nervous, late-night conversation, I told her that the nearby bazillions of bullfrogs, which hadn't missed a beat in three hours, would stop their "chir-eeep-ping" at the first sign that something large was moving in the area. (I suspected this to be a myth, but in television episodes of Daniel Boone in the sixties, that was always Mingo's clue.) Big mistake. When the bullfrogs stopped singing at midnight—presumably from exhaustion or union rules—Julie awakened me and, with the utmost solemnity, informed me of this urgent news from the forest. Sleep-dazed and incredulous that she had actually believed my story, I confessed that I was a complete idiot to tell her such a thing. She accepted my confession without qualification and dropped right off to sleep, while the bullfrogs and I lay awake and talked about bears.

After a gracious plenty of pancakes the next morning, Bennett, Kip, and I left to explore the mysteries of Sand Cave. As tough as these two seventh graders pretend to be, the idea of slipping into a wild cave with no guard rails and park service staff was a little daunting.

With no gear to slow us down, we pulled our canoe up where the mouth of the cave was visible from shore. Immediately, I felt a rush of cold breath from the black hole ahead, and it seemed to have been exhaled from the very bottom of the earth. Finding as promised a small pond of water in front of the cave mouth, I hoisted our canoe on my shoulders, carried it to the edge of the pool, and urged the boys to hop in. They were duly intrigued by the idea of paddling in this little pool of startlingly clear, cold water that seemed to rise up out of nowhere. After the boys made a few trips round the pond in the canoe, the dark opening at the rear beckoned them onward. I, being the biggest child in the group, urged them to take a looksee. In order to do so, they had to paddle back to the far edge of the pool to pick me up, so that I could mind their canoe and pick them up again after they finished exploring.

With me waiting in the canoe below, they climbed the rock cautiously, bunched and leading with a flashlight in a scene that recalled the cover of a Hardy Boys mystery. Carefully stoking their sense of adventure, I wondered aloud why there were no footprints at the cave entrance—a place surely untouched by rain for thousands of years. Could they be the first humans to approach this cave since ancient times? Might it be protected by a curse against all who attempt to enter? Would they find the skeletal remains of others who had tried?

Shrugging off my corny, spook house shenanigans, the boys made it into the first chamber. I impatiently demanded a full report on what they saw. With their flashlight they discovered a shaft above them that led upward into the darkness of the mountain. A passageway around a large boulder seemed to lead to another chamber in the cave, but, right on cue, their flashlight burned out.

I could hear the "You go!" "No, you go!" discussion that ensued from my place in the canoe, followed by the re-appearance of the Hardy boys at the entrance to the cave. Bennett cheerfully volunteered to take up my post in the getaway canoe while Kip and I rejoined the Leakey expedition. Once we were inside, it was as black as tar. A quick survey of my hand in front of my face revealed no glimmer of sunlight. Edging tentatively forward with my boot, I could feel a passageway. Kip held my hand as I led us into what seemed a grand chamber.

Leading with my boot again, I felt another passageway open up, narrower than the first, and I slid through. Kip tugged my hand in protest but, worried that he might lose me to the tomb of Tutankhamen, followed me in. The cool and motionless air, impenetrable by eyesight, imparted an other-worldly sense to our surroundings.

Standing there in what I could perceive with outstretched arms to be a large room, in my mind's eye I envisioned a tribal council of smiling skeletons seated against the walls, round about us. Kip saw them too, I know, because he was eager to be gone from this place. (It is times like these, when it falls to my twelve-year-old son to be the voice of reason, that I rest assured I have kept my pact with Peter Pan.)

How uncanny it is to imagine a place such as this, unmarked and open, accessible from the peaceful, tree-lined shores of a quiet river! I thought of the hordes of tourists standing in the queue for an eleven o'clock bus to take them to a lighted, stair-stepped cave. How much more intrigued would they be to stand with us, in this place, where some element of danger and discovery, however imaginary, gave each succeeding footstep a sense of great portent!

I inched my way into another crack in the rocks and could feel that beyond lay another room, but Kip pulled hard astern, and I relented. With no torch, we could have become disoriented, taken the wrong passageway back, and descended deeper still into the labyrinth—or at least so I imagined. Guided by the voice of our ferryman, we found our way back to a brighter world and greeted it with a renewed sense of adventure.

ROUTE OF THE SEVEN CARRIES

ST. REGIS CANOE AREA WILDERNESS
ADIRONDACK PARK

Imagine a balmy summer day—ladies in dresses and hats and parasols, men in handlebar moustaches shouldering heavy guide boats over carpets of pine needles through the woods, and you have a sense of what came to be known at the turn of the last century as the "Route of the Seven Carries." This place, now preserved as part of the St. Regis Canoe Area Wilderness, shares a history with the gilded age of wealth and leisure that brought the monied elite to places like Paul Smith's Resort, on nearby Lower St. Regis Lake. From such exclusive accommodations, those who wished to savor a little of what writer Adirondack Murray once called a forest that "stands as it has stood, from the beginning of time," where "the lumberman has never been," and "no axe has sounded along its mountainsides," could do so in just a day along this route. Taking our time over several balmy, summer days in 1998, we did the same.

The lumberman was not kept out of this region for long after Murray's arrival. Once the St. Regis area had been cut over, speculators swooped in and bought the cheap land. After making a fortune for himself as a

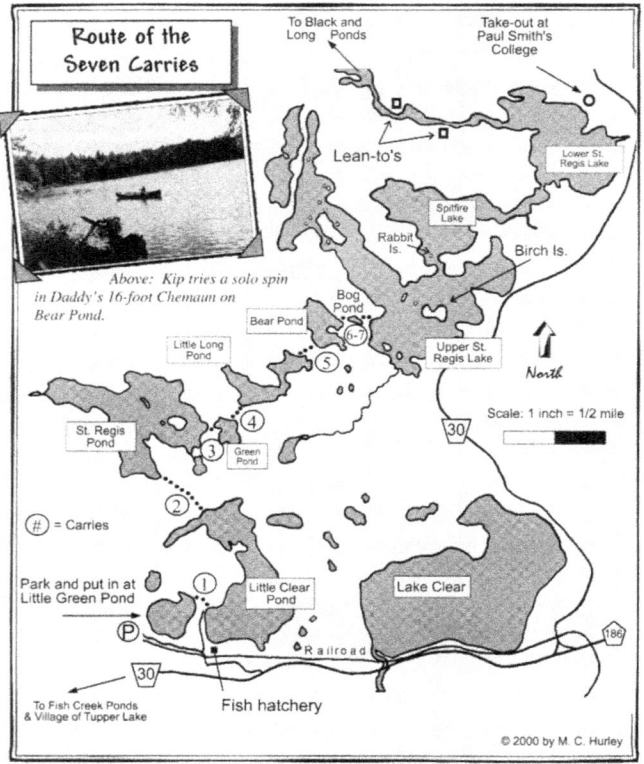

hotelier in the area around Upper St. Regis Lake that still bears his name, Paul Smith once bragged that "there's not a foot of land for sale on that lake this minute, and there's not a man in it but what's a millionaire, and some of them ten times over . . . I tell you if there's a spot on the face of the earth where millionaires go to play at housekeeping in log cabins and tents as they do here, I have it yet to hear about."

One of the great benefits of living in an era of wilderness renewal, as we do, is that you can experience these woods in very much the same condition as Murray once knew them-and as Paul Smith's guests could only imagine or fondly recall them, at the turn of the century.

I am pleased to report that the "seven" part of the Seven Carries Route is not merely the poetic license of some long-dead Adirondack travel-writer. There really are seven carries, beginning with the one from Little Green Pond, just north of Route 30, to Little Clear Pond. Coming north from the Village of Tupper Lake, on Route 30, you turn left into the driveway marked for the New York State Fish Hatchery Maintenance Area. Follow the road toward a sign that points to Little Green Pond, and make a left. The pavement changes to a narrow and potholed dirt road. You will see signs directing you to various campsites along the pond, but keep going. Where you see a sign for Upper Saranac Lake, the road forks to the right toward the parking lot for the put-in on Little Green Pond.

"Little" Green Pond is something of a misnomer, being several times larger than nearby Green Pond. I haven't a clue why it is so named, but there are so many ponds—little, green and otherwise—all over the North Woods that one can hardly expect the name-givers to keep track.

There is no fishing in Little Green Pond. I had heard some years back that ponds in this area were being treated with lye as a remedy for acid rain. Acid rain may explain why some are so exceptionally clear.

Most of the ponds on this route are healthy, and most are "trout water"—with all of the finicky variability that name suggests. You will catch neither bass nor pike nor pan fish, here, and even the trout are scarce in summer.

It had always been my hope to make this trip in the brisk days just after ice-out, when fisherman come from miles around in the yearly, ritual pursuit of St. Regis trout. Despite my constant efforts we went fishless on this summer trip, but the beauty of these woods and a supply of potatoes and beans amply filled the void.

From the put-in, my son Kip, then age 8, and I paddled across Little Green Pond to the campsite, near the carry, marked with the number one on a sign nailed to a tree. This was an attractive camp, but the nearby bog was filled with mosquitoes. In your short time on Little Green Pond, you must also endure a background of noise from both the road and families who drive in to make camp on the pond from the trunk of a car. This pond looks remote, but clearly it is not. If possible, plan to arrive early enough to allow progress farther than Little Green Pond for your first night's camp.

The carry (never a "portage" in the Adirondacks) from Little Green Pond to Little Clear Pond leads directly from campsite number one. A sign at the other end of the carry informs you that there is no fishing in Little Clear and Green Ponds. There is also a sign by the gate that prohibits boat launching, which obviously does not refer to canoes coming across the marked carry.

It was a beautiful and placid trip across Little Clear Pond, where no camping is allowed either on islands or on shore. The second carry, to St. Regis Pond, is well marked by a sign. At six-tenths of a mile, it is the longest of the trip. A boardwalk at the other end keeps your boots out of the muck. From the end of the boardwalk, one paddles to the right through the marsh to get out into St. Regis Pond. We took the second campsite to the right after leaving the carry. The first site also looked good but was occupied. Both are high on a hillside.

It was a rainy, second night in the lean-to, so we turned our attention to brownies baked in the reflector oven, firelight readings from Sterling North's novel, *Rascal*, potatoes and summer sausage fried with onions for dinner, and Swiss Miss before bed. (People in rainy parts of the world must be fat and well read.)

The reflector oven brought forth biscuits beneath raindrops on the awning, the next morning. We broke camp and headed across the lake in the direction of the short carry to Green Pond.

Like its "little" cousin, Green Pond was almost antiseptically clear, with not even a baitfish to be seen along shore. We were soon across and at the carry to Little Long Pond. According to the "Canoe Map," available from local outfitters and widely used in tills part of the Adirondacks, there is a campsite on Green Pond at the start of the carry. We didn't see any evidence of a site, though we did not explore thoroughly.

There should have been a site at the end of the carry into Little Long Pond, according to the map, but we didn't see any. Paddling out into Little Long Pond, on the right shore just before a hairpin turn, we saw a campsite that is not marked on the Canoe Map. Little Long Pond is alive and well. Kip netted crayfish, a newt, and some tiny minnows where the carry to Bear Pond begins.

The Canoe Map shows no campsites on Bear Pond, but we saw one to the right, about 100 yards northeast of the carry from Little Long Pond. As we came around the finger of land that juts out into Bear Pond on the way to the next carry, we saw another campsite on shore that was posted "no trespassing." It had two picnic tables. Near this site, the carry to tiny Bog Pond appears.

Bog pond is well named. The frogs must sing a mighty chorus here in the evening. It looks like quite the haven for bass and pickerel. Though our hopes were raised briefly by the resemblance of this place to more productive waters, our efforts at the rod went unrewarded.

At the seventh and final carry, civilization finally intruded on the insular, wilderness world that had been our home for the past five miles. The carry from Bog Pond ends at Upper St. Regis Lake on a gravel road leading to someone's summer home. This large lake is still very much the resort that Paul Smith made it, and you will likely encounter motorized craft of all variety.

After a dash across Upper St. Regis Lake that could be rough paddling in high winds, one passes a little bit of history at the inlet to Spitfire Lake. Here, on a dot of land that must surely have been larger when it served its famous purpose, a plaque reads: "On this island in 1886, Dr. Edward Livingston Trudeau conducted his historic experiment to determine the effect of environment on the incidence and progress of tuberculosis on a colony of rabbits. This plaque was placed by Trudeau Institute, Inc., in commemoration of this pioneering study in experimental epidemiology, October 7, 1972." Thank Dr. Trudeau and his colleagues that you have the lung capacity to paddle, as you'll likely need it trying to cross Spitfire Lake.

Spitfire is well-known as a sailing lake. It lies in such a way, apparently, that it regularly draws a good amount of wind. In summer you will see several sailboats moored there if not just as many underway. I am told there is an historic sailboat design which is found in its greatest numbers on Spitfire Lake, though I did not recognize any.

The entrance to Spitfire Lake can be difficult to spot. The best way to find it is to go straight across to Birch Island from the end of the carry between Bog Pond and Upper St. Regis Lake. As you get to the other side of Birch Island, look to the north for the red and green buoys which seem to be sitting right in front of a woods. Tucked behind them is the narrow inlet to Spitfire Lake.

Follow the right shore of Spitfire as it narrows down to a serene bog that wends its way into Lower St. Regis Lake. Coming through, here, I turned back to take a picture, only to see in my viewfinder the framing of a house going up in the woods on shore. I put the camera away. The new owners, like the "millionaires" who came to "play at housekeeping in log cabins" in Paul Smith's day, have no doubt spent a bundle of money for their dream home. They will have a pristine view of this bog. The rest of us will have a view of their house.

There is no public camping anywhere on Lower St. Regis Lake. Kip and I were permitted to stay at a site on the lake (filled with broken beer bottles) that is owned by Paul Smith's College, in order to meet our shuttle early in the morning. This site would not be anyone's first choice. The college has also built an unattractive, concrete building right on the shore. There are some lean-tos for camping farther up the river that are supposed to be very nice, but coming into the lake late in the day it would be chancy to depend on one of those being available. It is best to end the trip and take out here, just as Paul Smith's guests once did.

While we unloaded our canoe, a young campus police officer came by. Looking at our gear, he asked where we had been and, when I described our trip, remarked at what a "great idea" we had to canoe from campsite to campsite. I kid you not—he was utterly unfamiliar with the whole concept of recreational canoe camping, which had been virtually invented in the Adirondacks before spreading across North America. I stopped what I was doing to get a better look at the man. Almost too startled to speak but not wanting to appear rude, I asked him where he was from. "Born and raised here at Paul Smith's," he said. I restrained my incredulity long enough to say, simply, that voyaging by canoe is something for which his hometown was once well known. "Sounds like fun ," he said, and walked on.

He got that part right.

Peace River

Fort Meade to Wauchula

As I write this story, I am distantly reminded of the John Knowles' novel, *A Separate Peace*, that was required reading for a good many of us. Knowles told the tale of two boys standing at the threshold of manhood and the horror of World War II, who seek one last summer of refuge from the world that awaits them. They find it only briefly on a river in New Hampshire, and even there the stark reality of life and death manages eventually to intrude. My son Kip, who on this trip rarely looked back to see if I was following closely in his wake, has never known a moment of doubt in the goodness of mankind or an hour of uncertainty for his future. He is growing up in a world where young boys can hardly be expected to mow the grass much less make the world safe for democracy, but that's fine by me. Life offers us too few moments of peace for as often as it tests our character. Even at his tender age, he is chafing at the bit to go, to see, to do. The Peace River offered all of us that chance, last Thanksgiving, and a respite worthy of its name.

The Peace River is one of a great many that make Florida surprisingly rich in opportunities for canoe

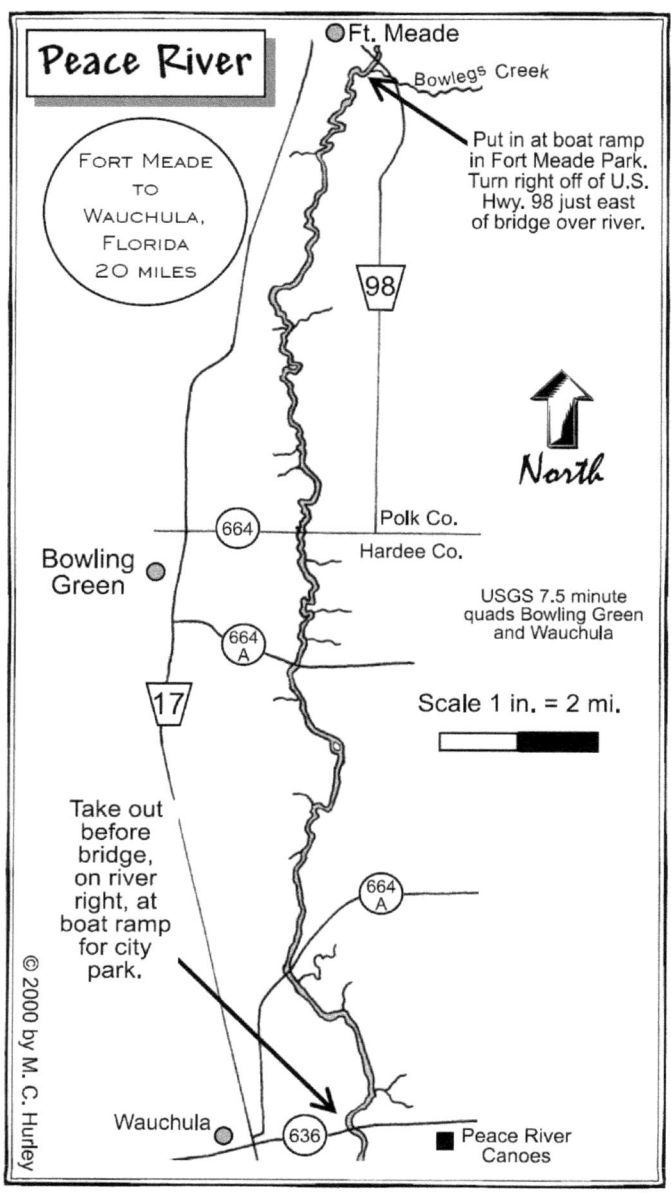

camping in the North Woods tradition—without the cold toes. In the 67-mile section that begins in Fort Meade, it is officially the "Florida Peace River Canoe Trail."

Floridians have wisely seen something worth preserving, here. You get a sense of their enthusiasm at the web site for "Paddle Florida" (paddlefl.com), where thirty-nine rivers and waterways in all are described in tantalizing detail. Stop someone with a canoe on top of his car at any orange stand or a gas station, and he'll talk about his favorite—the place you've really got to see if you really want to know what Florida paddling is all about. He'll tell you of the meanest gator he ever saw, the big shark's tooth he sifted from the river before the tourists knew to come there, and the funny-looking fossil he can't identify but will send to the Smithsonian one of these days. He'll tell you about the year the water got so low he discovered Ferdinand De Soto's fishing reel, and he'll offer to take you to the very spot.

I got one such invitation from Jim Anstis, an architect whose travels bring him now and again to North Carolina. When he looked me up in Raleigh one day, he spoke fondly of the St. Mary's River, in the northeastern corner of the state, but disappointingly of the fact that the water-level on that stream is almost always too low to paddle. I have heard the same lament from many others. And so it was in search of a less finicky flow and ideal off-season camping that we came to the Peace.

We were joined in this trip by ten readers who signed up to rendezvous at Fort Meade on the Friday after Thanksgiving. Under clear, warm, and bug-less skies our adventure began at the park just outside of town on Highway 98. After the bridge over the river on this road, a sign marks the entrance to the park on the right. A short drive through the park leads to a wide, grassy parking area with a concrete boat-ramp. Motorboats are allowed on the river but are rarely seen. We encountered one unhappy camper on the second day who warned us that a thief had stolen his boat motor the night before. (I must confess that, in this tranquil place, I was rooting for the thief.)

Imagining that some of us might paddle nearly the entire length of the canoe trail while others would take out farther upstream, we enlisted the aid of Peace River Canoes in Wauchula to run a shuttle. They offer friendly and inexpensive service, but waiting for their school bus to arrive and then drop off other paddlers along the river before taking us back to Ft. Meade was more time consuming than we expected. If you have the extra vehicles and don't need to rent a canoe, you may want to consider leaving a vehicle at the park by the take-out and running your own shuttle.

The section between Ft. Meade and Wauchula measures about twenty river-miles and is ideally suited for a leisurely, three-day, two night trip. Stop at any one of the local filling-stations to buy a wire-mesh screen, and bring it with you. Day-trippers and campers alike come to this river by the hundreds to sift the sand at the bottom of the shallow water for shark teeth. Just as our group paddled by, I saw one man pull a tooth from the water that was nearly three-inches long! Thankfully, the wearers of those dentures shipped farther out to sea several millennia ago.

It is nothing short of amazing that, with all of the people sifting the bottom of this river every year, there is no shortage of fossils for the taking. One elderly gentleman had made an avocation of it, and I could not resist a photograph of his canoe, proudly named "Fossil Hound," with a plastic wolf as a hood ornament to drive home his theme.

We put in at about noon in Fort Meade. You'll find the water to be lightly tea-colored but clean. The banks are forested in cypress and swamp-bottom hardwoods. If you are getting a very late start, there is some high ground for camping on the left bank above a cluster of cypress knees within ten minutes of the put-in. Once you get past the part of the river that is accessible by foot paths from Fort Meade Park, plastic fish-bait containers and other debris become less noticeable, as does the noise from the Highway 98 bridge. Another nice camping spot appears high on the left bank about one hour into the trip, followed by a good site high on the right bank about three miles downriver from Bowlegs Creek.

You will pass under two power-lines which are shown on the Bowling Green USGS quadrangle. Just after the second power-line, where the map shows Whidden Creek entering on the right bank, a dirt road leads to the river. Several people were fishing from lawn chairs, here, as we paddled by. A short distance farther downstream, a large picnic pavilion and a clearing appears on the right bank. If you come this far before making camp, you'll want to camp well below these areas.

The same caveats apply to swimming in the Peace River as I mentioned before in writing about the Suwannee. There are alligators in these waters, although they are spread out and hard to find. You'd be lucky to see one at all, but that doesn't mean they can't see you.

Attacks do occur every year in Florida, though usually not without a full measure of human stupidity to help them along. Don't let small children or dogs swim unattended, and don't feed, chase, or antagonize any alligators that you do see. We saw only one—a baby not more than three-feet long, sunning himself on a log. The fellow in our group who paddled ahead to claim our campsite reported seeing two adult gators as he sprinted downriver in the early-morning hours.

As the two boys whom I was trailing seemed more inclined to dawdle and talk than paddle, our group split into two flotillas that were far apart by nightfall. Half of the group paddled ahead and made camp in a farmer's field above some wide, rock ledges. This is reportedly a favorite camp for anyone running the river from Fort Meade, and unless you get there early it will probably be taken. It is not heavily wooded, but it offers an excellent view and a superb location for fossil hunting and swimming.

Kip and I and four others in our party made camp at around 5:30 in an area where the trees had been thinned to allow livestock to come to the river from nearby fields. The spot is located about one mile below the Rt. 664 bridge, shown on the map. Although we didn't know it at the time, our campsite was about fifteen minutes upriver from a Class-I ledge. This ledge flows into a deep pool with a rope-swing, and Kip took full advantage of both.

Firewood was ample all along the river, and we made a cozy night of it. Kip had taken a tongue lashing from me for "falling" into the water from the stern of his canoe that day during a moment of silliness, and he needed to dry out. This may be Florida, but it was chilly around

Thanksgiving, and Kip's seeming incapacity for remaining dry at these times of the year always has me undone. Whatever might be the number of outfits I pack for him, he will require one more. The surprising thing his, he never seems to get cold—wet or dry—and I always am.

Our campsite came with the delicious and unexpected bonus of its own orange tree. After an early morning breakfast, one of the boys spotted the golden treasures hanging just out of reach above us. Roy Fralick's 13-year-old grandson Robbie needed little encouragement to scamper up the trunk (photo on page 20) and toss down the winnings. Advice that wild oranges are so bitter they will pucker your lips for hours went unheeded and, it turned out, was unnecessary. The ones we picked were as sweet and juicy as any you can imagine.

Wild oranges truly are bitter, I am assured, but don't let that stop you from sampling them. This tree may have been an orchard strain planted by a local farmer, or perhaps it had cross-pollinated with one. Goodness knows there are enough orange groves in the area to present the opportunity for hybrids to spring up.

Leaving our campsite in the morning, we soon came to the ledge downstream. The boys had made a point of leaving camp far enough ahead of us that they would appear to be "on their own," yet not so far that we were not forewarned of anything of importance by their whoops and hollers. They successfully negotiated the short drop over the ledge without our assistance.

When we adults rounded the bend, we saw that the boys had got out of their canoe and were standing upon the ledge to guide us poor laggards across. Their voices too distant to be heard over the running water, on seeing us they became electrified with movement, waving arms as if to signal some grave danger ahead. After capturing our attention and bringing us to a halt, they pointed toward the best course over the ledge with all the self-assuredness of two Maine guides. Never mind that they pointed in different directions, it was comforting to know we were the object of so much concern.

The boys' warnings notwithstanding, the ledge of which I speak poses no hazard other than a grounding at low water. We shimmied and scooted over with no difficulty and paused to take a few photos while Kip and Robbie both went in for a swim—that being the end of the third and final pair of dry pants. It was Kip's characteristic good fortune that the weather was warming up nicely by now, in fine Florida style.

There is an ideal site on the right bank beside the rope swing, just after the ledge, that is big enough for no more than two tents. The soft trill of water running over the ledge would make sweet music for a camp, here. The river cuts a second channel around an island as it passes over the ledge, but all of the island is too low and thick with brambles to make it suitable for anything but bivouac camping.

One of the advantages of holding a rendezvous of readers of this journal, such as we had this weekend on the Peace, is to see the variety of ways in which people shelter and feed themselves. I have noticed that I am almost always the only one who cooks over an open flame. I also invariably end these trips resolved to put more forethought and creativity into the kinds of foods I pack. Someone, it always seems, has done something astonishingly clever and quick with pine nuts or pesto, while I toil over a pot of two-hour stew.

On this trip down the Peace, I enjoyed Roy Fralick's expertise in recreating his own delicious, split-pea soup. He first dehydrates it, then freezes it, then grinds it in a blender to a fine powder. Rusty and Becky Cox shamelessly prepared and ate two enormous steaks right before our eyes—a meal I have lost the habit of packing on so many North Woods voyages but which is perfect for portage-less trips on southern streams. The recipe that most intrigued me, however was immodestly named "Crab Cakes Commander." It requires a can of lump crabmeat and a packet of instant mashed potatoes. The potato flakes are mixed using about a half the amount of water ordinarily required, then folded in with the crabmeat. Suitable quantities of Old Bay seasoning are added, and the patty is fried in oil. As an old Baltimore boy, I was so taken with this idea that I tried it at home and can vouch for its success.

Another gem of rendezvous knowledge was Rusty Cox's recommendation of Dr. Bronner's Peppermint 18-in-1 Pure-Castile Soap—an eccentric lavage (if you couldn't guess from the name) available at trendier backpacking stores. Its inventor "Einstein-Heilbronner" Bronner has guaranteed it since 1948 as an effective shave cream, shampoo, dentifrice, soap, breath-freshener, facial pack, and who-knows-what else. I used this and smelled just like a Peppermint Patty.

I also have several of our fellow voyagers to thank for demonstrating the usefulness of headlamp-style flashlights. They free your hands to work and make any nighttime job go faster. Becky Cox offered me hers to use as I broke camp on the third day before dawn. I now have one on my standard checklist.

The wide, flat rock and overlying pastureland where half of our party camped appeared on the left bank after a long horseshoe bend in the river. We stopped here to sift the bottom in the photos you see on page 15 and found it to be littered with shark teeth. Interestingly, there are a lot more teeth from sharks in these rivers, it seems, than from alligators. Although the sharks have been gone long enough for the gators to be catching up by now, the sharks apparently left behind an awful lot of bridge work.

On the second day, the boys escaped again in their canoe and lit out far ahead of the pack. I have never been able to hold Kip back from anything—not even at the age of five, when he eloped on an island on the Carolina shore for a good hour before another boy's mother caught him and nailed his shorts to the ground. As his father, I find myself now at a difficult place in time where I am not sure when to step in and when to step back. At his age I had the run of the county on a bike—something we'd never dream of letting him do, but the time for more freedom is coming. He's already at the stern of his own canoe. He'll have his own adventures, and I won't always be a part of them. I hope he's ready. I hope I'm ready.

From the location of our first campsite to the takeout, we encountered areas suitable for camping much more regularly than we had farther upriver. The banks also got higher and a good bit sandier at the waterline. Shortly after the Rt. 636 bridge, a stream comes in from the left. Here I caught up with the boys, who had stopped to sift the stream for fossils. The stream was clear and wild and cool, which made me all the more disappointed to see that someone had cleared the pasture above it for a home site. It won't be wild for long. Seeing the evidence of this grading work, we moved on and made our second night's camp a half-mile downriver on a high sandbank on the left. Some of us camped in a pasture on higher ground, while the rest preferred to be on the river.

The second and final night of the trip was spent enjoying the company of those readers I had missed in our camp on the first night out. They were polite to listen quietly as I played what little classical guitar I could. I started playing a year ago with the idea of taking a guitar along on canoe trips. Emily Hershberger showed us that a flute is even more portable and just as pretty to hear.

After rushing down I-95 to get to this place, and dreading the long journey home to Carolina, I felt a quiet gladness to be within this tiny band for one more night. Stories were told of wars and ships, of local legends and tall tales, of voyages done and voyages to come. We huddled there on the sand, strangers just days before, now friends knitted together by the firelight. My son and I slept that night beneath the stars, beside a river, in what is yet a wilderness, sheltered yet awhile from the winds of change. May places like the Peace never vary, and may life keep for each of us the promise of many nights like these.

Mullica River

New Jersey Pine Barrens

I always thought that New Jersey got a bad rap. Yes, the snarl of roads between Trenton and New York may be the most congested in the nation. And of course, anyone uncertain whether chemicals truly are the state's biggest business need only roll down his window at a tollbooth to be sure, but there is more to this state—much more—than meets the eye and nose on the Jersey Turnpike.

Seekers of solitude and ideal conditions for canoeing should consider the 1700 square miles that comprise the Pinelands National Reserve. Within this ecologically diverse region on the state's coastal plain lies a wilderness unexpectedly rich in pure, fresh water known as the Pine Barrens. In the barrens, the steep ridges of New Jersey's western border on the Delaware River have given way to flat, sandy soil well suited for pine trees and not much else. Dozens of tea-colored streams have carved winding courses through otherwise forbidding thickets, leaving swelling mounds of sand at each turn that beckon us to leave our paddles and explore. Scientists say that nearly every species of vegetation known in the entire northeastern United States grows in New Jersey, but

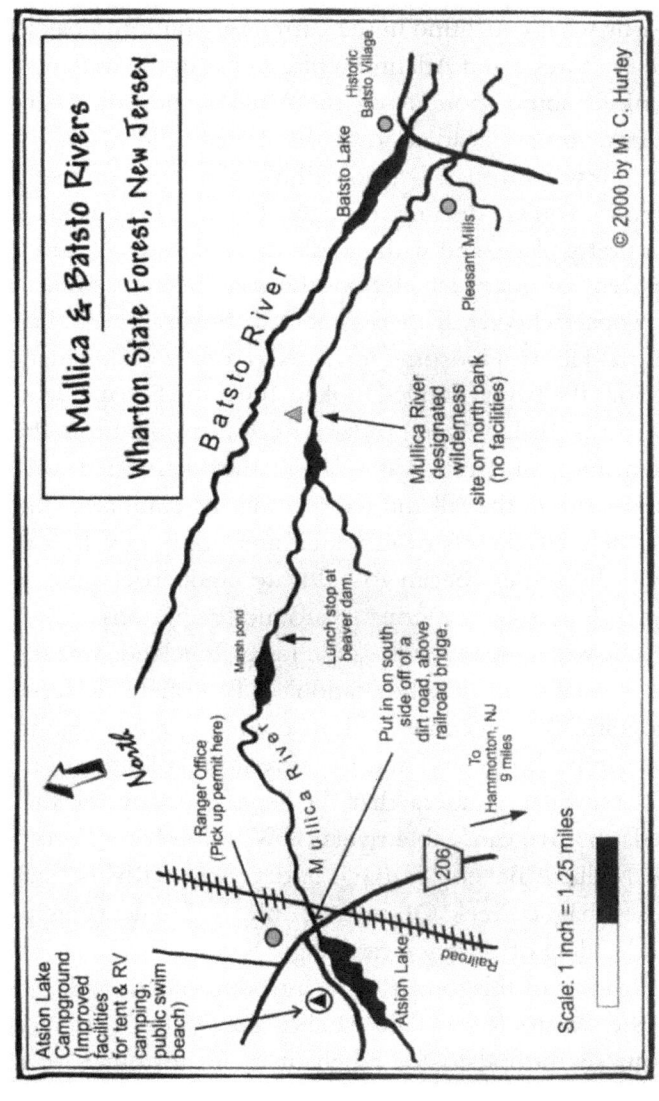

mostly what you'll find in the barrens are pine and oak in the dry forests and Atlantic White Cedar in the wetlands. Blink at some spots along the Mullica and you might believe you are headed down the Allagash, in Maine, or on your way through Quetico. Blink again, and you might suppose you are drifting through a Georgia bayou. Ah, it is a pretty place, and with paddle in hand you will find it "barren" of not much else but the cares of this world.

Those who recall their American history know that, before Henry Hudson sent a party of Englishmen to explore the bay of Sandy Hook in 1609, the Lenape (later known as the Delaware) Indians ruled this land. From the abundance of fresh water bogs, they harvested wild cranberries in the fall and fed them to the colonists, who put them to all sorts of new and interesting uses. Before long, the settlers began to cultivate cranberries here as they still do today in farms all around the barrens.

The wider area known as the Jersey Pinelands was the first installment in the nation's "Biosphere Reserve Program," which comes with its own long-range plan to manage both the land and the seventeen trillion gallons of freshwater aquifers that lie beneath it—water that feeds the five canoeable rivers of Wharton State Forest: the Mullica, Batsto, Wading, and Oswego Rivers, and Nescochague Creek. Of the five, only the Mullica, Batsto, and Wading offer canoe camping.

Readers of this journal were introduced two years ago to the Batsto River. The Mullica lies within a stone's throw of the Batsto for much of its length but is of a markedly different character. The Mullica changes in species of vegetation, width and rate of flow more often than the Batsto. In June of 1999, thirty readers of the journal and I carne to Atsion to rendezvous for the eight-mile trip to Pleasant Mills, with one night of camping at the group wilderness site along the way.

A trip on the Mullica begins with the obligatory matriculation at the state ranger-office on Route 206 in Atsion, a small house on the right side of the road as one heads north from Hammonton. Required permits for use of the only wilderness campsite on the river are sold, here. Up to half of the 100 permits available for this site may be reserved (often by large groups) in advance by mail, with the remainder held open for same-day walk-ins at Atsion. Reservation requests mailed to the park headquarters in Hammonton are routinely lost or not processed in a timely fashion, so you'll want to deal directly with the Atsion Office. The Atsion office is available by telephone, but they keep limited and variable office-hours.

Once you've completed the necessary rigmarole and have a legal permit, your next challenge will be to find the unmarked put-in. Turning left out of the ranger's office, go less than fifty yards back toward Hammonton, across the bridge, and turn left onto a dirt road. Go past the mailbox in what appears to be someone's driveway. Keep going on this road about one hundred yards until you spot the dirt parking-lot beside the river. We were warned not to park here, due to vandals, and brought our empty vehicles back to the lot at the ranger station instead.

Our group of fifteen canoes got underway at 10:30 in the morning. At the put-in, the river is no more than 15-feet wide and on this summer day had a one to two-knot current. Within ten minutes, we were at the railroad trestle shown on the map. Here, some boats ran up on the stumps of old pilings just below the surface, and folks had to step out to maneuver their way through. The Mullica was more of a brushy, overgrown creek than a river for the first two hours of the trip. Although there are almost no rocks, the key to not getting stuck on submerged logs is to pack light and bring a plastic boat All of the rental canoes we saw were aluminum, and they had an especially hard time making way in spots. However, there were only one or two true obstructions to the well-paddled canoe on the entire section of the river below Atsion.

After the first hour one enters a lily pond, which ends abruptly at an easy and exciting beaver dam with a two-foot falls. Because this is a dam and not a rapids, running it will be much the same at normal or low water. We took advantage of the tall bank before the dam to have lunch.

From this point onward, you will begin to spot sandy ridges and clearings that would make ideal campsites, but like Aladdin in the cave, you have promised your masters in the ranger's office that you will not stop until you reach the designated campsite.

Below our lunch stop, we followed the river through some low-lying grass and lily ponds for another mile before it returned to the seclusion of the forest. For the remainder of this section above the campsite, the woods remained fairly close by, with the river less than fifteen feet across in most spots. The Mullica wilderness campsite is limited to one hundred campers and, though accessible by a sand road, is off-limits to motor vehicles. Fire bans are always in effect during daylight hours, and fires are often banned altogether in summer due to dry conditions.

We knew a ban was in effect when we started, but after a soaking rain came while we pitched camp, I had assumed the ban was lifted. Not so. Lucky for me, a ranger wandered into camp to check permits before I started a campfire, and he told us that the ban was still in effect. Fines for violators can be stiff, I hear. He even lifted the lids on everyone's cooler to check for alcohol—another taboo.

Don't break out the Ripple when he leaves, either: This guy doubled back to check us again, a short while later. One must assume from the intensity of this surveillance effort that the woods are thick with criminals in canoes.

We arrived at the campsite at 2:30, after about two hours of paddling from our lunch stop. The campsite is said to be located two-thirds of the way to the take-out at Pleasant Mills. The entire site stretches for perhaps one hundred yards along the left bank. It is wide, very picturesque, and cleared of enough trees to provide many perfect spots on which to pitch a tent. Beside the campsite, a wide pool in the river proved irresistible to early-morning swimmers and was well suited to the purpose, being not too deep, with a soft, sandy bottom.

There is a farmhouse-style hand-pump at the campsite that calls forth fresh, sweet-tasting water from the sands, below. The entire site was free of trash and very well maintained. Two neatly-kept outhouses were placed discreetly back from the river.

A group of young people camping for the weekend were local kids who had thrown a trip together on short notice—hardly card-carrying REI types. They were quiet and well mannered. I have read in Robert Parnes' book,

Canoeing the Jersey Pine Barrens, that rowdies and slobs have become the bane of wilderness campgrounds in these parts, but so far I have not encountered anyone of that ilk in my two trips here.

The Mullica River site would be a nice place for a campfire when fires are allowed, but as with other designated campsites in the barrens, downed wood is scarce. I am told that the reason campfires are banned during the day is that the rangers sitting high above the forest canopy in lookout towers cannot distinguish the smoke of a bona fide campfire from the beginnings of a forest fire. The campfire ban lifts at 3:00 p.m. because, rather quaintly, that is when all the lookout rangers go home for the day.

We passed the evening in the enjoyable exchange of conversation among strangers with a shared passion, as has become the custom of these rendezvous. The children tumbled and played in my open, floor-less lean-to, each wanting to know how I live peaceably among the spiders and snakes that they imagine go about in the woods at night. (I sleep too soundly to notice them.) Carol Ostermark worked her magic on a dish of pine nuts and pesto that brought forth *oohs* and *aahs* from the assembled samplers. Her husband led the little children in song around the (non-) campfire in an endearing rendition of "My Old Man is a [fill in your occupation]." Jim Mandle and Fred Allerton continued their tradition of experimentation with new gadgets, gear and gastronomy largely unknown to the rest of us old dogs. Others shared their experiences on various rivers near and far. Rain now and again sent us scurrying beneath our tarps, only to see us emerge like spiders on the waterspout as each shower passed.

The gray morning dawned too soon after the late-night gabbing, and we were off again. The river resumed its narrow winding but soon broke into glorious, cedar-rimmed vistas. After the first hour of paddling, a noticeable S-turn preceded the tallest overlook of the trip. Although it was too early to stop here for lunch, some of us stopped anyway just to take in the view. After about an hour of paddling past this point, one comes to a pool some sixty-yards long beside a wide beach on the left bank. This was the best spot for lunch on the second day. Just half a mile beyond this beach, a narrow footbridge known as Constable Bridge spans the river ahead of a tiny island with an enormous pine tree perched (for the time being) in the middle of it.

You will first hear the traffic on the Route 542 bridge, then pass underneath it. The take-out is beyond the bridge but within sight of it, on the left bank. The boats with large motors putting in, here, told us that tidal waters were not far downstream. We simple paddlers had not seen enough of each other, but we had seen the best this river had to offer. Fond memories of the Mullica will be the ties that bind until another river calls us all together, again.

DELAWARE RIVER

DELAWARE WATER GAP

I t was a cold Christmas night in 1776 when General Washington and 2400 American soldiers made their nine-mile trek up and across the Delaware River from the Pennsylvania side, and surprised the redcoats at Trenton. If George Washington's troops only knew what a fertile, shining wilderness lay in the mountains miles upstream from the place where he spent that night skipping silver dollars, the rebels might have abandoned their cause to spend a few days canoe camping at the Delaware Water Gap, and today we might have been awash in warm beer and mutton pies.

The Upper Delaware River is indeed a treasure that lies hidden within the Pocono Mountains that divide Pennsylvania and New Jersey, but it is well known to generations of area residents. Almost anyone who came up through a Boy Scouting program in Pennsylvania, New Jersey, Delaware or New York has made a canoe-camping trip here, complete with the obligatory attempt at running Skinner's Falls without swamping.

From its smallest beginnings in the Catskill Mountains of Schoharie County, New York, the Delaware flows freely for a distance of more than 400 miles until it meets

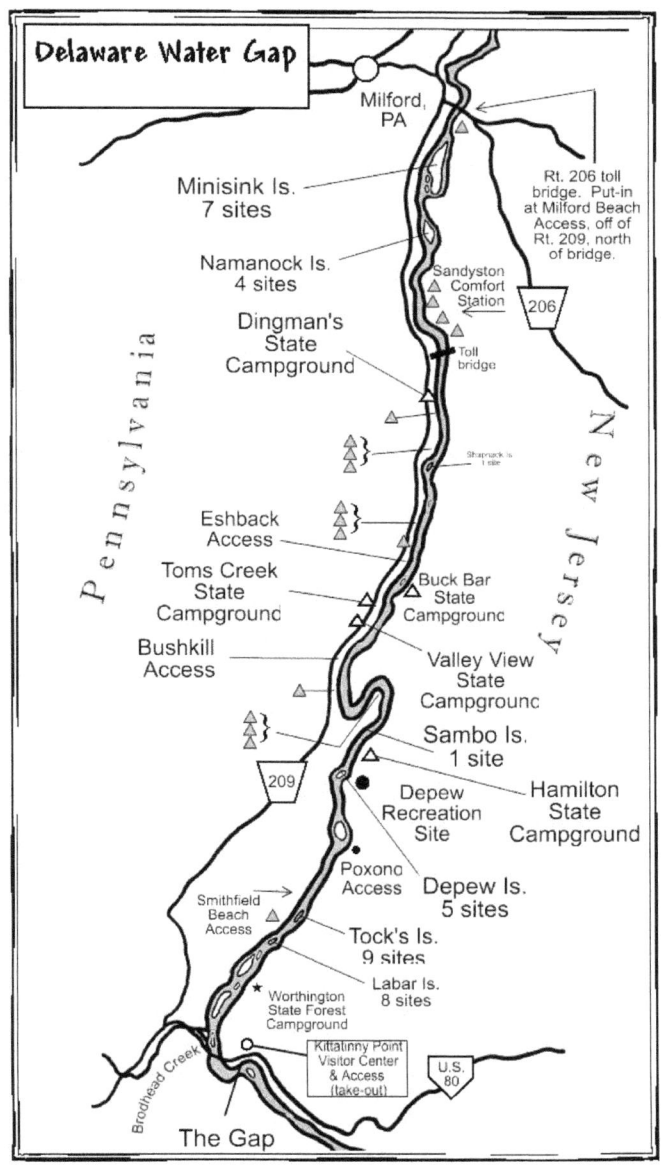

tidewater at Trenton. Like many of the rivers of the Eastern seaboard, it was vitally important to commerce in the years before the arrival of rail transport and, as a consequence, was once actually more developed in many sections than it is today. It is, to the credit of its many defenders, one of the few major rivers remaining in the United States that is free flowing along its entire length.

Officially designated a national recreation area by Congress in 1965, the area is also known for the hotly contested and narrowly averted plan to dam the river back in the seventies. Entire towns were evacuated and homes abandoned in the surrounding hills in anticipation that they would soon be covered by rising water from the planned Tock's Island Reservoir. But hippies moved into the abandoned properties and refused to leave while environmental activists pressed their case for keeping the river free-flowing. The hippies and the environmentalists won that battle when Congress, on November 10, 1978, granted a section of the river and about 2000 acres of shoreline protection under the National Wild and Scenic Rivers Act. The entire area has been managed by the National Park Service since 1987 under a mixed-use plan that affects some 70,000 acres in all. In 1992, Congress finally deauthorized the dam project.

The portion of the Delaware designated as a National Scenic River covers only about forty miles, from just above Milford to the "Water Gap" just below Stoudsburg, Pennsylvania. The term refers to an impressive ravine where the river flows between the sheer, sandstone walls of Kitattinny Mountain, with elevations of about 1500 feet on each side.

We began our trip at the Milford Beach Access after a

tortuous drive through one traffic jam after another in the little Pocono towns along the way. At the gated access point, a park service ranger asks the number of days you will spend on the water and charges a parking fee for each day. This buys a sign that you place in your car to keep it from being towed from the lot while you are on the river. There is ample parking, and when we arrived on Memorial Day Weekend, there was a good crowd of day-trippers on hand. True to my experience in most areas, however, the competition for campsites was not nearly as stiff as we expected.

The water is fairly deep at the put-in and was cloudy but not muddy after a lot of rain in late May. The grassy banks at this time of year were coming up in beautiful white and yellow wildflowers and were lined with sycamores and other hardwoods. The forest was completely leafed out and the water was fairly warm, even this early in the season.

We camped at the first available site on Minisink Island, fearing that we might not find another site in the crowded holiday conditions. However, I would recommend that you continue to follow the island down on the left shore, where there are some more desirable sites. The first site, where we camped, is right next to a radio-controlled model airplane club, and the whine of those little engines is hard to ignore. Road noise, too, diminishes as you go farther down the river.

Shortly below Minisink Island, a beautiful, open vista appears with a high, rock cliff on the right side at several points as you head downriver. During our trip the river was about two feet higher than normal, and the rapids and riffles had been washed out. I saw no section of the river that would present much of challenge even to a novice paddler, and the few strainers were (contrary to what may appear from the photo, below) easily avoided.

Shortly after breaking camp on Minisink Island, we came to a spot in the river that I mistook for Namanock Island but which actually is a corner of the end of Minisink Island that has been cut off by the river and is not shown on the park map. Take the left channel, here, on the New Jersey side, to head through a quiet canopy of the forest that is very intimate and pretty. An easy riffles leads into this channel, whereas the channel on the Pennsylvania side is wide and open.

Road noise is still fairly prominent along much of the river below Milford. The road tracks the river's right bank until around Bushkill.

Wildlife is abundant along the Delaware. We saw two bald eagles, one deer, a beaver, and sign of bear. The high water spoiled the fishing for the most part, but I was lucky to catch one smallmouth bass on a spinner in some clear water rushing past an undercut, grassy bank. This was my sister Suzie's and her husband Dick's first camping trip with me, and it was my pleasure to filet this fish (shown at right), sauté it in white wine and herbs, and serve it for dinner. They liked the marinade so well that I tried to find some more for my next trip, only to discover that my supermarket has stopped carrying it. It's the "Grill Creations" brand white wine and herb marinade, made by Durkee's, and comes in dry-mix packets that require only oil and water. Cases are available by mail from Edge Distributing in Chicago.

By noon on the second day we were at the toll bridge. Up to that point there had been only sporadic development—maybe three houses or so. The river was entirely flat, moving at a good current, and the scenery was very wild. You'll know you're at the toll bridge when you hear the banging noise of the cars going over it. The sound is like that of an aluminum canoe being drug over rocks.

On a short stop on the left bank for lunch, we spotted an old road that came up the bank on the New Jersey side. Some motor bikes roared by as we were stopped there. Nearby we saw an the remains of the foundation of a house above some concrete steps leading from the river. Despite the good omen of finding a live hellgrammite and duly impaling him on Kip's hook, the fishing did not improve for the remainder of the trip.

The campsites on the Pennsylvania side of the river, as one nears the Eshback Access, are all pretty low-lying and weedy. All sites are numbered on the park map. Campsite no. 36 is within walking distance and eyesight of the Eshback Access building and offers no privacy. Most of the sites on the Pennsylvania side below Dingman's Ferry Access were fairly low lying and less desirable than sites on the islands or on the opposite bank. I cannot comment on Dingman's Campground, on the Pennsylvania side, as one cannot see it very well from the river even though it is marked on the map as being right on shore.

By 2:00 in the afternoon we were at the Bushkill access. The Bushkill and Eshback Access points are close together. Bucks Bar is an island campsite and fairly nice. Again, however, the other sites to this point were low lying and weedy. Across from Bushkill, there is an RV camping area that I expect most folks will want to avoid.

We made our second night's camp at about 2:30 p.m. on the Peter's site, which is a lovely point of land just a mile or so below Bushkill Access. The site is wide, forested but well cleared and overlooks river. In the woods a short distance behind the site, a couple of low ridges hide the remains of the Walpack Fort, marked by a small, stone monument for the year 1755, when this fort was a British stronghold in the French and Indian War. It is now not much more than a few stones surrounding a large hole in the ground. Here you may ponder that battles that took place right in these woods where, two decades before the American Revolution, the question of whether we would be a predominantly English or French culture was finally answered. The Walpack Fort was the terminus of the "Military Road" that once led through these mountains to the headquarters of the colonial army of New Jersey, at Fort Johns. We saw some fresh bear scat on the ridge at Walpack Fort and decided to take our leave of the place, fearing new battles.

Although I rarely ever paddle the same river twice and therefore don't know what lies ahead when I choose a campsite, the Peters site it turns out was the best for several miles. As we headed south again past the U-turn at the Peters site, we came to the only section of the river described as a rapids on the park map above Kitattinny. A high slope on the left shore forested in pine and firs marks this part of the river. To me it was very reminiscent of the Allagash in Maine. The rapids were washed out when we came through, but they should not be much more than a Class I, even a low water.

There is a nice campsite high on the right bank—listed on the map as the "Walters" site—immediately after the

Smithfield Beach Access. A short distance farther downriver is Labar Island, which has several sites. However, the road on the New Jersey side is visible across from the island for that reason.

There are public bathrooms on the right bank across from the Labar Island site, and our group stopped there to take a break. A bit farther downriver the Worthington State Forest is marked by development on the left bank. A large, blue house is located there. There were several people camped at this spot with radios blaring. Across the river is Depew Island, which is private property. Here, a large resort lies in full view of the river, with a swimming pool, tennis club and a white building with a red tile roof.

After Depew Island, the flow of the river seemed to quicken a bit, preparing to enter The Gap. Notwithstanding the close proximity and growing noise of Interstate 80, the surrounding scenery is exceptionally pretty at this part of the river. A washed out, stone bridge and the overpass of the highway signal that the take-out is close by. The landing appears on the left bank as you look upon the towering cliffs of Kitattinny Mountain. A very nice park-service visitor's center is located at the take-out, complete with a gift shop and interpretive display. The Appalachian Trail crosses here and continues on its journey to Maine. But for us the lovely trip from Milford that ended here was journey enough, another in a long list of reminders that there remains on the founding coast of this country a remarkable wilderness waiting to be discovered.

TEMAGAMI CANOE COUNTRY

DIAMOND & WAKIMIKA LAKES CIRCUIT

Writing about one place to go canoeing in Canada is sort of like picking a good pasta restaurant in Italy, drinking only one beer in Germany, or tasting only one vintage of Bordeaux in France. The sum and substance of what this country offers to the canoeist is so overwhelming that one can scarcely find a superlative to ascribe to one location that would not be equally applicable to a hundred others. Temagami is, though—dare I say it—"special." At least it has been special to me ever since I saw the first illustrations of Hap Wilson, the writer and artist who made this area famous to a generation of paddlers and who still writes and paints nearby. His finely detailed and carefully rendered portraits of North Woods scenes are an inspiration for my amateur efforts to illustrate this journal. His widely-sold book, *Temagami Canoe Routes*, first published in 1978 by the Canadian Recreational Canoeing Association and now on its seventh printing, was our guide on this trip.

Unlike La Vérendrye, Algonquin, Quetico and other famous paddling destinations in Canada, Temagami is not a provincial park unto itself. In fact, it isn't a park at

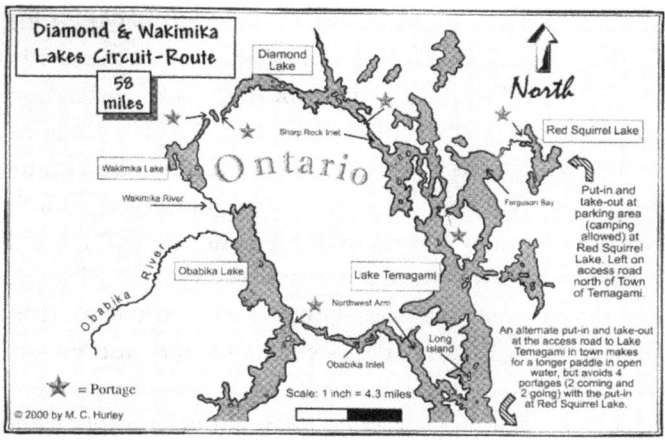

all but rather a tiny town in the province of Ontario, about sixty miles north of the city of North Bay. Temagami Canoe Country refers to a collection of seven provincial parks of various sizes located near the Town of Temagami that together total more than 263,000 acres—an area roughly half the size of the Great Smoky Mountains National Park. However, not all of the land considered to be part of the canoe country here lies within the boundaries of these parks. Non-park lands are interspersed along the canoe routes of Temagami to comprise an area larger in total size than Yellowstone National Park.

On this first trip to Temagami, we explored the Diamond-Wakimika Lake Canoe Route, part of which lies within Obabika Provincial Park. We paddled a fifty-eight-mile loop that roughly follows route number six in Wilson's book, although we did not begin at the Town of Temagami as he recommends. Recalling too well the windbound days we had spent during the previous summer in La Vérendrye, we decided against the long, northward paddle across an open water that those who put in at the Town of Temagami must face. Instead, we put in farther north, on Red Squirrel Lake. The trade-off for this route is that you add four portages (two coming and two going) that you otherwise would not encounter by beginning and ending in Temagami. Absent a strong north or northwest wind at the time of departure, I would recommend that anyone making this same trip leave from Temagami, as Wilson suggests. The scenery and crowds are really no better either way.

Anyone planning to spend the night in Temagami and begin the trip the next morning should make reservations at a local hotel, if possible. The Loon Shore Lodge looked like the nicest place in town. A cheaper option would be to camp at Finlayson Point, a small park on the left just before you come into town, but I do not know whether you can reserve a site there. When we arrived late at night, we were turned away by the ranger at the gate to Finlayson Point because every tent-site was taken. The few hotels in town were also full, so we headed to Red Squirrel and camped in the parking lot.

To get to Red Squirrel Lake by car, drive about six miles north of town, then turn left and head another eighteen miles down Johns-Manville Road, a dirt road in fair condition. After pitching our tents in the darkness, we awoke the next morning to discover a veritable forest of travel trailers and tents at this location, all occupied by serious meat-fishermen who had come with boats and outboards to ply Red Squirrel Lake for trout and walleye. Walking down to the lake that first morning, still bleary eyed from our flight from North Carolina, we were encouraged to see several large lakers and walleye on stringers tied to the pier, but we caught nothing but bass, ourselves, on the entire trip.

With enthusiasm to finally have some water in our wake, we stopped within sight of the put-in that first morning to cook breakfast at the first available campsite on the lake. Breaking out the kitchen kit and making a small fire, we soon had a hot breakfast in the boys' bellies and time left over for a swim.

On this trip we noticed that the water, even in lakes accessible to motorboats, was exceptionally clear and clean. In fact, Wilson goes so far as to state in his book that "almost all of the Temagami canoeing waters are clean and pure for drinking," and I certainly agree. At the encouragement of locals, we did not bother to purify any of our water except on Red Squirrel, and there only due to the concentration of gas outboards. The water was especially sweet to the taste, as well.

To come up Red Squirrel Lake toward the portage, one must turn and paddle north. A large island lies in the middle of the northern arm, and on the north shore of that island is a very pretty campsite. Another nice camp, and one to which we returned on the last day, is just beyond this island on the left shore, also on a point looking north.

The portage from Red Squirrel Lake to Ferguson Bay was fairly strenuous and fostered some misgivings about the decision to begin the trip at this location rather than Temagami. It begins at a rocky landing beside the outlet from the lake and runs approximately 800 yards, or a little less than half a mile. It goes straight up in the beginning, then crosses a road and heads downhill. Cans and paper trash left by other campers at the end of this portage certainly detracted from the overall appeal. The portage returns to the small stream leading from Red Squirrel Lake, and one follows this stream to the left to get to Ferguson Bay. Worn out from the portage, we stopped to watch the boys haul about two dozen mussels from the bottom of the river into a laundry sack. Mussels aboard, we continued our trip.

Following the little, nameless stream that leads into Ferguson Bay, we came to a pond that at first seem locked by a marsh. Following the weed line generally to the left, we spotted an opening in the grass that led back to the river and on to the bay. Entering Ferguson Bay on Lake Temagami, we encountered some occasional motorboat traffic and some sparse cottage development, but not enough to be obtrusive. A float plane regularly takes off and lands on Ferguson Bay. The lake and surrounding bluffs are stunningly pretty, but the wide expanse of the bay makes for an open-water crossing that can be difficult in a wind, as we discovered on the return leg.

I must say that the water of Lake Temagami is the clearest I have ever seen, anywhere. In bright sun we could see down to the bottom, twenty feet or more. I happened, in fact, to see two absolutely huge smallmouth bass that were not the least bit interested in what I began hurriedly throwing at them. The clarity of the water on sunny days just absolutely shuts down the fishing. We soon gave up on the bass, went for another swim, and did some blueberry hunting on a tiny island.

Coming into Pickerel Bay, we crossed our second portage—about a quarter mile—and began looking for a camp for the night. While I do not begrudge the motorboat traffic on Lake Temagami, the red and green floating channel-markers and reflective range finders do seem a bit unnecessary. The only campsite on Horseshoe Island marked on the map published by Canadian Natural Resources is located right next to a rangefinder on shore that is supported by a large, steel tower. We camped instead on the overlook at the southern end of the island, which appeared to be a natural site.

The map we used for this trip is the Obabika Lake quadrant, available from the Centre for Mapping at 1-800-465-MAPS. However, only the campsites on Lake Temagami are marked on this map. I can only assume this is due to the fact that the other bodies of water on the map—Diamond, Wakimika, and Obabika Lakes all lie within provincial parks, where sites are not restricted. There are maps available from the Canadian Recreational Canoeing Association that do show sites in the wilderness areas as well as portages, and we were very glad to have one of these with us, as well.

At our Horseshoe Island camp we sacrificed the bag of mussels to our ten-quart boiler. To everyone's general disappointment, these mussels were not a bit like the sweet morsels from two summers ago on Lake Opeongo, of which Kip and I had been boasting. In fact, they were as chewy as shoe leather—perhaps owing to the fact that we had fetched them from a stream rather than a lake bottom. We found not one colony of mussels in any lake on this trip.

Leaving Horseshoe Island, one must come through two narrows to reach Sharp Rock Inlet and the portage to Diamond Lake, beyond. As we came through the second inlet, we found the terrain a little disorienting, and a compass proved to be very useful, here. The long, narrow bay which appears to the right is Sharp Rock Inlet. As we headed in that direction, the heavens let go with rain, and we stopped for lunch near the mouth.

Sharp Rock Inlet is popular as a sheltered anchorage for houseboats that are rented on the lake. A couple of these barges were anchored close to the portage, reminding us that for all the distance we had come, we had not yet begun the "wilderness" part of this trip.

At the end of Sharp Rock Inlet, the first dock that you see does not mark the portage. A small stream continues to the left several more yards to another dock, where the portage crosses. It is just a short hop-over, but it is fairly rocky should be taken slowly. This portage reportedly marks the location of a "jack ladder" drawn in Wilson's book which, in my rush to get across, I failed to notice.

Leaving the portage into Diamond Lake through a wide, shallow bay, we saw several islands. To our surprise, there was also some cottage development, here, though less than what we saw on Temagami. Many of the first campsites we encountered were already occupied, but sites seemed to become more plentiful and less populated as we moved down the lake. At a nearby youth camp some folks had told us that this route is the most popular in all of Temagami, and that seemed to be accurate. In an area as large as this, though, the only real crowding is in the search for campsites and at portages. You tend not to see anyone for hours when you are on the lakes during the day.

On Diamond Lake, we camped near the entrance to the northern arm, where a marsh is marked on the map.

A tiny, mussel-shaped island there offered us a beautiful overlook and fresh bear dung—full of blueberries.

Coming down the lake we trolled for smallmouth bass. A gold Mepps no. 3 squirrel-tail spinner was our best performer. We had fine fishing on Diamond Lake, and although none of the bass topped more than about a pound, we had plenty for a shore lunch over a campfire the following afternoon. We picked a spot on a gravel bar where a stream tumbles in from Small Lake.

The shorelines of Diamond Lake begin to narrow at the southwestern end, heading toward the portage. There is a good campsite on the left shore just where two large rock bars appear in the middle of the lake, here.

The portage landing at the end of Diamond Lake is deep muck into which Kip promptly stepped, sinking up to his chest. It was funny to Kip but fairly serious to me. Standing hip deep in the mud beside him, it literally took all of my strength to lift him out onto a rock, and it could have been a troubling situation had I been unable to get him out before he sunk in much farther. The portage trail, here, also bears special mention. It is extremely rugged. At times it is nothing more than a series of large boulders that you must hop across while balancing the canoe on your shoulders. There is a risk of a sprained ankle or worse for anyone who is not both careful and strong. It is best to go across first with just a pack so that you can see where the best path is. I would rate this trip "intermediate" rather than novice, as Hap Wilson does, solely because of this portage. I would also recommend, if at all possible, that two people carry one canoe, although no one did this while we were there, and I did see several teenagers cross the portage without problems.

After all of our effort on the portage from Diamond Lake, we had only 200 yards to paddle across a little, no-name pond before we had to do it all over again. The portage from the pond leads up a hill, turns right onto a gravel road for a short distance, then goes left down into the woods to the northern arm of Wakimika Lake. The northern arm narrows in a marsh before opening up to the main lake and its long, sandy beach. If you turn left and head down the beach, there are several idyllic campsites tucked back in the forest, just behind the wide ribbon of soft sand.

With an early start on the morning of day four, we headed down the western shore of Wakimika Lake under cloudy skies—good for fishing, I thought. As I paddled young Will Mistrot along, he began catching the kind of bass that tell a man he is, at long last, in the "wild" part of the forest. Soon enough, Kip had caught the biggest smallmouth bass he or I have ever seen. We kept the two largest bass in hopes of having them for dinner, but they were both stiff and cloudy-eyed by the time we finished dragging them down the shallow, windy, beaver-dammed creek that connects Wakimika and Obabika Lakes. We not only had to toss the fish, but we managed to knock a hole Robin Lauer's wood-canvas Prospector, which he successfully repaired with duct tape.

At Obabika Lake we found an ample number of beautiful campsites with lovely rock outcroppings, and we picked a good one for the night. A thunderstorm visited suddenly but only briefly, and we managed to sustain a wood fire fit for cooking and heating dishwater before running to the tents for bed. The two boys had their own tent throughout the trip, and it brought back memories of my own trips at that age hear them talk to each other in their beds at night, like two old wives, about everything and nothing at the same time.

The portage from Obabika Lake to Obabika Inlet is easy to miss, if you are as easily confused as I am, I suppose. Watch carefully for the head of the trail on shore. It leads up a hill, then forks. Follow the left fork all the way to the landing. Along Obabika Inlet and the Northwest Arm of Lake Temagami, we enjoyed some of the most consistent fishing of the trip. Our stringer was so full by the time we navigated our way back to the main arm of Lake Temagami that the more recent additions barely had their tails in the water. After finding my vote for the most stunning campsite of the trip, atop Long Island, we fileted and cooked our catch in a variety of experimental recipes—some good, and some that everyone will thank me to forget—followed by our old standby, a homemade fruit pie from the reflector oven. Our sixth night was spent asleep on a bed of pine needles, hoping for fair weather for the morning dash up the lake.

The weather cooperated for our sojourn. With lighter packs, we were soon back across the portage to Red Squirrel Lake, which will be known forevermore to history as the place where the North Woods refrigerator was invented. Knowing full well how deep that lake must be to support a healthy crop of lake trout, we resolved to make the boys a strawberry milkshake from evaporated milk, water, and Alba mix shaken in a Nalgene bottle. In a mesh bag we deposited the milkshake and a large rock, lowered it by rope to the bottom of the lake, tied the rope to a life jacket, and went back to camp to finish dinner. An hour later, up came the milkshake—cold as

Christmas—from the bottom of the lake. We had shown the boys some of the most beautiful country the world has to offer and an experience they won't soon forget, but after a week in the woods, never underestimate the power of a cold, strawberry milkshake over the heart and mind of a ten-year-old child. Let's face it: it just doesn't get any better than that.

NORTH NEST KEY LOOP

EVERGLADES NATIONAL PARK

When I was a young boy, my father would return to the house where my mother, grandmother, and sisters lived in Baltimore only once in a great while. On one such occasion, he met me on the stone doorsteps of our St. Paul Street rowhouse with a curious object in his hands. It was a stuffed, baby crocodile. It had lost the battle with it captors, but its leathery form remained fixed in a pose of threatening defiance—not unlike the expression that Dad reserved for anyone who questioned his wandering ways.

He had obtained the trophy in Key West, he said, and he spoke of his travels there. He hardly need have described the balmy tropical weather he had found. The tan on the creases of his face, nearly as leathery and worn as that of the small souvenir, told the story.

I imagined what it must have been like—the palm trees, the warm sun, the absence of wide expanses of asphalt and city buses, the cool, blue water, and, most of all, the freedom of that place. The Keys, they were called. Not the "islands" or the "beach," but the Keys. It was nothing like Ocean City, Maryland, I imagined. The very

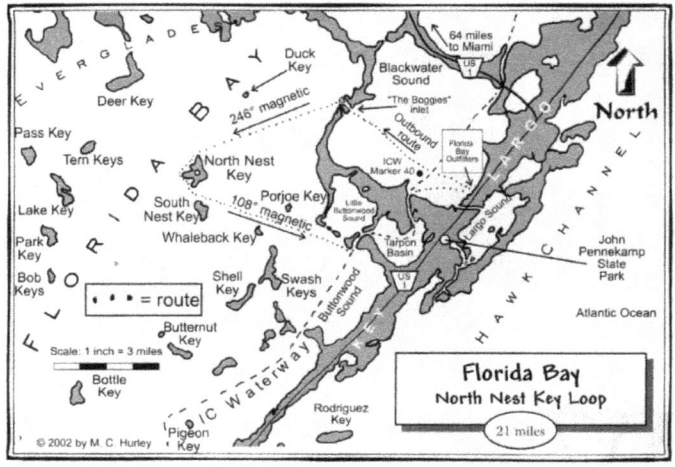

name of the place was something removed and exotic. There were no keys in Chesapeake Bay—no palm trees, no crocodiles, and no electric-blue ocean. I would go there one day, I thought, just as I knew even then that I would one day see the Adirondack Mountains, where my father had spent so much time as a boy. I would go to all such places, I dreamed, there to do the sorts of things that adventurous men do in faraway lands.

More than thirty years after that day in Baltimore, I realized my dream to explore the Florida Keys. This trip in the Fall of 2001 was not my first venture to the area, but it was the first that involved any real experience with the primitive, western side of the Keys—the side they call Florida Bay. In the area around Key Largo, Florida Bay is part of the Everglades National Park. The lonely, mangrove islands that lie scattered like green marbles across the pale, blue horizon are as desolate and inviting as they were when explorers first spied this land.

After I found a window of opportunity to go, a quick

foray onto Amazon.com produced several possible selections to help me form a plan. I chose a used copy of Johnny Molloy's book, *A Paddler's Guide to Everglades National Park*, from the University Press of Florida. When it arrived in the mail several days later, my eleven-year-old son Kip snatched it from my hands. Opening it, in seconds he settled on a destination: "Here, Dad," he said, "this looks like a good place." I looked at the page and saw Molloy's description for the North Nest Key Loop— 16 miles. After several hours of further reading, it was clear to me that Kip's initial choice would offer the best introduction to the Caribbean-style beauty of Florida Bay in a two-day, one-night excursion. Kip wanted to go, but an elbow fracture still healing after two months meant that he couldn't yet paddle long distances under his own steam. I would make the kayak trip alone and meet him in a few days at the Miami airport. The two of us would spend four days slumming it on the ocean side of Key Largo aboard our small sailboat.

The trip to North Nest Key begins at mile marker 104 on U. S. 1 in Key Largo, where Florida Bay Outfitters has a neat, little kayak and canoe shop with a distinctly local flavor. On arriving there I discovered that the route I was about to paddle is also the course of the annual "Bogart and Bacall" race sponsored by this outfitter. They came by the name honestly: The film "Key Largo" was filmed on the premises of the Caribbean Club, next door. The present-day establishment will scarcely remind you of the movie, but this is apparently where Bogart and Bacall made several famous scenes.

On arriving at the Caribbean Club late at night, after a sixteen-hour drive from Raleigh, I rushed to the edge of

Florida Bay just to see the water. Even in the dim light of the dock, I could tell that it was clear and clean. The Keys, at last! I was in the Keys!

Beginning from the small, sandy beach at Florida Bay Outfitters, a course generally 300 degrees to the west will take you past marker 40 of the Intracoastal Waterway toward the "Boggies." I have no idea what the derivation of that name might be. On the chart the Boggies appears to be a narrow pass to Florida Bay through the western shore of Blackwater Sound. From the water, the location of the pass is marked by a clump of land that forms the highest elevation along the thin line of mangroves on the horizon. As you approach, you will see the channel marker for the entrance to the pass.

Since crossing the Intracoastal Waterway you have been in Everglades National Park, but it is not until you come through the Boggies into Florida Bay that you first appreciate the wilderness character of the area. For me, it was like stumbling onto the pages of Robinson Crusoe or a scene from the movie "Castaway." There is, quite simply, no one and nothing to be seen but dozens of islands and blue-green water—everywhere. There are no sounds but the wind, the birds, and the dip of your paddle in the warm waves. It is so desolate, in fact, that when a boat finally did come ghosting by in the far-off distance, the skipper made a U-turn to check and see if I was lost. To him and his wife I owe the only picture you see of me on the water with this article.

Molloy's guidebook for some reason directs you toward Duck Key initially as you leave the Boggies and head into Florida Bay. I found it simpler to lay the rhumbline directly to North Nest Key on a course of 246 degrees magnetic. If possible, tape your compass to your kayak in your line of sight. When I left the Boggies on a clear afternoon, I could just barely make out the form of North Nest Key, but on a hazy day you might see no shape on the horizon toward which to steer.

Having paddled many miles for days on end on Canadian lakes, I was deceived somewhat by the distances over salt water. For one thing, Molloy describes this as a sixteen-mile loop. I may be wrong, but it certainly felt a lot more like the twenty-one miles I measured it to be on the chart. The wave action slows you down, and my lack of experience with a kayak paddle may have added to my fatigue. I had at one point considered entering the "Rum Runners' Challenge"—a 100-mile kayak trek from Key Largo to Key West—and I cannot tell you how pleased I was, about midway through the North Nest Key loop, that I had made other plans.

The Nest Keys have north and south islands. The southern island becomes more apparent as you travel farther into Florida Bay. Here is where your compass will come in handy to keep you on the right course. If you have a GPS, enter the location of North Nest Key as latitude 250854N and longitude 0803026W. Incidentally, the coordinates for almost any location identified on a map are available online at waypointregistry.org. Type in the name "Nest Keys" on this page, and the lat/lon comes right up, along with the particular USGS map-quadrangle for that location. As for maps, I would wait until you arrive in the area to purchase a waterproof chart at the West Marine or Boater's World on U. S. 1 in Key Largo. If you prefer to order in advance, waterproofcharts.com is a good, online source.

Approaching North Nest Key, head around the north side of the island and paddle along the shore of low-lying mangroves until you see a ribbon of sand open up. Along this shore, one or two small breaks have been cut into the mangroves to form campsites. There is also a beach for camping on the southern shore. There is supposedly an interior camping-area, but I had no interest in braving the mosquitoes to locate it. At the southwestern tip of the key there is a dock on which the park service has placed two portable toilets. Why two were needed on this little island I cannot imagine, but rest assured you will have ample opportunity for relief, here. An osprey has made more efficient use of one of the facilities in the form of a nest on the roof.

Everything Molloy and others say of the fierceness of the mosquitoes in this area is completely true. There will be no quiet, romantic evenings staring up at the stars from your campsite on the beach at North Nest Key or anywhere else in the Everglades, for that matter—unless you're looking through no-see-um netting. As soon as the sun begins to dip into the sea, you will be in your tent. The mosquitoes are present even in the dead of winter, but in the summer they are present in such numbers that it is considered foolhardy to venture into this part of the world. Your best bet is to choose a beach that is exposed to the wind. That will keep the little buggers at bay as long as the wind is blowing and you don't wander into the shelter of the trees.

North Nest Key is absolutely full of sea birds of all kinds. The pelicans roost in the mangroves in such numbers that they appear as ornaments on a Christmas tree. As you leave the island to the south, you will see tiny mangrove plants sprouting in the bay. They will one day catch enough sediment to form a connection to the main island. According to Molloy, this is how keys are "born" and grow.

The heading from the pass between the Nest Keys to Grouper Channel, where you will enter Tarpon Basin, is 108 degrees magnetic. Keep going until you see the channel marker, then head north through this channel. From here, you'll follow the channel markers across Tarpon Basin into another inlet that leads back into Blackwater Sound, where you began. As you paddle these inlets, stay close to shore and look down into the roots of the mangroves to see the fish that hide, there.

Although you can't really do it from the seat of a kayak or canoe, no trip to this part of Florida would be complete without seeing the ocean reefs at John Pennekamp State Park. This is a marine sanctuary with land-based camping and facilities. The state park protects the only living coral reef in the contiguous forty-eight states, and it is a beauty to behold. The park service runs a dive boat and snorkeling tours, but Kip and I spent four glorious days "camping out" on our 16-foot sailboat in Largo Sound and sailing to the reefs during the day. If you don't own a boat, you can pitch your tent and rent a motorboat from the park for the day. You won't find any stuffed, baby crocodiles, but the lure of the Keys remains as it has always been. It's a trip I waited thirty years to make and one you will never forget.

Lumber River

Hwy. 74 to Fair Bluff

I have neglected the Lumber River, and it is a shame I did. Readers and friends from around North Carolina would often ask my opinion of North Carolina's first "natural and scenic" river, and most were surprised to hear that I had never paddled it. Being concerned to offer my readers in Michigan and Maine and New York a suitable variety of stories about their home territories, I have floated fewer rivers in my own state than many, much less dedicated Tarheel paddlers. Of all the North Carolina rivers on my list, however, I had slighted the Lumber for so many years out of prejudice—prejudice that, being situated near the coast and on the border of South Carolina, it would measure up as just another dark, dreary, swamp-bottom stream with precious few places to make a footprint, much less to camp. I have never been as wrong about a river in my life. So wrong, in fact, that the Lumber has vaulted many places ahead to become my favorite Carolina stream.

The Lumber ambles its way through that part of Carolina known to golfers everywhere as the Sandhills. The topography, as that name suggests, is made up of rolling bluffs and swamp bottoms resting upon fine sand.

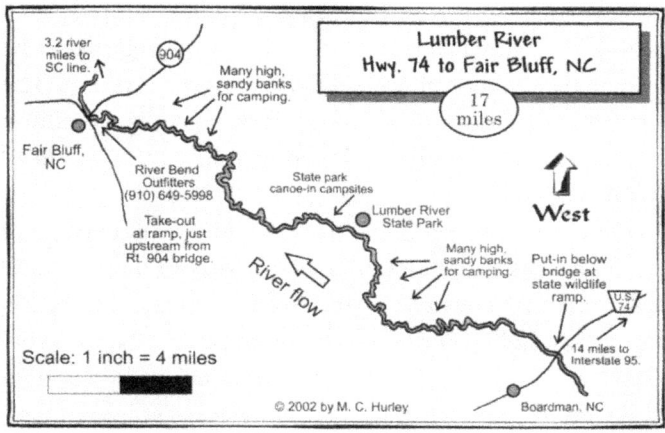

You can see the sand at almost every turn on this river, where mounds of it make excellent places to camp.

The low ground in the Lumber River Basin makes it unsuitable for many forms of development. As a consequence, the river has kept its wilderness character along much of its 115-mile length. Not surprisingly, it became the first river in North Carolina to receive protection under the National Wild and Scenic Rivers program and is still the only Eastern Carolina river to enjoy that status. It is also recognized as a state recreational water trail and national canoe trail. Portions of the river are classified as "natural and scenic," which is the designation reserved for rivers that are largely undeveloped and inaccessible by roads. The natural beauty of the bottomland forest in this section is interrupted only briefly by a few eyesores that fade quickly out of sight and mind. As one moves past the state park and toward Fair Bluff, the river becomes increasingly wild and undeveloped.

The put-in at Route 74 is a state wildlife ramp. It is an easy drive from Interstate 95 and can be negotiated by regular passenger-vehicles. There is ample parking. The current at this location is almost slack, so it bears mention that one turns to the right from the put-in to head downriver.

On the Lumber you will find a striking variety of plant life. The trees alone include sweet gum, red maple, laurel oak, swamp chestnut oak, bald cypress, flowering dogwood, holly, and loblolly pine. Wild grapes grow along the brushy banks. The woods seem to be teaming with wildlife, which explains the occasional sound of deer hounds baying in the distance. One poor dog got lost from his pack and, spying my canoe warily, decided to follow me down the river. After a mile or two, he answered the siren call of another deer scent and lit out, again.

His cries drifted to the river from deep in the forest for a while, then faded into the silence that surrounds the Lumber. That silence was regularly and abruptly punctuated by the hurried drumming of wings. Several flocks of wild ducks buzzed up and down the river, following its course like a highway in the woods. I would scarcely have needed a blind to have a fine supper of roasted fowl. Squirrels were also in busy abundance on shore, and the sandy shoals bore the tracks of many nocturnal visitors. At night, hoot owls serenaded me with that familiar question, never answered to their satisfaction: "Who, who cooks for you?" Beavers plying the tannic waters at night would occasionally slap their tails, creating a sound that distinctly recalls an eleven-year-old boy doing a cannonball off the low dive at the pool.

Aside from all its natural beauty, what I liked best about the Lumber is its suitability for canoe camping. There are shaded, soft sandbars along the river in abundance. Granted, I was paddling the water at record-low levels this past fall, but some of the sand banks clearly would still be exposed in all but flood conditions. You will have any number of beautiful, wilderness venues in which to pitch your tent and escape civilization, here.

Within forty-five minutes of one's departure from the put-in at the Route 74 bridge, the first deadfall appears. After this, there are a number of sandbars suitable for camping. The best of these is on the right bank, with a white, powdery beach and a good swimming hole, located approximately two river-miles from the put-in. After a ten-minute paddle beyond this site, Rough Horn Branch tumbles into the river noisily from the left.

There is some high ground on the left bank just after the point at which a dirt road comes in, on the left. A rope swing hangs from a tree on the left bank over the wide pool, here. Landing nearby, I explored the area to find some excellent, level campsites covered in pine needles and overlooking the river. Unfortunately, a little farther inshore I found an overflowing can of trash, strewn beer-bottles, and other evidence of late-night teen parties. There are some sizeable sand-mounds nearby that appear to be popular as a four-wheeling and dirt-bike course.

A large, open field appears on the left bank about three miles past the dirt-road access mentioned, above. It is privately owned, and a number of buildings are visible. They have thinned the trees to the river's edge, and, to control the resulting erosion, have dumped truckloads of cinder blocks down the bank. The view intrudes only briefly but looks just awful. It was a great consolation to find a beautiful sandbar on the right just another mile or two past this eyesore, and I made camp there for the evening.

There is a remarkable stillness as night falls in November on a swamp-bottom river. Every living thing in the woods is on the hunt in the fall, and everywhere animals are wary to be silent, lest they become prey. If it is solitude you seek, you will surely find it here.

I did see a number of couples coming down the river. Some were paddling for the day, while one man and his wife were bound for the canoe-in campsites at the state park. A wilderness site along the river is much to be preferred, unless you have a particular interest in the picnic tables, lantern hangers, and bathroom amenities that the state park offers in exchange for the nightly camping-fee. I prefer more primitive surroundings, but in typical fashion the State of North Carolina has done an excellent job with the Lumber River State Park.

The park comes into view just as the river opens up into a wide bay to the right, which is identified on the map as "Griffin's Whirl." The Lumber River State Park is divided into widely separated sections, and this location is known as the Princess Ann Access.

Looking straight across Griffin's Whirl, you can see the boardwalk that the park service has built. It leads to an overlook on the river. If you land here, you can follow the boardwalk along an interpretive trail with markers identifying many different types of plants. If you paddle a hundred yards past the overlook, two concrete boat-ramps appear on the right. Just above the ramps is a paved parking lot that leads to a covered pavilion, bathrooms and picnic areas. Also on the right bank, another hundred yards past the boat ramps, are the canoe-in campsites. There is a wide, unmarked landing here that would be easy to miss without any canoes pulled up on shore. Each campsite consists of a square, level, gravel area framed by railroad ties. Campfires must be built within those awful truck-wheel contraptions that the state uses for all of its campsites (another reason to rough it on the river). The picnic tables are convenient, though. When I arrived to explore the sites, a couple I met the day before invited me to share an elaborate breakfast they had spread out on the table in their camp. If you choose to stay at the park, a ranger will visit your tent to extract the eight-dollar daily fee. The canoe-in sites are first-come first-served, but you should call the park in advance. You can e-mail your questions or write to the ranger at Lumber River State Park, 2819 Princess Ann Road, Orrum, NC 28369. A helpful web page with information about the park can be found at www.ncparks.gov.

Leaving the state park, one enters the wildest section yet to be encountered on this trip. The river widens briefly, then returns to the familiar width of thirty feet or thereabouts, and a denser, wilder forest crowds in. There are not as many sandbars in the section below the state park as above, but you will still encounter half a dozen or more suitable for camping.

Many rivers around the nation, and particularly in the South, were once much more developed than they are today. On the way to Fair Bluff, you will see evidence of former development along the Lumber. The river derives its name from the bustling timber operations that first brought settlers to this area in the 1700s and powered the area economy for two hundred years. The photograph on the left of this page shows the remains of a wooden bridge from a more industrious era. Now, it is a stopping place for wood ducks and a curiosity for the passing canoeist.

Even though the area has been timbered for generations, there are some striking examples of old growth to be seen. The laurel oak, which is similar to the more commonly known live oaks in the southwest, grows to an impressive girth and height. There are several fine specimens of this tree on the park grounds and several more on the river toward Fair Bluff.

About a mile from the take-out, I came to a curious row of old pilings that ran straight down the middle of the river. Unlike the remains of the bridge that I had seen earlier, these pilings were in single file. I am not the sort that spends a lot of time pondering every artifact that appears along a river, but it bothered me to have no idea whatsoever why someone—obviously many years ago—would bother to drive a series of pilings in single file down the middle of the river for more than a hundred yards. Was it some ancient remnant of a feud to distinguish one man's "side" of the river from another, I wondered? The answer finally came from Stacy King, co-owner of River Bend Outfitters. He explained that at the turn of the last century, the pilings had been driven to give lumberjacks a place to "make up" rafts of logs to be floated to the coast at Georgetown, South Carolina, and sold for lumber. They would tie the logs to the pilings, then tie each log to the other until a sizeable raft was ready. When the river rose, three men would ride each raft on the journey to the coast, taking three weeks to make the trip.

Looking at the narrow width of the river and the occasional deadfalls, it struck me that a log drive must have been a tedious journey. No doubt it was, but we forget that the Army Corps of Engineers, in pre-conservation days, used to keep these and other rivers dredged and channeled for such traffic. Why, back in some of the tiniest little creeks around here, the remains of 19th century steamboats have been found in the deeper holes.

Speaking for myself, I'm glad that the Lumber has been left to the wild ducks, the beaver, and folks like me who have finally come to their senses and now realize what a treasure this place truly is.

Bear Island Canoe Trail

Hammocks Beach State Park

When I sit down to write each issue of the journal, I reach into a box of envelopes containing the maps, photographs, and notes taken for various trips and begin to peruse those that will best suit the needs of the season. This spring I reached down deep into this box and found a package of photographs I hadn't seen in a long time, from a special place on the North Carolina coast known as Bear Island. Looking through them, I recalled a misadventure, there, that ended happily but left an indelible impression on me as a young father.

It was 1995. Our son Kip had just turned five years old that summer. The seeds of the idea for a nationwide canoeing journal were taking shape in a monthly newsletter I was writing for the Croatan Canoe Club. The club would eventually founder after my interests took me beyond the rivers and lakes of Eastern North Carolina, but before it did an article on our trip to Bear Island appeared in the Summer 1995 issue of the club newsletter.

Bear Island is a three-mile lump of sand, sea oats, and maritime forest on the North Carolina seashore, near the town of Swansboro. It is roughly equidistant between Jacksonville and Morehead City. Locals will tell you that the name of the island derives from the occasional siting of black bears, there. These animals do swim over from the Croatan National Forest on the mainland from time to time, and they cause quite a stir among the beach-goers when they arrive. Historians claim, however, that the name originally was "Bare" Island. Whether that name derived from the amount of vegetation or other circumstances is open to debate, for now the southern end of the island is well-known as (an illegal) nude beach.

Stories of intrigue involving Blackbeard the pirate have touched this island and most others along the Carolina Coast. Blackbeard's storied treasure remains undiscovered, but the wreck of his flagship, the Queen Anne's Revenge, was discovered in 1996 just a few miles north of here, in Beaufort Inlet. After a succession of private ownership by wealthy planters, politicians, and sportsmen, the island was donated for use as a state park.

A trip to Bear Island begins at Hammocks Beach State Park on the mainland just outside Swansboro. Tidal marshes full of oyster beds and grass flats separate the mainland from the island. The flats are shot through with serpentine inlets that run like rivers with the tide. A canoe route through the marsh has been staked off by orange markers that are maintained by local scout troops. If you time your passage to and from the island with the direction of the tide, you can zip along at two knots without paddling a stroke.

Canoes are well suited to this trip, because you are protected from the wind for most of the way by the marsh flats. There are wet but lovely sandbars along the route that make excellent spots for lunch. The island itself is the best in the state for shelling, and on your way over you are likely to find live conch in the shallows. The well-marked oyster beds are commercially seeded and off limits to public harvesting. Be careful not to step out of the boat in these areas, as the oyster shells are razor sharp. Teva sandals or some similar footwear are a must, here.

The canoe route swings around the north side of the island, where the wind off of the Atlantic and the waves make for the toughest paddling, as seen in the photo on page 4. Once you pass the tiny inlet to the lagoon, however, the ride is placid. Paddling south in the lagoon, the dunes behind the beach rise up to your left, and the maritime forest lies to your right. The first (and, in my opinion, best) campsite is site number 13. It is located on the right, shortly after you enter the lagoon. You will have privacy, here, but a long walk to reach fresh water, the bathrooms, and the beach. Most folks prefer the oceanfront campsites. If you camp here, be sure to bring adequate sand stakes, or your tent may succumb to the onshore breeze in the middle of the night.

Bugs call the tune on Bear Island. Mosquitoes can be kept at bay with repellent, but the sand fleas are more persistent. If you're coming to the island anytime between March 1 and November 1, plan on making the regular application and re-application of one-hundred percent DEET a big part of the experience. If you can stand that, however, the rewards in scenery and solitude are as impressive as they come anywhere along the Carolina coast.

Julie and I camped here once with the kids. We brought way too much gear to be portaged over the dunes from the landing at the end of the lagoon. The campsites were two or three football fields away. The absence of a portage is a big advantage of site no. 13, and the reason why it's so often taken. If you plan to camp near the ocean, pack light for portaging.

When I came here with little Kip in 1995, we were joined by his playmate Zak Mathews and Zak's parents Nick and Missy. At that time my daughter Caroline was just three and much more fond of staying home with Mom than riding in tippy canoes. Kip, on the other hand, was a child of adventure. In the middle of the day we came down to wash off the sand in the outdoor showers at the bathhouse. No sooner had I stepped inside to use the loo than he had lit out for the horizon. When I emerged moments later to find him missing and a quick run around the bathhouse failed to reveal his whereabouts, the Mathews and soon the entire park police were enlisted in the manhunt. Kip was found about forty-five minutes later wandering up the beach and making friends along the way. It was one of those familiar moments of parenthood when you are too thankful to scold your child, though I received my share of scolding later from his mother.

I have not been to the southern end of the island, but the park service map shows additional campsites there, as well. The whole island was closed for an extended period after Hurricanes Bertha and Fran came back to back in 1996, and I understand the storms shifted the sandbanks in the marsh rather dramatically. Still, it remains a refuge for anyone seeking to experience the coast of North Carolina in the way that Captain John Smith, Sir Walter Raleigh and, yes, Edwin Teach, a/k/a Blackbeard the pirate once knew it. The ocean's impressive power to cleanse itself has overcome all of the insults of shipwrecks and oil spills that one might suppose would have despoiled these shores long ago. Crystal clear water and clean sands are cool on the feet and easy on the eyes. Loggerhead turtles still struggle ashore here each season to lay their eggs, completing a cycle their species has repeated for thousands of years. One hardly need ask why they return—who could ask for a prettier place?

EDISTO RIVER NORTH FORK

SHILLING'S BRIDGE TO ORANGEBURG

An unexpected perquisite of publishing this journal has been the frequent invitations from readers to join them and their families on their favorite rivers. Opportunities to accept such invitations amid the demands of work and school for our own children have been less frequent than we would prefer. Two springtimes ago, however, when Rick Wylie of Greenville, South Carolina sent photos of the Edisto River, just a few hours' drive from our home in North Carolina, the invitation seemed too good to resist.

For those who have a discerning ear and a gentle eye for such things, South Carolina has a distinctive allure. On one level—to some the only part of the state they ever know—it is the garish, neon lights of Myrtle Beach and the fireworks stands and billboards of "South of the Border" along Interstate 95. Others see it as a poor and racially divided state—the spiritual home of the segregationist Dixiecrats and its one-time standard bearer, Senator Strom Thurmond. Those old fires still smolder just beneath the surface, flaring up on occasion as they did to engulf Senator Trent Lott, only months ago. In many places, time seems literally to have stopped,

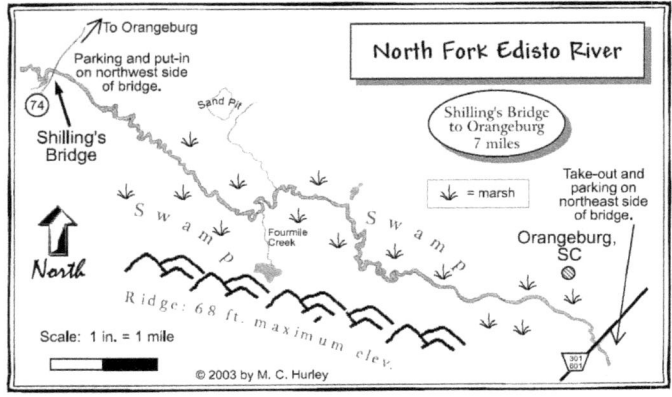

here, with the end of the Civil War. In lonely cotton fields and tobacco farms, this land still seems to be dithering about joining the union that its sons fought so bravely to preserve.

The network of South Carolina blackwater streams is vast. These waters have been stained a dark tea-color by the cypress roots and dense vegetation that line their banks, but it is this same tangle of vegetation that has kept the rivers remarkably clean. The North Fork of the Edisto (pronounced EHD-iss-toe) is a perfect case in point. It has too many stumps and deadfalls to make it navigable to water-skiers, and it is much too slow to interest today's throngs of whitewater thrill-seekers, all of whom can find ample water for their purposes in the western reaches of South Carolina, Georgia, and North Carolina. The high-levels of tannin and natural acidity that make it less hospitable to game fish also have kept it from being overrun by fishermen and revved-up, gleaming bass boats bristling with electronics and horsepower. The main stem of the Edisto along the lower sections has numerous sandbars for camping during low water. Terra firma for camping on the North Fork, on the other hand, is hard-won from the brambles and brush that jealously guard the sparse acreage of high ground along its banks. In what would appear to most to be reason to look elsewhere we found here, during the Spring of 2001, a diamond in the rough.

We saw not another boat for the duration of our journey. The very inhospitability of the North Fork has kept it a lonely and, in places, pristine example of the South Carolina Lowcountry in which General Francis Marion, the lauded "Swamp Fox" of the Revolutionary War, found refuge from the invading British army. Marion's heroics as a guerilla commander, fleeing danger in flat-bottomed bateaus along the blackwater streams of the Lowcountry, and camping out in the dense, swamp forest with his band of South Carolina farmers, was portrayed a few years ago by Mel Gibson in the movie "The Patriot." Marion was a Revolutionary War icon on a par with Washington—renowned for his ability to elude Lord Cornwallis' staid, British regulars, who regarded these swamps as an impenetrable wilderness. Today, a canoe trip on the North Fork of the Edisto is still a reliable means by which to escape the invasions of work, worry and modern life.

Gene Able and Jack Horan have written *Paddling South Carolina, A Guide to the Palmetto State River Trails*, first published in 1986 by Sandlapper Publishing in Orangeburg, with a revised edition in 2001. Copies are available through Amazon.com. I reviewed it in selecting the North Fork of the Edisto for this trip. The authors describe the seven-mile section of the North Fork that we ran, between Shillings Bridge and Orangeburg, as "one of the most popular stretches." As I stated, though, we saw not a single other paddler on the trip, and if it is as popular as the authors suggest, it must be that its short length makes it well suited to a day-trip as easily as an overnighter.

We began the trip after dropping off one vehicle under the Route 301 overpass, just outside Orangeburg. There is a park beside the overpass, on the east of the bridge, on the north shore. You can park and leave a car, here, for the duration of the trip. The parking area is open to the view of traffic passing on the highway, as an added deterrent against vandalism. Rick had brought an extra canoe that we had to leave atop his Jeep in the parking lot, and it was untouched when we returned.

There is ample room at the put-in at Shilling Bridge on State Road 74, seven miles east of Orangeburg. A dirt parking lot west of the bridge, on the north bank, marks the spot. There is a concrete ramp here, though it did not appear to be well-used. We found the river to be calm, clean and dark, moving at a gentle pace of a knot or less that lends a deliberate speed to even a modest effort at the paddle. Before we knew it, we were well downstream, swallowed up in an enchanting forest that arched completely over the width of the river in some spots.

The deadfalls and logs on the North Fork are no great obstacle to a well-paddled canoe. We lifted or shinnied our way around or over them without incident. Lunch stops, however, are few and far between. Most of the ground is moist and covered in brambles, so we made good use of a clearing on the south bank at the edge of a farmer's field that we encountered near mid-day.

I wish I could tell you that the North Fork had thwarted the invasion of developers as well as it had stymied General Marion's pursuers, back in 1776. As is sadly the case on so many southern streams, there are a few aging homesteads that interrupt the otherwise natural surroundings with an unwelcome squalor. These are likely to remain until and unless groups like the Nature Conservancy can buy them out or environmental legislation can curb further development as to force their eventual sale and removal. Some riverside shanties blend more readily into the surroundings, making no pretense of permanency. Others blend less well, but thankfully they are few in number and confined mostly to the upper reaches of the river.

I would not say that "South Carolina possesses an astounding array of rivers," as does Barry Beasley, author of South Carolina Rivers. It is hard to look at a map of Canada or Minnesota and be astounded by the amount of water anywhere else. Nonetheless, Beasley is quite correct in his observation that the diversity of this state's waterways is what amazes the uninitiated. One begins with breathtakingly cold, clear streams flowing through columns of rhododendron and rocks laden with bright green moss, in the ancient mountains of the west. That ecosystem compares starkly to the contemplative slowness of the rivers to the east, where the water seems anxious to pause and reconsider its journey before abandoning these shores altogether for the ocean waves of the Atlantic.

There are no designated campsites along this section of the Edisto. As one of the original thirteen colonies, public use of river lands in South Carolina is governed by the rule formally recognized in 1842, by the U. S. Supreme Court in Martin v. Waddell. In that case, the court stated: "When the Revolution took place the people of each State became themselves sovereign, and in that character hold the absolute right to all their navigable waters, and the soils under them, for their own common use." Subsequent decisions have so broadened the definition of "navigable" to include virtually any floatable stream used for public recreation. In all of the original colonies but a few, such as New York, the term "soils under" these streams (riparian land) is construed to include wet and dry land below the mean high water mark. The mean high water mark is readily visible by the erosion from past floods and, in a swamp like the Edisto, is higher than most of the stream bed. All such lands are deemed to be held in trust for the public. "Common use" has been construed to mean that while private landowners can build on these lands, they cannot prohibit members of the public from acceptable public uses. Such uses have, by more recent judicial decision, come to include camping and canoeing. What all of this legalese means for the modern-day Francis Marion, searching for a place to sleep for the night along streams like the Edisto, is that dry, low-lying land along the riverbed is available for camping. Discretion, politeness, and quiet after dark are still the watchwords of successful interaction with landowners. Such habits will get you a lot farther than legal opinions.

Most of the camping along the lower main branch of the Edisto is on fluffy, white sandbars, which generally are much more to my liking, but you would be hard pressed to beat the seven miles of the North Fork west of Orangeburg for solitude. Rick and his son Pierce and Kip and I selected a spot about midway on the right bank where we could see a stand of tall pines was growing—a sure sign of dry land. The floor of the forest was fairly thick with a low-covering of brambles, but we found a clear spot by what seemed an ancient oak. There was no evidence that we could find of anyone having camped there recently—or ever—but the spot was just big enough for our two tents and a dining fly.

The boys set about the task of finding wood for the fire while I pumped fresh bottles of clean drinking water from the river with a filter. Looking back at these pictures of my son Kip, just two years ago, it is astonishing to me to see how much he has grown—and how our time together is flying by. As you may by now have read, in the announcement on page 27 of this issue, this enchanting experiment in personal journaling which began with the first issue of Hurley's Pack & Paddle in Fall 1995, then became Hurley's Journal, and now is Paddle & Portage, will soon come to an end. Kip was only five years old when I started the journal. Not that any father needs an excuse to go camping with his children, but the consuming need to produce stories for this journal over the past eight years has had a pleasant and unexpected benefit: Kip by the age of twelve had paddled and camped on more than fifty different rivers and lakes in thirteen states and Canada. His sister, younger by eighteen months, had accompanied us on not quite that many but a ponderous number, as well. That is an achievement and an experience that would have been incomprehensible to me at their age.

Kip turned thirteen this year, and you would hardly

recognize him, today, from the pictures of the mop-topped little boy in the photographs of this trip, taken two years ago. Already I can foresee the distractions to come in the form of perfume and petroleum. There are so many of my own passions, so many of my own experiences that I want him to have. Like all fathers, though, I must continually remind myself that a son is not his father in miniature. He is a separate and distinct individual. He may—he will—follow other dreams, and different interests. The depth of my passion for wilderness exploration, for sailing to faraway destinations, and for writing about these experiences is borne in part, I know, by the experiences I desired but could not enjoy as a child. Kip has not been so deprived, and so he likely will find his passions elsewhere. Still, I hope that his woodland days have given him a love of adventure that he will pass on in some way to his own children.

Lying in such haunted woods, I imagine the ghostly figure of Francis Marion—huddled over a small cooking fire, his eyes ever on the misty horizon of the swamp, his conviction clear and his resolve undiminished. I am thankful to him and to the others that my son and I can enjoy this place in peace and freedom. When you camp here, recall and ponder the rich past that made your present journey possible. It is certainly true, as Weems described at the end of the war: "The American Revolution is a history of miracles, all bearing, like sunbeams, on this heavenly fiat: 'America shall be free!' "

Lake One / Snowbank Lake Circuit

Boundary Waters Canoe Area

If you spend much time at this canoe-camping thing, sooner or later you will have to grant interviews to inquiring family and friends who are intrigued by your sense of adventure. "Are there bugs?" they will want to know. "How do you go to the bathroom?" "If you get in trouble, can you call for help?" "Do you worry about bears?" "What if it rains?" Depending on who's doing the asking, you may choose to downplay these concerns. Your friends will want to believe you, when you do. That's because to them, people like you are a sociological oddity. Unless your friends grew up in places like the Adirondacks, Canada, or northern Minnesota, to them the idea of traveling through the great outdoors as an itinerant wanderer, moving from camp to camp by day and hiding in the forest by night, is something normally reserved for fugitives and terrorists. They will size you up and think: "He's a normal looking fellow. He seems to enjoy himself. Perhaps he's on to something with this canoeing business."

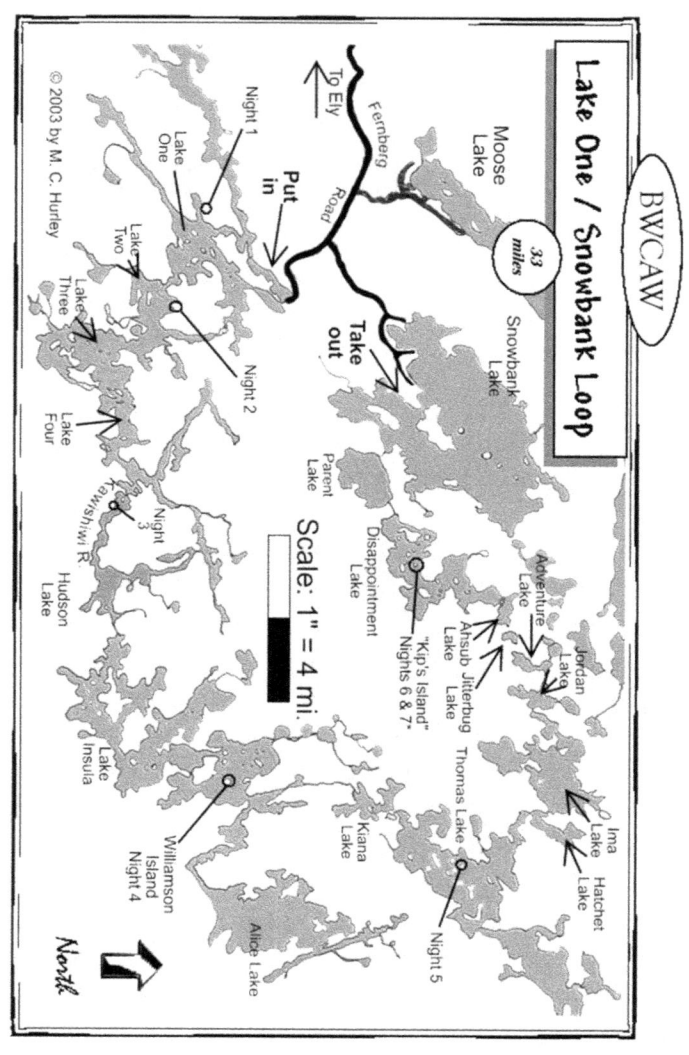

Succumbing to the flattery of their questions, sooner or later you will invite some of these inquirers (or they will implore you to invite them), to come along with you next year and experience just such an adventure, themselves. The following spring or summer, after spending prodigious sums on a new camping outfit, they will set out with you for the woods. Thus, the drama will begin anew. I have made casual acquaintances out of many close friends in just this way.

Invariably there are bugs—many, many little bugs—and rain. There are, of course, no bathrooms and never were; but more importantly, unless your friends have adhered faithfully to a training regimen of deep-knee bends in the weeks before their departure, the dig, squat, and balance-as-you-grasp-your-ankles method of relief will present them with a whole new set of challenges. Afterward, amid the tattered wreckage of rain-soaked sleeping bags, skinned knees, and a stubborn intestinal disorder, they will smile thinly and tell you how much they learned on the trip. As they do, an unspoken footnote to this polite conversation will literally rise like a plume of smoke from the corner of their mouths. Read the footnote, and it will tell you what they really "learned" is that electricity and running water and indoor plumbing are underrated. The whole experience will have confirmed their long-held suspicion that there is definitely something amiss with you—else why would you continue to subject yourself to this punishment? Next season, you will wonder aloud what ever happened to that nice couple, the so-and-so's, and someone will distantly recall that they are planning a trip to Disney World that year. After a few such failed encounters, you will begin to wonder whether a grown man's continued interest in sleeping in tents and cooking in the dirt is indeed some evidence of deep, unresolved psychological issues.

Actually, I exaggerate. I have alienated no more than a dozen friends this way—tops—and I have long since stopped wondering whether I have unresolved psychological issues. My diagnosis as an oddball was certified years ago. I have learned that in life there are two kinds of people: adventurers and everyone else. They are divided like continents. From one side to the other lies a great chasm of understanding across which no man may guide another. We must come to appreciate the adventurous life on our own or stay ashore.

Still, I occasionally cannot resist the temptation to recruit others to my way of leisure. And so it was at a family reunion last summer that this familiar dance began once again, as polite inquiries from my wife's cousin Edwin about past canoe trips developed into a serious discussion of gear, techniques, and likely destinations. Finally I could resist no longer the temptation to invite him and his wife and young children on a Boundary Waters adventure the following summer. He enthusiastically accepted. His wife and mine, at least for the time being, seemed to be on board with a plan to bring the four children. The ball was in my court.

Well familiar with the indignities that the North Woods can serve up to the inexperienced, and eager to make a good impression, I consulted the experts at Canoe Country Outfitters in Ely, Minnesota about possible routes. I was planning a week-long trip with children and wanted short paddling-distances each day, with easy portages. Canoe Country Outfitters has been in business since 1946. Owners Mark and Bob Olson are natives of the area and extremely knowledgeable about routes in the BWCA and Quetico. Their shop looks and feels more like a scoutmaster's basement than a retail store. In the several trips they have outfitted for me over the years, I have never had a moment's disappointment or received a piece of advice from them that wasn't dead-on. I trusted them to recommend some good choices, and true to form, Mark answered my inquiry by mail with a set of maps on which he had circled three possible routes leaving from points near their Moose Lake base-camp. Two were remote routes in the Quetico, on the Canadian side of the park, and one was closer by in the Boundary Waters, annotated with the words "sand beaches, island camping." I sent Mark's proposed routes to Julie's cousin and invited him to pick the one that best suited his family. He chose the BWCA route.

My wife, a veteran of many rain-soaked, buggy sojourns with me, was reluctant from the start to subject uninitiated members of her family to the same experience. Only the summer before we had endured swarms of mosquitoes followed by dangerous winds in Maine. By mid-spring, she had bugged out of this venture, and her support turned out to be the linchpin holding the plan together. Her cousin sent his regrets, and the expedition appeared to be evaporating before my eyes. My daughter Caroline gave notice that she would be occupied with other plans, during that week in August. Finally casting a doleful look that must have said "Et tu, Brute?" in the direction of my thirteen-year-old son Kip, I found an ally. He was bitten by the adventure bug years ago and knows he can do worse than to spend a week of his summer vacation catching fish almost at will, swimming in crystal-clear lakes, sunning himself on giant boulders, and generally pretending to be Lord High Governor of the North Woods. He and I would make the same trip of "island campsites" and "sandy beaches" I had planned for the cousins.

I will admit to some understanding of my wife's reluctance to make this trip. The bugs in summer in northern Minnesota can be as fierce as the scenery is stunning. I spent an almost insufferable week there camping in a lean-to, years ago, with no mosquito netting other than a hood for my head at night. The hum of the swarm was so deafening that I could scarcely fall asleep. For that reason we planned this trip around our trusty Eureka Timberline tent, which is impervious to bugs, rain, and wind, and planned to do our cooking under a 12-foot "Noah's Tarp" by Kelty, if foul weather came our way.

Arriving at the airport in Hibbing on a Northwest commuter flight from Minneapolis, we were greeted by the waiting shuttle driver who, like everyone else who assisted us on this trip, was a model of efficiency and service. Our conversation during the hour-and-a-half van ride to Ely soon turned to the driver's decision to leave his home in South Florida to move to Northern Minnesota. I remarked that the migration is usually in the other direction. He was quick to disagree, responding that the heat and humidity of summers in South Florida were oppressive to the point of distraction. "But what about the bugs up here?" I asked. This point he generally conceded, but he added with great relief that there were no bugs in Minnesota this summer.

"No bugs?" I replied, no less incredulous than if he had said there was no water in the lakes. After all, even the manicured suburbs of Raleigh, North Carolina are plagued with mosquitoes at this time of year. He explained that the preceding spring had been unusually dry, thus depriving the bugs of their usual hatching season.

When we got to Canoe Country Outfitters in Ely, Bob Olson confirmed the driver's good news. "You'll notice that there are almost no bugs in the woods, this year," he said. I could scarcely believe our good fortune. And the weather forecast for the week looked absolutely Bristol, to boot.

As I relished the days ahead, it occurred to me that this trip, with no bugs and good weather, was a lost opportunity to prove to Julie and her family that one need not, after all, be some sort of Sasquatch of the North to enjoy a week in the Boundary Waters. Instead, like a bucket of ice cream in a power failure, this bug-less week would be for the two of us to savor while it lasted.

Our trip began with a hurried departure late in the day from Ely to Lake One on Friday, the first of August. Our driver was Mark Olson's son, who recently competed his studies at the University of Wisconsin and is considering a career in fisheries biology in the park. He dropped us off where the paved road from Ely ends, at the landing to the lake. A U. S. Forest Service ranger was there but did not ask to see our permit. Each camper must obtain a permit allowing entry into the wilderness area through one of several designed entry-points. To preserve the wilderness experience, a limited number of canoes is allowed to enter the wilderness through each entry point, each day. You must enter through the checkpoint on the exact day stated on your permit, which meant that we couldn't wait until the next morning to recover from our early flight from North Carolina before starting our trip. Each entry permit specifies the number of days you may camp and an estimated exit date. However, you are not required to exit the park on the estimated date and could, if you desired, camp in the park all summer on a single permit. A permit for unlimited overnight use costs thirty-two dollars for two people. After the first two people in a party, you will pay ten dollars for each adult and five dollars for each person under the age of eighteen up to a maximum of nine people on a single permit. No more than nine people and four canoes may travel and camp together as a group in the park.

We found Lake One to be crowded, as predicted. With the ease of road access, families had set up base camps in several of the designated campsites. Each site is marked by a red dot on waterproof maps published by W.A. Fisher Co. of Virginia, Minnesota. Your outfitter will supply you with the maps you need. Fisher maps and a good Silva compass are de rigeur for any expedition in the Boundary Waters. It is quite easy to lose one's bearings, and although precise compass courses rarely are necessary, keeping a compass in front of you in the canoe as a general reference of your direction will help you identify land forms to keep from getting lost.

We found the westernmost campsite on Lake One to be unoccupied and pitched our tent in the waning daylight. This site was secluded but small and weedy, with little firewood. I would recommend you choose one of the sites farther out on the main lake, if you can.

We brought all of our own food and gear for this trip on the airplane with the exception of a canoe, paddles, life jackets, and stove fuel. Propane fuel canisters cannot be transported by air. No sooner had we pitched camp than we discovered that the fuel canisters we had purchased from the outfitter did not fit our stove. What would have been an incurable error, a few years ago, was remedied with a quick call by cell phone from our camp to the CCO store, that night. We were still close to the put-in. Without hesitation, Mark Olson promised to have a driver meet us there in the morning with a stove to fit the bottles we had and bottles to fit the stove we had brought. The driver arrived early and at no charge, with the goods as promised, and we continued our trip without missing a beat. I really can't say enough about the snappy service we received from Canoe Country Outfitters.

After eight years of having Daddy make all of Kip's meals and do the clean-up, we planned this trip to give Kip a chance, for the first time, to be totally in charge of the kitchen. I highly recommend this approach, as Kip took a keen interest in planning and preparing the menu. He picked out the groceries before we left and packed them. Out in the woods, I slept gloriously late while Kip rolled out of the sack, each morning, to make coffee and oatmeal. After dinner, he would boil water and clean the dishes. For my part, I cleaned the fish we caught and was responsible for pitching and taking down the tent and tarp each day. I got the better end of the bargain, and have to admit to feeling a little decadent in letting my son do most of the work, but I took quiet pride in his efforts.

We fish North Woods lakes generally by trolling, not casting. This method yielded unexpectedly good results throughout the trip, despite the fact that this appears to be one of the more well-traveled routes in the park. We were warned that the first week in August is the absolute busiest time of the year, so perhaps that explains the congestion we saw at the portages. Once out on the lakes, however, groups dispersed, and we generally found ourselves without another canoe in sight.

We had tremendous success with various lures, but the best performer for smallmouth and pike was a three-inch, floating Rapala minnow, trolled twenty-five yards behind the canoe, at normal paddling speeds. The best lure for walleye was a sinking or "Countdown" Rapala, or a deep-diving plug trolled slowly, in deeper water. When heading out from camp in the evening for a few hours of fishing, we would cast the same lures or a no. 3 Mepps spinner. Eight-pound-test line was tough enough to bring in eating-size pike or walleye without a leader, but Kip's rod was not ready for the smashing force of the walleye that took a lure he was trolling just off Williamson Island, on Lake Insula. I was paddling in the stern when the rod perched in front of Kip's seat in the bow whipped decisively backward into a deep u-shape, the way a rod does when the lure is solidly snagged on a log. Before I could slow the canoe, the rod had snapped in two. As I ruefully paddled back to try to retrieve the lure, Kip reported that he had a fish, and that it was still on. Several minutes later, pulling the line in hand over hand, he lifted a fat walleye over the side. For this insolence, we invited the walleye to dinner. I managed to "repair" Kip's rod by splinting the broken sections with green pine-branches and duct tape. The result was a misshapen excuse for a fishing rod, but to our great surprise we caught most of the fish for the remainder of the trip on it.

None of the portages on this trip was particularly strenuous. We doubled each portage, one of us carrying the canoe and the other a pack on the first leg, then both of us carrying packs on the second leg. Regular readers of the journal will recognize that Kip has shot up quite a bit in size since last summer, and it was certainly a treat to have him take a yeoman's load on the portages.

I recommend camping on Second Lake. Most folks we saw at this lake had either just begun their trip at Lake One and were eager to put some miles in their wake or were headed for a take-out at Lake One and anxious to make it there. Sensing that the campsite just north of where the portage comes into Second Lake might be rarely used, we camped there and found a hidden gem: a sloping beach for swimming and a cove filled with neglected pike.

Hudson Lake is really just a wide spot in the Kawishiwi River. The fishing there is not nearly as spectacular as the scenery. I recommend the site we found on this lake just beyond the portage from Lake Four. We paddled back down to the portage after dinner, landing the canoe on the rocks just above the falls. Kip caught several small bass in the eddy below the falls on a crappie jig, when all other attempts to catch something failed.

Lake Insula was a striking beauty with plenty of pike and walleye. I will not soon forget our view from the cliff on Williamson Island, where we played chess. A granite rock in the campsite, here, bears the name of the island

and provides a landmark.

From the clear, deep waters of Thomas Lake we paddled all day, past several campsites we might easily have chosen, in an effort to make Disappointment Lake. We feared we might not find an unoccupied campsite when we arrived, until Kip brought us ashore at an unnamed island on the south end of the lake. Here, high above the lake in an idyllic pine forest, we found soft, level ground, the prettiest views, and the best campsite of the trip. We named it "Kip's Island" in honor of its discoverer, stayed there two days, caught bass at will, and marveled at our good fortune. Since then, folks back home have tried to imagine the moon rising over this lake without a bug in sight, but we just sigh and tell them: "You had to be there."

Saranac River & Lakes

Adirondack Park

Many week-long canoe trips in the North Woods are ambitious affairs. The expanse of interconnected lakes and rivers beckons us to traverse the whole. In the shadow of the voyageurs, whose speed meant higher market-prices for their pelts, we devise careful itineraries of the distances to be covered each day and the portages to be conquered. Aiding each paddle stroke is the subtle tension of unspoken questions: "Will we make it, and when?"

There is of course a place—some would say a time—for trips like these. But the disadvantage of such schedules is what we miss while keeping them. In our haste to cover the day's distance and make camp, we may forgo the cast to that cluster of rocks that fairly yells "pike for the picking!"

In planning our Adirondack voyage, I had considered a number of such routes, but the fickle fate of a broken elbow one week before our departure dictated a slower pace. (For those of you who may be curious, suffice it to say that standing in roller blades while videotaping a child's birthday party should be classified as an ultrahazardous activity.) And so I devised what is

The Idler's Route

Put-in at Fish Creek; head to Upper Saranac Lake and first night's camp at Buck Island; second day, paddle down Upper Saranac to Bartlett's Carry en route to camp at Tick Island, in Weller Pond; spend third night at Norway Island in Middle Saranac; fourth day, follow Saranac River to Lower Saranac Lake and Duck Island; fifth night at Fern Island; take out at Ampersand Bay.

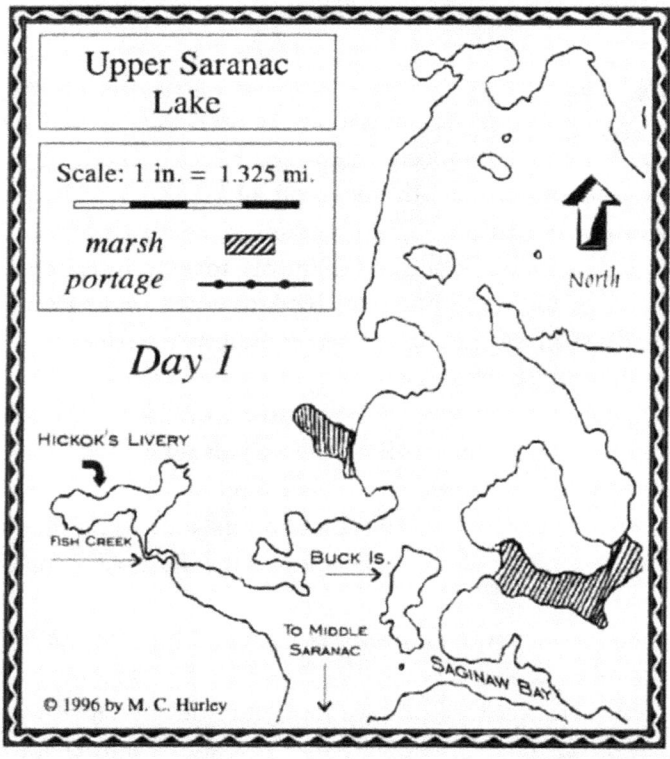

referred to here as an "idler's" route which, in addition to being well-suited to small children, novices, and the sick and injured, offers some of the best bass and pike fishing in the region.

Our trip began on June 16 at Fish Creek, approximately ten miles by Highway 30 from the Village of Tupper Lake, New York. As with my last trip in this region, we used Hickok's Boat Livery as our put-in. From Hickok's dock we paddled about two miles to our first night's camp at Buck Island in Upper Saranac Lake. Over the next six days, we fished, paddled, and lollygagged along a lazy route down Upper Saranac Lake to its connection with Middle Saranac Lake via Bartlett's Carry—an easy half-mile trot and our only portage—up into the sylvan beauty of Weller Pond, back into the east end of Middle Saranac, and through the Saranac River to Lower Saranac Lake. We took out at Ampersand Bay, on the east end of Lower Saranac Lake, after traveling only twenty-one miles in six days and five nights.

Four of us—two dads and two squirmy, six-year-old boys—drove all the way from North Carolina for the trip. (We had considered sending one dad and the boys by Amtrak sleeper-car via New York City for a pickup in Utica, and that might be an exciting adventure for those not inclined to make the drive with children.)

Almost anyone coming to this area from out-of-state will find it helpful to spend the night as we did at the Mount Morris View Motel on Highway 30, just north of Tupper Lake Village. One cabin has two double beds and two baths, and, more importantly, a kitchen with a full-sized refrigerator/freezer. The family who owns the motel was very helpful and courteous to us. We were able to buy all of our meats and juices at the Northern Born grocery in Long Lake and freeze them solid before

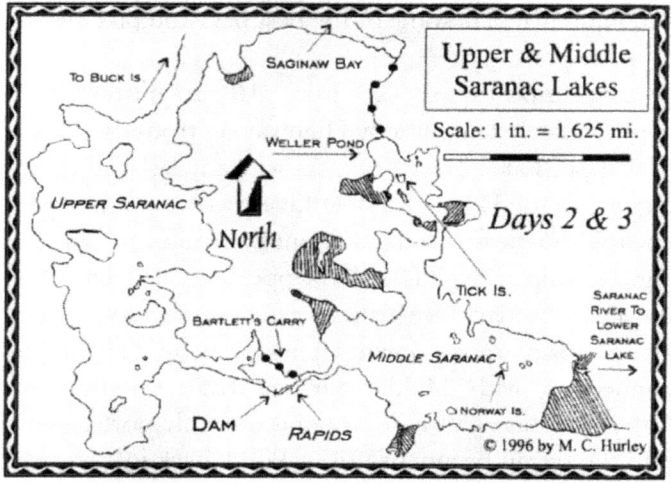

we headed out the next morning.

After making arrangements with Hickok's Livery to rent a second canoe and to be picked up six days later at Ampersand Bay, we readied our gear while the boys fished from the dock. Having baited my son's hook, I left it dangling above the water for a moment while I attended to some other item. A fair-sized fish made a leap at the worm above the surface. Shortly thereafter, our departure was delayed while we unhooked several fish for the boys and replaced their bait. It was clear that this trip would live up to its promise.

No reservation or fee is required for Buck Island or any of the other primitive sites on Upper Saranac Lake. Buck Island has several campsites. Site no. 10 where we spent our first night seemed to be the best. It offers level, shaded ground for tents and a large, flat rock sloping down to the landing area for swimming and sunning.

One of the many benefits of our itinerary was arriving

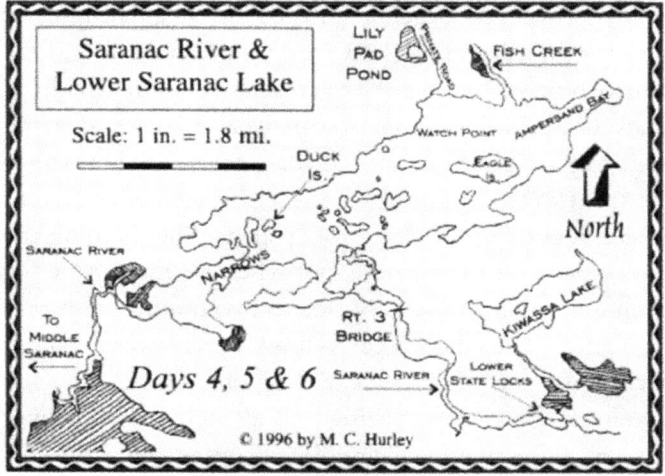

at the first night's camp in ample time to sort out cooking, sleeping, and kitchen arrangements and shake out our gear. The boys, having been cooped up on a long car-ride the day before, didn't have to wait long before getting to go swimming, fishing, and exploring on the island. By the next day, they were ready for the longest leg of the trip over to Tick Island in Weller Pond, a total of eight miles including the half-mile carry. After a luxurious breakfast, a leisurely swim, an unhurried departure from our camp on Buck Island, and three trips each over Bartlett's carry, we did not arrive at our second night's camp at Tick Island until after 6:00 p.m. We found no one camped on the island or anywhere else in this beautiful, mountain-rimmed oasis. It was clearly our favorite campsite of the trip. (Tick Island, incidentally, is named as the sister to nearby Tock Island—not for the insects living there.)

The inlet to Weller Pond is a delightful introduction to the clean, clear marshes that are characteristic of the

Saranac River and other streams of this area. Despite the beauty of Weller Pond, however, we generally found the best fishing to be on the larger lakes. Our first night at Buck Island offered a tasty appetizer of bass and perch filets to go with our steaks. The bass at this time of year—the third week in June—were found spawning in five to fifteen feet of water along rocky areas. Shepherding the boys took a lot of our time, but when we made time for fishing we pulled in bass of one to two pounds with easy regularity. The bass and yellow perch were caught exclusively on crank-baits and spinner-baits, with the deadliest producers being three-inch floater-diver Rapalas in perch and silver colors. These were cast a few feet off of rock islands and retrieved quickly. Middle Saranac Lake is fairly shallow with depths of twenty feet or less, and good fish were found in areas seeming to be well offshore, away from any discernible structure. In the area of Middle Saranac between Umbrella Point and Halfway Island, one fisherman took a nice pike on a locally popular, bronze-colored spoon with two red, plastic eyes and a treble hook, called a "redeye." It is retrieved fairly fast from deep water toward shore.

We caught more bass than any other fish, but a twenty-six-inch northern pike that hit a silver Johnson's Sprite among the rocks between Hocum Point Island and the north shore of Lower Saranac Lake was our biggest fish and best meal. Earlier, another pike had hit my Dardevle spoon in the weed beds of the Saranac River, about three hundred yards above the falls, but jumped and threw the hook. When fishing for pike in this area, big silver or bronze spoons with some flash of red appear to work best, and a wire leader should be used.

Our third night's camp at Norway Island afforded an impressive view from the top of its steep summit of pine and granite. Wood was somewhat scarce, here. We had enough for baking biscuits and heating dishwater, and we tried as always to leave a dry stack for the next party. Morning and evening fishing trips to nearby First and Second Islands yielded two nice bass before we moved into the lovely Saranac River on the fourth day.

The three Saranac Lakes of this trip are contained with the six million acres of Adirondack Park. Land use within the park has since 1971 been managed by the state Adirondack Park Agency. About sixty-two percent of the land is privately owned and includes a number of small towns. The remaining thirty-eight percent, about 2.3 million acres, is State Forest Land which, under an 1894 amendment to the New York State constitution, is required to be kept "forever . . . wild." A debate over the future of the park continues to rage among the area's 115,000 full-time residents whose livelihood depends upon commercial growth, the "forever wilders," and real estate developers. Some would like to see the moose and wolf reintroduced here and more of the park returned to a wilderness status, while others seek to subdivide large, wooded tracts for vacation and retirement homes.

The areas covered in this trip are a mix of wild and semi-wild lands. The shorelines of all three lakes are densely forested. At the start of the trip on Upper Saranac Lake, you will encounter cottages and boat houses on some parts of the lake. Middle Saranac Lake has virtually no development, and Weller Pond is completely wild. The Saranac River is undeveloped with the exception of a lock system for getting around the falls. Lower Saranac

Lake is surrounded by forested land on all but the far eastern shore near Ampersand Bay, where a few cottages and boat houses appear. Notwithstanding the occasional development on some parts of the trip, this is by far some of the prettiest water and woods, and offers some of the best island-camping, of any place in the Adirondacks.

Those who have traveled the Saranac Lake region in the past might not be familiar with the new reservation system implemented this year by the Department of Environmental Conservation (DEC), which is the agency responsible for the management of state campsites in Adirondack Park. With the exception of our first night on Buck Island, all of our campsites on this trip were reserved and paid for in advance under the new site-specific reservation program. The system is not without its imperfections, but on the whole it works well.

To reserve a site, you must call a reservation company in California at 1-800-456-CAMP that handles the reservations for all New York State public campgrounds and campsites. The numbers of the sites on each lake are on the map for Saranac Lake Islands Public Campground, published by DEC. (The Adirondack Canoe Map, which is de rigeur for canoeing this area, lists campsites but not the site numbers necessary for requesting reservations. Also, the canoe map shows several campsites on some islands in Middle and Lower Saranac Lakes where only one site is available for permitting.) If you don't have the campsite map, DEC will send you one at no charge.

Once you have the map referencing campsites in Middle and Lower Saranac Lakes by site number, the operator at 1-800-456-CAMP will take your reservation and credit-card payment over the phone. One substantial drawback is that the reservation procedure does not lend itself to canoe-camping from site to site. The operator will charge you a seven-dollar service fee for each site in your trip, even though the reservations are all made at the same time and all arrive at your door in the same envelope. That brings the tab to nineteen dollars per campsite. Also, the operator will not allow you to reserve more than three campsites for consecutive nights. If you are going to be traveling for more than three days and spending the night at a new site each day, you have to reserve the sites for nights four and afterward in someone else's name—a needless hassle. DEC welcomes written comments on the new reservation system at Bureau of Recreation, NYSDEC RM 679, P. O. Box 12063, Albany, NY 12214-5590.

The clear benefit of the site-specific reservation system is that it guarantees that your particular site will be unoccupied and waiting for you at the end of the day. When the ranger arrived by boat at Tick Island in the morning to collect our permit, he informed us that shortly before we arrived, late the preceding afternoon, he had run off a party that had camped on the island without a reservation. Because the DEC knows you're coming and makes sure the site is clear, there is more certainty in planning the trip. You can pick good campsites in advance, if you know which sites you want.

We did not, actually, know one site from another when we made our reservations. It's hard to go wrong in picking a campsite here, though, and we were well satisfied with all those that we picked with the possible exception of the last site at Watch Point/Shingle Bay.

This was a beautiful site with a stunning view above the lake, but it was too close to some cottage development on that end of the lake for our taste.

We opted to move to a new site every day for two reasons: to avoid being stuck in an undesirable site for more than a day, and to give this trip the feeling of adventure associated with a long-distance voyage without the long hours of paddling that six-year-olds might find too tedious. Moving daily also afforded a welcome routine for the boys, who eagerly anticipated exploring a new site with each sunrise. For those making the same trip, I'd recommend spending an extra night at either Tick or Duck Islands. Tick Island offered a rare, unexpected remoteness in a beautiful setting. Be sure to take the trail up the rear of that island to the rock overlook. Duck Island offered the prettiest tent-site of the trip.

The availability of firewood on some of these islands is a factor and will be more so, we imagine, later in the season when the downed wood has been picked over by other campers. The larger the island, the more likely that you'll be able to find firewood.

The one portage of the trip across Bartlett's carry is well-marked and fairly short. Be sure to put on bug spray before you begin, as the mosquitoes are waiting to greet you on the other end. Generally speaking, however, we encountered very little trouble with bugs on this trip. Despite a wet spring, we found no black flies on our arrival here in the third week of June, and the mosquitoes came out only at evening. The herbal repellent "Green Ban," available from The Boundary Waters Catalog, dealt effectively with the bugs. We only occasionally donned head nets. Had the black flies been a problem, we were told that applying Vick's Vap-O-Rub is an excellent repellent—a method which I have not tested but pass along here for what it may be worth.

After more than our share of days spent in the pouring rain on other trips, we led a charmed life in the Adirondacks this week in June. Five out of six days were dry. The water was just right for swimming, and we saw practically no one the entire time, owing, we were told, to schools still being in session in New York. Of the sixty-two available sites on Lower Saranac Lake, only eight including ours were occupied. Even old Uncle Nessmuk might have envied such isolation in his day, when throngs came to this region by steamer, stage, and rail in search of the classic beauty of the North Woods that, we happily found, still awaits us on the Saranac Lakes.

Sylvania Wilderness

Ottawa National Forest

While places like the Boundary Waters Canoe Area Wilderness, Algonquin Provincial Park, and the Adirondacks may get all the glory, to those who bother to look among the hidden gems of this nation's national forests for the best places to go canoeing, the Sylvania Wilderness is a diamond in the rough. I have Paul and Sandy Hoefgen of Hoefgen canoes in Menominee, Michigan to thank for being the first who whispered to me of this rare gem, and I have their blessing to shout about it to the readers of this journal.

Paul, his wife Sandy, and Paul's family before him have been busy making a few gems of their own, these past fifty years at the Hoefgen Canoe shop on the shores of Lake Michigan. They're the jaunty, fiberglass boats with the rakish bow profile. Paul and Sandy shipped me one of their canoes to review a while back ("Choosing a Tripping Canoe," Spring '98), and a friend quickly bought it out from under me. I made a point of borrowing one for this trip when I came through on my way north from Green Bay.

The Hoefgens and others often describe the Sylvania

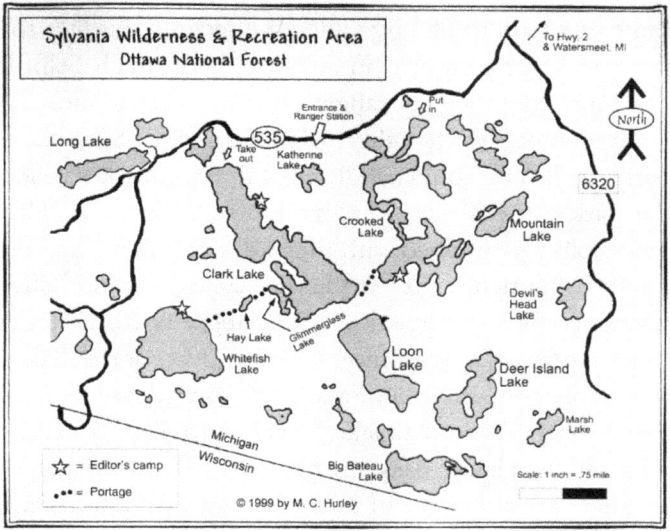

Wilderness as a miniature Boundary Waters. The water is pristine, the fishing is quite good, and the scenery is breathtaking. When the idea came up for a rendezvous of Midwestern readers of the journal, I had just the place in mind.

Like most trips in the Boundary Waters, a trip through Sylvania involves paddling lake to lake and camping at designated sites. Motors are not allowed with the exception of some local residents on Crooked Lake (who I presume lived in the park back when the government purchased the land in 1966 and have been granted some sort of long-term lease). Party size is closely controlled, and all glass bottles are banned.

Although I say that this park is a closely guarded secret, it remains quite popular with Michiganers and other locals who know the Upper Peninsula (the "U-P") for all the rugged beauty that it offers. For that reason, campsites tend to fill up rapidly. We secured the sites for this trip several months in advance, with much helpful coaching from the park ranger on which sites to pick.

By comparison to other wilderness areas, Sylvania is fairly small. You could paddle all of the major lakes inside the park's 21,000 acres in the course of a week. This accessibility, combined with the park's popularity among local fishermen, has made necessary some fairly restrictive fishing regulations. We caught northern pike, largemouth and smallmouth bass, but some lakes reportedly contain walleye and lake trout. Possession of bass is prohibited on all lakes except Crooked. If caught on prohibited lakes, bass must be released immediately.

There are a number of possible routes for a four-day, three-night trip, here. The natural and most popular starting places appear to be Crooked and Clark Lakes, both near the park entrance. The entrance to the park, four miles west of Water meet, Michigan off of Route 2, leads to a ranger substation and a forty-eight-site, improved campground with hot showers and flush toilets. One must check in at the Sylvania ranger substation to obtain permits for wilderness camping between May 15 and September 30. At other tin1es, no permits are required for camping in the wilderness area.

When permits are required, only five people are allowed to a campsite. Campsites and portages are designated on a park map, available at no charge from the forest service. Although not indicated on the map, some campsites are "doubles," allowing for more than one group of five to camp at that site. The ranger can tell you which sites these are on the lakes where you are headed.

Our itinerary called for the first night at the "Badger"

campsite on Crooked Lake, after about two miles of paddling from the put-in at the north end of the lake. After the put-in, we wound our way through some narrow channels where, incidentally, the northern pike fishing is rather good. In fact, we caught probably a dozen pike at various spots in Crooked Lake—one of the best being the wide, weedy bay in front of our campsite. What made that such a desirable location for pike, though, didn't do much for the nearby camping. The Badger site fairly hummed with common houseflies, and although they didn't bite, they hardly made for idyllic surroundings. Like all flies, though, they could not see at night. Once the sun went down the place was rather peaceful. To anyone making the same trip, however, I would recommend some site other than Badger on Crooked Lake.

One particularly lovely site we encountered lies on Mountain Lake. Our party of rendezvouers made a day trip there from our base camp on the first day. Whereas Crooked Lake is weedy, fertile and dark, Mountain Lake is crystal clear. It offers the added advantage of being off-limits to motorized traffic, which you will encounter occasionally on Crooked Lake. The first campsite on Mountain Lake, named "Bear," is the best. It sits on a little ridge bordering a couple of tiny trout-ponds on the north side and Mountain Lake to the south. Although it takes you out of the way, this site would be my choice for the first night for anyone making the same three-night loop.

Coming into the bay that leads to the portage to Clark Lake, the shoreline appears to be locked in vegetation. Paddle close to the edge of the marsh at the bottom of the bay until you spot the narrow channel that opens through the weeds to the head of the portage. The portage to Clark Lake is the prettiest of the trip, coming at the end into a verdant meadow.

Take some time to swim the wide, soft, sandy beach that greets you at the end of the portage to Clark Lake. The water here is as clean and clear as you will see anywhere, owing I understand to its acidity. This seems to have ruined the fishing, alas, but the swimming is practically Caribbean. Although the bottom of Crooked Lake is covered with bogs and weeds, Clark Lake is lined with rocks. The weeds return as you leave Clark and enter tiny Glimmerglass Lake, which is separated from Clark by a shallow, narrow inlet. After catching pike and bass at a furious pace on Crooked Lake, we were skunked coming and going on Clark and Glimmerglass Lakes, but the scenery was blissful indeed.

True to my experience in most spots in the North Woods, just one portage does a world of good for the fishing. After leaving Glimmerglass we came to Hay Lake, aptly named for the straw-like vegetation that stretches out from its shores. There the bass were ready to meet us, once again. You see our tiny band of rendezvouers pictured on page twenty, resting from the portage, here, and soaking up the beauty of this lake that seems to call to mind the very definition of Sylvania—"a realm of woodland beauty." The meaning of this term did not strike me at first, although I am well familiar with Nessmuk's frequent description of the Adirondacks as a "sylvan" paradise. I had rather assumed that the heirs to the Sylvania light bulb fortune had donated the land and had the place named after them. After hiking through these woods for any period of time, though, one quickly realizes how aptly named they are.

I cannot tell you what parts of these forests might contain virgin stands of timber, but some of the trees are truly enormous and of ancient age. Given the destruction of forest fires and logging in other national forests, it is a rare treat to walk through a mature hardwood forest such as you have in Sylvania. Mature forests are characterized by a minimum of undergrowth, owing to the light-absorbing properties of the large, high canopy of vegetation. Hiking along these portages has a theatric feel, as you can literally "see" the forest through the trees.

Whitefish Lake was the second camp on our itinerary, and the camping, swimming, and fishing here were of the same high quality generally prevalent in these woods. Whitefish is not a lake of great aesthetic beauty, being essentially round and devoid of islands, but there is a feeling of remoteness, here. It is worth noting that on Labor Day weekend, we saw no one on this lake except a young woman who hiked there alone, with no gear, very matter of factly went for a swim at the end of the portage, and left. Here's to the hale and hearty breed of women in Michigan, I say.

I can only guess that the catch-and-return policy on smallmouth bass, combined with the impediment of two portages, has made the fishing on Whitefish Lake what it is. Take a look at the fish in the picture on page 21, and by all means let me know your guess of its weight. I don't need to guess to tell you, though, that it was the biggest bass—smallmouth or otherwise—that I've ever taken on a line. I had been fishing along the shore of Whitefish after the rest of my party had gone ahead to get a jump on the portage back to Clark Lake and our final night's camp. When the wind piped up, I was paddling solo across the middle of Whitefish for all I was worth, trying to keep the bow of my 17-foot Hoefgen canoe headed to weather and not paying any attention to the Mepps spinner I was trolling from the stern. When the canoe reared back fairly to a stop, I almost lost rod and rig overboard before realizing I had connected with a moving object. It was par for the course that, when this fish came up and I realized it was the biggest of my "career," there wasn't another soul to be found. So, for my fellow Sylvania rendezvouers of little faith, who listened with skeptical smiles to my tale of a smallmouth dragon on Whitefish Lake, the proof is in the picture.

In the afternoon when we made camp at Whitefish, while others in our party were taking advantage of a balmy September day for a swim, I lay on a grassy bank just above the lake for a nap. I highly recommend it. On every trip, sooner or later, weather and temperature and opportunity come together to provide moments of solitary introspection like these. As I lay there upon the grass in the thrall of just such a moment, with a warm breeze gently prodding the branches of trees overhead, the rays of the late afternoon sun were enough to comfort but not to burn the skin. If one relaxes in that sort of environment long enough as I did that day, life begins to slow to an elemental pace, and you'd swear you can almost feel the earth turning.

Looking up at the boundless sky, you realize how truly insignificant you are—insignificant enough, perhaps, that they wouldn't hold it against you back at the office if you lay in that spot for a week or a month or two and worked out all the answers. It is at such moments when I am able to take the days of my life in my hand and mark the measure of where I've been, where I am, and where I am going.

Sooner or later we all learn that time is the only true wealth, and the value of time is what trips like these teach us. All of which is a wordy way to tell you, friend, that if you are in need of a good grassy bank for reflecting on your life and looking at the clouds for an afternoon, the first campsite to your right on Whitefish Lake is the place to do it.

All good things come to an end, and the final day of this journey came after an enjoyable evening spent sharing Ken Brown's talent for intoxicating ciders, cocoas, and teas while we all discussed the politics and affairs of the day before a warm fire. The diversity of experience and knowledge to be found among people who share a love of canoeing in the wilderness is one of the great benefits of this way of life. Before the day ended I paddled out into the middle of Clark Lake to see the loons. Growing suddenly thirsty, I dipped my cup into the water and drank it up. I had never tasted better, from the springs of the Smokies to the mountains of Maine. But then again, perhaps it wasn't so much the water I was thirsty for, but time—time to sleep and drink and fish and wonder, and eventually to recall, in places like these, what life is all about.

APPENDIX

Packing Systems

Loading the Duluth Kitchen Pack

The venerable Duluth Pack, faithfully made since 1882 by the Minnesota company of the same name, is to canoe camping what the Louisville Slugger is to baseball. When writers wax nostalgic for the "smell of canvas and leather" mixed with balsam and fresh air, they are conjuring a memory of North Woods canoeing influenced by the quality and character of Duluth's famous packs.

Duluth Packs are available by mail order through a toll-free number and a web page (duluthpacks.com). In this issue, you see Duluth's Kitchen Pack in all its boxy glory. It is constructed of the same durable green canvas, leather and copper rivets that distinguish the company's entire line. These packs are de rigeur for parties of four or more on extended trips. Following the numbered photographs on the facing page, use the key to learn here's how to load one with everything you'll need for elaborate meals:

Dinner on the 1st Night

Marinated steaks, beer bread with whipped, salted butter, mashed potatoes & gravy.

Place steaks and marinade in plastic bag, bag again, then freeze inside plastic container. Allow to thaw on the first day. Add can of beer to Daily Bread-brand bread mix, stir, bake in loaf pan in reflector oven, slice and butter. Whipped, salted butter (not margarine) will stay fresh for 2 or 3 days. Add steaming water to Real-brand mashed potatoes, top with dry-mix gravy.

Photo 1: The Open Country six-person cookset from Campmor is made of sturdier, heavier-gauge aluminum than you'll find in brands sold in most discount stores. A small kettle, a coffee pot, and six cups fit inside a 10-quart kettle. Use the larger kettle for stew and heating dishwater and the skillet as the lid for the kettle. Four small bowls will wedge inside the coffee pot.

Photos 2, 3, 4: The plastic plates that come with the Open Country set are too small, so buy six, 9-inch metal plates separately and nest them, upside down, in the cookset. Compress a canvas water bucket and lay it on top of the plates. Fill the bucket with river water and 2 squirts of chlorine bleach to wash hands.

Photo 5: Place a large, Lexan cutting board on the bottom of a 9.5 gallon, Rubbermaid "Roughneck" tote. The tote adds rigidity to the pack, keeps the contents organized, and doubles as a dishwashing tub. Place the packed cookset on the cutting board in the tote.

Photo 6: Wedge baking pans and a backpacker's grill between the cookset and the wall of the tote. Place a loaf pan as shown. Throw the pot-hanging chain of your cooking tripod in here, too.

Photo 7: A case for spices, firestarter, lighters, matches, extra baggies, scissors, a can opener, and small items fits next to the loaf pan.

Photo 8. The fully packed tote. Most meals will cook faster on a campfire, but carry a butane canister and a Microlite stove for quick soups and coffee. Stuff leather gloves (for working around the campfire), a water purifier, a measuring cup, and dish towels into the loaf pan.

Photos 9, 10: This steel reflector oven by Lefebvre's of Ontario folds flat and slides in first. Slide the tote in next, cookset-end first.

Photos 11, 12, 13: A canvas utensil roll snaps on and is held in place by two flaps. Tie the top with rope. Fill the cavernous side pockets with lunch snacks easy to reach.

Compact stoves are treacherous for balancing large pots. Use a small backpacking grill and dig a hole in the ground for the fuel canister to lower the stove.

Packing Systems

The Tandem Outfit

Nothing demands good planning like a week traveling through the wilderness by canoe. The first system presented here is for tandem paddlers who will "two-trip" or double the portages. The menu is made to be simple, allow lunch to be eaten on the go, and use everyday groceries that require no refrigeration.

No. 4 Duluth Pack: Lay envelope-style pack flat on ground; insert axe and collapsible saw sideways across bottom of pack; insert tarp folded square to match size of pack; with tarp against back of pack, lay tent bag and poles on top of axe and saw; sit pack upright, spread opening at top, and throw in the remaining gear: toiletry kit; bag of tarp stakes, assorted rope, stake-puller; bag of clothespins; snakebite kit; first-aid kit; wool shirts; plastic tent-mallet; flashlight; camera case; waterproof map case containing folded maps, paper, pencil and compass; knit caps; bailing sponge; bug head nets; canoe "legs"; quick-dry towel; duct tape; bug repellent; moccasins; sun block; raingear at top of pack; toilet paper in plastic bag inside front flap with trowel; small box of fishing lures and nail clippers; spare eyeglasses in case; leather gloves.

Sealine ProPack: This modern, waterproof dry bag

comes with shoulder straps and a waist belt for portaging. It will keep clothing and bedding drier than canvas packs. Stand pack upright and spread opening; insert rolled up and deflated camp-style air mattress and unroll outwards to made a cylindrical well lining the pack; repeat with the second mattress. Stuff loose sleeping bags into well and tamp down. For each person, fill one nylon mesh bag with clean clothes and a folded cotton laundry bag for soiled clothes. Stuff filled mesh bags into well. Compress and seal pack, folding over the top enclosure three times before buckling.

Duluth Kitchen Pack: This reinforced canvas pack has a deep interior well and two large side pockets. See "How to Load the Duluth Kitchen Pack" in this appendix for instructions on how to pack the following items: In a 9-1/2 gallon Rubbermaid "Roughneck" container (a rectangular basin used to do dishes) place the following items: 10 quart billy set containing 4 plates, large pot (also used to rinse dishes), medium pot, frying pan, 4 bowls, 4 cups, and coffee pot; 2 dish-pads; shoebox-size plastic box with lid containing firestarter and matches, butane lighters, seasoned salt, table salt, black pepper, bouillon, garlic powder, extra Ziploc bags, trash bag, pot pliers, squeeze bottles of antibacterial hand soap and dish washing liquid; 2 plastic cutting boards for rolling pies and biscuits and fileting fish; collapsible water bucket; pie pan; loaf pan; baking pan; spatula; serving spoon, paring knife, filet knife, measuring spoon, and 4-sets table knives, forks and spoons; water purifier; chain for iron cooking tripod (tripod carried loose in canoe); large mesh bag with string closure (for hanging dishes to dry). When full, slide the Rubbermaid container inside the middle compartment on top of the reflector oven, and tie the compartment shut with the earflaps. Stow plastic water bottles and extra backpack stove fuel in side compartments. Outside flap also sorts and holds eating utensils.

Duluth no. 3 Combo-Cruiser Pack: This is a traditional, woven-ash pack-basket that fits inside a deep, canvas pack with shoulder straps, a cover flap, and side pockets. It makes a rigid and easily portaged container for food. Protect the inside of the basket against spills with the heavy-gauge, reusable, plastic-bag liner sold by Duluth. Separate and store different types of food (e.g., vegetables or breakfast foods) in different-colored nylon-mesh bags inside the food pack. You can spot the color of the bag you need and rummage inside without having to dump the whole pack to find that candy bar. Pre-measure and re-package bulk ingredients in plastic bags. Double bag items like flour that will ruin if spilled or exposed to water. Store small, loose items such as cookies and jerky strips in plastic boxes and stow in pockets on outside of pack.

Day	Breakfast	Lunch	Dinner
1	In town	Candy bar, apple, peanuts	Sliced summer sausage, potatoes, green peppers and onions with seasoned salt and pepper, fried in canola oil.
2	Pancakes, bacon, coffee, orange drink	Cookies, raisins, jerky	Ham, instant mashed potatoes, gravy, fresh-baked cherry pie (Comstock® fruit-fillings come in a plastic jar with pull-tab top)
3	Biscuits, bacon, coffee, orange drink	Candy bar, apple, peanuts	Canoe Stew (see *HJ* "Ultimate List" for recipe), fresh-baked bread (Daily Bread Company mix), leftover cherry pie
4	Cinnamon toast, coffee, orange drink	Cookies, apricots, jerky	Breaded fish filets (u-catch-em), cottage fries with vinegar and spices, fresh-baked brownies (Snackwell mix needs only water)
5	Hot cereal, coffee, orange drink	Cookies, raisins, peanuts	Kraft Deluxe Macaroni & Cheese (Kraft's sauce comes pre-mixed in foil pouch, not can), ham, fresh-baked blueberry pie
6	Pancakes, ham, coffee, orange drink	Candy bar, apple, jerky	Herb & garlic pasta (dry mix by various brands—boil, add oil and seasoning), summer sausage, fresh-baked bread, leftover pie
7	Biscuits and jam, coffee, orange drink	Cookies, apricots, jerky	In town

Packing Systems

The Solo Outfit

Solo voyaging is by necessity an exercise in introspection and austerity. Introspection because you are, after all, alone. Austerity because you haven't the extra legs to carry a lot of gear. The following outfit is as austere as it needs to be. The soul-searching I leave to you:

No 4. Canvas Duluth Pack: toiletry kit; snakebite kit; bailing scoop; tarp; bug head net; sleeping bag; duct tape; sunblock; clothes; first aid kit; toilet paper; spare glasses; lines/rope; maps in plastic sleeve; gloves; bug repellent; compass; "canoe legs"; flashlight; ground cloth; Dutch oven; lean-to/tent; raincoat; coffee boiler; folding saw; trowel; utensil wrap; air mattress; stake puller; water filter; fishing tackle; clothespins; cutting board; stake mallet; wool camp shirt; camp towel; knit cap; loose items to be removed and stowed in canoe or on person (rod & reel, paddles, axe, jacket, PFD, hat, knife.

Canvas Duluth Day Pack (carry inside no. 4 pack on portages): Outside pouch: Choreboy scrubber/sponge; matches; lighters (2); firestarter in plastic bag; dish towel; leather work gloves; dish soap. Inside pouch: all food, water bottle, oil, spices.

Gear notes and tips: Tarp should be nylon with

reinforced grommets. Carry enough rope to hang tarp above campfire. A lean-to with two poles is lightweight and opens to campfire. In bad mosquito country, take a tent instead. Aluminum Dutch oven doubles as skillet. Use cloth covers for this and coffee boiler to keep campfire black off other gear. Canvas wrap sold by Duluth keeps utensils organized. Menu hints: Dried fruit in re-sealable bags keeps longer and is lighter than fresh. Eat for lunch and serve leftovers on your oatmeal. Carry extra Ziploc bags for non-burnable trash. Bannock bread mix: 1 cup all-purpose flour, 1 tsp. baking powder, dash salt, and 2 tbsp. dried milk. Add water, roll out, and cut into strips. Fry in pan or roll in sugar & cinnamon, twist on a green stick and bake over fire. Muesli mix: rolled oats, raisins, slivered almonds, powdered milk and raw sugar. Add water and eat as breakfast cereal. Drain and rinse smoked oysters sold in small tins in groceries. Vacuum-sealed cured ham keeps without refrigeration. Protect brownies and Hostess fruit pies in Tupperware.

Day	Breakfast	Lunch	Dinner
1	In town	Candy bar, dried apples	Fried potatoes and onion with summer sausage, brownie
2	Instant oatmeal, dried apples, Tang, coffee	Peanuts, cookies	Dried herb & garlic pasta mixed with summer sausage, cinnamon & sugar bannock baked on a stick
3	Homemade muesli	Candy bar, jerky	Sliced, cured ham, instant mashed potatoes, brownie
4	Jerky wrapped in fried bannock, Tang, coffee	Peanuts, dried apricots	Canned, smoked oysters in white sauce (make from dry mix) with spices, served over pasta, hot apple pie (single serving)
5	Hot oatmeal, dried apricots, Tang, coffee	Candy bar, jerky	Pan-fried fish filet (u-catchem) in corn meal, fried potatoes, cinnamon & sugar bannock baked on a stick
6	Homemade muesli, Tang, coffee	Peanuts, candy bar	Kraft Deluxe Macaroni & Cheese, brownie
7	Cinnamon & sugar bannock, Tang, coffee	Cookies, dried peaches	In town

Packing Systems

The Spartan List

After paddling the kinds of trips that involve long or frequent portages, one begins to long for that "ideal" lightweight outfit. In my case, speed and simplicity are the motivating factors. I need a quick and uncomplicated method to pack and unpack for multiple trips in a given season. Without going nuts about every ounce, here is the outfit I propose for go-at-a-moment's-notice, keep-it-simple canoe camping:

First, the Therm-a-Rest mattress stays. I'm forty-three years old—end of story. The bivy-style shelter offers a large weight-savings over conventional tents and makes campsite selection easy. You can sleep just about anywhere in one of these things.

For carrying food, a dry bag keeps away water that otherwise might rehydrate your noodles, blocks odors that attract animals, and offers a convenient handle for hanging from trees. Unlike the food, all of your kitchen equipment should be unaffected by rain or even an unexpected dunking and can go in an ordinary nylon sack. Bring an extra water bottle if you like, and keep one empty except when you're in camp. The Peak One "Trekker" mess kit is larger and slightly heavier than Coleman's featured "Solo" outfit, but I find the Solo too small to be useful. To do the dishes, simply fill the collapsible basin with hot, soapy water.

Your list should also include a filet knife, fish-fry, and oil to extend your food supply. The canvas utensil roll from Duluth adds weight but makes the list for its sturdiness. Ditto for the Duluth pack. It's not waterproof, but everything that needs to be dry is already sealed to stay dry before it goes in the larger pack.

This is the system I have used on short, quick trips, and it has performed as expected: no muss, no fuss, and next to no weight.

> The Spartan List:
> A Simple Solo System
> (Total weight: +/- 40 lbs.)
>
> **A.** Therm-a-Rest self-inflating mattress. **B.** Dry bag for food. **C.** Nylon kitchen-sack. **D.** Pack towel. **E.** Water bottle. **F.** Camera and film. **G.** Fishing tackle. **H.** Raingear. **I.** Bivy shelter. **J.** Lowe's compression sack containing sleeping bag and clothing. **K.** Dopp kit for toiletries and odd items. **L.** First aid kit. **M.** Bug headnet. **N.** Map case. **O.** Bug spray **P.** Duluth no. 3 or 4 pack.
>
> **Contents of Kitchen Sack (C):**
>
> 1. Peak one "Trekker" mess kit. 2. Duluth utensil roll. 3. Choreboy sponge 4. Dishwashing soap. 5. Glowmaster MicroLite Mini Stove 6. Butane stove fuel. 7. PUR "Hiker" water filter. 8. Firestarter and matches in Ziplok bag. 9. Collapsible wash basin. 10. Braided nylon rope, 50 ft.

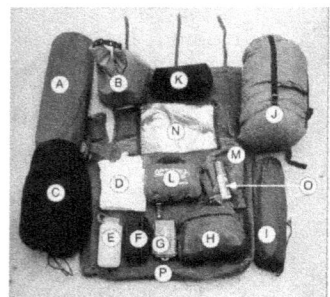 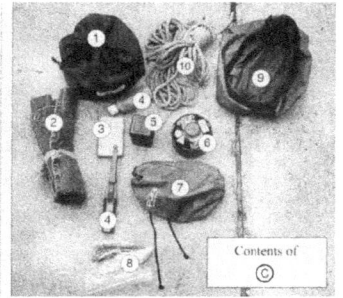

Camp Kitchen

Hobo Pie

There is nothing that better symbolizes the traditional canoe-camp than a reflector oven beside a wood fire. However, one alternative is a lighter, aluminum version of an old standby, the Dutch oven, available from New River Outdoors. Here's a Dutch oven recipe that will make you think you are eating beef pot pie six days out:

- Prepare tabouli per box directions and set aside.
- Use two boxes of Jiffy pie-crust mix to prepare double-thick upper and lower crusts. Coat bottom and sides of oven with olive oil. Mold lower crust to bottom of oven.
- Mix prepared tabouli with can of black beans (drained and rinsed), can of diced tomatoes, black olives, canned mushrooms, half of the shredded cheese, and a little olive oil. Pour onto lower crust and spread evenly. Top with remaining shredded cheese.
- Form and perforate top crust, place lid on oven, and set oven and under hot coals until top crust is golden (about an hour). Remove from coals and let set for 20 minutes. Serve warm and top slices with salsa and plain Greek yogurt. Serves 6.

World Famous! Canoe Stew

Many of you who ordered the Ultimate List may be wondering what you're supposed to do with all of those potatoes, carrots, beans, and onions you've been straining yourself to carry around in your food pack. "Vegetable stew" is noted on the suggested menu, but the coveted recipe for Canoe Stew has until now been the rare privilege of those few who have subjected themselves to the editor's cooking. So that all might know the savory taste of Canoe Stew, here at last is the secret recipe:

Ingredients

16 oz. dried blackeyed peas   2 large yellow onions
6 medium red potatoes   1 cup soy sauce
6 carrots   2 tsp. ground black pepper
2 tsp. garlic powder   4 beef bouillon cubes
1/2 cup cooking sherry (optional)   2 tsp. salt

Cover blackeyed peas in a 10 qt. pot with 3 qts. of water, or by about two inches. Bring to rolling boil and set aside one hour. Do not drain. Chop all vegetables thickly and add to beans and water with remaining ingredients. Simmer and stir occasionally for one hour or until potatoes are soft. Serves 12 adults.

Camp Kitchen

Spicy Campfire Popcorn

In the woods, popcorn is a welcome reminder of home, but products like Jiffy Pop leave trash and don't work well over campfires. You can make it from scratch, but just try keeping any hair on your arm or the lid in place as you shimmy a two-quart boiler over hot flames. Solve this problem with an aluminum Dutch oven. Dutch ovens are thick enough to dissipate heat evenly without the need for frequent shaking. Coat the bottom with enough canola oil (more viscous, less likely to burn) to nearly cover all kernels. Set the oven in coals, and try hard to wait for the popping to stop. Sprinkle with seasoned salt.

Camp Kitchen

How to Filet a Northern Pike

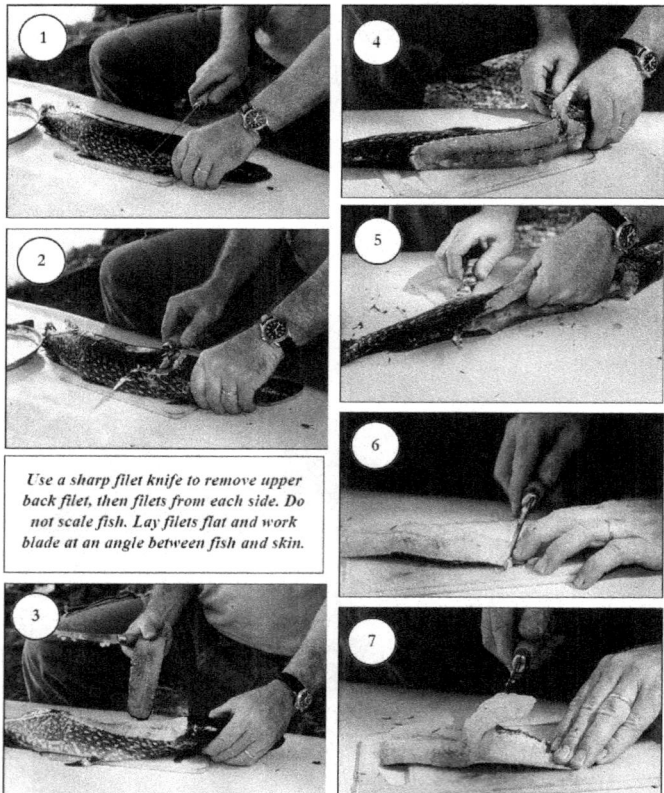

Use a sharp filet knife to remove upper back filet, then filets from each side. Do not scale fish. Lay filets flat and work blade at an angle between fish and skin.

About the Author

Born in Baltimore in 1958, Michael Hurley holds degrees in English Education from the University of Maryland and law from St. Louis University. He is admitted to the bar in Texas and North Carolina.

Michael's debut novel, *The Prodigal* (Ragbagger Press, 2013), won the 2013 Chanticleer Grand Prize and was shortlisted for several other literary awards. *Publishers Weekly* calls his second novel, *The Vineyard* (Ragbagger Press, 2014), a "well written" and "riveting tale." *Kirkus Reviews* calls it "addictive, escapist reading" and "deliriously satisfying." He is currently working on a third novel, *The Passage,* expected in late 2015.

Michael's first book, *Letters from the Woods,* published in 2005, was a collection of thirty-two essays from *Hurley's Journal*. It was a finalist for ForeWord Reviews Book of the Year. In 2012, Hachette Book Group published his sailing memoir, *Once Upon a Gypsy Moon*, about the 2,200-mile solo voyage that ended with the loss of his boat in the Windward Passage between Cuba and Haiti.

After more than thirty years in trial practice, Michael retired from the law in 2014 to write, sail, and pursue the secret of life full-time. He lives with his wife Susan and an Irish terrier named Frodo near Charleston, South Carolina. He keeps up with readers and life in general at www.mchurley.com.